FEMINIST INTERPRETATIONS OF MARTIN HEIDEGGER

RE-READING THE CANON

NANCY TUANA, GENERAL EDITOR

This series consists of edited collections of essays, some original and some previously published, offering feminist re-interpretations of the writings of major figures in the Western philosophical tradition. Devoted to the work of a single philosopher, each volume contains essays covering the full range of the philosopher's thought and representing the diversity of approaches now being used by feminist critics.

Already published:

Nancy Tuana, ed., *Feminist Interpretations of Plato* (1994)

Margaret Simons, ed., *Feminist Interpretations of Simone de Beauvoir* (1995)

Bonnie Honig, ed., *Feminist Interpretations of Hannah Arendt* (1995)

Patricia Jagentowicz Mills, ed., *Feminist Interpretations of G. W. F. Hegel* (1996)

Maria J. Falco, ed., *Feminist Interpretations of Mary Wollstonecraft* (1996)

Susan J. Hekman, ed., *Feminist Interpretations of Michel Foucault* (1996)

Nancy J. Holland, ed., *Feminist Interpretations of Jacques Derrida* (1997)

Robin May Schott, ed., *Feminist Interpretations of Immanuel Kant* (1997)

Celeine Leon and Sylvia Walsh, eds., *Feminist Interpretations of Soren Kierkegaard* (1997)

Cynthia Freeland, ed., *Feminist Interpretations of Aristotle* (1998)

Kelly Oliver and Marilyn Pearsall, eds., *Feminist Interpretations of Friedrich Nietzsche* (1998)

Mimi Reisel Gladstein and Chris Matthew Sciabarra, eds., *Feminist Interpretations of Ayn Rand* (1999)

Susan Bordo, ed., *Feminist Interpretations of René Descartes* (1999)

Julien S. Murphy, ed., *Feminist Interpretations of Jean-Paul Sartre* (1999)

Anne Jaap Jacobson, ed., *Feminist Interpretations of David Hume* (2000)

Sarah Lucia Hoagland and Marilyn Frye, eds., *Feminist Interpretations of Mary Daly* (2000)

Tina Chanter, ed., *Feminist Interpretations of Emmanuel Levinas* (2001)

FEMINIST INTERPRETATIONS OF MARTIN HEIDEGGER

EDITED BY
NANCY J. HOLLAND
AND
PATRICIA HUNTINGTON

THE PENNSYLVANIA STATE UNIVERSITY PRESS
UNIVERSITY PARK, PENNSYLVANIA

Library of Congress Cataloging-in-Publication Data

Feminist interpretations of Martin Heidegger / edited by Nancy J. Holland and Patricia Huntington.
    p. cm.—(Re-reading the canon)
  Includes bibliographical references and index.
  ISBN 0-271-02154-3 (cloth : alk. paper)
  ISBN 0-271-02155-1 (pbk. : alk. paper)
    1. Heidegger, Martin, 1899–1976. 2. Feminist theory. I. Holland, Nancy J. II. Huntington, Patricia. III. Series.

B3279 .H49 F395   2001
193—dc21   2001021447

Copyright © 2001 The Pennsylvania State University
All rights reserved
Printed in the United States of America
Published by The Pennsylvania State University Press,
University Park, PA 16802-1003

It is the policy of The Pennsylvania State University Press to use acid-free paper for the first printing of all clothbound books. Publications on uncoated stock satisfy the minimum requirements of American National Standard for Information Sciences—Permanence of Paper for Printed Library Materials, ANSI Z39.48–1992.

Contents

Preface *Nancy Tuana*	ix
Acknowledgments	xiii
Abbreviations	xv
Introduction I—General Background History of the Feminist Reception of Heidegger and a Guide to Heidegger's Thought *Patricia Huntington*	1
Introduction II—Specific Contributions Feminists Read Heidegger *Nancy J. Holland*	43

Part I: The Gender of Dasein

1	Geschlecht: Sexual Difference, Ontological Difference *Jacques Derrida*	53
2	The Problematic Normative Assumptions of Heidegger's Ontology *Tina Chanter*	73
3	Conflictual Culture and Authenticity: Deepening Heidegger's Account of the Social *Dorothy Leland*	109
4	"The Universe Is Made of Stories, Not of Atoms": Heidegger and the Feminine They-Self *Nancy J. Holland*	128

Part II: Poetics and the Body

5 The Absence of Monica: Heidegger, Derrida, and
   Augustine's *Confessions* — 149
   John D. Caputo

6 Sappho: The She-Greek Heidegger Forgot — 165
   Carol Bigwood

7 Feminine Figures in Heidegger's Theory of Poetic Language — 196
   Jennifer Anna Gosetti

Part III: Ethics, Home, and Play

8 Heidegger and Ecofeminism — 221
   Trish Glazebrook

9 House and Home: Feminist Variations on a Theme — 252
   Iris Marion Young

10 Thrownness, Playing-in-the-World, and the Question of
   Authenticity — 289
   Mechthild Nagel

Part IV: Thinking, Spirit, Moving Forward

11 From *The Forgetting of Air* to *To Be Two* — 309
   Luce Irigaray
   Translated by Heidi Bostic and Stephen Pluháček

12 "Through Flame or Ashes": Traces of Difference in *Geist's*
   Return — 316
   Ellen T. Armour

13 Revolutionary Thinking — 334
   Gail Stenstad

14 Stealing the Fire of Creativity: Heidegger's Challenge to
   Intellectuals — 351
   Patricia Huntington

   Contributors — 377
   Selected Bibliography — 381
   Index — 389

Preface

Nancy Tuana

Take into your hands any history-of-philosophy text. You will find compiled therein the "classics" of modern philosophy. Since these texts are often designed for use in undergraduate classes, the editor is likely to offer an introduction in which the reader is informed that these selections represent the perennial questions of philosophy. The student is to assume that she or he is about to explore the timeless wisdom of the greatest minds of Western philosophy. No one calls attention to the fact that the philosophers are all men.

Though women are omitted from the canons of philosophy, these texts inscribe the nature of woman. Sometimes the philosopher speaks directly about woman, delineating her proper role, her abilities and inabilities, her desires. Other times the message is indirect—a passing remark hinting at woman's emotionality, irrationality, unreliability.

This process of definition occurs in far more subtle ways when the central concepts of philosophy—reason and justice, those characteristics that are taken to define us as human—are associated with traits historically identified with masculinity. If the "man" of reason must learn to control or overcome traits identified as feminine—the body, the emotions, the passions—then the realm of rationality will be one reserved primarily for men,[1] with grudging entrance to those few women who are capable of transcending their femininity.

Feminist philosophers have begun to look critically at the canonized texts of philosophy and have concluded that the discourses of philosophy are not gender-neutral. Philosophical narratives do not offer a universal perspective, but rather privilege some experiences and beliefs over others. These experiences and beliefs permeate all philosophical theories whether they be aesthetic or epistemological, moral or metaphysical. Yet this fact has often been neglected by those studying the traditions of philosophy. Given the history of canon formation in Western philosophy, the perspective most likely to be privileged is that of upper-class white males. Thus, to be fully aware of the impact of gender biases, it is imperative that we re-read the canon with attention to the ways in which philosophers' assumptions concerning gender are embedded within their theories.

The new series, Re-Reading the Canon, is designed to foster this process of reevaluation. Each volume will offer feminist analyses of the theories of a selected philosopher. Since feminist philosophy is not monolithic in method or content, the essays are also selected to illustrate the variety of perspectives within feminist criticism and highlight some of the controversies within feminist scholarship.

In this series, feminist lenses will be focused on the canonical texts of Western philosophy, both those authors who have been part of the traditional canon, as well as those philosophers whose writings have more recently gained attention within the philosophical community. A glance at the list of volumes in the series will reveal an immediate gender bias of the canon: Arendt, Aristotle, de Beauvoir, Derrida, Descartes, Foucault, Hegel, Hume, Kant, Locke, Marx, Mill, Nietzsche, Plato, Rousseau, Wittgenstein, Wollstonecraft. There are all too few women included, and those few who do appear have been added only recently. In creating this series, it is not my intention to reify the current canon of philosophical thought. What is and is not included within the canon during a particular historical period is a result of many factors. Although no canonization of texts will include all philosophers, no canonization of texts that excludes all but a few women can offer an accurate representation of the history of the discipline, as women have been philosophers since the ancient period.[2]

I share with many feminist philosophers and other philosophers writing from the margins of philosophy the concern that the current canonization of philosophy be transformed. Although I do not accept the position that the current canon has been formed exclusively by power relations, I do believe that this canon represents only a selective history of the tradition. I share the view of Michael Bérubé that "canons are at once the location, the index, and the record of the struggle for cultural representation; like any other hegemonic formation, they must be continually reproduced anew and are continually contested."[3]

The process of canon transformation will require the recovery of "lost" texts and a careful examination of the reasons such voices have been silenced. Along with the process of uncovering women's philosophical history, we must also begin to analyze the impact of gender ideologies upon the process of canonization. This process of recovery and examination must occur in conjunction with careful attention to the concept of a canon of authorized texts. Are we to dispense with the notion of a tradition of excellence embodied in a canon of authorized texts? Or, rather than abandon the whole idea of a canon, do we instead encourage a reconstruction of a canon of those texts that inform a common culture?

This series is designed to contribute to this process of canon transformation by offering a re-reading of the current philosophical canon. Such a re-reading shifts our attention to the ways in which woman and the role of the feminine is constructed within the texts of philosophy. A question we must keep in front of us during this process of re-reading is whether a philosopher's socially inherited prejudices concerning woman's nature and role are independent of her or his larger philosophical framework. In asking this question attention must be paid to the ways in which the definitions of central philosophical concepts implicitly include or exclude gendered traits.

This type of reading strategy is not limited to the canon, but can be applied to all texts. It is my desire that this series reveal the importance of this type of critical reading. Paying attention to the workings of gender within the texts of philosophy will make visible the complexities of the inscription of gender ideologies.

Notes

1. More properly, it is a realm reserved for a group of privileged males, since the text also inscribe race and class biases that thereby omit certain males from participation.

2. Mary Ellen Waithe's multivolume series, *A History of Women Philosophers* (Boston: M. Nijhoff, 1987), attests to this presence of women.

3. Michael Bérubé, *Marginal Forces/Cultural Centers: Tolson, Pynchon, and the Politics of the Canon* (Ithaca: Cornell University Press, 1992), 4–5.

Acknowledgments

The following works included in this anthology are reprinted with permission:

Jacques Derrida's "Geschlecht: Sexual Difference, Ontological Difference" first appeared in *Research in Phenomenology* 13 (1983) and is reprinted with permission by Brill Academic Publishers.

An earlier version of Dorothy Leland's "Conflictual Culture and Authenticity: Deepening Heidegger's Account of the Social," will appear in *Feminist Phenomenology*, L. Fisher and L. Embree, eds., reprinted with permission by Kluwer Academic Publishers.

Iris Marion Young's "House and Home: Feminist Variations on a Theme" appeared originally as chapter 7 of *Intersecting Voices: Dilemmas of Gender, Political Philosophy, and Policy* (1997) and is reprinted with permission by Princeton University Press.

Abbreviations

Selected Works by Heidegger

BC   *Basic Concepts*. Translated by Gary E. Aylesworth. Bloomington: Indiana University Press, 1993.

BCP   "On the Being and Conception of *Physis* in Aristotle's *Physics* B.1." Translated by Thomas Sheehan, *Man and World* 9, no. 3 (1976): 219–70. Reprinted in *Pathmarks*, ed. William McNeill. Cambridge: Cambridge University Press, 1998.

BP   *The Basic Problems of Phenomenology*. Translated by Albert Hofstadter. Bloomington: Indiana University Press, 1982.

BT   *Being and Time*. Translated by John Macquarrie and Edward Robinson. New York: Harper and Row, 1962.

BT(s)   *Being and Time: A Translation of Sein und Zeit/Martin Heidegger*. Translated by Joan Stambaugh. Albany: State University of New York Press, 1996.

BW   *Basic Writings*. Edited by David Farrell Krell. New York: Harper and Row, 1977.

DI   *Hölderlin's Hymn "The Ister."* Translated by William McNeill and Julia Davis. Bloomington: Indiana University Press, 1996.

DT   *Discourse on Thinking*. Translated by John M. Anderson and E. Hans Freund. New York: Harper and Row, 1966.

EGT   *Early Greek Thinking: The Dawn of Western Philosophy*. Translated by David Farrell Krell and Frank A. Capuzzi. New York: Harper and Row, 1975.

EP   *The End of Philosophy*. Translated by Joan Stambaugh. New York: Harper and Row, 1973.

FC   *The Fundamental Concepts of Metaphysics: World, Finitude, Soli-

tude. Translated by William McNeill and Nicholas Walker. Bloomington: Indiana University Press, 1995.

FD *Die Frage nach dem Ding*. Tübingen: Max Niemeyer, 1984.

FL *The Metaphysical Foundations of Logic*. Translated by Michael Heim. Bloomington: Indiana University Press, 1984.

G *Gelassenheit*. Pfullingen, Germany: Günther Neske, 1959.

GA 1 *Gesamtausgabe*, B. 1, *Frühe Schriften*. Frankfurt am Main: Vittorio Klostermann, 1978.

GA 2 *Gesamtausgabe*, B. 2, *Sein und Zeit*. Frankfurt am Main: Vittorio Klostermann, 1977.

GA 4 *Gesamtausgabe*, B. 4, *Erläuterungen zu Hölderlins Dichtung*. Frankfurt am Main: Vittorio Klostermann, 1981.

GA 5 *Gesamtausgabe*, B. 5, *Holzwege*. Frankfurt am Main: Vittorio Klostermann, 1977.

GA 9 *Gesamtausgabe*, B. 9, *Wegmarken*. Frankfurt am Main: Vittorio Klostermann, 1976.

GA 13 *Gesamtausgabe*, B. 13, *Aus der Erfahrung des Denkens*. Frankfurt am Main: Vittorio Klostermann, 1983.

GA 24 *Gesamtausgabe*, B. 24, *Die Grundprobleme der Phänomenologie*. Frankfurt am Main: Vittorio Klostermann, 1975.

GA 26 *Gesamtausgabe*, B. 26, *Metaphysiche Anfangsgründe der Logik im Ausgang von Leibniz*. Frankfurt am Main: Vittorio Klostermann, 1978.

GA 39 *Gesamtausgabe*, B. 39, *Hölderlins Hymnen "Germanien" und "Der Rhein."* Edited by Susanne Zeigler. Frankfurt am Main: Vittorio Klostermann, 1980.

GA 40 *Gesamtausgabe*, B. 40, *Einführung in der Metaphysik*. Frankfurt am Main: Vittorio Klostermann, 1983.

GA 45 *Gesamtausgabe*, B. 45, *Grundfragen der Philosophie: Ausgewählte "Probleme" der "Logik."* Frankfurt am Main: Vittorio Klostermann, 1984.

GA 52 *Gesamtausgabe*, B. 52, *Hölderlins Hymne "Andenken."* Edited by Curd Ochwadt. Frankfurt am Main: Vittorio Klostermann, 1982.

GA 60 *Gesamtausgabe*, B. 60, *Phänomenologie des religiösen Lebens*, 1. "Einführung in die Phänomenologie der Religion" (Wintersemester 1920/21), edited by Matthias Jung and Thomas Regehly; 2. "Augustinus und der Neuplatonismus" (Sommersemester 1921); 3. "Die philosophischen Grundlagen der Mittelalterlichen Mystik," edited by Claudius Strube. Frankfurt am Main: Vittorio Klostermann, 1995.

GA 61   *Gesamtausgabe*, B. 61, *Phänomenologische Interpretationen zu Aristoteles Einführung in die Phänomenologische Forschung*. Frankfurt am Main: Vittorio Klostermann, 1985.

GA 65   *Gesamtausgabe*, B. 65, *Beiträge zur Philosophie (Vom Ereignis)*. Frankfurt am Main: Vittorio Klostermann, 1989.

GA 66   *Gesamtausgabe*, B. 66, *Besinnung*. Frankfurt am Main: Vittorio Klostermann, 1997.

ID   *Identity and Difference*. Translated by Joan Stambaugh. New York: Harper and Row, 1969.

IM   *An Introduction to Metaphysics*. Translated by Ralph Manheim. New Haven: Yale University Press, 1959.

N1–2   *Nietzsche: The Will to Power as Art* (N1) and *The Eternal Recurrence of the Same* (N2). Vols. 1 and 2. Translated by David Farrell Krell. New York: Harper and Row, 1991.

N3–4   *Nietzsche: The Will to Power as Knowledge and as Metaphysics* (N3) and *Nihilism* (N4). Vols. 3 and 4. Edited by David Farrell Krell. New York: Harper and Row, 1991.

NI, NII   *Nietzsche*. Vols. 1 and 2. Pfullingen, Germany: Günther Neske, 1961.

OWL   *On the Way to Language*. Translated by Peter D. Hertz. New York: Harper and Row, 1971.

Pa   *Parmenides*. Translated by André Schuwer and Richard Rojcewicz. Bloomington: Indiana University Press, 1992.

PD   "Plato's Doctrine of Truth." Translated by John Barlow. In *Philosophy in the Twentieth Century*, vol. 3, ed. William Barrett and Henry D. Aiken, 251–70. New York: Random House, 1962.

PLT   *Poetry, Language, Thought*. Translated by Albert Hofstadter. New York: Harper and Row, 1971.

PR   *The Principle of Reason*. Translated by Reginald Lilly. Bloomington: Indiana University Press, 1991.

QCT   *The Question Concerning Technology and Other Essays*. Translated by William Lovitt. New York: Harper and Row, 1977.

R   Preface (letter to Richardson) to *Heidegger: Through Phenomenology to Thought*, by William J. Richardson, VIII–XXIII. The Hague: Martinus Nijhoff, 1963.

SA   "The Self-Assertion of the German University." Translated by Karsten Harries. *Review of Metaphysics*, 38 (1985): 470–80.

SD	*Zur Sache des Denkens.* Tübingen: Max Niemeyer, 1969.
SdDU	*Die Selbstbehauptung der deutschen Universität. Das Rektorat, 1933/34: Tatsachen und Gedanken.* Edited by H. Heidegger. Frankfurt am Main: Vittorio: Klostermann, 1983.
SG	*Der Satz vom Grund.* Pfullingen, Germany: Günther Neske, 1957.
SZ	*Sein und Zeit,* funfzente Auflage. Tübingen: Max Niemeyer, 1984.
TB	*On Time and Being.* Translated by Joan Stambaugh. New York: Harper and Row, 1972.
US	*Unterwegs zur Sprache.* Pfullingen, Germany: Günther Neske, 1965.
VA	*Vorträge und Aufsätze.* Pfullingen, Germany: Günther Neske, 1954.
WD	*Was heisst Denken?* Tübingen: Max Niemeyer, 1954.
WIT	*What Is a Thing?* Translated by W. B. Barton Jr. and Vera Deutsch. South Bend, Ind.: Regenery/Gateway, 1967.
WT	*What Is Called Thinking?* Translated by J. Glenn Gray. New York: Harper and Row, 1968.

Introduction I—General Background

History of the Feminist Reception of Heidegger and a Guide to Heidegger's Thought

Patricia Huntington

One might wonder how Heidegger could be useful to feminist theory, given that he was not primarily a political thinker. Nor was he *explicitly* concerned with social ontology, contemporary issues of sexual identity, moral epistemology, or social ethics. He was above all else a profound thinker on the human condition as such. He offers the reader his lifelong meditations on the nature of human mortality. His works touch on themes such as the manifold ways that Dasein (human being) falls into unfreedom and inauthentic relations, what it means to be a thinker endowed with language, the poetic nature of human existence, and the urgent need in the era of technological rationality to restore a sense of balance, harmony, and quietude to existence. Heidegger's mature thinking, by virtue of its aspiration to unmask the instrumental underpinnings of Western philosophy, issues an original and serious challenge to the human race, but especially to Westerners. To the extent that fostering a healthier human condition holds implications for social ontology, ethics, philosophy of liberation, and spiritual freedom, Heidegger's deliberately suprapolitical corpus allows feminist theorists to engage and learn from his thought.[1]

It would be a laughable exaggeration to claim that feminist theory and praxis in the United States has sought out and mined Heidegger as a central resource. The reasons that feminist scholars shy away from Heidegger stem from the suprapolitical, seemingly esoteric, and nonempirical nature of his thought. The simple truth is that Heidegger's thought resists usage, "being put to work" for ends of any kind, in a fundamental way. Ironically, for this very same reason Heidegger's thought exerts its own quiet draw. Considerably greater interest in Heidegger exists among female scholars than many realize, an interest that has yet to be made intelligible to a wide audience and understood in itself. It is, thus, imperative to note that this anthology has important precursors, some of whose pioneering efforts are not represented here but will be detailed below. The essays here collected, even when written by some of the pioneers, are primarily newly written contributions to that earlier phase of scholarship.[2]

This anthology, being a collection in one volume of an array of approaches to Heidegger, is a first step toward making visible the extent and range of women's interest in Heideggerian themes, without claim to comprehensive representation of those interests. The collection of essays in this anthology both reflect the insights of and expand upon the pioneering feminist explorations that have to date not been regarded as a distinct body of work. They offer original and constructive ways to flesh out key Heideggerian concepts in order to reveal their import for feminist theorizing. Martin Heidegger is undoubtedly one of the most seminal thinkers in twentieth-century philosophy. Yet in spite of the massive body of secondary scholarship that exists in English, the place of Heidegger's immense legacy in shaping twentieth-century philosophy remains to be assessed. This anthology contributes to that evaluation by offering a range of considerations, both critical and appreciative, of the significance of Heideggerian thought. The aim is to do so from the standpoint of its potential contribution to feminist philosophy, even though advancing feminism was not a stated intent of Heidegger's authorship.

The main aspirations of this anthology are, thus, three. First, the aim is to give the reader an overview of work that illuminates Heidegger's potential contribution to gender studies. There has been no definitive anthology on feminist usages of Heidegger to date. As noted, the work compiled in this anthology can be considered phase two of feminist scholarship on Heidegger because, as a historic act, it provides a framework for recognizing past feminist studies of Heidegger and it collects past and current themes into a viable field of study. Second, Nancy Holland and I believe that this anthology will be eminently suitable for introducing feminist themes into any upper-level course or seminar on Heideggerian philosophy. Third, by addressing old and new themes that cover all periods of his writings, we firmly intend this anthology to invite, even encourage, future work on the intersections of feminism and Heidegger.

As Nancy and I have devised a two-part introduction, my tasks in writing "Introduction I" will themselves be twofold. In the first part, I offer a brief history of feminist interest in Heidegger and the thematic concerns that gave rise to that interest. The second part of Introduction I provides a general conceptual understanding of the two main phases of Heidegger's authorship. In section A, I explain the basic aspiration of Heidegger's thought and key concepts first developed in his early, pathbreaking work, *Being and Time*. In section B, I discuss the primary change that occurs in Heidegger's thought from the early to the later or mature works. Although the goal of overcoming metaphysics remains the same throughout both phases, the early Heidegger held that human beings could overcome metaphysical systems of representation through willed self-appropriation, while the later Heidegger ultimately rejects human will as the basis for overcoming metaphysics. At the end of section A, I offer a brief indication that the general philosophy of *Being and Time* presupposes a *gender-neutral view of Dasein*. Similarly, at the end of section B, I note how the later works harbor implications for *poetics, ethics,* and *spirituality*. Although I touch on *the four specific themes organizing this anthology*, I do so in each case only in a most preliminary fashion. My goal is to give only general background for comprehending Heidegger. These four themes receive full treatment in Nancy Holland's "Introduction II," where the specific contribution of each author finds articulation and the basic organization and unity of the anthology is made clearer.

History of the Feminist Reception of Heidegger

A notable socialist feminist, Sandra Lee Bartky, must be credited with writing the first article, to my knowledge, on the possible relation of

Heideggerian thought to feminist theory. Bartky was originally trained as a Heidegger scholar; her essay, "Originative Thinking in the Later Philosophy of Heidegger," appeared in 1970.[3] In this careful work in Heidegger scholarship, Bartky sorts out four meanings of the notion of "originative" or meditative thinking in order to evaluate later Heidegger's claim "that unless we learn to think originatively, the planetary domination of technology . . . will transform the earth into a desert" of European cultural hegemony. Bartky concludes in this article that later Heidegger's "notion of originative thought is far too vacuous and abstract to serve the needs of any radical world-renewing project."[4] In Bartky's critical assessment, Heideggerian thought, certainly the later philosophy but also the early work, provides no basis for undertaking concrete analyses of social relations. Because it cannot state definitively whether humans create or merely receive meaning, it finds itself unable to offer guidelines for a philosophy of liberation. The *"vacuity"* of the later thought, which stems from its pure formalism and lack of concretion, "dampens the spirit," serves up "a grotesque exaggeration of the historical importance of metaphysics," and, for want of granting human beings the creative power to pave a pathway to a new era, lapses into mere "prophecy" and quietism.[5]

Bartky's firm conclusions echoed debates about the pseudoconcreteness of Heidegger's thought that began around 1947 in the United States and Germany and have continued to resurface time and again on both European and American soil.[6] What is of vital importance for this history is that Bartky's scholarly evaluation, occuring in 1970 in the English-speaking world, seemed to hammer the final nail into the coffin of any potential consideration of Heidegger as a resource for the newly emerging body of feminist theory, just as the academic branch of the women's movement was getting under way and before Heidegger ever became a resource for women in their making sense out of their existence. The implication was that other brands of existential philosophy and phenomenology already in currency decisively trump Heidegger's sort in any attempt to make sense out of concrete existence and historical change. If we take Bartky's essay as the first of its kind, it seems that there was an initial period in which feminism's attitude toward Heidegger began as one of positive disinterest. We might call this a defined period, not of a failure to gestate rooted in mere ignorance nor unformed but potentiated interest, but rather antigestation. What Bartky printed explicitly and courageously—her argument in favor of refusing Heidegger as useless to developing any social theory with liberatory intent—it is safe to assume found pronounced if tacit sympathy among other female academics interested in examining women's situations. This sympathy continues to exist among female philosophers who either are not Heidegger experts, never took to Heidegger during graduate study, or, having initially been attracted to his work, deliberately abandoned interest when they turned to women's issues on the grounds given voice by Bartky.

Not until 1990, some twenty years later, did a positive reception of Heidegger appear within feminist-oriented scholarship. Ironically, this genuinely first phase of Heideggerian feminist scholarship begins with a new publication by Bartky, "Shame and Gender." Several definitively constructive usages of Heidegger by feminists appear in journals around the same time, even a few beforehand.[7] I nonetheless highlight Bartky's essay in part because she first wrote against undertaking such work and in part because this essay received widespread circulation in the feminist world, as it was published in her *Femininity and Domination*. Even given the acclaim of Bartky's book, however, the genuine emergence of a seriously Heideggerian-inflected feminism arrives squarely on the map through the decisive accomplishments of six books that appear throughout the 1990s, even as these six books depended upon other works to pave the way for their reception.

Jean Graybeal published *Language and "The Feminine" in Nietzsche and Heidegger* in 1990; Carol Bigwood's *Earth Muse: Feminism, Nature, and Art* arrived shortly after in 1993; with Ellen Mortensen's *The Feminine and Nihilism: Luce Irigaray with Nietzsche and Heidegger* following fast on Bigwood's heels in 1994; and my *Ecstatic Subjects, Utopia, and Recognition: Kristeva, Heidegger, Irigaray* then came out a few years later in 1998. Two highly important works in feminist theology written during the same time period are David W. Odell-Scott's *A Post-Patriarchal Christology* (published in 1991) and Marta Frascati-Lochhead's *Kenosis and Feminist Theology: The Challenge of Gianni Vattimo* (printed in 1998). I hasten to add that, throughout the 1990s, manifold journal articles and numerous dissertations on Heidegger in relation to gender were written. Moreover, a variety of additional books also appeared and incorporated important discussions of this topic either in a chapter or as part of a general, conceptual backdrop for the position to be developed. Much of this production occurred with scant knowledge of the range of similar work being done by others. In a vital sense, all these works plant seeds that contribute to generating a distinctly Heideggerian brand of thought on gender. Once again, I mark out these six works because their authors offered book-length or sustained projects in which they aspired, in significant measure, not merely to critique Heidegger or borrow a concept from Heidegger, but to reconstruct a gendered or postpatriarchal philosophy on the basis of the fundamental sensibilities of Heideggerian thought.

Before I remark on the thematic content of Bartky's essay and these six books, one question begs attention: what change in the soil of feminist theorizing occurred between 1970 and 1990 that not only catalyzed but also proved receptive to women's interest in Heidegger? What allowed for a radical shift away from the preliminary but deliberate refusal to take interest in Heideggerian thought within feminist social theory, a shift marked by the sudden, successive emergence in the 1990s of a body of scholarship by writers who aspire not solely to critique male-bias in Heidegger but instead turn to Heideggerian thought for the constructive purpose of developing new and vibrant orientations in feminism?

My personal view is that feminist interest in Heidegger had to wait for the Anglophone reception of the work of Luce Irigaray and, to a lesser extent, Jacques Derrida to take root and grow before bridges between matters of gender and Heidegger's brand of thought could be envisaged and received. It is neither accidental nor surprising that this anthology can appear at this moment in history. While the pathbreaking books by Graybeal, Odell-Scott, and Bigwood engender distinct homegrown forms of Heideggerian feminist thought in the 1990s, it is Jacques Derrida and Luce Irigaray who laid the groundwork in the 1980s for such possibilities to take root.[8] Derrida's three essays on the notion of *Geschlecht* in Heidegger's corpus—a polyvalent term meaning race, gender, species, and genus—at a minimum, perform two fundamental services. The three essays—commonly known as *Geschlecht* I, II, and IV—appeared in English in 1983, 1987, and 1993, respectively.[9] Together they constitute the only systematic analysis of the few references that Heidegger ever makes to the gender neutrality of Dasein and to gendered incarnation. Beyond the important work of cataloguing these references, Derrida's careful and detailed interpretations reveal that the Heideggerian concept of Dasein or human being is not entirely inimical to sexual difference.

Even so, Derrida's commentaries on *Geschlecht* (and his work in general) held at best ambiguous consequences for feminism's attitude toward Heidegger. Although they break open vital terrain on which a constructive turn to Heidegger could grow, the *Geschlecht* essays did not initially draw feminist attention to Heidegger, but rather impelled the continued cultivation of a Derridean or deconstructive strain within feminist scholarship. If they held promise for a positive feminist turn toward Heidegger, these essays also contained the seed for revitalizing Bartky's early 1970 claim that Heidegger's thought is too abstract to be of interest for feminism. Five years before Bartky's insightful use of Heidegger in 1990, Nancy Holland, in "Heidegger and Derrida Redux" (1985), attempted to repel a premature divide between the ostensibly more politically acceptable aspects of deconstruction and the politically suspect Heidegger, without thereby being naive about masculinist dimensions in Heidegger. Holland lays out very carefully the fundamental issue at stake in understanding the relation of Derrida's work to "its admittedly Heideggerian antecedant(s)" and to the general debate at that time over whether neither the left-leaning nor the right-leaning strain in Heidegger is desirable. By showing that Derrida regards both strains as inadequate to understanding Heidegger, Holland persuasively demonstrates that "one can never be certain that Derrida himself sees what he says . . . as a criticism of Heidegger rather than an amplification or radicalization of what is already present in the Heideggerian text."[10] Rather than resolve the question of the hidden potential within Heidegger for addressing the relation of gender to metaphysics, Holland decisively establishes Derrida's reasons for resisting premature rejection of Heideggerian thought from a profeminist, political stance.

In the academic climate of the 1980s, however, Bartky's earlier 1970 critique of Heidegger seemed fated to be rejuvenated in terms of postphenomenology. Diane Elam, in "Is Feminism the Saving Grace of Hermeneutics?" (1991), proclaimed that feminism cannot save hermeneutics from phallocentrism.[11] Rather, Elam argues, after Heidegger sexual difference can be recognized only on the basis of deconstructing such traditional methodologies. Elam's critique at once echoes Bartky's early distrust of Heideggerian thought but, very much against Bartky's own (generally non-Heideggerian) phenomenological sensibilities, expresses that distrust as a critique of hermeneutical phenomenology proper. Thus, by embracing the more politically inflected character of Derrida as it naturally fits, in contrast to Heidegger, with the prevailing postphenomenological currents in academic philosophy, the deconstructive strain of feminist scholarship played down Derrida's intrinsic relation to Heidegger. Despite Holland's thoughtful accomplishment as a Derrida scholar, this developing strain of feminist theory reinforced, whether intentionally or not, Bartky's earlier proclamation that Heidegger is too abstract to be of use to feminist ethics, social thought, or anything of currency. Still other feminists, against both Holland's compatibilism and Elam's incompatibilism, critiqued deconstruction along with its Heideggerian forerunner.[12]

In terms far more substantially related to woman's concerns, Irigaray's own, unique brand of work on the meaning of the "feminine" in Western metaphysics, in life, and in thinking about loving relations between men and women is heavily indebted to Heidegger. Once the separation of deconstruction from its Heideggerian roots is made, it must be asserted that Irigaray is arguably more substantially Heideggerian than deconstructive. And yet the initial reception of Irigaray in the United States emphasized the Lacanian and deconstructive aspects of her "philosophy" to the exclusion of its marked affinity with and female parallel to Heidegger's own project. Clearly, there are sound reasons to regard her work as exemplifying crucial Lacanian and deconstructive elements. Nonetheless, the reception of Irigarary in the English-speaking world neglected two elements essential to her own thought. I refer first to the methodology that evolved in the 1980s and second to her understanding of thinking as an activity distinct from theorizing or philosophizing. Irigaray adopts both orientations from Heidegger and, in the latter case, strives to develop a female variant of originary thinking—the very activity held to make Heidegger's thought pseudoconcrete and apolitical, if not downright mystifying in the ideological sense. Irigaray's saying that "[s]exual difference is probably the issue in our time which could be our 'salvation' " is emblematic of her avowed affinity to Heidegger in these respects.[13]

Many of Irigaray's works of the 1980s—her writings on Nietzsche and Heidegger proper as well as books such as *An Ethics of Sexual Difference, Sexes and Genealogies,* and *Thinking the Difference*—did not come into English translation until the 1990s. Yet these works mark a crucial change in style and sensibility after her critical efforts in the 1970s to reveal the phallic-centered nature of Freudian and Lacanian psychoanalysis as well as the Western philosophical tradition. Irigaray's work on Heidegger proper, written in 1983 right after and along with the Nietzsche book of 1982, marks off a new orientation in her thought and introduces a distinct constructive dimension into her methodology. Her critique of Heidegger, one little known to English speakers except through a short excerpt that appeared in 1991, went untranslated in full until 1999 and, though written earlier than most, appeared only after all other works of the 1980s had been translated.[14] The works of the 1980s were thus interpreted in accord with the preconceived idea—again, an idea that fit neatly and afforded feminism ready acceptance within prevailing academic trends—that the deconstructive and psychoanalytic features of *Speculum* and *This Sex Which Is Not One* provide the defining hermeneutic framework for her own philosophical project.

Although she develops a critique of Heidegger in 1983, Irigaray arguably begins this critique for the sake of adopting a Heideggerian understanding of the very nature of thought. For this reason, many of her works from the 1980s reveal pronounced Heideggerian overtones. These works are not primarily deconstructive but rather constitute a female variation on Heidegger's methodology of historical retrieval. In them, Irigaray tries to prepare the ground for recovering a substantial and originary manner of dwelling from out of the religious and Greek origins of Western tradition, a point I shall revisit below. So it is that she begins to develop her own brand of originary or meditative thinking by pressing more deeply than Heidegger into sexual difference. In this way, she gives birth to an essentially constructive and positively envisaged possibility for human flourishing when standing face-to-face before sexual difference. Even if she goes on to employ diverse methodologies in the 1980s, then at the very least the Heideggerian nature of her own understanding of the activity of thought proper takes shape and begins to blossom throughout that decade, even when she does not discuss Heidegger directly.[15] In addition to the failure to translate the Heidegger book until 1999, this dimension of her thinking was overlooked in part because many feminists and translators of Irigaray do not know Heidegger's work. And many feminists still found it more acceptable to fit Irigaray into the poststructuralist sensibilities of late-1980s and 1990s feminism or battle postmodernism out against modernist feminism where any reliance on Heidegger would surely take a beating, precisely for reasons initially articulated by Bartky and later advanced by others.[16]

Ironically, Bartky reappears at the inception of the first, positive wave of feminist interest in Heidegger. It would be erroneous to imply that Bartky has reversed her earlier view of the later Heidegger or even her general assessment that Heidegger offers little to women. Even so, chapter 6 of *Femininity and Domination* (1990) provides one of the first appropriations of a key concept from Heidegger's early work *Being and Time,* a work considered by numerous Heidegger scholars to offer a concrete, pragmatic view of human existence that avoids the pitfalls of pseudoconcreteness that is deemed characteristic of the later philosophy and, according to some of these scholars, plagues postphenomenology as well. In the chapter "Shame and Gender," Bartky adopts the Heideggerian notion of mood or attunement (*Gestimmtheit*) as an analytic tool for analyzing what she takes to be the primary modality of female embodiment within U.S. patriarchy: shame. Mood—one of the basic structures of being embedded in a world—is commonly understood to denote the reality that Dasein (human being) does not first stand in a cognitive relation to the world of its environs but rather finds itself attuned to that environs in a particular, affective way. All understanding occurs on the basis of a mode of affective attunement that colors our perception and the overall way in which the world appears intelligible to us. Heidegger argued that special moods, anxiety and boredom, reveal not simply the world as colored by a particular light but the very fact that attunement is an essential feature of human existence. In accord with the feminist goal of taking conceptual tools from canonical figures and extending them to gender analysis, Bartky relies on Heidegger's notion of attunement in order to undertake her own phenomenology of shame. She adds shame onto the list of primary moods, as, she argues, it is the defining mood within which women perceive their fundamental options in patriarchal society.

Even given Bartky's insightful article, the more substantial turn to Heidegger in feminist circles came to birth out of greater sensitivity to the spiritual impetus underlying Heideggerian thought. While a flourishing reception of Irigaray provided the historical conditions for a Heideggerian brand of feminist thought to emerge on American soil, the conceptual basis for the emergence of the first sustained, female-authored works on Heidegger by Jean Graybeal (in the same year as Bartky's article in 1990) and Carol Bigwood (in 1993) stemmed in significant measure, though not solely, from an affinity for Heidegger's spiritual sensibilities. Clearly David Odell-Scott's *A Post-Patriarchal Christology* (1991) stands even more firmly within a theistic interpretation of Heidegger. The two works by Graybeal and Bigwood, though based on an affinity with Heidegger's spirituality, nonetheless allowed for serious feminist consideration within a predominant, academic feminist orientation that is allergic to religiosity. Strictly speaking, Irigaray's own thought is definitively spiritualist, but the psychoanalytic and deconstructive renditions of her work ameliorate the substantial, as opposed to critical, aspects of her spirituality. Precisely for this reason, I do not intend to imply that every author who gave impetus to the first wave of Heideggerian feminist scholarship nor those in this anthology share theistic sensibilities. To the contrary, much scholarship continues to work within the classic philosophical orientation of being methodologically atheist. My suggestion is more simple yet not insignificant. The authors of the initial feminist books that appeared in the early 1990s, after the long hiatus from and in contradistinction to Bartky's "Originative Thinking" as well as her "Shame and Gender," absolutely did not regard Heidegger's spiritualism as remarkably lacking in concretion and wholly inefficacious when it comes to engendering a more humane world. These writers of the first sustained engagements with Heidegger began by rejecting that attitude toward Heidegger as misguided and, rather than defend him, simply offered reconstructions of Heideggerian thought in light of gender.

Bartky's preference for the early over the later philosophy, a preference common in Heidegger scholarship, enabled her to focus in the 1990 essay on a pragmatic and atheistic conception of human existence. Despite its prevalence within Heidegger scholarship, this focus overlooks the basic reality that the early Heidegger was already grappling with the questions that come to fruition in the later work. One way to understand the unity of theme from the early to the late works is precisely to address the notion of attunement in terms of its spiritualist connotations. While Bartky's essay centers on attunement as an essential structure of being finitely embedded in a historical and social context with no God's-eye view, Heidegger's own conception of attunement, even in *Being and Time*, grappled with the thicker reality that Dasein is a finite transcendence. Attunement articulates not simply the fact that, because human beings live within a concrete situation, all knowledge claims prove context dependent. Rather, it denotes for Heidegger our relation to the cosmos as an intelligible whole.

The twin notions of authenticity and inauthenticity in *Being and Time* refer not solely, as commonly held, to the distinction between holding naive identification with as opposed to taking critical, reflective distance on the prevailing discourses that are learned from the social context within which I am born and raised. It refers first and foremost to the more fundamental ontological reality that I can live solely on the basis of context-dependent values (whether critically or naively held), on the inauthentic side, or turn about-face and enter into an aware relation to my embeddedness in the cosmos proper, on the authentic side (as this is the only way in which I can truly win free from inauthentic compliance to a perspective or system of values). On this view, every Dasein or racial mode of existence is a guidepost to transcendence, to recovering an ontological sense of inherence in the cosmos proper, and not simply, as the modern view holds, a set of cultural values.[17] At stake is far more than critical reflection: namely, repose and equanimity. Where early Heidegger thinks of repose in terms of authenticity, the later Heidegger develops an understanding of a reciprocal relation between mortals and Being or cosmos proper. Although not centered on gender, Gail Stenstad's consistent exploration of attuning and event in Heidegger's thought paved the way for understanding the depth and ahistorical dimension of his notion of origin as well as what it means for a finite mortal to undergo transformation. Three essays in particular are significant: "Attuning and Transformation" (1991), "The Last God—A Reading" (1993), and "The Turning in *Ereignis* and Transformation of Thinking" (1996).[18] These form a backdrop for the question of Heidegger's religiosity.

By no means am I suggesting that all the work on Heidegger and gender that has emerged after Bartky's initial dismissal of the later thought grants a rich and full understanding of the spiritual significance of attunement. Although crucial work along these lines has been undertaken in feminist theology, most of this work is yet to come. I do suggest, though, that feminist interest in Heidegger—atheist or theist—often stems from a nascent, if tacit, intimation that Heidegger's thinking lays out a weighty sense of incarnation or embodiment. This includes Bartky's "Shame and Gender." And that intimation, in my view, strikes on the reality that weight stems from our material inherence in the cosmos and not simply from cultural and historical embeddness (a point awaiting greater exploration). It is thus not accidental that the first sustained works on Heidegger written by women and with an eye toward gender issues arose out of a felt kinship with the spiritualism of Heideggerian thought, precisely that aspect of Heidegger that leads other feminists to conclude that especially his later thought is not of use for feminist theorizing and praxis. I believe that this kinship and sensibility, embraced in Bigwood and Graybeal and nascent in other works, should (but may not) prove decisive in the next wave of Heideggerian-inflected, female-centered thought. The goal in this anthology, however, is the more limited one of bringing independently evolved concerns with Heidegger and gender together as a body and movement of thought.

Appearing in 1990 alongside Bartky's "Shame and Gender," Jean Graybeal's *Language and "The Feminine" in Nietzsche and Heidegger* proved pivotal in laying to rest another influential version of the view that Heideggerian thought is hopelessly antimodern and retrograde. I mean Julia Kristeva's claim, in *Revolution in Poetic Language* (1984, French edition 1974), that Heidegger's entire approach to subjectivity as rooted in existential care is a "logically and chronologically regressive mythological travesty" that merely hypostatizes a socially anxious subject and offers no resources for liberation from anxious concern.[19] Graybeal's sophisticated yet highly accessible and gracefully written book accomplishes numerous things. First, it stems from sympathy with Heidegger's "quest for non-metaphysical ways of thinking." Graybeal argues that both the early Heideggerian search for a joyous or authentic mode of life and especially the later Heideggerian notion of meditative thinking teach us how to live after the death of God, the Father. Moreover, living beyond "the death of 'the Father,'" rather than destroying religion, delivers us to a new understanding of religiosity, one that can "make new room for the 'feminine.'"[20] Second, her work tacitly explains why many women, at least during graduate school, feel great kinship with Heidegger. That kinship arises because there is an intimate connection between overcoming metaphysics and recovering lost, feminine styles of acting and being. Third, she demonstrates that the early Heidegger's conception of Dasein as rooted in care as well as later notions such as the source and mystery of existence all tap into the lost feminine dimensions of Western Being.

In order to advance her demonstration, Graybeal weaves a synthesis between Kristevan semiotics and Heidegger's understanding of the linguistic nature of human existence. And she explicitly defends Heidegger against Kristeva's critique that the Heideggerian subject lives a protected life, is much too happily identified with the traditional "religious or mythological definition of humanity," and remains unable to live freely without anxious need to fix the absolute meaning of reality by securing a linchpin in the symbolic edifice—that is, by getting the right concept of God, the Father, in place.[21] Although standing very much within the contemporary orientation toward symbolic analysis in postmodern theorizing, Graybeal goes beyond mere critique of gender blindness and seeks within Heidegger's thought new modes of existing that win free from the oppression of being caught within symbolically defined relations. Her work stands in keeping with a fundamental intuition that language and incarnation go hand in hand, a view as old as they come in religious and philosophical studies, but certainly, as her work implies, rejuvenated by Heidegger.[22]

Carol Bigwood's *Earth Muse: Feminism, Nature, and Art* (1993) leaped thick into Heidegger and placed his thought center stage within North American feminist theorizing.[23] Moving beyond Graybeal's subtle and probing exploration of the sytlistic affinities between feminine existence and meditative thinking, Bigwood developed a substantial, full-blown, and homegrown Heideggerian ecofeminst theory. Of decisive importance, Bigwood finds a more woman-friendly ethos in Heidegger than in more popular strains of deconstructive and poststructuralist feminist theorizing, strains that unfortunately inherit the "neo-Nietzschean" and "nihilistic" underpinnings of Derridean deconstruction. Although Bartky's "Shame and Gender" relied upon the fact that a phenomenological model of Dasein or subjectivity regards embodied attunement as a weighty occurrence, it is Bigwood who first challenges head on the claim that Dasein is pseudoconcrete when compared with Derrida. And, by arguing that poststructuralism tends to reduce female embodiment to thinned-out features of the linguistic construction of identity, she dispels Elam's view that feminism must be postphenomenological. In order to avoid the two extremes of gender skepticism (the view that we cannot talk about a univocal woman's standpoint) and essentializing woman's experience, Bigwood interprets Heidegger's view of Dasein as historical. This interpretation enables her to overcome the tendency within some postmodern theorizing to reduce woman's identity to an overly fluid and free-floating "cultural artifice" with "no real terrestrial weight."[24] Bigwood shows that subjects become stabilized in and through time; and women's perceptions disclose objective historical relations.

Moreover, because she regards the early and middle periods of Heidegger scholarship to be bogged down in masculinist sensibilities, Bigwood, *pace* Bartky, argues that it is the later philosophy that offers a genuinely female-sensitive ethos of receptivity to and nonagonistic dwelling with others on earth. In addition to rivitalizing Heidegger's understanding of embodiment, she shows how the Heideggerian notions of care, earth, and dwelling form a natural fit with a gender-sensitive ecology. Developing her own Heideggerian ecofeminist theory, with an original phenomenology of the hydroelectric plant, Bigwood compellingly exhibits that the later Heidegger, far from abdicating the weightiness of his early notion of Dasein, seeks to enhance our understanding of the textured nature of cohabitation. Although her brand of Heideggerian spiritualism is an earthbound as opposed to a cosmic one, Bigwood finds Heidegger immensely helpful in developing a notion of dwelling in the " 'world-earth-home' " that fosters open encounters "between cultures; races; the past, present, and future; and genders, and between the human and non-human."[25]

With the reception of Irigaray midstride in the Anglophone world, a reception that gave impetus to Bigwood's book, specific attention to Heidegger's influence on Irigaray could begin to dawn. This attention continues to press open the viability of his thought as a potential resource beyond Irigaray. Whereas Bigwood deliberately sought in Heidegger a thicker understanding of incarnation in the body and on earth, Ellen Mortensen in *The Feminine and Nihilism: Luce Irigaray with Nietzsche and Heidegger* (published in 1994 and based on her 1989 dissertation) explicitly critiques the methodological bias in Anglophone, feminist scholarship for its overly exclusive focus on the psychoanalytic dimension of Irigaray's work. Her book establishes that this focus covered over the importance of Irigaray's critiques of Nietzsche and Heidegger as central to her polemic with traditional philosophies, but also as essential to forming the basis for her own methodology and objectives. Treating nihilism as the key problem facing the twentieth century, Mortensen argues that Irigaray adopts Nietzsche's goal by effectuating a transvaluation of the notion of femininity. Yet Mortensen ironically concludes that Irigaray fails to remain outside the sway of metaphysics, as Heidegger informs us we must, the moment she names "Being" by positing the feminine as a transvalued value. In the last analysis, Mortensen also shows how Irigaray both relies on Heidegger when she treats the feminine as the forgotten of Western metaphysics and yet rejects Heidegger's "privileging of philosophical language" over other modes of disclosure.[26]

My own *Ecstatic Subjects, Utopia, and Recognition: Kristeva, Heidegger, Irigaray* (1998) sounded anew Mortensen's claim that Heidegger's influence on Irigaray has been inadequately understood by translators and theorists alike.[27] Even so, the intent of my book was neither to systematically analyze Heidegger's influence on Irigaray nor to compare the two thinkers. Like Bigwood (though not centered on ecology) I sought to construct a social theory and vision. My argument was that Heideggerian ontology can supply a solid basis on which to develop a social theory sensitive to difference. Given the ferocity of concerns over Heidegger's involvement with National Socialism and debates over the right and left Heideggers, it is difficult to avoid the question of the ostensible relation of Heidegger's thought to his politics. In keeping with Bigwood's and Caputo's respective views, I examined the masculine ethos that distinctively characterizes the middle period of Heidegger's thought and, rather than address his politics as a whole, offered this as a contribution to the broader debates.[28] Finally, in the second part of my book I generated a notion of critical utopian thought from Irigaray and Heidegger. My suggestion was that Heidegger offers Irigaray a way to envisage the future in an existentially rich but critically delimited manner that need not wed itself to a metaphysical "God" or communal form of life for all times.

Tina Chanter's *Ethics of Eros: Irigaray's Rewriting of the Philosophers*, having appeared in 1995, just after Mortensen's *The Feminism and Nihilism* (1994) and several years before my *Ecstatic Subjects* (1998), took one great stride toward revealing the relation of Irigaray to Heidegger and the Greeks. Chanter's book reflects the element of historical retrieval in Irigaray's thought. Precisely because it went against the grain of other approaches to Irigaray, Chanter's *Ethics of Eros* cultivated terrain for continued work of this kind to grow. Ellen Armour's "Questions of Proximity: 'Woman's Place' in Derrida and Irigaray" also makes an immensely useful contribution to spelling out in what ways Irigaray differs from Derrida.[29] Her source for this analysis is Irigaray's book on Heidegger. Krzysztof Ziarek's "Proximities: Irigaray and Heidegger on Difference" deserves mention in this context and certainly influenced my work. Although it appeared only recently in 2000, Ziarek's essay was written and presented much earlier, in 1994. "Proximities" constitutes one of the most serious attempts to date to specify exactly how Irigaray's understanding of the activity of thinking is decisively Heideggerian. The significance of Ziarek's work for transforming the initial interpretation of Irigaray and of the relation of her thought to Heidegger has yet to become fully appreciated, but will have appeared as part of his book *The Historicity of Experience: Modernity, the Avant-Garde, and the Event* in spring 2001, before this anthology arrives in print.[30] Joanna Hodge in "Irigaray Reading Heidegger," like Ziarek in his essay, delves with care into Irigaray's constructive reliance upon Heidegger's notion of originary thinking and the project of retrieval. Her important contribution deftly shows that Irigaray, though not positioned at root against Heidegger, "transforms Heidegger's violent readings of the texts constituting the history of philosophy into an amorous discourse."[31]

Chanter, Armour, Ziarek, and Hodge all advanced the effort to sort out the Heideggerian from the deconstructive strains of interpretation of Irigaray and opened the way for a deeper look at Heidegger. In addition to these influences, the main impetus behind my pressing a view of Heidegger and Irigaray as critical utopian thinkers in *Ecstatic Subjects* came from Drucilla Cornell's and Margaret Whitford's respective attempts to interpret Irigaray as offering a model of critical imagination. Numerous authors in *Engaging with Irigaray* also offered an important look at the question of utopia in Irigaray, most specifically Margaret Whitford and Jean-Joseph Goux.[32] Despite the position advanced in my book, I have since come to think that the depth of Irigaray's interest in meditative thought and spirituality moves in a direction altogether different from critical imagination and utopian thought. Treatments of Irigaray's methodology as a species of critical imagination or critical utopian thought, while eminently useful for social theory, nonetheless try to bridge the unbridgeable distance between Heideggerian historical retrieval and a psychoanalytic approach to image, word, symbol, and fantasy. Interpretations of Heidegger in relation to the search for a way to imagine the future without naively positing a final community of perfect harmony and self-transparency inevitably regard the Heideggerian strain in Irigaray as exerting an anachronistic pull. This view suggests that, by treating sexual difference as ontological difference, Irigaray not only privileges heterosexual relations in questionable ways but also inherits the retrograde preoccupation with a lost past that is ostensibly characteristic of Heideggerian temporality.[33] Scholars offering critical utopian interpretations of Irigaray, whether deliberately or not, want the deconstructive and psychoanalytic features of her thought to win out over the Heideggerian element of retrieval. They express a pervasive distrust of ontology that suffuses much feminist theory today.

The question of Irigaray's proximity to Heidegger ultimately hinges on whether she shares his understanding of *mythos* and language (*logos*). *Mythos*—a spontaneous expression of one's reciprocal participation in the source of existence (Being)—transcends the unconscious, the symbolic aspects of existence, and cultural values. This is the most difficult aspect of Heidegger to comprehend today and yet it is what makes his ontology defy association either with conservative nostalgia for an "origin" understood as some past form of life or with a fantastic future time. Nor does origin refer to a mere reservoir of unrealized meanings, whether taken as the unconscious or as the linguistic matrix of existence. It is precisely Heidegger's understanding of our originary inherence in a discernible reality that disallows mere classification of him as either a right or left Heidegger. That said, Irigaray has not squared off with the question of Heideggerian *mythos* in her own work. She jumps right back to employing psychoanalytic categories, such as the imaginary and the symbolic and the death drive, just after she has given birth to a meditation on sexual difference that enacts and gives life to a Heideggerian understanding of *mythos* or saying (*logos*). Irigaray's thought *intimates* without making entirely explicit a Heideggerian understanding of *mythos*, language or word. For this reason, Irigaray's texts give credence in varying degrees to each of the competing strains in Irigaray interpretation, those now emphasizing the Heideggerian and those highlighting the critical, deconstructive, or psychoanalytic elements of her text. Even so, Ziarek and others rightly press the Heideggerian moment because it operates as the most elemental inspiration of her work, as that with which she grapples.

If the parameters of feminist discussions about critical utopian thought categorically rule out apprehension that the ontological origin of human existence is irreducible to an archaic reservoir of unrealized meanings or not yet imagined possibilities, then it is the work in feminist theology that promises to appreciate this aspect of Heidegger, even though there, too, one finds an overdetermined preoccupation with deconstruction and psychoanalysis. Sadly, because of the overt commitment to Christianity, David Odell-Scott's *A Post-Patriarchal Christology*, although published in 1991, just after Graybeal and just before Bigwood, finds little audience in the broader world of postmodern feminist scholarship. Yet Odell-Scott ventures a fine study of "divine god-less thinking" in Heidegger and its implications for rethinking a postpatriarchal, Christ-centered faith. He argues that a *Theos*-centered (causal, metaphysical) and a *Christos*-centered (*logos* and context-based) theology prove incommensurable and only the latter allows for genuine difference to stand in opposition within divinity in a way that does does not fall prey to hierarchization.[34]

Other works of import in addressing Heidegger's understanding of the sacred include Sonya Sikka's *Forms of Transcendence: Heidegger and Medieval Theology* (1997) and her 1998 article, "Questioning the Sacred: Heidegger and Levinas on the Locus of Divinity."[35] The other Heideggerian-inflected, book-length study in theology, Marta Frascati-Lockhead's *Kenosis and Feminist Theology: The Challenge of Gianni Vattimo*, explores Vattimo's views of Heidegger and Nietzsche as they inform his search for emancipation from nihilism. In order to allow Vattimo's work to inform how we think about the relation of sexual difference to metaphysics and to nihilism, Frascati-Lochhead turns to Carol Bigwood's *Earth Muse*. Frascati-Lochhead presses for a more radical acceptance that, even though we never escape metaphysics wholly, this does not leave us with two undesired options: either a nihilistic-relativism that women fear will serve only the powerful or feminist essentialism. Although her orientation contrasts dramatically with that of Odell-Scott, Frascati-Lochhead finds that Vattimo's understanding of Heidegger's *Verwindung*—an overcoming of metaphysics from within metaphysics—allows for healing. Not only must feminists "strip traditional patriarchal theology of its metaphysical features," feminist theology must also undergo its own dissolution of "metaphyscial gynocentrism" by acknowledging "its belonging to the history of metaphysics" and *kenosis;* that is, the self-emptying of God through the incarnation must be met by a reciprocal self-emptying of the human person. "The destiny of feminist theology is, in this sense, one of *kenosis*."[36]

In addition to the *Geschlecht* essays and Irigaray's general corpus, I have highlighted six books, while relating numerous other books and essays solely to these, because each of these six books, in a specific way, clears away theoretic and attitudinal impediments to opening a path for a Heideggerian brand of woman-centered thought. Books of these kinds inevitably cultivate terrain for such a pathway to unfold. Throughout this same time period, from 1990 to 1999, a variety of other works pertinent to Heidegger and gender were accomplished. Questions concerning subjectivity in relation to language, time, and embodiment have germinated numerous strains of interest in Heidegger. These strains address a wide array of themes, including explorations of intersections between Heidgger and Kristeva, epistemology, the search for a lived ethos and various applied concerns in ethics, sexuality and authenticity, dwelling and home, the need to reinstate ontology within feminism, Heidegger's relation to female figures in his discussions of poetry, and pregnancy as a specific kind of female embodiment.[37] Since Nancy Holland and I started working on this anthology, it has become clear that numerous women among the new generation of philosophy students avidly and unabashedly explore connections between Heidegger and gender issues. And we have noted in the Selected Bibliography several dissertations, both older and newer, as some of this material will inevitably make its way into print.[38]

In light of the thematic range exhibited in the additional essays and books not discussed in this brief history, it should be obvious that there is no single canonical story to tell about the growth of this body of feminist work on Heidegger. Each of these additional works contains a seed that may yet grow into numerous strains. There is unavoidably something artificial in advancing any one story, even though the story has a sound basis in history. I wish to mention two other vital stories that have been emerging out of the same pool of chaos characteristic of new beginnings.

These are the ecological and the communications theory stories. Trish Glazebrook has now secured Heidegger's place in ecofeminism with her book, *Heidegger's Philosophy of Science* (2000). Her work, though different in orientation, follows in Bigwood's and, perhaps more directly, Michael Zimmerman's, steps. Zimmerman was one of the first people to discuss Heidegger's importance for ecological theory in relation to gender issues, as distinct from gender-neutral usages of Heidegger in enviromental theory. John Llewelyn as well contributed to this development. And more recently, Nancy Holland (1999) has taken interest in this area.[39]

A second noteworthy story emerged out of Stephen K. White's exemplary attempt to introduce into Habermas scholarship greater sensitivity to the political importance of Heidegger, specifically for Heidegger's kinship with feminist issues. His "Heidegger and the Difficulties of a Postmodern Ethics and Politics" initiated this effort in 1990, and White followed up in 1991 with a suggestive and direct discussion of feminism in *Political Theory and Postmodernism*. Although not addressed specifically to a feminist audience, Calvin Schrag's Heideggerian theory of communicative praxis offers the most viable alternative to a Habermasian model of communicative ethics in the twentieth century. Ramsey Eric Ramsey, Schrag's student, explicitly links Heidegger to a gender-sensitive ethics and social theory in his beautifully written *The Long Path to Nearness: A Contribution to a Corporeal Philosophy of Communication and the Groundwork for an Ethics of Relief*, published in 1998. Alison Jaggar (among others) has called for such an alterantive to Habermas as the missing link today in feminist social theory and, while I await her model, Ramsey's continuance of the Schragian legacy points to one such alternative that calls for further development. Although not centered on a phenomenological theory of communication, Nicholas Kompridis's insightful work promises to continue the effort to correct for narrowness and insensitivity to gender in Habermas's conception of reason by appeal to Heidegger, among others.[40]

Still, the seeds of other stories—such as that about Heidegger, gender, and aesthetics—remain to geminate, flourish, and be told. To come full circle to the story I am telling, I return to the question of spiritual attunement. The question of attunement—what sustains us in well-being throughout life journey—and its relation to gender differentiation has been taken up at the heart of Irigaray's project. If this was not evident in her dissertation, *Speculum*, it is evident now. The main intuition underlying her current work stems from Heideggerian inspiration. It thus calls us to look at Heidegger in his own right, and doing so would transform Irigaray scholarship. The most elemental question her work poses is whether sexual difference *can* be understood short of entertaining the *actuality* that it harbors positive and constructive potential beyond value-centered thought and the mere historical transmission of traditions and values. Sexual difference contains within itself guidelines for transcending the battle between the sexes and, insofar as sexual difference simply reveals in crystalline form other struggles of human existence, it points us beyond struggles of all kinds. This is a phenomenon of reality and not simply of meaning, ideas, or values.

Much work in feminist theology, as Frascati-Lochhead nicely points out, has not moved beyond interpreting religion as a set of values, on the one hand, and, I would add, transcending the suppositions of deconstruction and psychoanalysis, on the other. As noted above, both the deconstructive and the Heideggerian strains of Irigaray interpretation indeed do strive to address her call for a constructive notion of sexuate difference. For this reason, many authors press Irigaray toward questions concerning how to effectuate a transvaluation of values that does not fall prey to metaphysics—yet again. Even so, the critical framework for these discussions often remains entangled in the a priori assumption that the highest possible achievement for human being is to delimit rational, symbolic, or phantasmagoric ideals. But continued exploration of Heidegger's influence on Irigaray will necessitate a more direct confrontation with the real possibility of transcendence proper, albeit a transcendence fitting for earthbound and sexuate mortals. Even given the important work done in feminist theology, it is not clear that feminist theory in general is ready for the task of addressing whether there is a *real* relation of sexual difference to questions of transcendence and what kind of relation it is. This obvious omission occurs because most feminist theory is based on a categorical rejection of *the search for transcendence as such*. Not simply false approaches to transcendence, but transcendence proper has been indicted as the main source of woman's oppression. In this categorical atmosphere and on this desertlike terrain, a women-centered concern with religious transcendence could flourish only as does the cactus flower. What occurs instead is that only a deconstructive approach to religion seems viable (and this hardly yields a rich spirituality) or else women are left to engender historically relative and gender-relative symbolic practices, rituals, or cultural beliefs. Neither way leads to the intersection of sex and transcendence proper.

It is not inconsequential, then, that Bigwood and Graybeal engender a new sensibility that holds that the problem of metaphysics and religion is not merely a symbolic one but a substantial and vital one. This intuition underlies the explicitly Heideggerian impetus of Irigarary's thought, even though Irigaray herself has not adequately worked out a spiritual understanding of sexual difference in relation to the cosmos that transcends symbols. I believe wholeheartedly that this is exactly what she seeks to do, but that she is caught between the work of delimiting reason from within the bounds of symbolic systems and a Heideggerian understanding of originary thinking. In my comment I intend no disparagement, for if Irigaray has not fulfilled her goal, neither has anyone else, myself included, with the possible exception of Odell-Scott and Frascati-Lochhead, who planted a seed with their theological works. My comments point, rather, to the fact that Irigaray returns us to Heidegger, whose thought, while not explicitly involved in the task, provides thick guidelines for posing the question of sexual difference explicitly in terms of understanding mortal existence as an intersection between finitude and transcendence.

Let us then return to this anthology. The authors in this volume have divergent aims and understandings of Heidegger, aims that well exceed the question of transcendence under discussion.[41] As with all historical processes, the next phase of feminist interest in Heidegger must proceed as it freely will to explore multiple usages of his thought and to give birth to multiple strains of theory that either adhere substantially to his basic precepts or produce new varieties by grafting a branch of his thought onto another stalk, even stalks foreign to his own roots. There is something in the saying Let a thousand flowers bloom. My purpose here is not to constrain the expansive cultivation of such blossoming, but rather to suggest that, in the last analysis, the stubborn resistance of Heideggerian thought to "being put to use" requires a confrontation in actuality with his spiritual call, for his sounding this call is what both attracts women to his thought and repels them. Traversing more deeply the spiritual significance of Heidegger leads down a path that leaps beyond symbolic, linguistic, and psychoanalytic renditions of gender and god, to name the two things currently defining yet also limiting feminism. Squaring off with the religious roots of Heideggerian thought will, in turn, necessitate rethinking Irigaray scholarship as well.

I now turn to a discussion of the main philosophical concepts developed by Heidegger that allow for a rapproachment of feminism in its currently evolved interests and Heideggerian phemonenology. This guide is intended for the nonscholar and scholar alike.

A Guide to Heidegger's Thought

A. *The Early Work on Finitude and Authentic Self-Appropriation*

Heidegger wrote *Being and Time* as a sustained effort to overcome metaphysical thinking. Because it abstracts from and stills the fundamental quality of life, namely its kinetic or dynamic nature, metaphysics leads to a series of distortions and misunderstandings. It distorts the phenomenon whereby entities in the world make themselves intelligible to human understanding, and correlatively, it misrepresents our understanding of the human condition. All Western philosophy to date has transpired as a form of metaphysical thought, including modern philosophies that aspire to transcend metaphysics. Heidegger aims to shows us that encapsulated in all varieties of Western philosophy is one central dilemma that characterizes the human condition. This is the dilemma posed for *human understanding* insofar as human existence is *time-bound and itself kinetic*. How, in effect, can a finite human being, who only knows the world from within a concrete interpretive horizon of meaning, nonetheless transcend itself so that it can come to know phenomena without employing categories that falsify that phenomena? Because Dasein—Heidegger's technical term for human being—is temporal, it realizes its possibilities of understanding only through becoming. The problem faced by philosophy, then, is whether Dasein can bring to light a "transcending" understanding, one that allows the entity under consideration to appear in its dynamic nature, without stilling the kinetic flux of life.

Metaphysics kills off the life in phenomena by reducing entities to static things that can be conceptualized any way Dasein deems useful. The entire enterprise of Heideggerian thought, from the early works to the mature thought, endeavors to demonstrate that the true art of philosophy refuses to abstract from existential finitude but instead engages phenomena in its vital manifestation. *Being and Time* calls this enterprise fundamental ontology and shows that genuine philosophical thought requires the theorist to realize an authentic self-understanding. For authentic self-understanding proves a precondition of delineating a premetaphysical understanding of Being as such. Although Heidegger's understanding of the art of self-realization changes its face throughout his works, the pivotal aim of both the early and the mature works is to explain how Dasein can let things show themselves forth from out of themselves.

Heidegger's preliminary answer to the dilemma—that as human beings we are finite and yet it is incumbent upon us as self-aware beings to understand reality—can be found in his notion of *disclosure*. Heidegger defines truth as unconcealment (*aletheia*) or disclosure as such, rather than adhering to the typical philosophical definition of truth as correct perception. The notion that truth is unconcealment lies at the heart of Heidegger's understanding of the kinesis of life. It was the Greeks, according to Heidegger, who saw all entities as *phainomenon*, that is, as beings that harbor within themselves a dynamic movement of self-showing (BT, 29). Truth, defined as *aletheia*, denotes the fact that an entity can show itself forth in terms of a particular possibility only on condition that another aspect of the entity recede into the background. This reality is contained in the term *a-letheia* (un-concealment) where the alpha privative indicates the movement whereby something is brought out of concealment (*lethe*) by and into the light of human understanding. Heidegger holds that there are several kinds of unconcealment, ranging from the most originary to derivative forms. At fundament, unconcealment (*aletheia*) refers to the originary event of disclosure as such. Two derivative kinds of unconcealment obtain for Dasein and presuppose the first. These include the unthematized way that entities disclose themselves when Dasein is absorbed in a world of practical concern. And the most derivative stems from the act whereby we abstract from practical engagement with entities in a world in order to regard things as objects and on the basis of objectification to theorize the nature of both things and the subject of reflection.

The full substance of Heidegger's answer to the question, How can finite, time-bound Dasein know entities without distortion? is given through the elaboration of the basic intuition underlying *Being and Time*. That intuition holds that disclosure, the revelation of entities as meaningfully present, both happens to Dasein and yet can only occur through Dasein.[42] In *Being and Time* and the works written between 1928 and 1930, Heidegger claims that Dasein is unique among entities in that it alone stands in a questioning, that is to say, aware, relation to itself. Heidegger takes over and modifies the medieval conception of the *lumen naturale*. It is not that the human mind is illuminated from beyond. Rather, Da-sein, in its very manner of existing, is the site of disclosedness, the place where world is cleared such that entities light up and appear as meaningful. There is, then, a kinesis that is peculiar to Dasein. Da-sein, which literally means there-being, denotes the fact that human being is the site where world opens up and entities reveal themselves within a field of possibility (a world).

To be self-aware means that Dasein is, by virtue of its peculiar kinesis, the very activity of standing "in-between" a world and the event of disclosedness that makes possible a meaningful reception of entities. Simply put, Dasein both dwells in the world and yet is the clearing of world. As a finite, temporal entity, Dasein always already dwells within a particular world of meaning. And yet, as the site where disclosure occurs, Dasein is transcendence. Dasein ek-sists or stands outside itself. Dasein's ontological structure reaches beyond entities (beings) in their empirical manifestation within a horizon of meaning, and for this reason Dasein understands entities at an originary level in terms of their intelligibility proper (their beingness, their disclosedness). Only because Dasein is this transcending can it be absorbed in a given world and see entities as they appear within that particular referential totality.

Prior to any explicit attempt to theorize things in a world, phenomena appear first and foremost through Dasein's concerned, pragmatic engagement in a world. Entities do not first appear to Dasein simply as static and inert objects (present-at-hand) but rather as *meaningfully present* (ready-to-hand). By meaningful presence, I mean that things appear in terms of their possible usages. They appear, then, within a world or a referential totality (BT, 87). For example, a hammer appears "as useful for nailing" within the world of construction. But in another world of significance, say the world of writing, the hammer sitting on my desk "as useful for nailing" recedes from view and in its stead the hammer appears "as" altogether suited to be a paperweight. In that Dasein always dwells "in" a world, the disclosure of entities occurs within a hermeneutical field "as something," although the "as" remains unthematized in a philosophic sense. And yet Dasein can dwell within a world and entities can reveal themselves to Dasein only by virtue of Dasein's ek-stasis; that is, its transcendence of world. It is thus appropriate to talk about Dasein in the middle voice as both the recipient awareness of world and the site that lights up beings in a referential totality such that Dasein can engage them on the basis of its prethematic understanding of their possibilities.[43]

One of Heidegger's most significant contributions to philosophy consists in his showing that the problem of self-knowledge is not answered by abstracting from primordial engagement in a world. Dasein is this engagement. Hence, the act of theoretical abstraction from finitude yields a truncated conception of the nature of human reflection as a reflexive act and fails to enable us to understand existence. Once we must think from within existence, the primary problematic confronted by philosophy—how do we know what we know—must be restated. For the problem does not center on stepping outside context in order to capture the totality of the world. It centers rather on how one can arrive in media res in an aware relation to the unconcealment that conditions the self-showing of entities within any given referential totality or world. How can Dasein arrive at an understanding such that the self-showing of entities within a referential totality does not obscure two basic things: the nature of the vital role played by Dasein as the site of disclosure and awareness of unconcealment proper.

In seeking a genuine answer to this question, Heidegger requires us to make a distinction between truths of fact and truths of existence. Whereas the former deals with correctness of perception, the latter deals with authenticity of self-comprehension. The whole thrust of *Being and Time* aims to show that correct perception rests upon living authentically.[44] If human existence, as finite, precludes standing outside life and holding an objective viewpoint, then how is it possible for Dasein to arrive at an authentic self-awareness, one that brings beings as a totality into view? *Being and Time* offers a twofold answer to this question, one part existential and the other philosophical or thematic. The first answer pertains to whether it is possible for the human self to arrive at a coincidence with itself, so that its actions and expressed understanding of its motivations coincide. Given that Dasein is always oriented to new possibilities, it seems impossible that it could arrive at this self-coincidence. Heidegger shows, against common sense, that Dasein can face its outermost possibility, namely, death.

To act thoughtfully as if one's death is at hand brings one into a self-relation that frees one to see oneself as a transcending mortal, even though one may not die in actuality and some possibility remains unrealized. In facing death, one's possibilities for action are freed from conventional world-horizons and thus afford one the ability to abide disclosure as an event that lifts one out of time, delivers one to and for one's freedom, even as one must undergo time. Although Dasein is stretched "between" beings as a totality and yet transcends every totality, Dasein must nonetheless explicitly realize itself as this *finite transcendence* in order to become what it is, namely, a free yet finite mortal. This act of self-appropriation is called authenticity. There is a way within time that Dasein can bring its most basic structure and possibilities into view and thereby see itself for what it is, the clearing of disclosure. Most important, the reality that one can live authentically supplied Heidegger with the second answer to his question. Out of the posture of authenticity, a human being can develop a genuine and nondistorting ontological account of the human subject, of the kinetic nature of phenomena, and of the nature of unconcealment.

One clear reason for feminists to turn to Heideggerian thought is that the early works articulate a model of the human knower as pragmatically engaged in a world of meaningful concern. The early philosophy redeems everyday forms of understanding, in that these are less derivative than abstract knowledge. It forcefully argues that the way to arrive at a broad understanding of any person or thing cannot entail abstracting from one's embeddedness in a context. It entails rather the intensification of one's inherence in existence. Heidegger supplies a rich vocabulary for reconceptualizing human nature as care—custodian for what appears—rather than as the rational animal who lords over the earth. He demonstrates that Dasein is intersubjective (*Mitsein*) and embodied. Yet in spite of the concreteness of Heidegger's philosophy, a fundamental question arises.

In *Metaphysical Foundations of Logic*, Heidegger defends the gender neutrality of Dasein and this defense raises questions about whether his analysis of human existence can be filled out in terms of gender specificity or whether it harbors fundamental commitments that elide the reality of gender difference. One most basic question that feminists must pose to Heidegger is, Can the gender neutrality of Dasein support a social theory concerned with gender difference? Heidegger defends the gender neutrality of Dasein because his methodology seeks to think of human being as holistically engaged in world. This holistic method enables his thought to move beyond the body/mind problem in that neither mind nor body, cognition nor affection, is regarded as the more basic source of knowledge. When Heidegger argues that concerned engagement with others in a world provides a more primordial basis for grasping the nature of human understanding than theoretical knowledge, he deliberately does not claim that a bodily knowledge antedates theoretical abstraction. To say that Heidegger has a holistic approach means that concerned engagement, though prethematic and pre-predicative, entails both an affective attunement to the world and an attentive awareness appropriate to that engagement.

A basic thesis of Heideggerian philosophy, as noted, is that Dasein transcends things in their empirical particularities because it has a prethematic understanding of entities in terms of their intelligibility or disclosedness proper. Dasein is the site of disclosure and a being disclosed within a given horizon of meaning. The implication is that, although being incarnated into sexed bodies is a defining feature of worldly embodiment, sexual difference can take on multiple meanings in the world only because Dasein transcends gender difference in a certain regard. Insofar as it is the site of disclosure, Dasein is gender neutral. Heidegger's insistence on the neutrality of Dasein implies that gender does not encompass the totality of who one is. Such a conception of self is a consequence of being thrown into a body and a world. To Heidegger's own mind, this neutrality does not negate the reality that we live as embodied. But it does suggest that an authentic relation to one's embodiment would involve a moment of transcending finitude; that is to say, it would arise out of the activity whereby one recovers explicit awareness of being the site of disclosure. That act counteracts fallenness into conventional modes of understanding the body and the sexes. For this reason, this act breaks open a thoughtful relation to gendered embodiment and to the connotations gender carries in a given set of conventions.

B. *The Mature Notion of Meditative Thinking*

While the pragmatic conception of Dasein as concernfully engaged in one or another world of affairs was given definitive expression in *Being and Time*, there is a marked change in the later works. Whereas the early works focus on the role of Dasein's ontological structure as the site of disclosure, the later works shift away from analyzing Dasein. They focus instead on Being as such or the Event whereby Dasein is appropriated into unconcealment. The later works, even as they address poetics, technology, and language, reflect the mature Heidegger's deliberate attempt to think Being (disclosure proper) without reference to entities. Heidegger understands this shift in focus as essential to realizing more completely his original aspiration to foster a form of thinking that is premetaphysical or nonrepresentational.

Thus, in spite of this well-acknowledged shift in emphasis, the main question driving his thought (his *Seinsfrage*) remains the same throughout all periods of his work. That Dasein occupies a middle position between the way entities (beings) reveal themselves within a specific interpretive horizon and their beingness (the event of intelligibility) is the perplexing issue addressed by the entirety of Heidegger's life works. The reality that human beings do not create phenomena and yet phenomena can appear meaningfully only in relation to Dasein's activity is a momentous event, one that defines the very nature of existence and delineates to the human species its most basic task. To be this middle position requires Dasein to realize a special actively passive posture (designated by the middle voice) that "lets" things reveal themselves in their beingness. The basic problem for human thought is to interpret things in such a manner that they come forth as they are and not as distorted through the imposition of classification systems.

Although it is vitally important to recognize the thematic continuity in the Heideggerian corpus, it would be equally remiss to hold that a shift in emphasis is all that occurs in the later works. The main shift in emphasis away from Dasein and toward the Event of Appropriation yields subtle changes in tone, style, and topic. In the later works, Heidegger no longer strives to write a systematic philosophical ontology but instead offers poetic meditations. He talks less systematically of finitude and more poetically of mortality. We no longer find Dasein's defining characteristic described as pragmatic engagement in a world of concern. Instead Dasein's unique quality is now defined as a distinctive reciprocity it enjoys with the Event of disclosure. I agree with those who contend that such stylistic and emphatic changes indicate no substantial break in Heidegger's leading question. I further recognize that his turning away from Dasein to Being was instrinsically necessitated by his *Denkweg*, or path of thought. Yet far more significant than such stylistic and topical changes is a transformation in attitude that both funds and transfigures the explicit nature of his thought. The mature works break with the notion of authentic self-appropriation and advocate instead a posture of releasement from human will, a letting be that leaps into meditative thinking. The shift in emphasis from Dasein to Event demands and expresses, then, a marked transubstantiation in Heidegger's comprehension of the primordial task allocated to Dasein by its very nature, even though Heidegger had all along been thinking of this task and the essential relation of Dasein to Being.[45]

A profound ambiguity did pervade *Being and Time*, one that ultimately proved a deficient articulation of the nature of human finitude and human thought. That ambiguity centered precisely on the fact that in *Being and Time* Heidegger still made all systems of meaning take their point of reference from Dasein, even as he sought to decenter "man" as the source of knowledge and meaning. *Being and Time* falls into crisis because the difficulty of interpreting disclosedness in a way that does not reduce the self-showing of things to Dasein's willful intents or its capacity to make the world over fantastically according to its image, collides upon the notion of self-appropriation. Heidegger restates the difficulty by substantially modifying his notion of letting be. On the one hand, Dasein's ontological structure is to be released in that Dasein exists always already appropriated into a constellation of meaning. Letting be (*Gelassenheit*) in its first connotation thus denotes the Event of Appropriation that gathers beings into a meaningful constellation and attunes Dasein to the gathering. But letting be also refers to an attitude on the part of Dasein.

Being and Time sought but failed to articulate an adequate understanding of the attitude that alone enables Dasein to become what it is.[46] The implication is that the thematic emphasis in *Being and Time* evinced an error of existence, namely, that Heidegger misconceived Dasein's most basic possibility. And because the philosophical project of overcoming metaphysics rested on a proper understanding of Dasein's existential condition, it too could not be completed. The mature thought demands a new task as a precondition of arriving at self-understanding. The task is no longer one of self-appropriation but rather one of renouncing will, as Heidegger puts it in *Discourse on Thinking*. The attitude whereby the subject receives disclosure through nonwilling differs sharply from the notion of self-appropriation, which entails an aggressive wresting a thing from concealment by projecting a horizon of meaning over it, albeit a horizon that intended to bring its intelligibility proper into view.

Just as the early Heidegger offered a twofold answer in *Being and Time* to the problem of attaining a primordial disclosure of things, so too do his mature works give a double answer. For the early Heidegger, the model whereby we appropriate ourselves authentically and take critical distance on traditions had a transhistorical status. And yet the theoretical project of fundamental ontology, which aimed to break with metaphysical representations of man, had to work itself out through a confrontation with the history of philosophical categories and problems as we had inherited them. The mode of breaking free of tradition required working through tradition. Similarly, the mature works offer a transhistorical understanding of the task of releasement. In essence, self-appropriation is rooted in will. The mature Heidegger professes that the source of metaphysics stems from the will to surmount. Unlike in the early work, Heidegger now shows that human being cannot realize its freedom from conventions except by relinquishing will. We relinquish will through thinking, which Heidegger at times calls simply *Denken* (thought) and at other times refers to as meditative as opposed to calculative thought. Thinking in the mature works is decisively nonrepresentational. Heidegger distinguishes meditative thinking from all forms of conceptualization, including opining, ratiocination, cognition, representation, and speculation (contemplation). There is an activity that transcends representation, even though representational systems continue to abound in the world at large and the mind remains aware of their operation. This is the activity alone that releases Dasein into the realm where each entity discloses itself in its proper measure. No longer must Dasein will to overcome metaphysics, as this is impossible, but only wake up to metaphysics.

Heidegger also works out the nature of releasement in relation to the historical epoch within which we live and thus not only in transhistorical terms. We live in the age of *Gestell*, or technological Enframing (QCT), an era that marks the culmination of the history of metaphysics. Heidegger offers a *Seinsgeschichte*, or History of Being, in an effort to reveal that Western history unfolded through a progressive uprooting of our understanding of *technē* from *poiēsis*. Recall Heidegger's view that all phenomena have an intrinsic principle of self-showing. Heidegger has many names for phenomena—names such as *poiēsis* and *physis*—all of which denote the kinetic nature of entities. Thought, which is inherently conjoined to things as an enabling condition of their self-manifestation, is also a form of *poiēsis*. Heidegger defines *poiēsis* as "bringing forth" (*Hervorbringen*). All thought is a kind of bringing forth and yet some forms of reflection cover over, that is abstract from, their basic operation as bringing something forth into view. Heidegger claims that the Greeks understood *technē*—the particular kind of thinking peculiar to the fine arts and to craft—as a form of bringing forth and not thus as simple techniques that one wields to master the material of the craft one allegedly invents. To the contrary, *technē* involves being receptive to the possibilities granted by the thing itself and is thus a participatory activity that brings forth by letting the thing become its intrinsic possibilities (QCT, 12–13).

Metaphysics is unleashed at the inception of Western philosophical history because Plato, though he understood unconcealment and the essentially poetic character of thought, nonetheless theorized truth as correct perception. This move deracinates reason by unfastening it from its participatory act and leads to the eventual view of reason as the techniques by which we represent reality to ourselves. The mature Heideggerian philosophy offers sustained investigations into the ways that manifold canonical figures in Western philosophy each grappled with but failed to overcome the uncoupling of *technē* from the poetic nature of human existence. According to Heidegger, it is Nietzsche who ultimately reverses that history, though he too fails to overcome metaphysics, when he proposes that all thought is rooted in a will to surmount. Heidegger's ultimate definition of metaphysics is equally applicable to modern epistemologies as it is to classical metaphysics. Heidegger defines metaphysics as *onto-theo-logy* or the activity whereby one accounts for the totality of entities (beings) through the science of giving reasons (logos) until one reaches the supreme explanatory principle, Being as such (theology). Precisely this science of providing a "nexus of grounds," which allow the first principle to come into view, strives to transcend Dasein's temporal and finite inherence in life. Yet by abstracting from our own poetic essence as disclosive, we reduce entities to objects of human cognition only then to impose upon them the classification systems we regard as most accurate or suitable to our interests. And we wind up with a profoundly truncated conception of the nature of human reflection as the reflexive act whereby we can come to know things. In effect, human reason comes to be understood as the very ground of reality. And the will of Western civilization comes to dominate the globe.

Heidegger's mature thought suggests that mortal humans become free from the momentum of culture and history on condition that they relinquish will and allow themselves to be appropriated into the basic Event of Appropriation (unconcealment). Heidegger understands that Event in terms of a reciprocity between Dasein and Being. Being needs Dasein in order to come to thought. And yet Dasein also needs Being in order to be gathered into its originary repose before the self-revelation of entities. Although there is a transhistorical truth for Heidegger that human being is essentially poetic and can only arrive at equanimity through releasement, he also holds that the age of technological rationality manifests a most acute stage of the dis-ease of the will to surmount that has been the hallmark of all Western metaphysics. We have arrived, Heidegger warns, in a peculiar era in which the threat that we will forget once and for all our essentially poetic nature is very real. The age of Enframing is marked by an aggravated form of objectifying reason, one wherein we are tempted to reduce all entities not simply to re-presentable things but additionally to objects at our disposal, objects that seem to call out our total will to manipulation. In this era, what we tend to overlook is precisely that this basic orientation of the age permeates even human relations. Once we neglect to foster our deepest capacity to encounter things, ourselves, and one another as disclosive, we seem to pass over into a thoroughgoing inability to exist humanely. For only as self-disclosive does every living thing offer us food for thought, ways to understand and let be.

The historical dilemma, then, is this: human being cannot prevail over the age of *Gestell* by will, but rather must twist free of the historical consequences of Western metaphysics by recovering a capacity to embrace the intrinsic beauty housed in the singularity of each and every being. Heideggerian thought harkens back to an ancient wisdom. And he turns to the poets for assistance, as it is the poets who proclaim and offer a threshold to that which we have forgotten, the gift of each thing to every other. In the final analysis, all that affords equanimity is available to us in the mystery that all things are autodisclosive and provide us immeasurable and unceasing food for thought and delight, untold vistas of revelation, and a profound equanimity in the face of life journey.

In my remaining comments, I sketch three subthemes within Heidegger's project of overcoming metaphysics that have been of interest to feminist theory. These themes center on the role of poetics in building forms of life, the implications of Heideggerian thought for ethics, and whether meditative thinking offers a new spirituality or revolutionary social praxis. Not only is Heidegger one of few thinkers who bequeath the twentieth century a theory of poetics, but he also understands poetry and thinking to stand in close proximity to one another. It is of the very essence of human existence to dwell in a poetic responsiveness to the autodisclosive nature of all beings. Although the philosopher's primary vocation is not to write poetry, the thinker, and not simply the poet, has a special role to play in revealing the poetic nature of life journey. Moreover, Heidegger recognizes that art is one of the most vital ways in which truth can be understood as disclosure. And, because all thought transpires in and through word or language, Heidegger's work considers the relation of thought to word. In *Being and Time*, the emphasis falls on inauthentic babble—speaking out of conventional understandings—as distinct from authentic saying, in which one wrests from a thing disclosure of its nature through speech. The later works distinguish sharply between categorizing entities and responding to what calls Dasein to attentively receive it. Through word, Dasein lets things come forth into presencing for a while, to become illuminated by and to illumine Dasein's own understanding.

One important topic for feminism thus pertains to the kind of poetic ethos that can be fleshed out of Heidegger as a basis for establishing harmonious communal or intersubjective relations. There is a shift away from the willful ethos characteristic of the writings of the period from 1929 through 1936, works that can be said to carry pronounced masculine overtones, whereas the mature thought establishes a poetic ethos that is decisively more feminine and receptive in nature. The later works harbor potential resources for feminists in their thinking about what kind of fundamental attunement to life journey can establish open, rather than closed, communal ties. Still, even as it proffers positive contributions to feminism, Heideggerian poetics may need to be linked more explicitly to material reality. A person's ability to arrive at repose through a poetic relation to life journey may occur differently depending upon the gendered character of her or his body.

Another crucial issue stems from Heidegger's claim that poetic texts and the originary myths of the Greek and Christian worlds contain within them traces of what has been left "unthought" and forgotten in Western metaphysics. Heidegger sees the epochs of Western history as modes of dispensation in which it is given to Western Dasein to see the totality of entities within a particular horizon of meaning. These epochs can be understood in terms of the key words that open up that constellation of meaning: *idea* in Plato, *energeia* in Aristotle, *objectivity* for the moderns, *will to power* for Nietzsche, and finally *Gestell* (technological Enframing) in the twentieth century. To experience the historical dispensations of Being, whereby an epoch is granted or sent forth, is to cover over and forget the very Event of unconcealment proper. It is this Event that throws us into time and disposes us to follow the current constellation of beings as a totality. Yet forgetfulness means that we fall into time and fail to break free from the momentum of the age. Originary myths and poetic word offer guides into the unthought, namely, what was covered over at the inception of Western metaphysics (*poiēsis* and *alētheia*) and what harkens in the present to be recalled.

To the degree that we do not manage to leap out of a particular historical constellation of beings as a whole and into the Event that inaugurates it, we fail to find releasement from the sensibilities of the age. In addition, we cannot halt the forward momentum of history as the progressive unfolding of metaphysics. This failure is manifested as the continued belief that human reason invents the novel out of whatever the age regards as current, rather than meets the unpredictable and new through releasement from the compulsion to bring history under the control of human reason, prediction, and calculation. It is, then, an important endeavor to explore the significance of Heidegger's view that the unthought provides the basic threshold to freedom. Heidegger's meditations on poetic texts offer a provocative counterpoise to instrumental forms of thought; they strive to strengthen a sensibility that transcends our entanglement in technological domination of nature and Earth. Nevertheless, a serious feminist concern, first raised by Irigaray, is whether Heidegger's thought can deliver a future freed from domination, given that it never explicitly addresses the possibility that the feminine itself might be the unthought of Western metaphysics.

Although Heidegger never sought to develop an ethics out of his ontology, it does not follow that his corpus fails to give rich suggestions for ethics. His treatment of poetics harbors such suggestions, even though Heidegger's thought and his concern for human life are self-professedly antihumanist. Late Heideggerian thought does not center on philosophical anthropology. Nor does it assume that the ultimate cause of human struggle can be found within history. To the contrary, Heidegger holds that what conditions all historical struggle, whether one comprehends those struggles primarily as disputes over material inequities or as rooted in ideology, is the problem of how to be in but not of time. Fallenness into time is the ultimate source of unnecessary pain. For this reason, the solution to human conflicts will never be complete until we relinquish the basic drive to master reality that is unleashed through fallenness.

No matter how abstract Heidegger's *Seinsgeschichte* appears at first look, it is not without insight into the ultimate source of human conflict and suffering. There are ethical implications latent both in the concept of authenticity developed in *Being and Time* and in the mature notion of meditative thinking. Whereas authenticity focuses on what it means to take critical distance on conventional ways of interpreting life journey, the later model of letting be has been of keen interest to ecofeminist theory. The mature works advance a non-hierarchical and premetaphysical understanding of the relation of Dasein to the other. His is a fine model of a nondominating relation to earth, to human mortality, and to all life. Once again, though, the rich resources in Heidegger's thought have not eliminated all questions for feminists. Women question whether the later nondominating ethos explicitly values and appreciates the kinds of speech and playful human interaction characteristic of female practices and female-centered pleasures.

Finally, central to both the theme of poetics and that of ethics is the mature Heidegger's embrace of a nonrepresentational, meditative form of thought as key to nondominating relations to others and to overcoming the compulsion to bring historical development to center around Western man. What remains to be asked is what nonrepresentational thought can offer to social theory. Can meditative thinking offer support for the task of effectuating social change? The question poses a glaring challenge, especially since Heidegger insists that thinking yields neither usable knowledge (science) nor practical wisdom and does not lead us to act (WT, 159). Feminist interest in Heidegger must articulate the ways in which nonrepresentational thinking can sustain a better future for men and women, foster an alternative understanding of spiritual freedom, even ground a revolutionary practice of social change, or, according to Heidegger's own portrayal, fund compassionate acceptance of the uniqueness of every person and living thing. Addressing this Heideggerian challenge brings the history of Western metaphysics to an end without an ending. For it extends an invitation to current and future generations of scholars to explore these fruitful Heideggerian pointers toward a better way to live.

Notes

1. In the period from 1928 to 1935, Heidegger writes such political tracts as the *Rektoratsrede*, his speech delivered when he assumed the position of rector of Freiburg University. Such texts are exceptional and Heidegger's later works become apolitical.

2. Two exceptions include Derrida's "Geschlecht, Sexual Difference, Ontological Difference" and Irigaray's "From *The Forgetting of Air* to *To Be Two*." Derrida's article initiated discussions about Heidegger and gender. Irigaray's contribution, which comes from the Italian introduction to her Heidegger book, though published here in English for the first time, reflects her pioneering book on Heidegger, *L'oubli de l'air chez Martin Heidegger* (Paris: Éditions de Minuit, 1983); English edition, *The Forgetting of Air in Martin Heidegger*, trans. by Mary Beth Mader (Austin: University of Texas Press, 1999).

3. Sandra Lee Bartky, "Originative Thinking in the Later Philosophy of Heidegger," *Philosophy and Phenomenological Research* 30 (1970): 368–81.

4. Bartky, "Originative Thinking," 368 and 369, respectively.

5. Bartky, "Originative Thinking," 376, 375, 377, 380.

6. Representative samples include Günther Stern (Anders), "On the Pseudo-Concreteness of Heidegger's Philosophy," *Philosophy and Phenomenological Research* 8 (December 1947): 337–71; Karl Löwith, *Heidegger: Denker in dürftiger Zeit* (Frankfurt am Main: S. Fischer, 1953); Paul Hühnerfeld, *In Sachen Heidegger: Versuch über ein deutsches Genie* (Hamburg: Hoffmann und Campe, 1959); Karsten Harries, "Heidegger as Political Thinker," *Review of Metaphysics* 29 (June 1976): 642–69; Winfried Franzen, *"Die Sehnsucht nach Härte und Schwere: Über ein zum NS-Engagement disponierendes Motiv in Heideggers Vorlesung 'Die Grundbegriffe der Metaphysik,'"* in *Heidegger und die praktische Philosophie*, ed. Annemarie Gethmann-Seifert and Otto Pöggeler (Frankfurt am Main: Suhrkamp, 1988), 78–92. More recent debates over the concreteness of Heideggerian thought are too numerous to mention. Certainly Habermas has been a key critic in recent years, and John Caputo's *Demythologizing Heidegger* (Bloomington: Indiana University Press, 1993) locates specific areas of inattention to concreteness, without tossing the baby out with the bathwater.

7. I use 1990 as a historical marker because two constructive uses of Heidegger in journal articles (Bartky's and Maren Klawiter's) and Jean Graybeal's book all emerged. Maren Klawiter's "Using Arendt and Heidegger to Consider Feminist Thinking on Women and Reproductive/Infertility Technologies" came out in *Hypatia* 5, no. 3 (1990): 65–89. Although she focused on technology, Klawiter nicely anticipated that ecological interest in Heidegger would eventually address gender. Her article foreshadowed as well the little-known fact that some nursing students in the United States are sympathetic to Heidegger's view that human being is defined by care as opposed to reason. The Bartky and Klawiter essays emphasize the nature of human embodiment and thus establish the gender of Dasein as a vital topic of concern to feminists. One year later, Stephen K. White's *Political Theory and Postmodernism* (Cambridge: Cambridge University Press, 1991), discussed below, forges a substantial link between Heidegger and difference feminism. Although largely focused on media and image analysis, Patrice Petro's *Joyless Streets: Women and Melodramtic Representation in Weimar Germany* (Princeton: Princeton University Press) appeared in 1989 and relied on Heidegger, Benjamin, and Kracauer to develop a theory of perception. One early article was written in 1988 by E. Imafedia Okhamafe, "Heidegger's *Nietzsche* and Nietzsche's Play: The Question of Wo(man), Christianity, and Humanism" (*Soundings* 71 [Winter 1988]: 533–53). Okhamafe's article centers on Nietzsche's treatment of woman but toward that end she disputes Heidegger's interpretation of Nietzsche. She argues that Heidegger's interpretation "avoids the problem of woman and Christianity" (536) and, further, that "Heidegger's avoidance of Nietzsche's problematizing of the situations of Christianity and woman enables him to maintain from within his scheme a homogenous or metaphysical reading" (542). Her view opposes that articulated by Derrida in his 1983 and 1987 *Geschlecht* essays whose crucial role in the emergence of a feminist reception of Heidegger I discuss directly. Several dissertations that, again, made positive use of Heidegger were written around this same time. Andrea C. Staskowski's "Conversations with Experience: Feminist Hermeneutics and the Films of West German Women" (Ph.D. diss., University of Iowa, 1990) made a compelling argument that Heidegger, Gadamer, and numerous radical feminists provide better frameworks for understanding these women's films than does any variety of poststructuralist feminism. Also in 1990, Wanda Deifelt wrote "Toward a Latin American Feminist Hermeneutics: A Dialogue with the Biblical Methodologies of Elisabeth Schuessler Fiorenza, Phyllis Trible, Carlos Mesters, and Pablo Richard" (Ph.D. diss., Northwestern University), a work of significance for feminism's relation to religion. Another interesting dissertation in 1991 examined Eeva-Liisa Manner's poetry in light of Heidegger's understanding of poetry (Tuula Margareta Hokka, "Writing of the Soil, Smoke of the Sun: Perspectives on the Poetry of Eeva-Liisa Manner and Its Modernity" [in Finnish] [Ph.D. diss., Helsingin Yliopisto, Finland]). I mention these because they were written around 1990, the historical marker for the emergence of a constructive use of Heidegger. For other dissertations of interest (between 1992 and 2001), see the Selected Bibliography.

8. I wish to note that Hélène Cixous's work is most sympathetic to Heidegger and should be one of the primary sources encouraging feminist interest in Heidegger.

38   Introduction I

9. Jacques Derrida, "Geschlecht: Sexual Difference, Ontological Difference," (commonly known as *Geschlecht* I) can be found in *Research in Phenomenology* 13 (1983): 65–83 and was originally published in Michel Haar, ed., *Martin Heidegger* (Paris: Cahier de l'Herne, 1983). "Geschlecht II: Heidegger's Hand," trans. John P. Leavey, Jr., is published in *Deconstruction and Philosophy: The Texts of Jacques Derrida*, ed. John Sallis (Chicago: University of Chicago Press, 1987), 161–96. "Heidegger's Ear: Philopolemology (*Geschlecht* IV)," trans. John P. Leavey, Jr., is published in *Reading Heidegger: Commemorations*, ed. John Sallis (Bloomington: Indiana University Press, 1993), 163–218.

10. Nancy J. Holland, "Heidegger and Derrida Redux: A Close Reading," in *Hermeneutics and Deconstruction*, ed. Hugh J. Silverman and Don Ihde (Albany: State University of New York Press, 1985), 219 and 225, respectively.

11. Diane Elam, "Is Feminism the Saving Grace of Hermeneutics?" *Social-Epistemology: Journal of Knowledge, Culture and Policy* 5 (October–December 1991): 349–60.

12. Derrida and the deconstructive stain of feminism, like Heidegger, came under similar scrutiny for abstracting from subjectivity and essentializing femininity, as did other strains of feminist poststructuralism. Kelly Oliver's "Nietzsche's Woman: The Poststructuralist Attempt to Do Away With Women" (*Radical Philosophy* 48 [Spring 1988]: 25–29), though not directed against Derrida, gives a clear statement of one concern about male appropriations of the discursive positions of female voices. Although these debates were too widespread and varied to reproduce here, of note is that Holland later addresses more specifically the gender neutrality of Heidegger's concept of Dasein, while again taking up a constructive approach to Derrida and Heidegger, in "Derrida and Feminism," *APA Newsletter* 91 (Fall 1992): 40–43. In relation to debates over the reception of Derrida, John Caputo's work between 1984 and 1993 also laid the groundwork for a nonnaive look at Heidegger in relation to gender and oppression.

13. Luce Irigaray, *An Ethics of Sexual Difference*, trans. Carolyn Burke and Gillian C. Gill (Ithaca: Cornell University Press, 1993), 5.

14. Thanks go to Mary Beth Mader, who devoted her dissertation in large measure to translating *L'oubli de l'air chez Martin Heidegger*. For full reference, see n. 2 above.

15. Irigaray claims deliberately to employ different methods in "Thinking Life as Relation: An Interview with Luce Irigaray," interview by Stephen Pluháček and Heidi Bostic, *Man and World* 29 (1996): 350–51.

16. Although fewer in number than those criticisms directed against Heidegger for his ostensible lack of concretion, variations of this critique of French feminism within feminist circles are also too many to enumerate. Nancy Fraser and Sandra Lee Bartky, eds., *Revaluing French Feminism: Cultural Essays on Difference, Agency, and Culture* (Bloomington: Indiana University Press, 1992) give a good entry into such concerns.

17. Heidegger shares this view in common with the Spanish existentialists Miguel de Unamuno and Jose Ortega y Gasset, who formulated such conceptions of race before he did.

18. Gail Stenstad, "Attuning and Transformation," *Heidegger Studies* 7 (1991): 75–88; "The Last God: A Reading," *Research in Phenomenology* 23 (1993): 172–84; "The Turning in Ereignis and Transformation of Thinking," *Heidegger Studies* 12 (1996): 83–94.

19. Julia Kristeva, *Revolution in Poetic Language*, trans. Margaret Waller (New York: Columbia University Press, 1984), 129.

20. Jean Graybeal, *Language and "The Feminine" in Nietzsche and Heidegger* (Bloomington: Indiana University Press, 1990), 2, 4, and 2, respectively.

21. Graybeal, *Language and "The Feminine,"* 126.

22. Graybeal's synthesis of Kristeva and Heidegger is a precursor to Noëlle McAfee's "Abject Strangers: Toward an Ethics of Respect," in *Ethics, Politics, and Difference in Julia Kristeva's Writing*, ed. Kelly Oliver, 116–34 (New York: Routledge, 1993) and to Jennifer Anna Gosetti's "Language and Subject in Heidegger and Kristeva," *Philosophy Today* 43, supplement (1999): 76–87.

23. Carol Bigwood, *Earth Muse: Feminism, Nature, and Art* (Philadelphia: Temple University Press, 1993).

24. Bigwood, *Earth Muse*, 7, 26, 24, 44 respectively.
25. Bigwood, *Earth Muse*, 10.
26. Ellen Mortensen, "Woman's (Un)truth and *le féminin*: Reading Luce Irigaray with Friedrich Nietzsche and Martin Heidegger," in *Engaging with Irigaray: Feminist Philosophy and Modern European Thought*, ed. Carolyn Burke, Naomi Schor, and Margaret Whitford (New York: Columbia University Press, 1994), 225. Mortensen's *The Feminine and Nihilism: Luce Irigaray with Nietzsche and Heidegger* (Oslo: Scandinavian University Press, 1994) is currently out of print. This essay offers a nice taste of what she accomplished.
27. Patricia Huntington, *Ecstatic Subjects, Utopia, and Recognition: Kristeva, Heidegger, Irigaray* (Albany: State University of New York Press, 1998).
28. John Caputo shows that a distinct ethos colors the work of the 1930s in "Heidegger's *Kampf*: The Difficulty of Life and the Hermeneutics of Facticity," in *Demythologizing Heidegger* (Bloomington: Indiana University Press, 1993), 39–59. Bigwood states but does demonstrate the basis for holding the same view, as doing so would divert from developing her ecofeminist theory. Although I had not read it at the time, Kathleen Wright's "Heidegger's Hölderlin and the Mo(u)rning of History," *Philosophy Today* 37 (Winter 1993): 423–35, laid the groundwork for the analysis I undertook (see n. 37 below).
29. Tina Chanter, *Ethics of Eros: Irigaray's Rewriting of the Philosophers* (New York: Routledge, 1995), esp. chap. 4. Ellen T. Armour, "Questions of Proximity: 'Woman's Place' in Derrida and Irigaray," *Hypatia: A Journal of Feminist Philosophy* 12 (Winter 1997): 63–78.
30. Relevant works include Krzyzstof Ziarek's "Love and the Debasement of Being: Irigaray's Revisions of Heidegger and Lacan," *Postmodern Culture* 10, no. 1 (1999): paragraphs 1–29 (online); "Proximities: Irigaray and Heidegger on Difference," *Continental Philosophy Review* 33 (2000): 133–58; and "Sexuate Experience: Irigaray and the Poetics of Sexual Difference," *The Historicity of Experience: Modernity, the Avant-Garde, and the Event* (Evanston: Northwestern University Press, 2001).
31. Joanna Hodge, "Irigaray Reading Heidegger," in *Engaging with Irigaray*, 195 (see n. 26 above). In addition to her *Heidegger and Ethics* (London: Routledge, 1995) and other essays, Hodge developed two essays in particular that, while not explicitly focused on gender, advanced an understanding of how the 1930s changed Heidegger's relation to politics. These are "Nietzsche, Heidegger, and the Critique of Humanism," *Journal of the British Society for Phenomenology* 22 (January 1991): 75–79; and "Forgetting: Europe, Tradition, Philosophy," *Journal of the British Society for Phenomenology* 26 (October 1995): 255–67.
32. Drucilla Cornell, *Beyond Accommodation: Ethical Feminism, Deconstruction, and the Law* (New York: Routledge, 1991); Margaret Whitford, *Luce Irigaray: Philosophy in the Feminine* (London: Routledge, 1991). Whitford's "Irigaray, Utopia, and the Death Drive" and Jean-Joseph Goux's "Luce Irigaray Versus the Utopia of the Neutral Sex" both appear in *Engaging with Irigaray*, 379–400 and 175–90, respectively. See n. 26 for full reference.
33. See Cornell's clear remarks in "The Future of Sexual Difference: An Interview with Judith Butler and Drucilla Cornell," ed. Pheng Cheah and Elizabeth Grosz, *Diacritics* 28.1 (Spring 1988): 19–42, especially 30–33.
34. David W. Odell-Scott, *A Post-Patriarchal Christology* (Atlanta, Ga.: Scholars Press, 1991), 197–208.
35. Sonya Sikka, *Forms of Transcendence: Heidegger and Medieval Mystical Theology* (Albany: State University of New York Press, 1997) and "Questioning the Sacred: Heidegger and Levinas on the Locus of Divinity," *Modern Theology* 14 (July 1998): 299–323. Although I have not singled out *Deconstruction, Feminist Theology, and the Problem of Difference: Subverting the Race/Gender Divide* (Chicago: University of Chicago Press, 1999), because it does not advance a substantive Heideggerian position, Ellen Armour's work is informed by an acknowledgment of the Heidggerian roots of Irigaray and Derrida. Because her concern in this book is to enable "white feminism to think racial

difference" by "uncovering and clearing the ground that has nurtured the divide between race and gender" (3), Armour turns to Derrida and Irigaray, who derive their methods from Heidegger in ways that enable us to see the radicality of Irigaray's methology (110). Also noteworthy is Philippa Berry's "The Burning Glass: Paradoxes of Feminist Revelation in *Speculum*," in *Engaging with Irigaray*, 229–46 (see n. 26), as it shows how Irigaray appropriates Heidegger in order to deconstruct the spirit-matter dualism in Western thought. Her essay initiates and calls for more thorough explorations of Irigaray's relation to religion, in particular medieval mysticism. Berry's essay supports the key point I am asserting, namely, that understanding Heidegger's religiosity will require scholars to reexamine Irigaray.

36. Marta Frascati-Lochhead, *Kenosis and Feminist Theology: The Challenge of Gianni Vattimo* (Albany: State University of New York Press, 1998), 9, 211, and 10 respectively.

37. Grouping them thematically and not chronologically, I mention key essays. Noëlle McAfee (1993) and Jennifer Anna Gosetti (1999) have, following Graybeal, written insightful essays that weave the ontological elements of Heidegger together with Kristevan semiotics into a theory of subjectivity (see n. 22 above). Kathleen Wright's "Heidegger's Hölderlin and the Mo(u)rning of History" (1993) anticipated the need to address Heidegger's failure to oppose political violence and its relation to his forgetfulness of woman figures, a theme taken up by others previously mentioned (see n. 28). Terri Elliot challenges Nancy Hartsock's standpoint epistemology from a Heideggerian perspective in "Making Strange What Had Appeared Familiar," *The Monist* 77 (October 1994): 424–33, and thus advances concerns over the feminist turn away from ontology. Rosalyn Diprose's book on ethics and female embodiment, *The Bodies of Women: Ethics, Embodiment, and Sexual Difference* (New York and London: Routledge, 1994), was based on her dissertation (1991); together these provided one of the first statements (only one year after Graybeal) that Heidegger's concept of authenticity allows us to think about sexual difference in ways that resist dogmatic cultural discourses. The particular question of ethos as it informs ethics offers a conceptual basis for Nancy Holland's recent book, *The Madwoman's Reason: The Concept of the Appropriate in Ethical Thought* (University Park: Penn State University Press, 1998), which addresses ethics in terms of a concept of appropriate action. Also related to ethics, Anne Cladwell's "Fairy Tales for Politics: The Other, Once More," *Philosophy Today* 41 (Spring 1997): 40–50, discussed Heidegger as part of her argument that Derrida's ethical demand to respect alterity is limited, whereas Irigaray teaches us how to live well with alterity. On the basis of Heideggerian sensibilities, Gail Stenstad's "Anarchic Thinking: Breaking the Hold of Monotheistic Ideology on Feminist Philosophy," in *Women and Values: Readings in Recent Feminist Philosophy*, ed. Marilyn Pearsall (Belmont, Calif.: Wadsworth, 1993), 248–53, developed a model of anarchic thinking that affirms multiple voices in feminism. Amy Mullen's "Purity and Pollution: Resisting the Rehabilitation of a Virtue," *Journal of the History of Ideas* 57 (July 1996): 509–24, explored how Kierkegaard and Heidegger link purity to questions of sexuality and authenticity. Iris Young's "House and Home: Feminist Variations on a Theme" (chap. 7 of her *Intersecting Voices: Dilemmas of Gender, Political Philosophy, and Policy* [Princeton: Princeton University Press, 1997] and reprinted here), although critical of Heidegger, indicates that the influence of Heidegger on feminism has extended outside the circle of Heidegger scholarship proper. Another fine use of Heidegger to explore female embodiment, "Dasein Gets Pregnant," by Lanei Rodemeyer, appeared in 1998 (*Philosophy Today* 42, supplement: 76–84).

38. Since Gosetti's work has moved beyond the dissertation, I note Maria Christine Cimitile's and Brian Bowles's dissertations. In "The Truth in Mimesis: Phenomenological Transformation in Gadamer, Heidegger, and Irigaray" (Ph.D. diss., University of Memphis, 1999), Cimitile critiques interpretations of Platonic mimesis as imitation. She initiates an important area of research into the relation between Heidegger's understanding of truth as unconcealedness and Irigaray's notion of mimcry. Brian Bowles, in his "Heidegger's Retrieval of Aristotelian [πάθος]: On the Place of 'the Bodily' in Heidegger's Thought" (Ph.D. diss., Loyola University of Chicago, 2001), undertakes a much needed systematic exploration of the bodily dimension of *Being and Time* that will be of

import. Although they are not many in number, I also wish to mention that a few works on Heidegger and race or Africana philosophy have been developed. While not all treat gender, these works are of relevance to feminism: Tsenay Serequeberhan's *The Hermenuetics of African Philosophy: Horizon and Discourse* (New York: Routledge, 1994); Roy Martinez's "Existential *Angst* and Ethnic Cleansing," *Soundings* 77 (Spring/Summer 1994): 201–10; and Steven E. Jones's "Disconnected Connection: The Road to Being a Black Man" (Ph.D. diss., University of Maryland, College Park, 1996). Jones relies on Serequeberhan to undertake a phenomenology of being Black and being a man.

39. Trish Glazebrook, *Heidegger's Philosophy of Science*, Perspectives in Continental Philosophy, no. 12 (New York: Fordham University Press, 2000). See also her "Heidegger and Experiment," *Philosophy Today* 42 (Fall 1998): 250–61 and "From *Physis* to Nature, *Techne* to Technology: Heidegger on Aristotle, Galileo, and Newton," *Southern Journal of Philosophy* 38 (Spring 2000): 95–118; Michael E. Zimmerman, "Feminism, Deep Ecology, and Environmental Ethics," *Environmental Ethics* 9, no. 1 (1987): 21–49; *Heidegger's Confrontation with Modernity: Technology, Politics, and Art* (Bloomington: Indiana University Press, 1990); and "Rethinking the Heidegger-Deep Ecology Relationship," *Environmental Ethics* 15 (Fall 1993): 195–224; John Llewellyn, *The Middle Voice of Ecological Conscience* (New York: St. Martin's Press, 1991). Ladelle McWhorter's anthology, *Heidegger and the Earth: Essays in Environmental Philosophy* (Kirksville: Thomas Jefferson University Press, 1992) does not explicitly address gender, but nonetheless contributes to thinking about Heidegger and ecology. Gail Stenstad has a fine essay in that collection. I want to mention Yoko Arisaka's very interesting essay, "Women Carrying Water: At the Crossroads of Technology and Critical Theory," in *New Critical Theory: Essays in Liberation*, ed. William S. Wilkerson and Jeffrey R. Paris (Lanham, Md.: Rowman and Littlefield, 2001). She offers a gender-sensitive look at Nepalese women, their water needs, and how to introduce technology into their lives. Although she draws solely on critical theory and existentialism as her explicit theoretic sources, Arisaka's approach has definite Heideggerian undertones.

40. Stephen K. White, "Heidegger and the Difficulties of a Postmodern Ethics and Politics," *Political Theory* 18 (February 1990): 80–103; *Political Theory and Postmodernism* (Cambridge: Cambridge University Press, 1991); Ramsey Eric Ramsey, *The Long Path to Nearness: A Contribution to a Corporeal Philosophy of Communication and the Groundwork for an Ethics of Relief* (Atlantic Highlands, N.J.: Humanities Press, 1998); Nikolas Kompridis, "Heidegger's Challenge and the Future of Critical Theory," in *Habermas: A Critical Reader*, ed. Peter Dews (Oxford: Blackwell, 1999), 118–50. See also my comments on the possible relations of Schrag's work to gender issues in "Between the Scylla of Discursivity and the Charybdis of Pantextualism," *Human Studies* 21 (April 1998): 197–206.

41. See Nancy Holland's "Introduction II," where she indicates precisely how each contributor to this anthology builds on, develops, or amplifies the first phase of interest in Heidegger that spanned 1990 to 1998. In general terms, the authors in Part I, "The Gender of Dasein," offer closer examinations of early Heidegger's views of subjectivity, intersubjectivity, and temporality than have been undertaken to date. Careful studies of this kind, in the multicultural milieu, need to be undertaken. Part II, "Poetics and the Body," contains three fine contributions to an area that has received scant attention. Typically, the most rigorous scholarly work on Heidegger and poetics has not been gender specific. The essays in Part III, "Ethics, Home, and Play," represent current attention that has arisen over Heidegger's potential contribution to ethics (earlier examples include White and Bigwood, while Hodge, Ramsey, and Holland are more recent; see n. 40 for others). And they nicely extend interest into applied concerns over ecology, woman's relation to home, and the role of play in ethics. All contributors to Part IV attend to the initial stumbling block for feminism, namely, whether originary thinking harbors within itself vibrant potential for revolutionary programs of change. Rather than tacitly assume an affirmative answer to this question, these authors make explicit what they consider to be radical dimension of Heideggerian thought.

42. I invoke Tom Sheehan's vocabulary of meaningful presence. See his "Heidegger," in *A Com-*

panion to the Philosophers, ed. Robert L. Arrington, Blackwell Companion to Philosophy, 12 (Malden, Mass.: Blackwell, 1998), 288–97; and his entry "Martin Heidegger," in the *Routledge Encyclopedia of Philosophy*, ed. Edward Craig (New York: Routledge, 1998), 307–23.

43. Noteworthy here is that an entity takes on meaningful presence "as something" or in terms of its "possibilities" ultimately because Dasein, as a kinetic yet self-aware entity, is mortal. Because Dasein undergoes its own existence as possible, it knows its own mortality, its death. It carries its death, albeit unrecognized, in every decision to actualize one rather than another possibility. Transcendence, understood by one who is time-bound, points toward the final absence, death. Ultimately it is because Dasein knows its own absencing (both as death and as that which remains unrealized in any act) that the absenting in every mode of presencing peculiar to phenomena is intelligible to it.

44. Heidegger held that the Greek philosophers knew this distinction. The Greeks posed the problem of the philosophic search to articulate the nature of reality first and foremost as a problem of the truth of one's being. Prior to any distinction between truth and falsity of perception (correctness of perception) lies something more basic still, namely, the truth of one's existing, of one's inherence in the totality of what is (beings as a whole). The Greeks rightly clarified the nature of human understanding when they showed that understanding was not a matter of abstracting from one's inherence in a mode of disclosedness of entities in order to re-present the thing under a concept. To the contrary, the art of understanding, as Heidegger argues of Plato, entailed an entire attunement of the soul, a turning of one's entire being in such a manner that things can show themselves without dissemblance.

45. William J. Richardson, in his massive and highly influential *Heidegger: Through Phenomenology to Thought* (The Hague: Martinus Nijoff, 1963), first distinguished between Heidegger I and Heidegger II or the early and late Heidegger. The subsequent reception of Heideger in the United States took place in terms of this division or subdivisions thereof (e.g., the middle and early-early periods). Thomas Sheehan has notably sought to dispel the mistaken view that what Heidegger calls the Turn in thinking correlates to periodic, stylistic, and substantial shifts in his corpus. I agree with Sheehan that the Turn denotes an aspect of the Event by which Dasein is appropriated into disclosure and that this appropriation requires a personal response. My own sentiment, however, is that we cannot underestimate the nature of this personal transformation, its impact on Heidegger's authorship, and its significance for philosophy, as it implies that thinking renounces projection altogether. See Sheehan's "Martin Heidegger" (n. 42 above), esp. 315–16; and his "Kehre and Ereignis: A Prolegomenon to *Introduction to Metaphysics*," in *A Companion to Heidegger's "Introduction to Metaphysics*," ed. Gregory Fried and Richard Polt (New Haven: Yale University Press, 2001).

46. Reiner Schürmann, in his "Heidegger and Meister Eckhart on Releasement," *Research in Phenomenology* 3 (1973): 95–119, clarifies that releasement both is Being's way to be and an attitude that Dasein can adopt.

Introduction II—Specific Contributions

Feminists Read Heidegger

Nancy J. Holland

The essays in this volume have been divided into four interwoven groups, as indicated by the titles of the respective sections. Despite a certain amount of unavoidable overlap, these groupings are intended to be both thematic and chronological, beginning with *Being and Time* and ending with more forward-looking articles by Gail Stenstad and Patricia Huntington. While of necessity somewhat arbitrary, these groupings and this part of the Introduction are intended as a rough guide for readers interested in a specific topic or period in Heidegger's work.

The earliest essay in this collection, Jacques Derrida's "Geschlecht: Sexual Difference, Ontological Difference," is the first of four essays Derrida has published on the same subject over roughly the past twenty years.[1] Starting his investigation from Heidegger's apparent silence with regard to gender, especially in *Being and Time*, Derrida attributes this to the "fact" that sexual difference seems to remain an ontic, rather than ontological, feature of Dasein. In the Marburg lectures of 1928, however, Heidegger explicitly asserted the gender neutrality of Dasein, which Derrida terms a "pre-dual sexuality," a powerful positivity of which our understanding of the two sexes (Heidegger's limitation) would only be a derivative or even privative form. Derrida's guiding question here is whether this neutrality of Dasein does not in fact simply repeat the traditional philosophical denial of sexual difference—which would in fact establish the male as the only "true" sex—and the corresponding erasure of sexuality per se.

Tina Chanter makes a similar point in her essay, "The Problematic Normative Assumptions of Heidegger's Ontology," but broadens it to include Heidegger's more general denial of the significance of any differences between humans (her list of examples includes gender, race, class, ethnicity, and sexuality as a minimum set). She attributes this denial to certain underlying normative assumptions Heidegger makes, and looks in some detail at aspects of *Being and Time* that facilitate his repetition of these traditional exclusions. These exclusions, she argues, allow Heidegger's culturally specific understanding of Dasein to remain protected from critical interrogation. Chanter organizes her critical reading through the lenses of the body, others, and temporality/history, using Descartes as the exemplar for the tradition from which Heidegger, she argues, fails sufficiently to distance himself. She also offers a nuanced schematic interpretation of how Dasein temporalizes itself, and illuminates ways in which some aspects of Heidegger's work can be seen to contribute significantly to the development of feminist thought.

In her essay, "Conflictual Culture and Authenticity: Deepening Heidegger's Account of the Social," Dorothy Leland draws on Charles Guignon's application of Heidegger's thought in *Being and Time* to psychotherapeutic practice to create a broader, more radical understanding of authentic living on the basis of a concept of "conflictual culture." Leland emphasizes the extent to which Guignon, and Heidegger, ignore the internal diversity in any given social group and hence the conflicting, and potentially subversive, values that can be found within the social order from which authentic Dasein must draw its moral choices. In contrast, Leland uses the writings of women from the Native, Hispanic, and black populations of the United States to illustrate how the "shared medium of intelligibility"[2] may not in fact be shared and may not even be fully intelligible to some of those living within a particular cultural space.

One of the points Leland makes has to do with schools of Heidegger interpretation in the United States, specifically the "Berkeley school," which has developed around the teaching of Hubert Dreyfus. Dreyfus's reading of *Being and Time* suggests a distinction in Heidegger's use of the term *inauthenticity* that recognizes the continued immersion even of authentic Dasein in the they-self of a given cultural context and thus does not apply the normative weight of authenticity uniformly across all forms of "inauthentic" existence. The effect of the difference Leland points out can be seen in the contrasting uses made of some of the same passages from *Being and Time* in Chanter's essay and in my " 'The Universe Is Made of Stories, Not of Atoms': Heidegger and the Feminine They-Self." The latter article also continues Leland's interest in the interconnections between Heidegger's work and psychotherapy. I draw on a form of neo-Freudian theory and Simone de Beauvoir's *The Second Sex* to investigate, first, how Heidegger's account of authenticity and the they-self might provide the basis for an understanding of the possibility, and limitations, of feminist consciousness, given a feminine they-self in a masculinist world, and second, how sense might be made of the claim that gender (in a sufficiently broad sense) actually is an ontological, rather than ontic, feature of Dasein.

The authors of the essays in the following part move beyond *Being and Time*, and beyond Heidegger's own texts, to look at his work from the perspective of poetics and the (female) body, using ancient texts to trace the "unthought" of those Greeks and early Christians whose thought Heidegger uses as foils for his own, and drawing on the contemporary texts of Derrida, Luce Irigaray, and Julia Kristeva to link the female figures of this "unthought" to the body and to the question of sexual difference explored in the first section. The later Heidegger's frequent linking of the poet and the philosopher underscores the importance of key poetic texts as avenues into the deepest understanding of Being in any historical situation, among the ancients as well as among ourselves, and by putting modern philosophy and ancient poetry into a common perspective, these essays illuminate the possibilities those avenues might open for feminist thought.

Rather than examining the general silence with regard to gender in *Being and Time*, in "The Absence of Monica: Heidegger, Derrida, and

Augustine's *Confessions*," John Caputo takes as his focus the specific silence about Saint Monica in Heidegger's Freiburg lectures on Saint Augustine in 1920–21. Caputo considers Heidegger's exclusion in light of "Circon-fession," Derrida's meditation on weeping, Augustine, and his own mother's death.[3] Caputo's concern is with Heidegger's political militarism and philosophical voluntarism in the period before 1936 and its later transformation into an understanding of Being that Caputo points out is compatible with contemporary ecofeminism, even while he recognizes that such uses of Heidegger's work should not blind us, as it were, to the continued masculinism and systematic insensitivity to human pain and suffering in Heidegger's thought.

Carol Bigwood moves back even further in time to address "Sappho: The She-Greek Heidegger Forgot," a reading of Sappho's life and poetry as the "unthought" of Heidegger's readings of ancient Greeks texts. For Bigwood, it is feminine laughter, rather than Caputo's concern with women's tears, that is missing in Heidegger's understanding of the ancients, and Sappho's poetry, widely admired in her own time, that might provide another, woman-centered avenue to the meaning of Being for the Greeks. She places her own work in the context of Irigaray's readings of Heidegger and, seeing Heidegger in the feminine, finds traces of Aphrodite in his later writings, especially *On the Way to Language*. She finally suggests a sense in which Heidegger and Sappho both might be understood as poets of "love and time."

In "Feminine Figures in Heidegger's Theory of Poetic Language," Jennifer Gosetti measures Heidegger's distance from the modern (Cartesian) subject in view of his critique of what Gosetti terms "poetic-lyrical subjectivism." She centers her discussion on Heidegger's characterization of language as a non-egocentric, but not unproblematic, "abode of the self," which she shows to be related to his reading of female figures. Gosetti's concern is to enrich Heidegger's understanding of the poetic and its feminine dimensions by linking it to Kristeva's notion of the semiotic. The ancient female figure under consideration here is Antigone, or rather Heidegger's interpretation of Sophocles' character in his lecture course *Hölderlin's Hymn "The Ister."* For Gosetti, Antigone represents an "unthought" that would introduce an embodied, female self into Heidegger's text, enrich our critical understanding of the disembodied, Cartesian male self, and given Kristeva's semiotics, make possible a more radical critique of subjectivity itself.

The third group of essays seeks to expand Heidegger's thought into the realms of both feminist political theory and ecological ethics. This is a vital part of a collection such as the present one, not only because it is a natural growth out of the later Heidegger's own concerns with our relationship to the natural world, but also because of the frequent criticism that his work offers no grounding for ethics or political thought, at best, or might even have elements actively opposed to a liberatory feminist project. These three authors take Heidegger's work as a starting point and, by developing it beyond its own limits and putting it in the context of contemporary feminist and ecological debates, illustrate both the dangers and the opportunities it offers for moral and political theory.

In her essay, "Heidegger and Ecofeminism," Trish Glazebrook discusses Heidegger's lectures on Aristotle's *Physics*, his work on technology, and related texts in light of contemporary work in ecological ethics and ecofeminism. From this perspective, another reading of the gender neutrality of Dasein, Derrida's "powerful positivity" of a "pre-dual sexuality" can be developed, a reading that Glazebrook argues opens ecofeminism to a greater plurality in its challenge to the phallicism (that is, the often totalitarian male-centeredness) of much ecological thought. Such an approach suggests both an important political use of Heidegger's work and an alternative ecological paradigm that could avoid incorporating an androcentric bias into our very understanding of "nature" and the "human."

Glazebrook ends with a discussion of the concept of home in the later Heidegger, a topic that is further developed in Iris Marion Young's "House and Home: Feminist Variations on a Theme." Starting with the distinction between *building* and *preservation* in "Building, Dwelling, Thinking," Young draws on Irigaray to underscore the privilege that Heidegger gives to the former, and discusses similar distinctions in the work of Beauvoir and Hannah Arendt. Young herself uses Heidegger's concept of preservation to argue against a trend in feminist thought that would reject the home and homemaking as sites of women's oppression, but she also acknowledges that these concepts are deeply ambiguous in women's life experience. She then offers an alternative way of understanding home that can provide grounds for a liberatory reconceptualization of safety, privacy, and the relationship between one's self and one's physical and historical place in the world.

Mechthild Nagel's "Thrownness, Playing-in-the-World, and the Question of Authenticity" returns to *Being and Time*, specifically the discussion there of play, as seen through the work of Hans-Georg Gadamer.

She considers how Heidegger's use of the concept works against the usual understanding of play as agonistic, or conflict-centered, in a way that opens it to "antifoundational feminist play theory." At the same time, however, she cites Young and others in an investigation of Heidegger's analyses of the "fore-structure" of interpretation, projection, and authenticity to trace his continued allegiance to a traditional, that is masculinist, ontology of play. In doing so, she emphasizes the resources Heidegger's thought can provide for our understanding of life-affirming, feminist play, as described by María Lugones, but also his continuing allegiance to Cartesianism.

The final four essays expand Heidegger's thinking even further outward and onward, toward the realm of religion and into the future. Luce Irigaray's Introduction to the Italian edition of *L'oubli de l'air chez Martin Heidegger*,[4] "From *The Forgetting of Air* to *To Be Two*" (published here in English for the first time in an excellent translation by Heidi Bostic and Stephen Pluháček) echoes her other recent work rethinking the thought of authors such as Nietzsche, Plato, Aristotle, Descartes, and Levinas[5] in an effort to make us all no longer men/Man, "because we are men and women." In the case of Heidegger, her focus is on the relationship between breath and Being as similarly concealed, forgotten, and unacknowledged sources of life, and in that way also similar to the maternal/female body. She refers here, as does Bigwood, to the linkage between Heidegger and Eastern thought, even while recognizing Heidegger's enduring attachment to the ground of Western philosophy.

Ellen Armour draws on both Irigaray and Derrida in "mining" Heidegger's work for what might be useful to feminist religious thought. " 'Through Flame or Ashes': Traces of Difference in *Geist*'s Return" considers Irigaray's calls for a new understanding of god in light of similar concerns in Heidegger's later work, but also in light both of feminist criticism of such a project and of Derrida's critique of Heidegger's concept of *Geist* in *Of Spirit* and elsewhere.[6] These texts add the elements of fire and earth to Irigaray's discussions of air and water as sensible transcendentals, maternal elements under erasure in the work of Heidegger and Nietzsche, respectively. These new elements, Armour argues, provide the basis for a reading of Heidegger that would go beyond Irigaray and Derrida toward a new feminist understanding of the theological meaning of his work.

In contrast to Armour's essay, which draws us deeper into contemporary continental thought in its reading of Heidegger, Gail Stenstad's

"Revolutionary Thinking" links his thought on the possibility of radical transformation with the work of feminists from the other side of the Atlantic such as María Lugones, Elizabeth Spelman, Susan Griffin, Lorraine Code, and Annette Baier. Working largely from untranslated texts in the *Gesamtausgabe*, Stenstad discusses in particular the concept of *Auseinandersetzung*, ending with a call for anarchic thinking that could be the basis for a nonconfrontational revolution in human life.

Patricia Huntington's "Stealing the Fire of Creativity: Heidegger's Challenge to Intellectuals" provides even more of a clarion call to feminists, and anyone else who cares to listen. Organized around the central concept of a lived possibility of well-being, Huntington's argument is that Heidegger challenges us as intellectuals to rethink the grounding and nature of our own thought. In a careful critique of her own recent book, Huntington illustrates how Heidegger, in *What is Called Thinking?* and elsewhere, asks us to accept the groundlessness of our thinking so that we may disown our creativity and thus free ourselves to and for truly revolutionary, anarchic, even playful feminist thought.[7]

Thus these authors give a largely, although not exclusively, positive response to the questions raised by Patricia Huntington in the first part of this Introduction. Even those most critical of his ideas admit their relevance to the feminist philosophical enterprise, and many go further to show how his thought may be productive in the work we do. They propose ways in which Heidegger's emphasis on the self-revealing "letting be" of things can be helpful to a liberatory understanding of the social world; they offer illustrations of how his account of technological rationality can help provide the intellectual space for a strong feminist critique of the gender biases inherent in the modern worldview and in its historical antecedents as well; they suggest ways in which his rejection of rigid dualisms and his openness to poetry and the natural world create one possible framework for our understanding of the multiple complexities and the diversity of women's lived experience across time, space, and cultural barriers of all sorts. But the question still remains of whether Heidegger may not be the last, or the most recent, of the long line of dead white men who have created the intellectual and material boundaries within which we continue to live our lives. We may still ask whether he is, as he says of Nietzsche, the last great metaphysician, or a guide to something that might lie beyond.

Notes

1. *Geschlecht* is an untranslatable German word that can mean, Derrida reminds us in a footnote (see page 53), "sex, race, family, generation, lineage, species, genre/genus." "Geschlecht" was published in 1983 in Michel Haar, ed., *Martin Heidegger* (Paris: *Cahier de l'Herne*); the English translation appeared in *Research in Phenomenology* 13 the same year. "Geschlecht II: Heidegger's Hand," trans. John P. Leavey, Jr., was presented at a conference, "Deconstruction and Philosophy: The Texts of Jacques Derrida," in 1985 and published in a volume of the same name, edited by John Sallis, in 1987 (Chicago: University of Chicago Press); "Heidegger's Ear: Philopolemology (*Geschlecht* IV)," trans. John P. Leavey, Jr., was published in John Sallis, ed., *Reading Heidegger* (Bloomington: Indiana University Press, 1991); "*Geschlecht* III" has been described recently as "forthcoming" (Jacques Derrida, *Politics of Friendship*, trans. George Collins [New York: Verso, 1997], 269). Related texts include Jacques Derrida, *Of Spirit*, trans. Geoffrey Bennington and Rachel Bowlby (Chicago: University of Chicago Press, 1987), and Jacques Derrida and Christie V. McDonald, "Choreographies: Interview," *Feminist Interpretations of Jacques Derrida*, ed. Nancy J. Holland (University Park: Penn State Press, 1997).

2. Charles Guignon, "Authenticity, Moral Values, and Psychotherapy," in *The Cambridge Companion to Heidegger*, ed. Charles Guignon (Cambridge: Cambridge University Press, 1992), 226.

3. Jacques Derrida, "Circum.:" in Geoffrey Bennington and Jacques Derrida, *Jacques Derrida* (Bloomington: Indiana University Press, 1997).

4. Translated into English by Mary Beth Mader as *The Forgetting of Air in Martin Heidegger* (Austin: University of Texas Press, 1999).

5. On Nietzsche, see Luce Irigaray, *Marine Lover of Friedrich Nietzsche*, trans. Gillian C. Gill (New York: Columbia University Press, 1991); on the others, see *An Ethics of Sexual Difference*, trans. Carolyn Burke and Gillian C. Gill (Ithaca: Cornell University Press, 1993).

6. See n. 1 above.

7. Patricia Huntington, *Ecstatic Subjects, Utopia, and Recognition: Kristeva, Heidegger, Irigaray* (Albany: State University of New York Press, 1998).

Part One

The Gender of Dasein

1

Geschlecht

Sexual Difference, Ontological Difference

Jacques Derrida

—to Ruben Berezdivin

1928

Of sex, one can readily remark, yes, Heidegger speaks as little as possible, perhaps he has never spoken of it. Perhaps he had never said anything,

First and wholly preliminary part of an interpretation by which I wish to situate Geschlecht within Heidegger's path of thought. Within the path of his writings too, and the marked impression or inscription of the word Geschlecht will not be irrelevant. That word, I leave it here in its language for reasons that should become binding in the course of this very reading. And it is indeed a matter of "Geschlecht" (sex, race, family, generation, lineage, species, genre/genus) and not of *the Geschlecht*: one will not pass so easily toward the thing itself (the Geschlecht), beyond the mark of the word (Geschlecht) in which, much later, Heidegger will remark the "imprint" of a blow or a stamp (Schlag). This he will do in a text we shall not discuss here but toward which this reading will continue, by by that name or the names under which we recognize it, of it "sexual-relation," "sexual-difference," or indeed of "man-and-woman." That silence, therefore, is easily remarked. Which means that the remark is somewhat facile. A few indications, concluding with "everything happens as if . . . ," and it would be satisfied. The dossier could then be shut, avoiding trouble if not risk: it is as if, in reading Heidegger, there were no sexual difference, nothing of that in man, or put otherwise in woman, to interrogate or suspect, nothing worthy of questioning, *fragwürdig*. It is as if, one might continue, sexual difference did not rise to the height of ontological difference, on the whole as negligible, in regard to the question of the sense of being, as any other difference, a determinate distinction or an ontic predicate. Negligible for thought, of course, even if not at all for science or philosophy. But insofar as it is opened up to the question of being, insofar as it has a relation to being, in that very reference, *Dasein* would not be sexed. Discourse on sexuality could then be abandoned to the sciences or philosophies of life, to anthropology, sociology, biology, or perhaps even to religion or morality.

Sexual difference, it was said, could not rise to the height of ontological difference. If one wished to find out what height is in question, the thought of difference not rising to any, the silence would not be lacking. That could then be found arrogant or, precisely, provoking, in a century when sexuality, common place of all babbling, has also become the currency of philosophic and scientific "knowledge," the inevitable *Kampfplatz* of ethics and politics. Not a word from Heidegger! It could even be found a matter of grand style, this scene of stubborn mutism at the very center of the conversation, in the uninterrupted and distracted buzzing of the colloquium; for in itself it has a waking and sobering value (but what exactly is one speaking about around this silence?): Who, indeed, around or even long before him has not chatted about sexuality as such, as it were, and by that name? All the philosophers in the tradition have done so, from Plato to Nietzsche, who for their part were irrepressible on the subject. Kant, Hegel, Husserl have all reserved it a place; they have tried at least a word on it in their anthropology or in their philosophy of nature, and really everywhere.

Is it imprudent to trust Heidegger's manifest silence? Will what is thus ascertained later be deranged from its pretty philological assurance by

---

which in truth I know it is already magnetised: "Die Sprache im Gedicht, Eine Erörterung von Georg Trakls Gedicht" (1953), in *Unterwegs zur Sprache* (1959, 36 ff.).

some known or unedited passage when, while searching out the whole of Heidegger, some reading machine will hunt out the thing and snare it? Still, one must think of programming the machine, one must think, think of it and know how to do it. Relying on which words? Only on names? And on which syntax, visible or invisible? Briefly, in which signs will you recognize his speaking or remaining silent about what you nonchalantly call sexual difference? What do you think by those words or through them?

In order that such an impressive silence be today remarked on, to let it appear as such, marked and marking, what, on the whole, would be satisfactory? Undoubtedly this: Heidegger would have said nothing about sexuality by name in the places where the best educated and endowed "modernity" expected it with a firm foot, under its panoply of "everything-is-sexual-and-everything-is-political-and-reciprocally" (note in passing that the word "political" is of rare usage, perhaps null, in Heidegger, another not quite irrelevant matter). Even before a statistic were taken, the matter would seem already settled. But there are good grounds to believe that the statistic here would only confirm the verdict: about what we glibly call sexuality Heidegger has remained silent. Transitive and significant silence (he has silenced sex) which belongs, as he says, to a certain *Schweigen* (*"hier in der transitiven Bedeutung gesagt"*), to the path of a word [*parole*] he seems to interrupt. But what are the places of this interruption? Where is the silence working on that discourse? And what are the forms and determinable contours of that non-said?

You can bet on it, there's nothing immobile in the places where the arrows of the aforesaid panoply would assign the point named: omission, repression, denial, foreclosure, even the unthought.

But then, if the bet were lost, the trace of that silence would not merit detouring? He doesn't silence anything, no matter what, the trace does not come from no matter where. But why the bet? Because before predicting anything whatever about "sexuality," it may be verified, one must invoke chance, the aleatory, destiny.

Let it be, then, a so-called "modern" reading, an investigation armed with psychoanalysis, an enquiry authorized by complete anthropological culture. What does it seek? Where does it seek? Where may it deem to have the right to expect at least a sign, an allusion, elliptical as it may be, a reference, to sexuality, the sexual relation, to sexual difference? To begin with, in *Sein und Zeit*. Was not the existential analytic of *Dasein* near enough to a fundamental anthropology to have given rise to so many misunderstandings and mistakes regarding its pretended *"réalité-humaine"* or human reality as it was translated in France? Yet even in the analyses of being-in-the-world as being-with-others, or of care either in its self or as *Fürsorge*, it would be vain, it seems, to search even for the outline of a discourse on desire and sexuality. Hence the consequence could be drawn that sexual difference is not an essential trait, that it does not belong to the existential structure of *Dasein*. Being-there, being *there*, the *there* of being as such, bears no sexual mark. The same then goes for the reading of the sense of being, since, as *Sein und Zeit* clearly states (§ 2), *Dasein* remains in such a reading the exemplary being. Even were it admitted that all reference to sexuality isn't effaced or remains implied, this would only be to the degree that such a reference presupposes quite general structures (*In-der-Welt-sein als Mit- und Selbst-sein, Räumlichkeit, Rede, Sprache, Geworfenheit, Sorge, Zeitlichkeit, Sein zum Tode*) among many others. Yet sexuality would never be the guiding thread for a privileged access to these structures.

There the matter seems settled, it might be said. And yet! *Und dennoch!* (Heidegger uses more often than one would fain believe this rhetorical turn: and yet, exclamation mark, next paragraph).

And yet the matter was so little or ill understood that Heidegger had to explicate himself right away. He was to do it in the margins of *Sein und Zeit*, if we may call marginal a course given at the University of Marburg/ Lahn in the Summer Semester 1928.[1] There he recalls certain "directive principles" on "*the problem of transcendence and the problem of SEIN UND ZEIT*" (§ 10). The existential analytic of *Dasein* can only occur within the perspective of a fundamental ontology. That's why it is not a matter of an "anthropology" or an "ethic." Such an analytic is only "preparatory," while the "metaphysics of *Dasein*" is not yet "at the center" of the enterprise, clearly suggesting that it is nevertheless being programmed.

It is by the name of "*Dasein*" that I would here introduce the question of sexual difference.

Why name *Dasein* the being which constitutes the theme of this analytic? Why does *Dasein* give its "title" to this thematic? In *Sein und Zeit* Heidegger had justified the choice of that "exemplary being" for the *reading* of the sense of being: "Upon which being should one read off the sense of being . . . ?" In the last instance, the response leads to the "modes of being of a determinate being, *that* being which we the questioners ourselves are." If the choice of that exemplary being, in its "privilege," becomes the object of a justification (whatever one think of it and whatever be its axiomatics), Heidegger on the other hand seems to proceed by decree, at least in that passage, when it becomes a matter of *naming* that exemplary being, of giving it once and for all its terminological title: "That being which we ourselves are and which includes questioning as one of its possibilities of Being [*die Seinsmöglichkeit des Fragens*], we name being-there [we grasp it, we arrest it, apprehend it 'terminologically,' *fassen wir terminologisch als Dasein*]." That "terminological" choice undoubtedly finds its profound justification in the whole enterprise and in the whole book by unfolding a *there* and a *being-there* which (nearly) no other pre-determination should be able to command. But that does not remove the decisive, brutal, and elliptical appearance from that preliminary proposition, that declaration of name. On the contrary, in the Marburg Course, the title of *Dasein*—its sense as well as its name—can be found to be more patiently qualified, explained, evaluated. Now, the first trait that Heidegger underlines is its *neutrality*. First directive principle: "For the being which constitutes the theme of this analytic, the title 'man' (*Mensch*) has not been chosen, but the neutral title '*das Dasein.*'"

At first the concept of neutrality seems quite general. It is a matter of reducing or subtracting every anthropological, ethical or metaphysical predetermination by means of that neutralisation, so as to keep nothing but a relation to itself, bare relation, to the Being of its being; that is, a minimal relation to itself as relation to Being, that the being which we are, as questioning, holds with itself and its own proper essence. This relation to self is not a relation to an ego nor to an individual. Thus *Dasein* designates the being that "in a determined sense" is not "indifferent" to its own essence, or to whom its own Being is not indifferent. Neutrality, therefore, is first of all the neutralisation of everything not bearing the naked trait of this relation to itself, of this interest for its own Being (in the widest sense of the word "interest"). This implies an interest or a pre-comprehensive opening up for the sense of Being and for the questions thus ordained. And yet!

And yet the unfolding of this neutrality will be carried out with a leap, without transition and from the following item on (second directive principle) towards a sexual neutrality, and even towards a certain asexuality (*Geschlechtslosigkeit*) of being-there. The leap is surprising. If Heidegger wanted to offer examples of determinations to be left out of the analytic of *Dasein*, especially of anthropological traits to be neutralised, his only quandary would be which to choose. Yet he begins with and keeps himself limited to sexuality, more precisely to sexual difference. It therefore holds a privilege and seems to belong in the first place—to follow the statements in the logic of their enchaining [together]—to that "factual concretion" which the analytic of *Dasein* should begin by neutralising. If the neutrality of the title *"Dasein"* is essential, it is precisely because the interpretation of that being—which *we* are—is to be engaged *before* and *outside* of a concretion of that type. The first example of "concretion" would then be belonging to one or another of the two sexes. Heidegger doesn't doubt that they are two: "That neutrality means *also* [I underline—J.D.] that *Dasein* is neither of the two sexes [*keines von beiden Geschlechtern ist*]."

Much later, and at any rate thirty years later, the word "*Geschlecht*" will be charged with all its polysemic richness: sex, genre, family stock, race, lineage, generation. Heidegger will retrace in language, by means of irreplaceable path-openings (that is, inaccessible to a current translation), though labyrinthine, seductive and disquieting ways, the imprint of roads usually shut. Still shut, here, by the two. Two: that can not count anything but sexes, it seems, what are called sexes.

I've underlined the word "also" ("that neutrality means also . . ."). By its place in the logical and rhetorical chain, this "also" recalls that among the numerous meanings of that neutrality, Heidegger judges it necessary to begin not so much with sexual neutrality—which is why he also says "also"—yet, nevertheless, *immediately* with it *after the only* general meaning that has marked neutrality up to this point in the passage, to wit the *human* character, the title "*Mensch*" for the theme of the analytic. That is the only meaning which up till then he has excluded or neutralised. Hence a kind of precipitation or acceleration which can not be neutral or indifferent: among all the traits of man's humanity found thus neutralised with anthropology, ethics, or metaphysics, the first that the very word "neutrality" makes one think of, the first that Heidegger thinks of in any case, is sexuality. The incitement cannot be due merely to grammar, that's obvious. To pass from *Mensch*, indeed from *Mann*, to *Dasein*, is certainly to pass from the masculine to the neutral, while to think or to say *Dasein* and the *Da* of *Sein* from that transcendent which is *das Sein* ("*Sein ist das transcendens schlechthin,*" *Sein und Zeit*, p. 28), is to pass into a certain neutrality. Furthermore, such neutrality has to do with the nongeneric and nonspecific characters of Being: "Being as fundamental theme of philosophy is not a genre of a being (*keine Gattung*) . . ." (ibid.). But once again, if sexual difference can't exist without relation to saying, words, or language, still it can't be reduced to a grammar. Heidegger rather than describing it designates it as an existential structure of *Dasein*. But why does he all of a sudden insist with such haste? While in *Sein und Zeit* he had said nothing of it, asexuality (*Geschlechtslosigkeit*) figures here at the forefront of the traits mentioned when recalling *Dasein's* neutrality, or rather the neutrality of the title "*Dasein*." Why?

The first reason may be suspected. The very word *Neutralität* (*neuter*) induces a reference to binarity. If *Dasein* is neutral, and if it is not man (*Mensch*), the *first* consequence to draw is that it may not be submitted to the binary partition that one most spontaneously thinks of in such a case, to wit "sexual difference." If "being-there" does not mean "man" (*Mensch*), *a fortiori* it designates neither "man" nor "woman." But if the consequence is so near common-sense, why recall it? Above all, why should one go so much trouble to get rid of a thing so clear and secure in the continuation of the Course? Should one indeed conclude that sexual difference doesn't depend so simply on whatever the analytic can and should neutralise, metaphysics, ethics, and especially anthropology, or indeed any other domain of ontic knowing for example biology or zoology? Should one suspect that sexual differences cannot be reduced to an ethical or anthropological theme?

Heidegger's precautionary insistence leaves one thinking, in any case, that here things are not a matter of course. Once anthropology (fundamental or not) has been neutralised and once it has been shown that it can't engage the question of being where it is engaged as such, once it has been observed that *Dasein* is reducible neither to human-being nor to the ego nor to consciousness and the unconscious nor to the subject or the individual, nor even to an *animal rationale*, one might conclude that the question of sexual difference doesn't have a chance of measuring up to the question of the sense of being or of the ontological difference, that even its very riddance wouldn't deserve privileged treatment. Yet incontestably it is the contrary that happens. Heidegger has just recalled *Dasein's* neutrality, and there he is right away trying to clarify: neutrality also as to sexual difference. Perhaps he was then responding to more or less explicit, naive or sophisticated, questions on the part of his hearers, readers, students, or colleagues, still held, aware or not, within anthropological space. What about the sexual life of your *Dasein*? they might have still asked. And after having answered the question on that terrain by disqualifying it, in sum after having recalled the asexuality of a being-there which is not an *anthropos*, Heidegger wishes to encounter another question, even perhaps a new objection. That's where the difficulties will grow.

Whether a matter of neutrality or asexuality (*Neutralität, Geschlechtslosigkeit*) the words accentuate strongly a negativity which manifestly runs counter to what Heidegger thereby wishes to mark out. It is not a matter of linguistic or grammatical signs at the surface of a meaning that remains for its part untouched here. By means of such manifestly negative predicates there should become legible what Heidegger doesn't hesitate to call a "positivity" (*Positivität*), a richness, and, in a heavily charged code, even a power (*Mächtigkeit*). Such precision suggests that the a-sexual neutrality does not desexualize, on the contrary; its *ontological* negativity is not unfolded with respect to *sexuality itself* (which it would instead liberate), but on its differential marks, or more strictly on *sexual duality*. There would be no *Geschlechtslosigkeit* except with respect to "two"; asexuality could be determined as such only to the degree that sexuality would mean immediately binarity or sexual division. "But such asexuality is not the indifference of an empty nothing (*die Indifferenz des leeren Nichtigen*), the feeble negativity of an indifferent ontic nothing. In its neutrality, *Dasein* is not just anyone no matter who, but the originary positivity (*ursprüngliche Positivität*) and power of essence [*être*] (*Mächtigkeit des Wesens*)."

If *Dasein* as such belongs to neither of the two sexes, that doesn't mean that its being is deprived of sex. On the contrary, here one must think of a pre-differential, rather a pre-dual, sexuality—which doesn't necessarily mean unitary, homogeneous, or undifferentiated, as we shall later verify. Then, from that sexuality, more originary than the dyad, one may try to think to the bottom a "positivity" and a "power" that Heidegger is careful not to call sexual, fearing undoubtedly to reintroduce the binary logic that anthropology and metaphysics always assign to the concept of sexuality. Here indeed it is a matter of the positive and powerful source of every possible "sexuality." The *Geschlechtlosigkeit* would not be more negative than *aletheia*. One might recall what Heidegger said regarding the *Würdigung des "Positiven" im privativen Wesen der Aletheia* (in *Platons Lehre von der Wahrheit*).

From hence, the Course sketches a quite singular movement. It is very difficult to isolate in it the theme of sexual difference. I am tempted to interpret this as follows: by a kind of strange and quite necessary displacement, it is sexual division itself which leads to negativity, so neutralisation is *at once* the effect of this negativity and the effacement to which thought must subject it to allow an original positivity to become manifest. Far from constituting a positivity that the asexual neutrality of *Dasein* would annul, sexual binarity itself would be responsible, or rather would belong to a determination that is itself responsible, for this negativation. To radicalize or formalize too quickly the sense of this movement before retracing it more patiently, we could propose the following schema: it is sexual difference itself as binarity, it is the discriminative belonging to one or another sex, that destines or determines to a negativity that must then be explained. Going a bit further, sexual difference thus determined (one over two), negativity, and a certain "impotence" might be linked together. When returning to the originality of *Dasein*, of this *Dasein* said to be sexually neutral, "originary positivity" and "power" can be reconsidered. In other words, despite appearances, the asexuality and neutrality that should first of all be subtracted from the sexual binary mark, in the analytic of *Dasein*, are in truth on the same side, on the side of that sexual difference—the binary—to which one might have thought them simply opposed. Does this interpretation sound too violent?

The three following sub-paragraphs or items (§ 3, § 4, § 5), develop the motifs of neutrality, positivity and originary power, the originary itself, without explicit refrence to sexual difference. "Power" becomes that of an origin (*Ursprung, Urquell*), while elsewhere Heidegger will never directly associate the predicate "sexual" to the word "power," the first remaining all too easily associated with the whole system of sexual difference that may, without much risk of error, be said to be inseparable from every anthropology and every metaphysics. Moreover, the adjective "sexual" (*sexual, sexuell, geschlechtlich*) is never, at least to my knowledge, used, only the nouns *Geschlecht* or *Geschlechtlichkeit*, which is not without importance, these nouns being all the more capable of irradiating sense to other semantic zones. Later we will follow there some other paths of thought.

But without speaking of it directly, these three sub-paragraphs prepare the return to the thematic of *Geschlechtlichkeit*. They first of all efface all the negative signs attached to the word "neutrality." This word does not have the emptiness of an abstraction, neutrality rather leads back to the "power of the origin" which bears within itself the internal possibility of humanity in its concrete factuality. *Dasein*, in its neutrality, must not be confused with the existent. *Dasein* only exists in its factual concretion, to be sure, but this very existence has its originary source (*Urquell*) and internal possibility in *Dasein* as neutral. The analytic of this origin does not deal with the existent itself. Precisely because it precedes them, such an analytic cannot be confused with a philosophy of existence, with a wisdom (which could be established only within the "structure of metaphysics"), or with a prophesy that would teach such or such a "world view." It is therefore not at all a "philosophy of life." Which is to say that a discourse on sexuality which would be of this order (wisdom, knowledge, metaphysics, philosophy of life or of existence) falls short of every requirement of an analytic of *Dasein* in its very neutrality. Has a discourse on sexuality ever been presented not belonging to any of these registers? It must be noticed that sexuality is not named in that last paragraph nor in the one that will treat (we will return to it) a certain "isolation" of *Dasein*. It is named in a paragraph in *Vom Wesen des Grundes* (the same year, 1928) which develops the same argument. The word is found in quotation marks, as if incidentally. The logic of *a fortiori* raises its tone somewhat there. For in the end, if it is true that sexuality must be neutralised "with all the more reason" (*"a plus forte raison"*), as Henri Corbin's translation says, or *a fortiori, erst recht,* why insist? Where is the risk if misunderstanding? Unless the matter be decidedly not obvious, and there is still a risk of mixing up once more the question of sexual difference with that of Being and the ontological difference? In that context, it is a matter of determining the ipseity of *Dasein*, its *Selbstheit* or being-a-self. *Dasein* exists only for its own sake [*a dessein de soi*] (*umwillen seiner*), if one can put it thus, but that does not mean either the for-itself of conscoiusness nor egoism nor solipsism. It is starting from *Selbstheit* that an alternative between "egoism" and "altriusm" has a chance of arising and becoming manifest, as well as a difference between "being-I" and "being-you" (*Ichsein/Dusein*). Always presupposed, ipseity is therefore "neutral" with respect to being-me and being-you, "and with all the more reason with regard to 'sexuality' " (*und erst recht etwa gegen die "Geschlechtlichkeit" neutral*). The movement of this *a fortiori* is logically irreproachable on only one condition: It would be necessary that such "sexuality" (in quotation marks) be the assured predicate of whatever is made possible by or from ipseity, here for instance the structures of "me" and "you," yet as "sexuality" not belong to the structure of ipseity, and ipseity that would not as yet be determined as human being, me or you, conscious or unconscious subject, man or woman. Yet if Heidegger insists and underlines ("with all the more reason"), it is because a suspicion continues to weigh on him: What if "sexuality" already marked the most originary

Selbstheit? If it were an ontological structure of ipseity? If the *Da* of *Dasein* were already "sexual"? What if sexual difference were already marked in the opening up of the question of the sense of Being and of the ontological difference? And what if, though not self-evident, neutralisation were already a violent operation? "With all the more reason" may hide a more feeble reason. In any case, the quotation marks always signal some kind of citing. The current usage of the word "sexuality" is "mentioned" rather than "used," one could say in the language of *speech act theory*; it is cited to be compared, warned about if not accused. Above all one must protect the analytic of *Dasein* from the risks of anthropology, psychoanalysis, even of biology. Still there perhaps remains some open door for other words, or another usage and another reading of the word "*Geschlecht*," if not of the word "sexuality." Perhaps another "sex," or rather another "*geschlecht*," will come to be inscribed within ipseity, or will come to derange the order of all its derivations, for example that of a more originary *Selbstheit* making possible the emergence of the *ego* and of you. Let us leave this question suspended.

If this neutralisation is implied in every ontological analysis of *Dasein*, that does not mean that "the *Dasein* in man," as Heidegger often says, need be an "egoistic" singularity or an "individual ontoically isolated." The point of departure within neutrality does not lead back to the isolation or insularity (*Isolierung*) of man, to his factual and existential solitude. And yet the point of departure within neutrality does indeed mean, Heidegger carefully observes, a certain original isolation of man: not, precisely, in the sense of factual existence, "as if the philosophising being were the center of the world," but as the "*metaphysical isolation* of man." It is the analysis of this isolation which then raises again the theme of sexual differences and of the dual partition within *Geschlechtlichkeit*. At the center of this new analysis, the very subtle differentiation of a certain lexicon already signals translation problems which will only become aggravated for us. It will remain ever impossible to consider them as either accidental or secondary. At a certain moment we ourselves will be able to notice that the thought of *Geschlecht* and that of translation are essentially the same. Even here the lexical hive brings together (or swarms scattering) the series "dissociation," "distraction," "dissemination," "division," "dispersion." The *dis-* is supposed to translate, though only by means of transfers and displacements, the *zer-* of *Zerstreuung, Zerstreutheit, Zerstörung, Zersplitterung, Zerspaltung*. But an interior and supplementary frontier still partitions the lexicon: *dis-* and *zer-* often have a negative sense, yet sometimes also a neutral or non-negative sense (I would hesitate here to say positive or affirmative).

Let us attempt to read, translate and interpret more literally. *Dasein* in general hides, shelters in itself the internal possibility of a factual dispersion or dissemination (*faktische Zerstreuung*) in its own body (*Leiblichkeit*) and "thereby in sexuality" (*und damit in die Geschlechtlichkeit*). Every proper body of one's own [*corps propre*] is sexed, and there is no *Dasein* without its own body. But the chaining together proposed by Heidegger seems quite clear: the dispersing multiplicity is not primarily due to the sexuality of one's own body; it is its own body itself, the flesh, the *Leiblichkeit*, that draws *Dasein* originally into the dispersion and *in due course* [*par suite*] into sexual difference. This "in due course" (*damit*) insists through a few lines' interval, as if *Dasein* were supposed to have or be a priori (as its "interior possibility") a body found to be sexual, and affected by sexual division.

Here again, an insistence on Heidegger's part to observe that dispersion like neutrality (and all the meanings in *dis-* or *zer-*) should not be understood in a negative manner. The "metaphysical" neutrality of isolated man as *Dasein* is not an empty abstraction operating from or in the sense of the ontic, it is not a *neither-nor*, but rather what is properly concrete in the origin, the "not yet" of factual dissemination, of dissociation, of being dis-sociated or of factual dis-society: *faktische Zerstreutheit* here and not *Zerstreuung*. This being dissociated, unbound, or desocialized (for it goes together with the isolation of man as *Dasein*) is not a fall nor an accident nor a decline [*déchéance*] that has supervened. It is an originary structure affecting *Dasein* with the body, and *hence* with sexual difference, of multiplicity and lack-of-binding [*déliaison*], these two significations remaining distinct though gathered together in the analyses of dissemination (*Zerstreuung* or *Zerstreutheit*). Assigned to a body, *Dasein* is separated in its facticity, subjected to dispersion and parcelling out (*zersplittert*), and thereby (*ineins damit*) always disjunct, in disaccord, split up, divided (*zwiespältig*) by sexuality toward a determinate sex (*in eine bestimmte Geschlechtlichkeit*). These words, undoubtedly, have at first a negative resonance: dispersion, parcelling out, division, dissociation, *Zersplitterung*, *Zerspaltung*, quite like *Zerstörung* (demolition, destruction), as Heidegger explains; this resonance is linked with negative concepts from an ontic point of view, immediately drawing forth a meaning of lesser value. "But something else is at issue here." What? Another meaning, marking the fold of a mani-fold multiplication. The characteristic sign (*Kennzeichnung*) by which such a multiplication can be recognized is legible to us in the isolation and factual singularity of *Dasein*. Heidegger distinguishes this multiplication (*Mannigfaltigung*) from a simple multiplicity (*Mannigfaltigkeit*), from diversity. The representation of a grand original being whose simplicity was suddenly dispersed (*zerspaltet*) into various singularities must also be avoided. It is rather a matter of elucidating the internal possibility of that multiplication for which *Dasein*'s own body represents an "organising factor." The multiplicity in this case is not a simple formal plurality of determinations or of determinities (*Bestimmtheiten*), it belongs to Being itself. An "originary dissemination" (*ursprüngliche Streuung*) belongs already to the Being of *Dasein* in general, "according to its metaphysically neutral concept." This originary dissemination (*Streuung*) is from a fully determined point of view *dispersion* (*Zerstreuung*): difficulty of translation which forces me here to distinguish somewhat arbitrarily between dissemination and dispersion, in order to mark out by a convention the subtle trait which distinguishes *Streuung* from *Zerstreuung*. The latter is the determination of the former. It determines a structure of originary possibility, dissemination (*Streuung*), according to all the meanings of *Zerstreuung* (dissemination, dispersion, scattering, diffusion, dissipation, distraction). The word *Streuung* appears but once, it seems, to designate that originary possibility, that disseminality (if this be allowed). Afterwards, it is always *Zerstreuung,* which would add—but it isn't that simple—a mark of determination and negation, had not Heidegger warned us the previous instant of that value of negativity. Yet, even if not totally legitimate, it is hard to avoid a certain contamination by negativity, indeed with ethico-religious associations, that would seek to bind that disperson to a fall and a corruption of the pure originary possibility (*Streuung*), which appears then to be affected by a supplementary turn. It will indeed be necessary to elucidate also the possibility or fatality of that contamination. We will return to this later.

Some indications of that dispersion (*Zerstreuung*). First of all, *Dasein* never relates to *an* object, to a sole object. If it does, it is always in the mode of abstraction or abstention from other beings which always co-appear at the same time. And this multiplication does not supervene because there is a plurality of objects; actually it is the converse that takes place. It is the originary disseminal structure, the dispersion of *Dasein*, that makes possible this multiplicity. And the same holds for *Dasein*'s relation to itself: it is dispersed, conformably to the "structure of historicity in the widest sense," to the extent that *Dasein* occurs as *Erstreckung*, a word whose translation remains dangerous. The word "extension" could all too easily be associated with *extensio*, which *Sein und Zeit* interprets as the "fundamental ontological determination of the world" according to Descartes (§ 18). Here something else is at issue. *Erstreckung* names a spacing which, "before" the determination of space as *extensio*, comes to extend or stretch out being-there, the *there* of Being, *between* birth and death. Essential dimension of *Dasein*, the *Erstreckung* opens up the *between* that links it at once to its birth and to its death, the movement of suspense by which it *is tended* out and extended of itself *between* birth and death, these two receiving meaning only from that intervallic movement. *Dasein* affects itself, and that auto-affection belongs to the ontological structure of its historicity: "*DIE SPEZIFISCHE BEWEGTHEIT DES erstreckten Sicherstreckens NENNEN WIR DAS Geschehen DES DASEINS*" (§ 72). *Sein und Zeit* links together precisely this intervallic tension and dispersion (*Zerstreuung*) (notably in § 75, p. 390). *Between* birth and death, the spacing of the *between* marks at once the distance and the link, but the link according to a kind of distension. This "between-two" as rapport (*Bezug*) drawn into relationship (*trait*) with both birth and death belongs to the very Being of *Dasein*, "before" any biological determination, for instance ("*Im Sein des Daseins liegt schon das 'Zwischen' mit Bezug auf Geburt und Tod*," p. 374). The link thus enter-tained, held or drawn between [*entretenu, entre-tendu*], over or through the dis-tance between [*entre*] birth and death, is itself entertained *with* dispersion, dissociation, unbinding (*Zerstreuung, Unzusammenhang*, etc. Cf. p. 390 for example). That link, that between, *could not take place* without them. Yet to take them as negative forces would be to precipitate the interpretation, for instance render it dialectical.

The *Erstreckung* is thus one of the determinate possibilities of essential dispersion (*Zerstreuung*). That "between" would be impossible without dispersion yet constitutes only one of its structural dependents, to wit temporarily and historicity. Another dependent, another possibility— connected and essential—of originary dispersion: the originary spatiality of *Dasein*, its *Räumlichkeit*. The spatial dispersion is manifested in language for instance. Every language is first of all determined by spatial significations (*Raumbedeutungen*).[2] The phenomenon of so-called spatialising metaphors is not at all accidental, nor within the reach of the rhetorical concept of "metaphor." It is not some exterior fatality. Its essential irreducibility can't be elucidated outside of this existential analytic of

Dasein, of dispersion, historicity or spatiality. The consequences therefore must be drawn, in particular for the very language of the existential analytic: all the words Heidegger uses necessarily refer back to these *Raumbedeutungen*, beginning with the word *Zerstreuung* (dissemination, dispersion, distraction) which names the very origin of spacing at the moment when as language it submits to its law.

The "transcendental dispersion" (as Heidegger still names it) thus belongs to the essence of *Dasein* in its neutrality. "Metaphysical" essence, we are more precisely told in a Course presented above all at that time as a metaphysical ontology of *Dasein*, whose analytic constitutes only a phase, undoubtedly preliminary. This must be taken into account in order to situate what is here said about sexual difference in particular. Transcendental dispersion is the possibility of every dissociation and parcelling out (*Zersplitterung, Zerspaltung*) into factual existence. It is itself "founded" on that originary character of *Dasein* that Heidegger then called *Geworfenheit*. One should be patient with that word, subtracting it from so many usages, current interpretations or translations (for instance dereliction, being-thrown). This should be done foreseeing what the interpretation of sexual difference—which right away follows—retains in itself of that *Geworfenheit* and, "founded" on it, of transcendental dispersion. [There is] no dissemination that fails to assume such a "throw" [*jetée*], the *Da* of *Dasein* as thrown [*jetée*]. Thrown "before" all the modes of throwing [*jetée*] that will later determine it, project, subject, object, abject, trajectory, dejection; throw that *Dasein* can not make its own in a project, in the sense of *throwing itself* as a subject master of the throw. *Dasein* is *geworfen*; that means that before any project on its part it is thrown, but this being-thrown is not yet *submitted* to the alternative of activity or passivity, these [concepts] still too much in solidarity with the couple subject-object and hence with their opposition, one could even say with their objection. To interpret being-thrown as passivity could reinscribe it within the derivative problematic of subjecti(vi)ty (active or passive). What does "throw" mean before these syntaxes? And being-thrown even before the image of the fall, be it Platonic or Christian? There is being-thrown of *Dasein* "before" there even appears—in other words, "before" there occurs for it there—any thought of throwing amounting to an operation, activity, or an initiative. And that being-thrown of *Dasein* is not a throw *in* space, in what is already a spatial element. The originary spatiality of *Dasein* is drawn toward [or has to do with, *tient à*] the throw.

It is at this point that the theme of sexual difference may reappear. The disseminal throw of being-there (understood still in its neutrality) is particularly manifest in the fact that *Dasein* is *Mitsein* with *Dasein*. As always in this context, Heidegger's first gesture is to observe an order of implication: sexual difference, or belonging to a genre, must be elucidated starting from being-with, in other words, from the disseminal throw, and not inversely. Being-with does not arise from some factual connection, "it cannot be explained from some presumably originary generic being," by a being whose own body would be partitioned according to a sexual difference (*geschlechtlich gespaltenen leiblichen Wesen*). On the contrary, a certain generic drive of gathering together (*gattungshafte Zusammenstreben*), the union of genres (their unification, rapprochement, *Einigung*), has as "metaphysical presupposition" the dissemination of *Dasein* as such, *and thereby Mitsein*. The *Mit* of *Mitsein* is an existential, not a categorical, and the same holds for the adverbs of place (*Sein und Zeit*, § 26). What Heidegger calls here the fundamental metaphysical character of *Dasein* is not to be derived from any generic organisation or from a community of living beings as such.

How does this question of *order* matter to this "situation" of sexual difference? Thanks to a prudent derivation that in turn becomes problematic for us, Heidegger can at least reinscribe the theme of sexuality, in rigorous fashion, within an ontological questioning and an existential analytic. As soon as it is not placed upon a common *doxa* or a bio-anthropological science, the one and other sustained by some metaphysical preinterpretation, sexual difference remains to be thought. But the price of that prudence? Is it not to remove sexuality from every originary structure? Deduce it? Or in any case derive it, confirming all the most traditional philosophemes, repeating them with the force of a new rigour? And that derivation, does it not begin by a neutralisation whose negativity was laboriously denied? And once the neutralisation is effected, does one still arrive at an ontological or "transcendental" dispersion, at that *Zerstreuung* whose negative value was so difficult to efface?

In this form these questions remain, undoubtedly, summary. But they couldn't be elaborated simply in an exchange with the passage in the Course of Marburg which names sexuality. Whether it be a matter of neutralisation, negativity, dispersion, or distraction (*Zerstreuung*), indispensable motifs here, following Heidegger, for posing the question of sexuality, it is necessary to *return* to *Sein und Zeit*. Although sexuality is not there named, its motifs are treated in a more complex fashion, more differentiated, which does not mean, on the contrary, in an easier or more facile manner.

We must remain content here with several preliminary indications. Resembling in the Course a methodical procedure, neutralisation is not without link to what in *Sein und Zeit* is called the "privative interpretation" (§ 11). One could even speak of method, since Heidegger appeals to an ontology to be accomplished by or on the "way" of a privative interpretation. That way allows the "a priori's" to be extracted, while a note on the same page, crediting Husserl, says that it is well known that "a priorism is the method of every scientific philosophy which understands itself." This precisely in the context of psychology and biology. As sciences they are founded on an ontology of being-there. The mode of being of life is accessible, essentially, only through being-there. It is the ontology of life that requires a "privative interpretation": "life" being neither a pure *Vorhandensein* nor a *Dasein* (Heidegger says this without considering that the issue requires more than a mere affirmation: it seems to be obvious), it is accessible only by a negative operation of subtraction. It may then be asked what is the being of a life which is *nothing but* life, which is neither this nor that, neither *Vorhandensein* nor *Dasein*. Heidegger has never elaborated that ontology of life, but one can imagine all the difficulties it would have run into, since the "neither . . . nor" conditioning it excludes or overflows the most basic structural (categorial or existential) concepts of the whole existential analytic. It is the whole problematic that is here in question, the one that subjects positive knowings to regional ontologies, and these to a fundamental ontology, which itself at that time was preliminarily opened up by the existential analytic of *Dasein*. No chance (once more, one might say, and show) if it is the mode of being of the *living*, the animated (hence also of the psychical) which raises and situates that enormous problem, or in any case gives it its most recognisable name. This matter cannot be engaged here, but in underlining its all too often unnoticed necessity, it should at least be observed that the theme of sexual difference could not be dissociated from it.

Let us for the moment keep to that "way of privation," the expression picked by up Heidegger in § 12, and this time again to designate the a priori access to the ontological structure of the living. Once that remark is elaborated, Heidegger enlarges upon the question of those negative statements. Why do negative determinations impose themselves so often within this ontological characteristic? Not at all by "chance." It is because one must detach the originality of the phenomena from what has dissembled, disfigured, displaced or varnished them, from the *Verstellungen* and *Verdeckungen*, from all those pre-interpretations whose negative effects should in their turn be annulled by the negative statements whose veritable "sense" is truly "positive." It is a schema that we have recognised before. The negativity of the "characteristic" is therefore not fortuitous any more than the necessity of alterations or dissemblances which it attempts in some manner *methodically* to correct. *Verstellungen* and *Verdeckungen* are necessary movements in the very history of Being and its interpretation. They can not be avoided like contingent faults; one may not reduce inauthenticity (*Uneigentlichkeit*) to a fault or sin into which one should not have fallen.

And yet. If Heidegger uses so easily the word "*negative*" when it is a matter of qualifying statements or a characteristic, he never does it, it seems to me (or, more prudently, much less often and much less easily), to qualify what, in pre-interpretations of Being, makes still necessary those methodical corrections of a negative or neutralising form. *Uneigentlichkeit*, the *Verstellungen* and the *Verdeckungen* are not in the order of negativity (the false or evil, error or sin). And one can well understand why Heidegger carefully avoids speaking in this case of negativity. He thus avoids religious, ethical, indeed even dialectical schemas, pretending to rise "higher" than they.

It should then be said that no negative signification is ontologically attached to the "neuter" in general, particularly not that transcendental dispersion (*Zerstreuung*) of *Dasein*. Thus, without speaking of negative value or of value in general (Heidegger's distrust for the value of value is well known), we should take account of the differential and hierarchical accent which regularly in *Sein und Zeit* comes to mark the neutral and dispersion. In certain contexts, dispersion marks the most general structure of *Dasein*. This we have seen in the Course, but it was already the case in *Sein und Zeit*, for example in § 12 (p. 56): "The *being-in-the-world* of *Dasein* is, with its factivity, always already dispersed (*zerstreut*) or even parcelled out (*zersplittert*) into determinate modes of *being-in*." Furthermore, Heidegger proposes a list of these modes and of their irreducible multiplicity. Yet elsewhere, dispersion and distraction (*Zerstreuung* in both senses) characterise the inauthentic ipseity of *Dasein*, that of *Man-selbst*, of that *One* which has been distinguished from ipseity (*Selbst*) as authentic and proper (*eigentlich*). As "anyone," *Dasein* is dispersed or distracted (*zerstreut*). The whole of that analysis is well known, we're only detaching that which concerns dispersion (cf. § 27), a concept one can again find at the center of the analysis of curiosity (*Neugier*, § 36). That, let us recall, is one of the three modes of falling (*Verfallen*) of *Dasein* in its everyday-being. Later we shall have to return to Heidegger's warnings: falling, alienation (*Entfremdung*), and even downfall (*Absturz*) are not meant here as the theme of a "moralising critique," a "philosophy of culture," a dogmatic religious account of the fall (*Fall*) from an "original condition" (of which we have neither ontic experience nor ontologial interpretation) or of a "corruption of human nature." Much later, we will have to recall these warnings and their problematic character, when within the "situation" of Trakl, Heidegger will interpret the decomposition and the dessentialisation (*Verwesung*), that is to say also a certain corruption, of the figure of man. It will still be a matter, even more explicitly this time, of a thought of "*Geschlecht*" or of *Geschlecht*. I put it in quotations because the issue touches as much on the name as on what it names; and it is here as imprudent to separate them as to translate them. We shall ascertain it, it is there a matter of the inscription of *Geschlecht* and of *Geschlecht* as inscription, stamp, and imprint.

Dispersion is thus marked *twice*, as general structure of *Dasein* and as mode of inauthenticity. One might say the same for the neutral: in the *Course*, while it is a question of *Dasein*'s neutrality, no negative or pejorative index; yet "neutral," in *Sein und Zeit* may also be used to characterize the "one," to wit what becomes the "who" within everyday ipseity: then the "who" is the neutral (*Neutrum*), "*the one*" (§ 27).

This brief recourse to *Sein und Zeit* has perhaps allowed us better to understand the sense and necessity of that *order of implications* that Heidegger tends to preserve. Among other things, that order may also render an account of the predicates made use of by all discourse on sexuality. There is no properly sexual predicate; there is none at least that does not refer, for its sense, to the *general* structures of *Dasein*. So that to know what one speaks of, and how, when one names sexuality, one must indeed rely upon the very thing described in the analytic of *Dasein*. Inversely, if this be allowed, that disimplication allows the general sexuality or sexualisation of discourse to be understood: sexual connotations can only mark discourse, to the point of immersing it in them, to the extent that they are homogeneous to what every discourse implies, for example the topology of those "spatial meanings" (*Raumbedeutungen*) which are irreducible, but also all those other traits we have situated in passing. What would a "sexual" discourse or a discourse "on-sexuality" be without evoking farness [*eloignement*], an inside and an outside, dispersion and proximity, a here and a there, birth and death, a between-birth-and-death, a being-with and discourse?

This order of implications opens up thinking to a sexual difference that would not yet be sexual duality, difference as dual. As we have already observed, what the Course neutralized was less sexuality itself than the "generic" mark of sexual difference, belonging to one of *two* sexes. Hence, in leading back to dispersion and multiplication (*Zerstreuung, Mannigfaltigung*), may one not begin to think a sexual difference (without negativity, let us clarify) not sealed by a two? Not two yet or no longer? But the "not yet" or "no longer" would still mean, already, some dialectical appropriation.

The withdrawal [*retrait*] of the dyad leads toward another sexual difference. It may also prepare other questions. For instance, this one: How is difference deposited among two? Or again, if one kept to consigning difference within dual opposition, how can multiplication be stopped in difference? Or in sexual difference?

In the Course, for the above given reasons, *Geschlecht* always names sexuality such as it is typed by *opposition* or by duality. Later (and sooner) matters will be different, and this opposition is called decomposition.

Notes

1. *Metaphysische Anfangsgründe der Logik im Ausgang von Leibniz, Gesamtausgabe*, vol. 26.
2. Cf. also *Sein und Zeit*, 166.

2

The Problematic Normative Assumptions of Heidegger's Ontology

Tina Chanter

Several approaches suggest themselves as ways in which a feminist critique of Heidegger might be explored. Among the most fruitful sites of enquiry I would include the following topics:

1. Bodies
2. Others
3. Temporality and History

My strategy in this essay will be to raise some feminist concerns around each of these topics, and to suggest that perhaps the most far-reaching feminist critique of Heidegger consists in exposing a normative bias that is built into his ontological method in such a way as to cover over its prejudices. Once the normative assumptions of Heidegger's discourse are uncovered, it becomes possible to see not only that Heidegger neglects feminist concerns when treating certain topics, but also how his philosophy is formulated in such a way as to render such concerns irrelevant. Heidegger's ontology has pretensions to a neutrality and universality that I do not believe it can sustain. I will suggest that his philosophy operates in a way that exhibits a systematic blindness not only to its own gender bias, but also to a range of other normative assumptions it makes. My claim is that Heidegger methodologically rules out in advance any serious consideration of significant differences between individuals (whether those differences are specified in terms of gender, race, class, ethnicity, sexuality, or some other culturally loaded difference). This characteristic of his methodology leads him to posit, almost by default, a culturally specific version of Dasein that he takes to be exemplary, but whose exemplarity is never made available for critical interrogation.

While in this essay I am certainly critical of Heidegger's project for the exclusions it permits in the name of impartiality, my aims and motivations do not derive from a wholly negative reading of Heidegger. At the same time as acknowledging that there are crucial lacunae in Heidegger's ontological approach, I suggest that Heidegger foreshadowed certain gestures that have been taken up and developed in various strains of feminist thought and race theory. Heidegger's rethinking of history is perhaps the privileged example of this tendency, and it is of particular interest in that it exhibits both the greatest strengths of Heidegger's philosophy and its spectacular failures. I also want to recognize that even the contours of my critique of Heidegger borrow significantly from his own critical interrogation of what has come to be known as the metaphysics of presence.

Bodies

We seem to exhibit a persistent, confused avoidance when confronted with bodies. Judeo-Christian thought offers us plenty of models that envisage the soul, in the absence of salvation, as trapped in, mired by, or condemned to the material aspects of existence. The metaphor that represents the eyes as windows of the soul reflects a deep tendency to see ourselves as imprisoned in, or entombed by, our physical materiality. It is hardly surprising that philosophy has imbibed the ways in which bodies continually confound us in our attempt to think about our relation to the world and to formulate adequate responses to it. Neither have feminists been immune to the apparently allergic reaction philosophers have to bodies, notwithstanding its recently adopted program of self-medication, whereby it has assiduously addressed itself to the previously neglected "problem of embodiment"—with decidedly mixed results. We are still trying to overcome the vestiges of somatophobia, a difficult task already, but one that is compounded by rampant cries of "essentialism!" every time someone tries to tackle the task.[1] It is one thing to accede intellectually to the ideological impact that patriarchal denials of bodily significance continue to exert on feminist theory, and quite another to successfully or completely live down their legacy. Ideologies, as we know, remain robust precisely because they are good at finding devious ways of mutating.

The history of feminist thought demonstrates a complex relationship to bodies. Beginning with denial, it has evolved into the corrective maneuvers of compensation, but its gestures are still compromised by the resistance of bodies to analysis. The recent attempts of feminist theory to engage bodies reflect an ambiguity that characterizes so much contemporary thought: on the one hand, Heidegger's influence has been indispensable in formulating many influential feminist inquiries and projects, and in this sense his importance for feminism is a given; but on the other hand, feminist theory must dispense a great deal of energy in setting straight the record of neglect and denial. Feminists must avoid succumbing to the continuing temptation of repeating an inherited aversion to bodily significance. As a result, Heidegger's influence on feminist thought remains enigmatic and obscure. It has filtered through to feminism by indirect routes—through Merleau-Ponty, Sartre, Beauvoir, Lacan, Foucault, Derrida, and Deleuze. Without Heidegger, Merleau-Ponty could not have articulated his acute brand of politically infused and psychoanalytically oriented phenomenological discourse on the body in quite the way he did. Without Heidegger, Beauvoir couldn't have mobilized Hegel's master-slave dialectic, and welded it together with Sartre's optimistic commitment to freedom in quite the way she did. Even if, more recently, the reaction of French intellectuals to Heidegger has been more dismissive, if not ascerbic, than that of the existential phenomenologists, it cannot be disputed that Heidegger's thought constitutes something like a transcendental condition for it.

To get down to details, one of the most perplexing enigmas of Heidegger's work is that on the one hand its metaphysical proclivities imply a radical critique of the disembodied Cartesian subject, but on the other hand there is almost no effort to produce a positive experiential account of the lived body. In Heidegger's attempt to overcome Descartes's subject/object or mind/body dualism he specifies that the two terms of the dualism are not ontologically equivalent. By speaking of "Dasein" rather than the subject, Heidegger hopes to accomplish two things. First, he wants to definitively sever any ontological continuity between the way Dasein exists and the way other objects exist, insisting that the being of Dasein is distinct from the being of any other object. Second, he wants to establish that Dasein's very way of being includes within it an understanding of the world. By the term *world* Heidegger designates the environment "wherein" Dasein exists (see BT, 93/SZ, 65). That is, Dasein's mode of existence differs from all other objects, in that its mode of existence consists partly in an understanding of the issues that make up its concerns, both in its immediate environment and in the public spheres in which it moves and that have significance for Dasein. In other words, unlike other entities, Dasein's very way of being is constituted to some extent by its understanding of other entities and their relation to its own being. As there-being, Dasein is always already engaged in the world, and not set over against it, not in ontological opposition to it.

According to Heidegger, Descartes fails to investigate the ontological status of "I am." Descartes, says Heidegger, "takes the Being of 'Dasein' ... in the very same way as he takes the Being of the *res extensa*—namely as substance" (BT, 131/SZ, 98). The meaning of Descartes's concept of substantiality remains ontologically unclarified and is assumed to be incapable of clarification (see BT, 127/SZ, 94). By characterizing the subject as *res cogitans*, a thinking thing, or a thing that thinks, Descartes treats the subject as if it were ontologically equivalent to a thing, but with the added capacity for thought. In Heidegger's language, this amounts to treating the being of Dasein as if it were present-at-hand. The question of the specific being of humans remains forgotten (see BT, 75/SZ, 49).

Descartes's basic ontological orientation, suggests Heidegger, remains consonant with traditional sources. Both the Aristotelian definition of man as a "rational animal" (where humans are understood as ontologically equivalent to animals, with the extra capacity for reason added on, or somehow attached), and the Christian understanding of man as made in the image of God (where humans are understood as finite beings, created by an infinite being, somehow transcending their finitude through their understanding) are misleading and ontologically mystifying. What we need, according to Heidegger, is not a model where the body and the soul (or nature and spirit) are thought to constitute humans, where the parts stand in an uneasy relation to the whole, but rather an idea of Dasein's being as a whole. Hence, for Heidegger, "man's '*substance*' is not spirit as a synthesis of soul and body; it is rather *existence*" (BT, 153/SZ, 117). The self is conceived not as a thing that thinks, but as a way of being. Dasein's existence thus gets defined not through any core substantial reality, but only in its definite ways of being, and through its possible ways of being. That is, Dasein exists as its possibilities, both at the ontical and ontological levels, both as situated in relation to the definite, concrete possibilities that define its existence as an entity and as situated in relation to its fundamental existential possibilities that constitute the possible ways for it to be.

In traditional ontology, Heidegger points out, 'Being' is used in such a wide sense that it embraces the 'infinite' difference between created beings and the perfect being. For Descartes, created beings are divided into two kinds of substances, *res cogitans* and *res extensa* (see BT, 125–26/SZ, 92). Whether explicitly or implicitly, the idea of being that is assumed here, on Heidegger's reading, is presence-at-hand (*Vorhandensein*).

Descartes's mistake is to pass over (along with the rest of the tradition) the phenomenon that Heidegger calls "the world" and the Being of entities that are ready-to-hand. By default, both the being of Dasein and the being of other objects are treated as present-at-hand by the tradition. In order to rectify what he regards as an ontological misinterpretation Heidegger undertakes an analysis of the equipmental relations that structure Dasein's dealings with the world. The import of this analysis has become familiar to readers of Heidegger through the example of the chain of references involved in the act of hammering in a nail. Heidegger points out that in order to make sense of such an act, we refer not to the objective status of the hammer as an object (as present-at-hand), nor to the isolated act by itself, but rather to a series of meaningful references that explain the significance of this single act in terms of the overall projects Dasein undertakes. The meaning of the simple act of hammering is thereby cashed out in terms of the end to which it is directed, the meaning and purpose of this project, and its relationship to Dasein and to others who are affected by, and who contribute to, Dasein's projects.

One of the outcomes of Heidegger's analysis of Dasein's circumspective concern, expressed in its equipmental relations, is that the world of equipment evokes a network of significations, alliances, priorities, and so on, the totality of which make up Dasein's self-understanding. Hence Heidegger insists that equipment refers to a plurality of references, rather than to a single object. Another outcome of Heidegger's analysis is that Dasein's self-understanding is structured by its tendency to derive its meaning from its meaningful relations with the world. In other words, Dasein first understands its own being at the level of the ready-to-hand, since it carries over its understanding of the world in which it operates, and applies this understanding to its own being. The ambiguity underlying this interpretive possibility of Dasein, far from being accidental, is in fact a structuring feature of Dasein.

The distinctive priority that Dasein has over other entities, and the reason Heidegger chooses it as the vehicle for raising the question of being, is its ontico-ontological priority. Dasein is both an entity in the world, and its being is an issue for it, or its way of being includes within it an understanding of its way of being. Part of what it means for Dasein to understand itself is for it also to have a working understanding of other beings. When Dasein hammers a nail into the wood, it does so because it answers to a specific need that can be articulated within a context of significant projects, which might include wishes, desires, ends, and so on. What explains the singular act, in other words, is the purpose for which that specific act is undertaken. Dasein might be acting as a carpenter. In hammering a nail, a carpenter takes for granted a range of unarticulated assumptions and an implicit context. Dasein's act might be explained in a number of ways: Dasein might be said to be acting in accordance with sustaining a career, fulfilling obligations for a particular client, creating a specific object for a specific purpose, and so on. It is noteworthy that the direction in which Heidegger's early ontological analysis tends does not leave much room for aesthetic considerations. The carpenter might, for example, stand back and admire the grain of the wood she is using or appreciatively notice the smell of the wood chips. It is not until several years after *Being and Time* that Heidegger will pay serious attention to aesthetic experience.[2]

I suggest that an unresolved tension emerges from Heidegger's analysis of Dasein's engagement in the world as ready-to-hand. Heidegger maintains that Dasein's way of existence is conceptually distinct from the way in which any other objects exist. He reserves the term *Existenz* for this specific way of existing that belongs to Dasein, as distinct from the ways in which other objects can exist, namely either as ready-to-hand (*Zuhan-*

den), where an object is taken up as useful by Dasein, or simply as present-at-hand (*Vorhanden*), as when an object falls outside the circuit of usefulness and reverts to being merely an inert object. Although at the conceptual level Heidegger is at pains to rigorously distinguish between Dasein's specific mode of existence and that of other objects, in fact Dasein fails, not just initially but systematically, to comprehend this difference. Dasein first gains its understanding of itself from the world in which it lives, and since it is therefore seduced by the tendency to interpret itself as if it could be reduced to the level of the ready-to-hand, Dasein is structured by its very relation to the world. It is very difficult to separate Dasein's *Existenz* (the specific mode of existence that Dasein has) from the mode of existing that Heidegger characterizes as ready-to-hand. Indeed, Heidegger acknowledges repeatedly that for the most part Dasein does interpret itself in terms of the ready-to-hand, for that is what is closest to it. At the same time, Heidegger labels such interpretations as everyday, average, fallen, and inauthentic, suggesting that Dasein needs to rise above such interpretations in order to achieve ontological clarity. The question arises, then, What, if anything, serves to distinguish Dasein's proper mode of existence from Dasein's obfuscation of itself as ready-to-hand, a tendency that easily reverts to Dasein taking itself as present-at-hand?[3] To the extent that Heidegger answers this question, his distinction between the authentic and the inauthentic modes of Dasein's being might be cited. To point to the distinction between authenticity and inauthenticity is to raise a whole series of further problems that have persistently plagued Heidegger's interpreters. Before indicating the interpretive dilemmas provoked by a consideration of Heidegger's differentiation between authenticity and inauthenticity, let me draw to a close my discussion of Heidegger's critique of Descartes's ontology by suggesting that the nature of Heidegger's critique leads him away from any sustained consideration of lived bodily experience.

Heidegger's critique of traditional ontology, with which, as we have seen, he identifies Descartes's classic dualism, unfolds by means of an interpretation that dislodges the priority of substance, thinghood, or (to use Heidegger's terminology) the assumption that all entities are present-at-hand. That is, on the traditional view, all entities exhibit the same mode of presence, and that mode of presence is essentially characteristic of a metaphysics that models its conception of reality on substance. Thus inert physical matter, or objects as defined by their spatiotemporal location, come to represent the prevailing idea of what constitutes reality.

Descartes took the defining characteristic of objects to be their extension, while the defining characteristic of the substance he called mind was designated as thought. Heidegger objects that in assigning to thinking beings the same kind of being as that of extended substances, Descartes has overlooked the possibility that there might be a way of existing that is peculiar to human beings, and that this unique way of being consists of our having an understanding not only of ourselves, but also of other entities in the world (including other objects and other subjects). This understanding, according to Heidegger, is part of the very fabric of Dasein's being, and as such it constitutes a relation with objects other than Dasein. The task, then, on Heidegger's view, is not to establish an initial connection between subjects and objects, or to bridge the gap between mind and body, but rather to provide an account of the relational way in which Dasein exists in the world. Because Heidegger stresses this relational aspect of Dasein's existence, one would expect a much fuller exploration of embodied existence. Heidegger emphasizes that Dasein is integrated into the world, rather than separated off from it.

I suggest that Heidegger's account of Dasein remains more consonant with the disembodied transcendental subject that Heidegger claims Kant inherited from Descartes than Heidegger admits. The explanation for this, in my view, lies in the dominant role that understanding plays in Heidegger's analysis of Dasein, the extent to which he appeals to the necessity of formulating a concept of the understanding, and the lack of any sustained account of bodily experience. Except insofar as bodies signify as a contributing factor to the meaning of Dasein's projects, and their significance is thereby subsumed by Dasein's ways of understanding, Heidegger pays very little attention to them.

One of the guiding efforts, if not the principal objective, of *Being and Time* can be identified as the progressive clarifying and deepening of Dasein's self-understanding. The idea is first introduced under the guise of Dasein having its being as an issue for itself. Subsequently, the notion of understanding is reinterpreted under the rubric of possibility, and finally as projection. Toward the end of *Being and Time*, Heidegger introduces the idea of formulating a concept (*Begriff*) of the understanding (*Verstehen*), an idea that he will develop in the *The Basic Problems of Phenomenology*. My point in sketching the outlines of this development is to emphasize that no matter how far Heidegger imagines having departed from the Cartesian notion of the subject as a thinking being, or from the medieval notion of the subject (which Heidegger reads as approximating to the same view), whereby the intellect determines, or takes the measure of, the thing, through adequation, the legacy of a disincarnate intellect remains. Although Heidegger makes a point of refusing the salience of the distinction between *praxis* and *theoria*, preferring his governing distinction between the ontic and the ontological, the fact remains that his ontological project remains bound to that of theoretical clarification. Of course, as a philosophical project, it is inevitable that there be a privileging of the theoretical. My point is that in *Being and Time*, there is a progressive move away from the concrete starting point of Dasein's world and toward a disembodied understanding of Dasein. Heidegger's project thus errs on the side of the intellect, or the mind, rather than that of the materiality of the world, reinforcing the Western tendency to prioritize the abstract over the concrete that Heidegger would discredit.

It is important to note that the understanding within which Dasein operates, at first, is at a level that is both unreflective and unthematized. Dasein grasps how to operate tools in the world, and how to negotiate the physical conditions of the world, by maneuvering around obstacles without having to stop and measure the space to be negotiated in relation to the proportions of the body. I can move around a room, walk through a doorway, or get into a car, due to an operational understanding I have of the relation between my body and its physical environment. Dasein, in Heidegger's language, has a preontological understanding of the world. The ontological structures that Heidegger draws out of this preontological experience, and designates *existentialia*, that is, the fundamental or basic structures of Dasein's existence, amount to a systematic ordering or synthesis of the multiple possibilities for Dasein's existence in the world. If it is true that Heidegger not only acknowledges a nontheoretical understanding of the world, but also privileges such dealings, articulating them under the rubric of circumspective concern, it is no less certain that the theoretical burden of Heidegger's analysis leads him away from such ontic concerns, and toward their ontological clarification. Heidegger, of course, insists upon the necessity of the ontical as that in which ontology is rooted. And yet, his objections notwithstanding, there is an undeniably moral tone, which sometimes approaches a quasi-religious fervor, in his exhortations that Dasein disentangle itself from the curiosity and idle talk of the they. It is hard not to read into the language of fallenness with which Heidegger describes Dasein's lostness in the they echoes of the theological fall from grace. For Dasein to remove itself from the fallen state of the inauthentic they, mired in ontical concerns, might then be understood as approaching the heady heights of ontological enlightenment.

If one problem with Heidegger's account of Dasein's multifarious relations with the world is that it always seems to have decided in advance in favor of ontology and against the ontic level of experience, another problem is that it is geared almost exclusively to the world of work. Descriptions of Dasein's involvement with objects and with others are oriented around the equipmental world, with the result that both the picture of Dasein that emerges and the *existentialia* that it yields are largely task oriented. Dasein engages in certain types of activity for the sake of an end that it has in view. A very one-sided view of Dasein is thus provided by Heidegger, one that either ignores what most would regard as important aspects of experience, for example, sexuality, eroticism, enjoyment, and pleasure, or, at best, treats them as only important as subordinate to Dasein's successful negotiation of its equipmental relations and its ultimate ontological task of clarifying the significance of such dealings. To the extent that Heidegger pays attention to the physical ways in which we move around the world, for example, he does so largely in the service of Dasein's instrumentalism. It is in order to accomplish certain tasks that Dasein's bodily experience is taken into account.[4] The outcome is that the bodily dimensions of experience are only admitted to Heidegger's analysis in the most rarefied and abstract way. The structures that dominate division 1 of *Being and Time* are consistent with the prominent role played by the understanding. They are geared to the accomplishing of work-oriented tasks and are expressed in relations such as the "in-order-to" and "for-the-sake-of-which," structures whose implicit temporal dimensions, specifically the priority accorded to future-oriented projects, will be parsed out explicitly in division 2 of *Being and Time*.[5]

It is also worth noting that because Heidegger, in *Being and Time* (though in his later work he will retract this principle), subordinates spatiality to temporality, he deprives himself at the structural level of the opportunity to elaborate fully the complexities of bodily experience and the ways in which humans negotiate lived space. A thorough investigation of Dasein's spatiality is ruled out by the extent to which Heidegger's analysis of spatiality is directed according to a corrective task. His analysis is largely restricted to correcting the container model, whereby Dasein's worldhood is reduced to the conception of space ontologically suitable to the relation between a vessel and the water it contains. Any attempts to explore the positive characteristics of spatiality that are implied by this critique are truncated by the formal requirements of his analysis. In making spatiality derivative of temporality, he treats spatiality only in the very limited context of the ready-to-hand relations that constitute circumspective concern. This equipmental context is itself subjected to a reinterpretation in temporal terms. Spatiality thus tends to be exempt from systematic consideration in *Being and Time*. At the very least its consideration is truncated, and subordinated to the thematic and organizing concern of temporality.

Parallel Between Marx and Heidegger

We have seen that Dasein mistakes the nature of its identity when it understands itself in terms of the ready-to-hand, transferring to itself the character of the things to which it relates "proximally and for the most part," as Heidegger is fond of saying. Immersed in a complex network of relations that make up its circumspective world, Dasein takes itself to be more or less equivalent to that which is closest to it—things. I have suggested that Heidegger's concept of Dasein lacks bodily expression. To clarify my point, allow me to briefly introduce a theoretical structure that can serve as a parallel to highlight how Heidegger fails to retain Marx's reference to a domain that resists incorporation into the abstract, theoretical world. Heidegger's structure of Dasein's self-understanding can be compared with the notion of ideology, drawn from Marx and filtered through the lens of Althusser.

In Marxian terminology, human activity includes within it a relationship that individuals maintain with the otherness of nature, through physical labor, even as the process of labor constitutes an exchange between the biological and the spiritual. The transformation of raw materials into products, a process that occurs in and through the mixing of human labor with nature, results in objects that resist easy categorization as either natural or artificial. Not only does the product as such, that which is created through human labor, defy attempts to reduce it to either side of the nature/culture divide; so too the addition of labor to raw materials constitutes an aspect of the thing produced that is difficult to attribute to biology on the one hand or society on the other hand. Once it is produced, the artifact acquires an independence both of the worker and from the work process that led to its production; yet there remains a sense in which the materiality of the worker's labor represents an irreducible aspect of the product. That irreducibility resides, in part, in the physical process of labor, supported and enabled by the worker's being able to secure access to the basic biological necessities of life (food, shelter, clothing, and so on). The bodily processes of sustenance and rejuvenation, as well as the skills required by techniques of physical labor, skills that are inscribed in bodily movements, among other things (whether these skills consist of those of an experienced wood laborer, or word processor), are factored into the Marxian theory of labor.

Through the alienation of labor that the proletariat experiences under capitalist systems, workers are alienated from the product of their labor. The concrete objects that workers create, but do not own, are experienced as standing over and against the worker, in opposition to the very people that created them. Further, the product of labor takes on an alien and abstract quality in acquiring a commodity value, which replaces its use-value, or its value as a useful object. The worker is thereby alienated not only from the creative process of labor that issued in the object, but also from the product itself, from him- or herself as a worker and producer, and therefore also from him- or herself as a human being. Since, for Marx, the productive and creative capacity of humans is definitive of what it means to be a human being, this last aspect of alienation includes the worker's alienation both from him- or herself as an individual, and from other individuals, as members of the human species. Through the various forms of the worker's alienation—from the process of labor, from the product of labor, from the value that the product takes on in a capitalist market, and from him- or herself both at the level of the individual and at the level of the species—the worker finds him- or herself reduced to a thing.

The genius of capitalism rests in its ability to elicit the support of the worker, so that the worker participates in ensuring the continuation of his or her own oppression, by reproducing the conditions of oppression that reduce him to a mere thing. The worker's false consciousness facilitates his or her own collusion with the aims of capitalism. As the worker works, not only is the accumulation of material goods, in the form of capital, secured through profits gained according to the theory of surplus value;[6] but also the worker reproduces the conditions of his or her own alienation. In addition to reproducing the material conditions of exploitation, by maximizing profits for the capitalist owners, thereby producing more capital, widening the gap between workers and owners and providing surplus capital to be reinvested in the capitalist system, the worker submits to the ideology of capitalism. Capitalism treats the worker as if he or she were no more important than a thing. It represents the worker as inessential and dispensable. In fact, however, capitalism depends upon the worker being a worker: without the worker, capitalism would collapse. The worker's own disenchantment with him- or herself is a result of the worker's false consciousness.

In short, to take seriously the notion of ideology is to understand that the ruling class not only controls the allocation of material resources, which the worker needs to survive at the biological level, but also determines the worker's thought patterns, behaviors, gestures, self-image, and so on. The false consciousness of capitalist ideology infects the worker and can be understood not so much as a system of concepts or ideas, but rather in an imaginary and fantastic way, as Althusser has emphasized. The worker succumbs to false consciousness because he or she is captivated by the system that he or she, as a functioning member of the working class, continues to reproduce. Psychologically invested in the system that contains and defines the worker, there is little option but to identify with the image that capitalism holds up for the worker, exercising the worker's investment in that image.

The worker is captivated by capitalist ideology, believing falsely in his or her own unimportance, rather than recognizing his or her structural necessity to the mechanism whereby capitalism ensures its own operation. We might say, then, that the worker lacks conceptual clarity about his or her own place, role, and function within the capitalist system, instead buying into the myth that he or she counts for nothing, or certainly for no more than a thing. In much the same way, Heidegger suggests that Dasein mistakes itself for a thing when it takes itself as equivalent to those things with which it is constantly in relation in the ready-to-hand. Like the worker's ideological mystification, Dasein's mistake does not amount to a conceptual error, precisely insofar as it does not amount to a well-considered, reflective, ontologically clarified, conceptual judgment. Indeed it is precisely Dasein's lack of conceptual clarity that makes its mistaken view of itself akin to ideology.

What can be learned from this parallel? First, whereas for Heidegger, Dasein's aspiration for truth seems to steer Dasein away from the concrete, physical, or material world, Marx thinks that the distinctive character of humanity lies in the creative productive capacity. That is, on the one hand, for Marx, what defines humans as humans involves the relation that they sustain, in and through their creative aspect as producers, with the nature that they transform into products. On the other hand, the thrust of Heidegger's discourse, especially in its requirement that if Dasein is to be true to itself, it must engage in an ever more rigorous quest for clarity in its self-understanding, leads Dasein inexorably away from ontic concerns.

In contrast, Marx's dialectic is firmly situated within the demands of a materialist conception of history.[7] As such, it must continue to negotiate the reality of, and interrelation between, matter and spirit. The material world imposes itself in the guise of biological needs, natural limitations, and bodily materiality, while the spiritual or creative aspect of human nature, that which specifies humans as human, is such as to confront that material reality and transform it into something other than natural, other than what it was, to add to it a value that transcends its natural state. Of course, it is crucial to add that if Marx retained a reference to bodily materiality, he did little to take account of women's experience—bodily or otherwise. Thanks to feminist critiques of Marxist theory, such as those by Gayle Rubin and Heidi Hartmann, which make good this neglect, we are not without guidance on how to make Marxian concepts of labor and ideology applicable to women.[8]

Should the worker manage to overcome his or her own alienation, by getting rid of the ideological claims invented either by the prevailing class system or by patriarchal gender relations, that is, if he or she is able to see beyond his or her alienated state, to refuse the myth of being no more worthy than a thing, the worker will be able to lay claim to the product of his or her own labor. The truth for the worker is that without his or her compliance, capitalism or patriarchy would cease to function effectively. At least theoretically, then, the worker therefore has it within his or her power to incite collective action, and overthrow the system.[9] But how, if at all, can Heidegger's Dasein alleviate the conditions of his or her own inauthenticity? Is such an outcome even possible? It would seem that the best that can happen is that Dasein oscillates, in a constant tension, between inauthentic involvement in things in the world, which induces Dasein to see itself as on a par with the things to which it relates, and an authentic attunement to its true character, as possibility, as freedom. To the extent to which Heidegger's project remains fundamentally tied to the ongoing clarification of Dasein's own initially inadequate understanding of its place in the world, and its relation to things and others, it is hard to see how Dasein can avoid an unmitigated theoretical abstraction if it is to maintain an authentic understanding of itself. Of course, the obvious riposte to this is that it doesn't: Dasein, one might argue, cannot sustain a state of authenticity. It can only maintain it in the blink of an eye, for a moment, in the *Augenblick*. Of this, more below.

With this briefly sketched parallel between the Marxist theory of ideology and Heidegger's notion of Dasein's potential for self-understanding, I hope to have at least indicated that Heidegger does not leave much room for the material, bodily, physical aspects of existence. In his eagerness to avoid equating Dasein's ontological status with that of a present-at-hand thing, he seems to divorce his analysis from the tangible realm, providing us with no path back to the material, except insofar as he allows that it remains a necessary starting point and guide for the analysis. In fact, this affirmation turns out to be rather tenuous, since the task to which Dasein is beholden, namely that of ontological clarification, requires it to move beyond the preontological, operational understanding of its world in its inarticulate immediacy, and toward the rarefied climate of ontological clarity. Dasein's task is to wrest itself away from its initial tendency to see itself on a par with the things that make up its world, away from its concrete involvement with the world, and to conceive of its own lack of determination by such concrete concerns—be it only for the moment of authenticity.

Heideggerians might reject this criticism, by emphasizing that to be authentic in Heidegger's sense is not a state sustainable beyond the instantaneous: the moment of vision provides no more than a temporary clarity that allows Dasein to reorient itself toward the world in a way that no longer obfuscates Dasein's own ontological status in that world. The moment of vision, Heideggerians might argue, includes within it an ecstatic openness to the future and the past. It opens onto the future through anticipatory resoluteness and gathers up the present in the light of its past. It accedes to its destiny not in an aberrant moment, for that moment is isolated neither from the historical processes that led up to it nor from the future possibilities that Dasein has yet to realize. The gathering of temporality into the ecstatic unity of the moment of vision, it might be argued, is no fleeting and insubstantial realization, but endures in its impact and reinstalls Dasein's involvement with the world. Even if these are fair comments—and I will endeavor to show in the following two sections that they are not—it remains the case that the concrete level of Dasein's preontological involvement in the world is qualified as inauthentic by Heidegger, while ontological clarity of authenticity is reserved for the moment of vision, a notion that is at best elusive and at worst too vague to be of much help. Does Heidegger mean by the moment of vision some kind of insight that Dasein has into the character of its existence? Presumably not, since the notion of insight fails to reflect the horizonal structure of projection that Heidegger emphasizes, suggesting a notion of grasping, whereby Dasein imposes its will on the world.

Others

It is no secret that feminism has got quite a lot of mileage out of the idea, encapsulated most pithily perhaps by care ethics, that women's approach to morality (and, by association, to practically everything else) is characteristically more empathetic, more open to emotional considerations, and more responsive to connectedness and attachment than men's. To put it in a way that highlights my immediate concern, women are taught to care for and be oriented toward others, while men are encouraged to separate from their mothers and become autonomous individuals. In short, women are other-directed, and men are self-directed; women are context-bound, while men strive for objectivity and distance; women, in part because of their privileged relationship to child rearing, are caring and nurturing, while men are rational and abstract.

While there are good reasons to be cautious about accepting care ethics lock, stock, and barrel, there is also no doubt that some of its implications are worth considering very carefully. I am going to leave aside the legitimate complaints about the failure of care ethics (at least in its earliest manifestations) to address diversity within the group women, its consequent harboring of a naive universalism, and its general lack of metaphysical clarity about the status of its central claim that women speak in a different voice. Let me focus instead on what I take to be the most important achievements of care ethics, namely its legitimization of an idea that it shares with a number of other (ultimately perhaps more interesting) versions of feminism. That is, the idea that the values that have been enshrined in traditional moral theories, such as justice, rationality, and rule-governed behavior, tend to privilege an approach to ethics that comes more readily to boys than it does to girls. Not only are the values celebrated by Enlightenment thinking (autonomy, individuality, and reason) typically assumed to constitute and shape the moral fabric of society, they are also assumed to be neutral, objective, and universal, when in fact, feminists suggest, they embody a view that is biased toward a masculine point of view, that is not shared by women, and that is therefore partial to men. Moreover—and this is the kicker—traditional moral theory presents itself as if it were unmarked by all these qualifications. It represents itself as gender neutral, accessible to all, and the only obvious route to goodness. It adopts a hypermorality about itself. It isn't enough that it remains the dominant model of morality; it assumes the right to judge other approaches by its own standards about itself. And if the rest of us raise questions about its ascendancy, we are liable to accusations of immorality . . . which sort of prejudges the issue, doesn't it?

In this section I will suggest that, despite Heidegger's formal stipulation that others are at the same ontological level as Dasein, his conception of Dasein as highly individualized and unique ultimately prejudices his philosophy against a serious and sustained consideration of others. It needs to be acknowledged at the outset that Heidegger makes the claim that "Dasein is essentially Being-with [*Mitsein*]" (BT, 156/SZ, 120), and he asserts that this claim has an "existential-ontological" status. Such a claim suggests that Heidegger treats others as if they were on a par, ontologically, with Dasein. A number of other claims support such a view, as when Heidegger says that "*Being-with* and *Dasein-with* (*Mitsein* and *Mitdasein*)" are "equiprimordial with Being-in-the-world" (BT, 149/ SZ, 114), or when he stipulates that "the kind of being which belongs to the Dasein of Others differs . . . from readiness-to-hand and presence-at-hand . . . they are *like* the very Dasein which frees them, in that *they are there too, and there with it.* . . . Being-in-the-world, the world is always the one that I share with Others" (BT, 154–55/SZ, 118). Heidegger takes pains to emphasize that Dasein is not to be understood as an isolated "I" whose relation with others must be established. Rather, Dasein's relation to others is assumed, " 'the Others' already are there with us" (BT, 152/ SZ, 116). Heidegger goes on to say, "By 'Others' we do not mean everyone else but me—those over against whom the 'I' stands out. They are rather those from whom, for the most part, one does not distinguish oneself—those among whom one is too" (BT, 154/ SZ, 118).

It is clear that Heidegger wants to construe others as ontologically equivalent to Dasein, and to underline the fact that others do not occur in the world in the same way as entities that are ready-to-hand or present-at-hand. Others thus have an existential privilege akin to Dasein that sets them apart from all other entities. Despite this, I will suggest that the architectonic structure of Heidegger's analysis exacts certain demands and requirements that result in a severely attenuated role for others. Heidegger's rhetoric leans toward sketching the place of others as derivative of Dasein. This point can be specified in several ways. I will organize my discussion under four topics: Heidegger's concept of world; the distinction between authentic and inauthentic; the "who" of Dasein; and the role that death plays in Heidegger's analysis.

World

First, and most immediately, Heidegger tends to describe others as if they were a characteristic or attribute of Dasein's world, with the result that others might be included in the world, but the world is always Dasein's world. Thus, when Heidegger says, "The world of Dasein is a with-world [*Mitwelt*]" (BT, 155/SZ, 118), we understand that he is asserting the unparalleled importance of others in Dasein's world, but we must also concede that what remains unquestioned is that the world belongs to Dasein. Similarly, Heidegger talks of being with others as being part of the "character" of Dasein (BT, 154/SZ, 118), and describes "being-with" as an "existential characteristic of Dasein" (BT, 156/SZ, 120). Again, Heidegger claims that "Being-with is in every case a characteristic of one's own Dasein" (BT, 157/SZ, 121).

In his discussion of being-with-others, Heidegger's guiding question is, Who is Dasein in its everydayness? (see BT, 149/SZ, 114). In answering his guiding question about the "who" of Dasein, Heidegger takes his orientation from the phenomenon of Being-in-the-world (see BT, 153/SZ, 117). We have already seen that Heidegger is critical of Descartes, along with the rest of the tradition of Western metaphysics, for overlooking the phenomenon of the world, in the specific way that Heidegger understands this term (see BT, 128/SZ, 95). We know that the phenomenon of the world is central to Heidegger's analysis. At the same time, however, it should be recalled that "Being-in-the-world is always fallen" (BT, 225/SZ, 181). Since the analysis of the they proceeds in terms of this way of being, it will necessarily also be fallen or inauthentic. Heidegger confirms this when he says, "The Self of the everyday Dasein is the *they-self*, which we distinguish from the *authentic Self*—that is, from the Self which has been taken hold of in its own way.... As they-self, the particular Dasein has been *dispersed* into the 'they,' and must first find itself" (BT, 167/SZ, 129). Dasein's relations to others is described by Heidegger primarily in terms of its fall or dispersion into the they-self, that is, Dasein's tendency to interpret itself and its ideas in terms of opinions that it unthinkingly takes over from the public realm. This leaves little room for any systematic consideration of the possibilities of informed, thoughtful, or authentic collective social or political action at the level of protesting prevailing socioeconomic conditions.

Authenticity and Inauthenticity

Given that Heidegger's discussion of others is oriented to Being in the world, which, as we just saw, is always fallen, and given that, as we have also already seen, the question that Heidegger uses to guide his analysis of being with others is articulated with reference to everydayness, it should hardly be surprising to find that the discussion is overwhelmingly devoted to inauthentic, fallen, everyday relations. And this is indeed what we find.

Heidegger's discussion of others includes a brief description of a particular way of being with others that he identifies as authentic, namely a kind of "solicitude" (*Fürsorge*) that "*leaps ahead*" of the other (BT, 158/SZ, 122), thereby helping the other to become "transparent to himself" (BT, 159/SZ, 123). With the exception of this brief passage, the account that Heidegger provides of possible ways to be with others yields a largely negative picture and is dominated by what Heidegger calls "the they" (*das Man*). It is hard to miss the disparaging terms in which Heidegger casts what he calls the "dictatorship of the 'they,' " into which "one's own Dasein" is dissolved (BT, 164/SZ, 126). Heidegger says, "We take pleasure and enjoy ourselves as *they* [*man*] take pleasure; we read, see, and judge about literature and art as *they* see and judge; likewise we shrink back from the 'great mass' as *they* shrink back; we find 'shocking' what *they* find shocking. The 'they,' which is nothing definite, and which all are, though not as the sum, prescribes the kind of Being of everydayness" (BT, 164/SZ, 126–27). The "they," which answers to the question of who everyday Dasein is, turns out to be the " 'nobody' to whom every Dasein has already surrendered itself in Being-among-one-another [*Untereinandersein*]" (BT, 166/SZ, 128). Under the sway of the opinions of the neutral "they," that is, under the dominion of views that get attributed to the they, but which no particular Dasein owns up to, Dasein exhibits a "failure to stand by one's Self" (BT, 166/SZ, 128). The they-self is the inauthentic self, from which Dasein must win itself back.

The "Who" of Dasein

Heidegger wants to avoid the problem of solipsism. Heidegger's notion of the they-self can be seen as an alternative to positing a subject, defining this subject as essentially a mind that thinks, or a thinking being, and then confronting the Cartesian difficulty of how to bridge the gap not only between mind and body, but also between my mind and the minds of others. Rather than having to solve the problem of how to connect an isolated I to others, Heidegger construes the problem almost in reverse. Dasein is initially lost in the they, adrift among the shifting and groundless opinions of the public with which it finds itself surrounded, and a part of. It must gather up its forces, break away from the aimless gossip of public opinion and find its authentic self, come back to itself. The rhetoric with which Heidegger describes this move away from inauthenticity and toward inauthenticity suggests that in order to be authentic, Dasein must sever its ties from the they, cut itself off from others—in short, it must approximate itself, at least in some respects, to the isolated Cartesian I from which Heidegger seems to be trying so hard to get away from! This aspect of Dasein—Dasein confronting its fate alone—is the aspect that is perhaps expressed most fully in Heidegger's consideration of death, and I will return to it in a moment.

While I think that it does successfully capture a certain strain in Heidegger's thought, the preceding sketch I have drawn of how Heidegger's notion of the they approaches the problem of others in a way that avoids solipsism needs to be complicated. It ignores the way in which Heidegger takes up and reworks the two characteristics of Dasein that he sketches at the beginning of section 9 of *Being and Time,* namely Dasein's mineness (*Jemeinigkeit*) and the fact that Dasein's essence lies in, or is grounded in, its existence.[10] It also leaves out of account the complexities surrounding the ontologico-ontical status of Dasein that Heidegger introduces here:

> Just as the ontical obviousness of the Being-in-itself of entities within-the-world misleads us into the conviction that the meaning of this Being is obvious ontologically, and makes us overlook the phenomenon of the world, the ontical obviousness of the fact

> that Dasein is in each case mine, also hides the possibility that the ontological problematic which belongs to it has been led astray. *Proximally* the "who" of Dasein is not only a problem *ontologically;* even *ontically* it remains concealed. (BT, 152/SZ, 116)

If the who of Dasein is ontically concealed, this is because—despite Heidegger's insistence on the formal constitution of Dasein as an entity that is in each case I myself (see BT, 150/SZ, 114)—proximally and for the most part Dasein is not "in each case mine." That is, it is not an isolated I, but rather, as immersed in the everyday, it is precisely the they-self. Dasein's usual way of being is inauthentic, which means that ontically it is not in fact itself, but rather "itself" is a collection of opinions and views that it unwittingly takes over from others. At the ontological level, however, Dasein is not to be equated with the they. Far from it. To be oneself is to retrieve oneself from dispersal in the they, to return to oneself, or to come back to oneself, after having been lost in the they.

If we bear in mind Heidegger's assertion that the "who" of Dasein "is not only a problem *ontologically;* even *ontically* it remains concealed" it is possible to make sense of what otherwise appear to be conflicting claims that Heidegger makes in his discussion of being with others. What we have, in effect, is three different levels at which such claims can operate: ontical, ontological, and ontico-ontological. First, there is the "ontically obvious" level, which asserts that "it is I who in each case Dasein is" (BT, 150/SZ, 115). Heidegger says, "It may be that it is always ontically correct to say of this entity that 'I' am it" (BT, 151/SZ, 116), but ontologically such assertions can be misleading. We might say that this level of understanding provides us with a starting point, but as preontological it remains at the unexamined, vague, average understanding Dasein has of its way of being. In answering the question of the "who" of Dasein at this level, we mistake the ontico-ontological character of Dasein. We answer something like "I myself am Dasein"—but on Heidegger's view, at least from the point of view of the existential analytic, we are wrong to do so. In doing so, we are opting for "the most usual and obvious of answers" instead of retaining the "priority" of "ontico-ontological assertions" that would yield a properly "phenomenological" (BT, 151/SZ, 115) interpretation. Rather, Heidegger seeks to show that proximally, Dasein exists not as itself for the most part, but rather in the way that "they" exist. Ontically, then, the answer to the question of "who" Dasein is lies concealed at first. To clarify the ontical status of Dasein as it is for the most part, that is, as it exists inauthentically, would be to demystify Dasein's idea that it is itself, and reveal to it that it is in fact, for the most part, the "they-self." This answer to the question of "who"Dasein is provides an ontically clarified concept of the self: Dasein's ontico-ontological understanding of its own "self" needs to be interpreted as the "they-self" that it gets lost and dispersed into. This ontico-ontological level is the second level of interpretation. Ontologically, there is yet another obfuscation that Heidegger must clear away, and this brings us to the third level, the ontological level. So long as we attempt to answer the question of who Dasein is by taking as our clue an understanding of the self based on substantiality, our answer remains at the level of the present-at-hand. Heidegger wants to interpret Dasein at the ontological-existential level, and this involves combating the idea that Dasein is a self-identical substance that somehow maintains its coherence throughout a series of changing experiences (see BT, 150/SZ, 114). Rather than appealing to substance as providing the underlying unity that makes the I identical with itself, Heidegger appeals to the ontological conditions of possibility that allow Dasein to be either true to itself or to fail to stand by itself.[11] That is, he appeals to the idea that Dasein can either be authentic or inauthentic. If we recall that authenticity and inauthenticity are "grounded in the fact that any Dasein whatsoever is characterized by mineness" (BT, 68/SZ, 42), we cannot help but be struck by the circular movement of Heidegger's analysis.

To be authentic, the self cannot remain mired in the they-self, but must elevate itself from the average everydayness of the they and become free for itself. Dasein must stand alone, but it must do so not out of a naive and misguided understanding of its own isolation from others, as if that were a given, but rather in the knowledge that it has had the strength to tear itself away from the opinions of the they. Heidegger will interpret this standing alone in terms of authentic resoluteness. Thus, Heidegger says that Dasein's mineness "indicates an ontologically constitutive state, but it does no more than indicate it" (BT, 150/SZ, 114). In other words, it is ontologically appropriate to define Dasein with regard to its mineness, but one cannot do so without first going through the interpretation of Dasein's lostness in the everyday. In this state, Dasein is phenomenologically not defined by itself at all, but precisely by others. Only by regaining its sense of itself as free to make its own choices does Dasein come back to itself, into its own, and only then can it be said to be constituted by "its Being . . . in each case mine" (BT, 150/SZ, 114).

If we stand back from the intricate details of Heidegger's argument, the main question that emerges is this: in the final analysis does Heidegger's treatment of being-with-others amount to any more than a distraction from Dasein's ontological journey toward its quest for its own authenticity, a detour by which Dasein deviates from its own path of self-discovery, to which it is destined to return? How far does Dasein ultimately stray from the original priority conferred on the self by its mineness? Is Heidegger's ontology bound to a philosophical view that fails to move much beyond the solipsistic tendencies modern philosophy has inherited from Descartes? Let me turn to Heidegger's understanding of death in an attempt to confirm that Heidegger's account of Dasein reveals a strong tendency to reassert the individualistic traits of the metaphysical commitments he tried to overcome.

Death

Interpretively, death would seem to present Heidegger with a problem at first sight. Heidegger's attempt throughout *Being and Time* is to provide a picture of Dasein's being-as-a-whole. The fact of Dasein's mortality appears to be an obstacle for rendering clearly the totality of Dasein: if Dasein still has some part of its life to live out, it would seem that any analysis of its structure must remain incomplete until such time as death arrives. Yet when Dasein dies, it is no longer Dasein—it no longer exists. The conundrum that death would seem to pose is that Dasein's finitude entails that part of it remains outstanding, for so long as Dasein is alive it has not yet completed itself, but as soon as Dasein dies, it is no longer Dasein. The problem turns out to be falsely conceived, on Heidegger's view. It operates on the assumption that it shares with so many other metaphysical problems, namely that Dasein can be ontologically understood as akin to things that are present-at-hand. Heidegger suggests that rather than see death as an obstacle that interferes with the attempt to get the whole of Dasein in view, being-toward-death should be understood as integral to Dasein's way of being, as constitutive of Dasein's being. We are always on our way to death. Since to die is precisely no longer to be Dasein, Dasein's finitude should be understood as constitutive of Dasein's very existence. Dasein's specific way of existing, *Existenz*, is conceived as distinct from the existence of other things. Dasein's finitude is essential to its way of existing, just as it is thereby also crucial for

Heidegger's rethinking of temporality. Temporality, for Heidegger, must be thought of on the basis of death, and not vice versa. Metaphysical philosophy posits an abstract, ongoing, infinite time, and then reads death against this backdrop of time both as that which passes, and as that which can only ever be real in the present. The tension between time as essentially transitory and as lacking reality outside the present, is one that Heidegger doesn't think the Western tradition of philosophy has ever successfully addressed. By reorienting his reflections about time away from the traditional priority philosophers have granted to the present, and toward the future, Heidegger, by the same token, privileges death over the now. This is not to say that he is naive about the impossibility of ever escaping the ineluctable privilege that the present maintains, since even the future cannot be envisaged outside a present, and the past cannot be remembered outside a present.

Representation, memory, imagination may give us a certain freedom toward the present, but they equally serve to underscore the ineliminable priority of the present. One of Heidegger's great contributions is his constant insistence that the present cannot easily release itself from the hold of the past, any more than it can divorce itself from the impending future. To abstract the present from the weight of the past, or from the responsibility of the future, is to buy into a model of time that is borrowed from science, rather than to take seriously Dasein's status as a finite being, and to understand that our finitude shapes our very access to, and understanding of, temporality.

As finite beings, we are always on the way to death, and in this sense death is certain. What is not certain is when we will die, and in this sense death is indefinite (see BT, 303/SZ, 258). We typically cover up the certainty of death, by assuming that death is in the future, when in fact it is possible at any moment. The solution is not to constantly fear death, but rather to see that the "not yet" of death is part of what it means to exist. Heidegger thus conceives of the "not yet" of death as belonging to Dasein's very mode of existence, as belonging to Dasein's way of being. Rather than seeing the time which Dasein has yet to live as interfering with any attempt to grasp Dasein as a totality, Heidegger suggests that Dasein's finitude be understood as characteristic of Dasein's way of being. Death is not to be thought of as an additional, accidental event, without which Dasein's structure cannot be understood, or without which Dasein remains incomplete, but rather as the inevitable end to Dasein. Hence the fact that there is still some time outstanding for any given Dasein is only a problem for understanding so long as we insist on imposing on Dasein an ontology that is appropriate to things. Once we see that the possibility of death structures our way of being, that it can happen at any moment, and that it will happen at some moment for every Dasein, the fact that it has not happened yet does not get in the way of understanding Dasein. Death merely has to be taken seriously as characteristic of Dasein's mode of existence. Thus Heidegger conceives of death as the "possibility of impossibility."

Heidegger stresses that no one can take my place in dying (see BT, 284/SZ, 240). He says "coming-to-an-end implies a mode of Being in which the particular Dasein simply cannot be represented by someone else" (BT, 286/SZ, 242). Clearly, this position is indisputable at an empirical level. No one can stand in for me when it comes to dying. Yet it is also true that one can sacrifice one's life for another, and it is far from clear whether Heidegger ever seriously takes on the questions raised by this possibility. Levinas suggests, and I concur, that Heidegger preempts the moral issue of what it means to substitute oneself for another, by insisting on construing death as the individualization of Dasein. Heideggerians will object that in understanding death as the supreme individualization of Dasein, Heidegger does not rule out the possibility that Dasein might choose to go to its death for another, but the objection misses Levinas's point. That Dasein might make the choice of sacrificing its life for another does not alter the basic assumption that governs Heidegger's analyses of death. He still posits Dasein's freedom as basic, and this is precisely what the Other, according to Levinas, puts in question.

Heidegger simply does not think that the possibility of sacrificing oneself for another is as basic as the empirical truth that even if someone goes to his or her death for another, everyone must still die his or her own death. He also insists that in death, all our relations with others are undone (BT, 294/SZ, 250). I submit that while this might well be true for Dasein itself, it is certainly not true for the others that Dasein leaves behind. Heidegger devotes little consideration to bereavement and mourning, and his sparse discussion leaves much to be desired. For all the work that the concept of anxiety does for Heidegger, in disclosing Dasein's "uttermost possibility" (BT, 310/SZ, 266), in bringing Dasein face-to-face with the possibility of impossibility, or with the experience of nothingness, it does not ultimately disrupt the circuit of Dasein's self-understanding. It merely consolidates Dasein's resolve. In the end, Heidegger's Dasein stands alone against the world, resolute in its finitude.

Dasein's isolation is uncompromising. It begins and ends in the closed circuit of Dasein's own self-understanding.

Temporality and History

Typically, women have been more associated with spatiality than temporality. As we have seen, Heidegger privileges time over space, and in doing so, he prioritizes a traditionally masculine trope over a traditionally feminine trope, but without marking it as such. He thereby endorses and reiterates the priority of a masculinized temporal ordering, which becomes the ultimate framework for interpreting the meaning of Dasein's existence. While maintaining that his analysis of Dasein is neutral with respect to sex, gender, race, and class, Heidegger in fact presents us with a picture of a very specific Dasein. Heidegger's Dasein is one who is largely untroubled by its bodily existence (except insofar as bodily needs are subordinated to goal-oriented ends, as in the for-the-sake-of-which), one who assumes the priority of self over other, and one for whom spatiality is subordinated to temporal ordering. Is it accidental that all these facets of Dasein's existence articulate traditionally masculine characteristics?

Plato's maternal chora—for all its indeterminacy and resistance to being named anything, let alone a concept, has more resonance for space than it does for time. Julia Kristeva's revival of the Platonic chora of *Timaeus* has not only given life to its maternal and spatial connotations, but also to its preverbal associations. By relating the chora to the transition from the pre-Oedipal to the Oedipal, Kristeva preserves its diachronic, retroactive character that Plato had first set forth. Chora names that which cannot be named, that which lies outside of complete incorporation into the symbolic realm, and yet that which, were it not for the symbolic, could not be said to exist. In this sense the chora represents the impossibility of remaining outside a masculine symbolic: inchoate matter requires the form of symbolic order, even as it incurs a loss whose effects will never be entirely recuperated. One could pose the following question to Heidegger: is there any aspect of preontological experience whose meaning will not be taken up by an ontological schema? Is there any residue of experience that resists ontological analysis? Can the preontological level be signified in any other terms than the ontological? If the answer is no, as I suspect it is, Heidegger remains Hegelian in ways that

Kristeva has put into question. Ontological analysis has the effect of sublating a preontological realm. What Kristeva has tried to point toward, by insisting on the differentiation between the semiotic and the symbolic, is the impossibility of having the language of the symbolic or the ontological capture everything that resonates as semiotic or preontological. Even if Heidegger attempted to capture the difference between Being and beings, the question remains of whether, in the final analysis, he leaves room for any other register than the ontological to hold sway.

Kristeva's essay "Women's Time" is a good place to look for an attempt to combat the rather exclusive way in which women have been rendered according to space but not time, matter but not form, the landscape of nature, but not the historical record of culture.[12] To the extent that women have been figured within a temporal lexicon, they are associated with beginnings, rather than endings. Beauvoir, among others, has pointed out that women's most obvious affinities are with generation, rather than corruption, life-preserving tasks such as mothering, rather than death-defying activities such as hunting. We cannot forget, of course, that psychoanalysis has done its part to associate women with the death drive, but it is an open question of whether the topographical schemes that render women as akin to death remain overdetermined by the same masculine imaginary that has represented women as other with a capital O: women are not human. Animal-like, godlike, on a par with nature, on a par with the elements, below or above, embodying everything sinful in the figure of Eve, or everything divine, as in the projection of female deities, but never simply the same as man—never human, always inhuman. Women are associated with the death drive *from a masculine point of view*.

To the extent that Heidegger's corrective task vis-à-vis the tradition consists of challenging the traditional priority of the present and replacing it with an emphasis of the future, he might be seen to reinscribe the relative neglect of those temporal dimensions over which women have been guardians—birth, new beginnings, generative power. Of course, to say that Heidegger simply swapped an emphasis on the present for an emphasis on the future is hugely oversimplifying, because he tried to emphasize the future's priority in a way that also allowed for the way in which all three ecstases (past, present, and future) equally codetermine one another. In other words, he wanted the priority of the future to facilitate an account of temporality that stressed above all the unity of all three ecstases that subtended whatever privilege the future assumed. His overall point was not to make the future the most important dimension of temporality, whereas traditionally the present had taken pride of place. The point, rather, was to demonstrate how each ecstasis was dependent on a pre-ontological understanding of the other ecstases. One cannot understand the present without a kind of co-understanding of the past out of which it derives, or the future toward which it is headed—this is what Heidegger wanted to show. To say that he wanted to emphasize, above all, the unity of the ecstases, is to say that whatever privilege Heidegger's account of being-toward-death gave to the future, that privilege was intended to redound to the account of Dasein's finite temporality as a whole.

Despite these caveats, it is still fair to say that accompanying, and perhaps grounding, Heidegger's relative emphasis of the future (as it relates to ending life) over the present, is a relative neglect of the past (as it relates to beginning life). There is scope, then, for asking how the predominantly female experience of motherhood might inform an alternative account of temporality, one that does not so much emphasize death and ending as birth and beginning. Heidegger admits that he has focused almost exclusively on Being-towards-the-end, and neglects the question of beginning (see BT, 425/SZ, 373). But, having acknowledged the problem, rather than rectify the problem, he justifies the neglect. Why? Heidegger couches the problem of "Dasein's stretching along between birth and death" as a problem of the "connectedness of life" (BT, 425/SZ, 373). He dismisses the usual understanding of how one phase of life is connected to another as resting on a notion of time as present-at-hand. To see life as a "sequence of Experiences" is to see what is really actual as the present-at-hand now, with past experiences as no longer actual, and future experiences as not yet actual. At the bottom of the problem of connectedness, Heidegger discerns a problem of identity—how does the self remain the same self throughout different times? What accounts for the persistence, or self-sameness, of the I who experiences otherwise diverse and disconnected stages of life? Connectedness, Heidegger suggests, should not be thought of as a framework that serves to link together fragmentary moments, but rather as the ecstatic structuring of Dasein itself. Resisting the notion that we need to discover the essence or substrate of the self beneath the flow of time, Heidegger prefers to understand the flow of temporality as itself constitutive of Dasein's "identity," or rather, in Heidegger's terms, Dasein's being. The stretching along between birth and death must not be thought of on the basis of a container model, according to Heidegger. Both the beginning and end of Dasein's life, in some sense *are*—they exist not as arbitrary boundaries to Dasein's present, which may or may not be there. Rather they are necessary dimensions of Dasein's present, which help to constitute the present as what it is. Connectedness, or stretching along between birth and death, is not to be thought of as akin to the motion of a thing. The movement by which Dasein stretches itself along, or connects its diverse experiences to itself, is what Heidegger calls historizing (*Geschehen*), a term that is to be distinguished from our usual idea of history, understood as the object of a science. To study history as an object of science is to do what Heidegger calls "historiology." But Dasein can only engage in such a study of the history of objects because it is itself historical.

This is not the place to rehearse elaborate details of Heidegger's notion of temporality. However, a few pointers are in order, especially if we are going to grasp Heidegger's thoughts about historical consciousness and understand the difference between our normal notion of history and the sense that Heidegger gives the terms *historicity* and *historicality*. A good deal of Heidegger's argument about time hinges on the ambiguity of the concept of *ousia*. Usually rendered by Aristotle's translators as "substance," it can also be rendered as "essence," "existence," or "being."[13] Heidegger claims that "in ontologico-Temporal terms" *ousia* signifies "presence" [*Anwesenheit*]" and hence entities are grasped as "present" [*die Gegenwart*]. That is, they are understood in terms of that particular aspect of time that we designate the present, as distinct from the past and future. According to Heidegger, the Greeks—not only Aristotle, but also Parmenides and Plato—"take time itself as one entity among others, and try to grasp it in the structure of its Being, though that way of understanding Being which they have taken as their horizon is one which is itself naively and inexplicitly oriented towards time" (BT, 48/SZ, 26). That is, entities "are conceived as presence (*ousia*)," but "without any acquaintance with the fundamental ontological function of time" (BT, 48/SZ, 26) that operates in order to allow this interpretation. The ambiguity Heidegger identifies in the Greek conception of *ousia* resides in its equivocation between the ontological and the ontic. Not only does it designate both the essence or whatness of a being (independently of its existence) and the existence or thatness of being—that it exists. It is also used in an ontic sense, to mean "that which is always available in the everyday Dasein of humans: useful items, the homestead, property assets, possessions, that which is at any time for everyday use, that which is immediately and for the most part always present [*Anwesende*]" (FL, 145). Heidegger thinks that for Aristotle—and therefore for the tradition that he inaugurates—time "shows itself in circumspective concern" (BT, 473/SZ, 421). What this means is that, whether explicitly or not, the idea of being that is assumed is presence-at-hand (*Vorhandensein*).

Throughout *Being and Time* Heidegger works with a tripartite structure that will ultimately be resolved into the three temporal ecstases. He sets it out in terms of the fundamental *existentialia*, or basic ontological characteristics of Dasein: existentiality, facticity, and falling. These fundamental characteristics, which describe the basic ways in which Dasein exists, are respectively mapped onto the relations with which Heidegger has described Dasein's involvement in the world, that is, Dasein's being-ahead of itself, its being-already-in, and its being-alongside (see BT, 235/SZ, 250). One can see how these relations prefigure Heidegger's ultimate reinterpretation of the temporal categories future, past, and present. In their undifferentiated states, the future is understood as ahead-of-itself (*Sich-vorweg*) (see BT, 386/SZ, 337), the past as having-been (*Gewesenheit*), and the present as *Gegenwart* (see BT, 397/ SZ 346).[14] Heidegger lays out the structure of Care in section 41. Compiling what he says there with the other structures that are worked out in various stages of *Being and Time*, we can summarize his findings with the following chart:

Structure of Care (paragraph 2, p. 237)[15]

Existentiality	Being an issue for itself being-ahead-of-itself for-the-sake-of-which	grounded in the future
Facticity	thrownness being-already-in-the-world in-order-to	grounded in the past as having-been
Being-fallen	they being-alongside fleeing uncanniness	grounded in making-present

Temporality makes possible the unity of existence, facticity, and falling. Heidegger understands the future past and present in the following terms:[16]

Assumptions of Heidegger's Ontology   103

    future   towards oneself
    having been back to
    present   letting-oneself be encountered by

Allow me, for the sake of brevity and clarity, to also present the following suggestion for how to render Heidegger's temporal interpretation of the structural items of care, that is, understanding as futural; state-of-mind as thrown, that is, as having-been; and falling in its existential meaning as present.

Being and Time: Structural Items of Care Interpreted Temporally

1. Understanding (Verstehen) as Futural
Section 68a, Temporality of Understanding

Undifferentiated	Inauthentic	Authentic
Ahead-of-itself (Sich-vorweg) (386)	**Future (Zukunft)** Awaitng (Gewärtigen) (386)	**Future** Anticipation (Vorlaufen) (386)
	Present (Gegenwart) making-present (Gegenwärtigen)	**Present** moment of vision (Augenblick)
	Past (Gewesenheit) Having-forgotten (Vergessenheit)	**Past** Repetition (Wiederholung)

Horizonal Schema: for-the-sake-of-which (416)

2. State-of-Mind (as thrown), 68b
Temporalizes itself primarily in having-been (Gewesenheit)

Undifferentiated	Inauthentic	Authentic
Having-been (Gewesenheit)	**Past** (Fear) Forgetting (Vergessen)	**Past** (Anxiety) Repeatability (Wiederholbarkeit)
	Present making-present (Gegenwärtigen) (394)	**Present** Gegenwart hält den moment of vision (Augenblick) *at the ready (auf dem Sprung)* (394)

| | Future
lost present
(verlorenen Gegenwart) (395) | Future
Future of
resoluteness (Zukunft der
Entschlossenheit) (395) |

Horizonal Schema: that in the face of which it has been thrown and that to which it has been abandoned

3. Temporality of Falling (Verfallen), 68c
Falling has its existential meaning in the present (397)

Undifferentiated	Inauthentic	Authentic (Does not strictly apply) (397)
Present (Gegenwart) (397)	Curiosity (Die Neugier) Never-dwelling-anywhere Aufenthaltlosigkeit	[moment of vision (Augenblick)]

Temporalizes itself out of itself (399)

Horizonal Schema: In-order-to

Allowing these summary charts to stand in for a full account of temporality, let me to turn to the question of history, the final substantive topic I wish to address, against the background of this overview of Heidegger's notion of temporality.

At the beginning of section 72, Heidegger reminds us that an understanding of Being belongs to Dasein's very state of Being. He stipulates that this understanding must be interpreted primordially, in order for us to gain a *concept* of this understanding. Conceptual clarity is to be produced out of an initially prereflective (preontological) grasp of Being. There is a sense, then, in which Dasein's understanding, or its way of Being, presupposes the very Being that is asked about. Another way of putting this would be to say that, in its understanding, Dasein projects a sense of Being, and thereby assumes precisely the object of inquiry, albeit in a vague and unthematic way. Because Dasein's understanding is itself a way of Being, Dasein already operates within the horizon of Being. The task remains to elucidate more exactly what is being projected. This idea of Dasein's understanding always already positing in some vague sense what Heidegger sets out to discover (the meaning of Being) gives some guidance about why temporality is so important, as the "primordial condition for the possibility of care" (care being the name Heidegger gives to the overall structure of Dasein). Dasein is immersed in a world, through circumspective involvement, "always already." This dimension of experience, the "always already," Heidegger designates by the term *thrownness* (*Geworfenheit*).

Heidegger appeals to the idea of Dasein handing itself a "possibility which it has inherited and yet chosen" (BT, 435/SZ, 383). Some of the more sophisticated versions of postmodern feminism have taken over precisely such a model. I have in mind those versions of feminism that take seriously the various processes by which subjects are constructed by cultural influences, and in this sense are created by history, but which stop short of allowing the vague idea of "construction" to completely obliterate any concept of agency. The problem with the direction in which Heidegger takes his analysis is that he is too much in thrall to unspecified notions such as "heritage," which, in the aftermath of his association with Nazism, begin to look very suspicious. Having repeatedly insisted, throughout *Being and Time*, that authenticity is not simply a moral category, and having resisted the idea that it means anything like good, he says, for example, "If everything 'good' is a heritage and the character of 'goodness' lies in making authentic existence possible, then the handing down of a heritage constitutes itself in resoluteness" (BT, 435/SZ, 383). The assumption that everything that is handed down to us is good seems enormous and untenable, to say the very least. Heidegger's appeals to the simplicity of the fate to which Dasein is brought back sets off further alarm bells. Because of this, the extent to which Heidegger's understanding of history allows others back into the picture, after having largely banished them in their guise as "the they" is more than disturbing. For the question that is posed is, What others, and in whose name do these others speak? It is hard to avoid the conclusion that the others that Heidegger has in mind, the others who represent the good, the others whose heritage history hands down to us as our fate, are those who the Nazis believed were destined to rule.

I have deliberately not assumed one particular version of feminism in the foregoing. In recognition of the fact that feminism is a diverse set of sometimes conflicting theories, I have referred to different traditions of feminism at different points. I have suggested that feminists who are situated within the continental tradition are saddled with the uneasy legacy of Heidegger's discomfort with bodies, a legacy that we are still trying to live down. I have shown why I think that Heidegger's analysis of Dasein reiterates to some extent the solipsism he wanted to avoid. Dasein remains solitary, without much allegiance to others, in its alleged neutrality

106   The Gender of Dasein

with regard to race, sex, gender, and ethnicity. It also remains very much beholden to the transcendental subject from which it wants to break away. For all its ingenuity, Heidegger's reworking of the question of time does not manage to extricate Dasein from an ultimately rather traditional emphasis on subjectivity as the locus of understanding. Even in the face of death, Dasein stands alone. In authentic anticipation, Dasein is thrown back on its own devices—those of mastery, control, and dominance. To the extent that Heidegger does take the impact of others seriously, he imports notions of tradition and heritage that we should approach only with extreme caution. For the idea of history that seems to be foreshadowed is one that harks back to a quasi-Hegelian view, where whatever happens happens and then gets regarded as necessary. Under the sway of fate, Dasein can apparently cling to traditions that pronounce themselves as destiny, traditions that discriminate on the basis of sex, race, ethnic identity, sexuality, class, and so on, without acknowledging the partiality and bias of these traditions.

I have provided an account of Heidegger's Dasein as progressively clarifying its understanding of itself by wresting itself from the concrete world. Dasein's self-understanding amounts to an overcoming of ontical concerns, or rather their transmutation into ontological comprehension. This journey of self-clarification is at the same time a severing of Dasein from inauthenticity, a severance that takes shape as a repudiation of others, who figure for the most part as "the they." To the extent that the material, bodily aspects of the world are left behind by Dasein in its quest for self-understanding, they are associated with the domain of those inauthentic others. The care of the self is left to those vague, shadowy figures who are still caught up in the ontological obfuscation of the they.[17] If my account is legitimate, the consequences for feminism are profound. For those others, from whom Dasein tries so hard to divorce itself, also play the role of caretakers of Dasein's material, bodily needs, and such roles are occupied overwhelmingly by women and minorities.- Since Heidegger's Dasein is allegedly neutral, there is no room for him to acknowledge the political implications of the division of labor that is implied by his account. Since his ontology is one that has universal pretensions, there is no place for an acknowledgment of the sexist, racist, and classist structures on which his account implicitly relies.

The only point at which others are admitted back into the ontological system is the point at which they become responsible for handing down to us a heritage, yet one that celebrates tradition as fate. For Heidegger, "fateful Dasein, as Being-in-the-world, exists essentially in Being-with-Others, its historizing is a co-historizing and is determinative for it as destiny [Geschick]. This is how we designate the historizing of the community, of a people [Volkes]" (BT, 436/SZ 384). Dasein's heritage is specified, or rendered explicit as "repetition." Heidegger says, "*Repeating is handing down explicitly*" (BT 437/SZ, 385). "The authentic repetition of a possibility of existence that has been—the possibility that Dasein may choose its hero—is grounded existentially in anticipatory resoluteness; for it is in resoluteness that one first chooses the choice which makes one free for the struggle of loyally following in the footsteps of that which can be repeated" (ibid.). Given the era that Heidegger is writing in, and the destiny that he ended up embracing, the invocation to these others, and to Dasein's nebulous hero, is surely one that we must regard with acute suspicion. For, with hindsight, neither Dasein's authentic choice, nor the hero it loyally follows; neither the community, nor their destiny, has remained nebulous.[18]

Notes

1. See Elizabeth V. Spelman's discussion of somatophobia in *Inessential Woman: Problems of Exclusion in Feminist Thought* (Boston: Beacon Press, 1988), 126–27.

2. See, for example, Heidegger's 1936 essay, "The Origin of the Work of Art" (see PLT).

3. To take oneself as present-at-hand is not necessarily to theorize one's being as present-at-hand, but is more likely to consist in precisely the failure to theorize Dasein's specific way of being.

4. Levinas, Merleau-Ponty, and Sartre have provided phenomenological accounts of the lived body that go some way toward supplementing Heidegger's disembodied account of Dasein's experience, but all of them reproduce, in some measure, Heidegger's failure to take seriously gendered experience.

5. See for example BT, 235/SZ, 191 and BT, 376/SZ, 328.

6. Very briefly, surplus value is produced through the difference between the price that a commodity can command and what it costs to maintain the worker as a worker, or to keep the worker alive and healthy enough to be able to work. That is, it is the difference between the commodity produced and the cost (for example) of minimum wages, wages that allow the worker to remain alive by producing the cost of the bare necessities of life, but deny the consumption of luxury goods. The worker is allowed to live only in the sense of mere existence, but not allowed to enjoy the products of his or her labor.

7. See, for example, Karl Marx and Frederick Engels, *The German Ideology*, ed. C. J. Arthur (New York: International Publishers, 1986).

8. See Gayle Rubin, "The Traffic in Women," in *Toward an Anthology of Women*, ed. Rayna Reiter (New York: Monthly Review Press, 1975); Heidi Hartmann, "The Unhappy Marriage of Marxism and Feminism: Towards a More Progressive Union," in *The Unhappy Marriage of Marxism and Feminism: A Debate on Class and Patriarchy*, ed. Lydia Sargent (London: Pluto Press, 1981), 1–41.

108 The Gender of Dasein

9. As J. S. Mill first pointed out, and Simone de Beauvoir reiterated, the traditional conditions that dictate women's living situations entail their relative isolation as housewives in households presided over by husbands, and do not lend themselves to the collective solidarity of laborers under capitalism.

10. The two characteristics that Heidegger takes up as "clues . . . for answering the question" of "who" Dasein is "formally indicat[e] the constitution of Dasein's Being" (BT, 152/SZ, 117). They are "the priority of *'existentia'* over *essentia,* and the fact that Dasein is in each case mine [*die Jemeinigkeit*]" (BT, 68/ SZ, 43).

11. Heidegger develops the notion of "constancy" in relation to Dasein's authenticity.

12. Julia Kristeva, "Women's Time," in *The Kristeva Reader,* ed. T. Moi (Oxford: Basil Blackwell, 1986), 187–213.

13. See translators' note 1 to BT, 47.

14. By "undifferentiated" Heidegger means the general character of the future, past, or present, without regard to authenticity, or inauthenticity.

15. See BT, 235–37/SZ, 191–93; BT, 364/SZ, 317; BT, 375–76/SZ, 327–28.

16. See BT, 377/SZ, 328.

17. In Levinas's critique of Heidegger, these figures take on the explicit shape of the feminine.

18. Some material from this chapter appears in a different version in *Time, Death and the Feminine: Levinas with Heidegger* (Stanford: Stanford University Press, 2001).

3

Conflictual Culture and Authenticity

Deepening Heidegger's Account of the Social

Dorothy Leland

In an essay titled "Authenticity, Moral Values, and Psychotherapy," Charles Guignon explores ways in which Heidegger's concept of authenticity illuminates the role of moral discourse in psychotherapy.[1] Guignon agrees with Medard Boss, Ludwig Binswanger, and others that Heidegger's ontology of *Dasein* has profound implications for psychotherapy. But he finds their interpretations of Heidegger to be flawed. According to Guignon, psychotherapists influenced by Heidegger have tended to invoke an existentialist interpretation of Heidegger's *Dasein* analytic, an interpretation that preserves the core value of modern individualism, described as "freedom understood negatively as freedom from constraint" (AMP, 223). On this interpretation, authenticity is construed as "the stance of the rugged individualist who, upon experiencing anxiety in the face of the ultimate absurdity of life, lives intensely in the present and creates his or her own world through leaps of radical freedom" (AMP, 215).

In contrast, Guignon holds that Heidegger's ontology of Dasein undercuts all forms of modern individualism. On this account, human being is inextricably bound to some historical culture and exists only as a process or activity of taking up and taking over what already has been made available within that culture. Authenticity and inauthenticity refer to ways in which one takes up and takes over one's cultural heritage—its possibilities, its patterns of living and doing, its stories and interpretations. Whereas inauthentic Dasein lives in forgetfulness of this heritage, authentic Dasein " 'remembers' its rootedness in the wider unfolding of its culture, and it experiences its life as indebted to the larger drama of a shared history" (AMP, 234).

Guignon's interpretation of Heidegger on authenticity provides one compelling way of working through texts that are not always clear and that sometimes appear to be contradictory. Significantly, his account belongs to an influential strand of Heidegger interpretation that I call the "Berkeley school" (because it is spun around the writings and teachings of Hubert Dreyfus), which assimilates much of Heidegger's thought in *Being and Time* to that of the late Wittgenstein of the *Philosophical Investigations*.[2] According to the Berkeley school, unlike the Sartre of *Being and Nothingness*, who is viewed as supporting an extreme form of individualism rooted in the notion of radical freedom and choice, the Heidegger of *Being and Time* portrays human being as embedded in networks of shared social practices in a way that undercuts individualistic and mentalistic conceptions of the self. In *Heidegger and the Problem of Knowledge*, Guignon puts the matter this way: "Heidegger defines being human, or Dasein, as essentially Being-in-the-world, that is, as being contextualized in equipmental contexts, in a culture, and in history. These contexts define the self without residue—the Cartesian mind as a center of experiences divides out without remainder. What makes us unique as individuals is not an 'internal space' or substantial self distinct from our roles in the world."[3]

One key to this interpretation is a reading of Heidegger's analysis of *das Man* in *Being and Time* (and other writings from the same period) that hinges on a distinction between conformity and conformism. As Dreyfus notes, this reading attempts to rescue Heidegger from his own confusions: "Heidegger, influenced by Kierkegaard's attack on the public in *The Present Age*, does everything he can to blur this important distinction" (HD, 154). As developed by Dreyfus, as an *existentiale* or basic structure of Dasein, *das Man* refers to our being as participants in a public world, always already engaged in activities within shared contexts of significance. In this sense, Dreyfus argues, *das Man* is better translated as "the one" or "the anyone" rather than as "the they," since this latter translation suggests that "*I* am distinguished from *them*, whereas Heidegger's whole point is that the equipment and roles of a society are defined by norms that apply to *anyone*" (HD, 152). Social norms define both the in-order-tos that constitute the being of equipment and the for-the-sake-of-whiches that give equipment its significance. It is because such norms apply to anyone that the world of Dasein is a "with-world."

Social norms presuppose "averageness" or commonality, but this averageness is distinct from the blind conformism and mediocrity that Heidegger, following Kierkegaard, ascribed to the public. In becoming enculturated into the practices definitive of a social world, we become familiar with the average or common (prevailing) significance of things. I come to understand the significance of chairs within my social world by learning how to sit on them and by learning that chairs are normally used for sitting. In this sense, enculturation involves conformity to norms. This conformity to norms is distinct from conformism understood as a tendency to latch onto whatever falls into the "range of the familiar, the attainable, the respectable" (Heidegger, BT, 152). In the latter case, conformism is not a matter of acting on the basis of a prior familiarity with the in-order-tos and for-the-sake-of-whiches made available by one's culture; rather, it involves absorbing oneself in a narrow range of these possibilities and closing oneself off from a deeper mode of self-understanding. As conformist *Dasein* "flees into" the realm of the familiar, attainable, and respectable, it also "falls away" from its "ownmost possibilities," including the possibility of deliberately and selectively choosing from the range of possibilities offered up by one's cultural heritage.

Although a reading that self-consciously endeavors to clarify distinctions that Heidegger "confused" can rightfully be criticized for foregrounding in Heidegger's work something other or more than Heidegger intended, I find the Berkeley school approach to Heidegger's *das Man* analysis compelling. It provides a useful framework for working out accounts of human agency in which the communal nature of human being takes center stage. However, the framework is limited, particularly if applied to the historical/cultural realities in which we actually live. For example, Heidegger's *das Man* analysis presents the "with-world" of shared social practices as if it were free from deep social divisions. It floats free from systems of dominance and subordination and from an analysis that links the prevailing practices of a culture to such systems. As a result, the framework obscures the way in which groups can be differently situated within a given historical/cultural realm. It obscures also the ways in which differences in one's factical situation can complicate the task of authentic living.

In this essay, I use Guignon's analysis of authenticity and psychotherapy to illustrate this problem. After summarizing this analysis, I introduce the concept of "conflictual culture" and show how Guignon's view of what is involved in authentic living is oversimplified within the context of such a culture. On the view I present, we get a different picture of what is involved in authentic living when this picture is drawn from the standpoint of individuals whose "thrownness" includes being members of marginalized or oppressed social groups. I point out some conceptual tools needed to understand how authenticity might work itself out for members of such groups, and I use these tools to show how authenticity might be linked to political struggle.

Guignon on Authenticity and Psychotherapy

Guignon sketches his account of authenticity on the backdrop of the notion of "average everydayness"—roughly, the way most of us are most of the time. On Heidegger's view, in our average everydayness, we are engaged in concrete, practical activities (for example, paying bills, buying groceries, convening a meeting, writing my sister). According to Guignon, "[W]hen we look at our 'average everydayness,' . . . we are led to what might be called a 'manifestationist' view of human agency. For the manifestationist, there is no way to draw a clear distinction between an inner, core self, and what is merely outward show. Instead . . . our very identity as agents is defined and realized only through our ways of becoming manifest in the world" (AMP, 224). The notion here is that we define who we are through our actions. Rather than viewing actions as the expression of some inner core of being ("self" or "person"), actions are viewed as the "coming-into-being " of the self or person. For example, it is not because I am a conscientious person that I pay my bills on time;

rather, this action is one among others that defines my coming-into-being as conscientious. The coming-into-being of the self or person is temporalized as a "happening" that unfolds throughout a lifetime. According to Guignon, this means that a "person's identity can be grasped only in terms of his or her life story as a whole" (AMP, 225).

The "happening of a life" has authentic and inauthentic forms.[4] Inauthentic life is characterized by an absorption in the demands of the present. This affects the character of one's self-understanding, which gets determined by one's immediate preoccupation, present successes and failures, assessments of feasibility and unfeasibility, and so on. In such absorbed preoccupation with present demands, life is reduced to a series of means-ends strategies for coping with the exigencies of the day. In Guignon's words, "As a series of strategies for coping with practical concerns, our everyday lives are contracted into a series of episodes—the 'one damned thing after another' of mere functioning or 'getting by.' . . . The outcome of this disjointed way of living is alienation from oneself, an inability to see anything as really mattering, and a feeling of futility only partially alleviated by occasional intense 'peak experiences' that are supposed to 'make it all worthwhile' " (AMP, 228). According to Guignon, the inauthentic form of life is a perfect breeding ground for a variety of demoralization disorders that seek relief from contemporary psychotherapy.

As used by Guignon, the phrase "alienation from oneself" means alienation from a "higher" form of life—authentic existence.[5] Authentic life involves a "radical breakdown of our complacent absorption in everydayness" (AMP, 228), and a concomitant facing up to the fact that as finite beings "we are 'delivered over to ourselves' in the sense of being responsible for making something of our lives" (AMP, 229). Guignon describes this as taking a stand on one's being-toward-death, interpreted as facing up to the fact that everything one does contributes to the realization of some final configuration of one's life as a whole.

Authenticity has a distinctive temporal structure that gives coherence, cohesiveness, and integrity to a life course. "Where inauthentic existence is lost in the dispersal of making-present, an authentic life is lived as a unified flow characterized by cumulativeness and direction. It involves taking over possibilities made accessible by the past and acting in the present in order to accomplish something for the future" (AMP, 229–30). Guignon adopts the narrativist vocabulary of Paul Ricoeur and others to provide an alternative description: where inauthentic existence is contracted into a series of episodes, authentic existence is protracted as a coherent story. It is a life guided and given focus by what Hans-Georg Gadamer calls an "anticipation of completion" and Frank Kermode calls a "sense of an ending" (AMP, 230).

As I've described it thus far, Guignon's account of authenticity seems at least consistent with the existentialist version of authenticity (as a leap of radical freedom) that he rejects. What is key to differentiating these accounts is the concept of freedom. According to Guignon, the existentialist version of authenticity adopted by Boss, Binswanger, and others is rooted in the core value of modem liberalism, where freedom is understood negatively as freedom from constraints. More specifically, on the existentialist interpretation, authenticity is viewed as freedom from the constraints of social norms. It involves rising above the crowd to realize one's uniqueness and to assert one's nonconformity. For Guignon, such an ideal of unbounded freedom is self-defeating. This is because nothing is really binding where all things are possible, since this means that no choice can be presented within one's experience as superior to any other. Moreover, the ideal is not consistent with Heidegger's characterization of human being, whose agency is made possible by the social practices constitutive of being-with others.

Guignon's alternative account of authenticity builds on what he takes to be two basic Heideggerian insights: that one's personal life story is always rooted in the wider drama of a communal history, and that one's participation in public forms of life functions as an enabling condition for action. Thus, rather than viewing authenticity as freedom from communal forms of life, Guignon proposes that authenticity is instead "a fuller and richer form of participation in the public context" (AMP, 228). The basis of this fuller and richer participation is a kind of self-focusing, in which we take up available social roles and cultural possibilities with a lucid sense of what we are trying to make of our life as a whole. Stated in a narrativist mode, "[I]f we think of living out our own lives as composing our own autobiographies, then authentic self-focusing might be thought of as a way of imparting a narrative continuity to our life stories."[6]

Authentic self-focusing also can be directed toward one's culture viewed as an heritage and as a source of repeatable possibilities. The attunements, commitments, possibilities of self-interpretation, and so forth that circulate within a cultural world are products of history, and by focusing on the historical unfolding of one's cultural world, we can become connected to this history as a source of potential. "Where inauthentic Dasein just drifts along with the latest trend, authentic Dasein 'remembers' its rootedness in the wider unfolding of its culture, and it experiences its life as indebted to the larger drama of a shared history. As a result, authenticity involves encountering one's possibilities as drawn from the 'wellsprings' of a 'heritage' and living one's life as part of the 'mission' or 'destiny' of one's historical community as a whole" (AMP, 234). As a wellspring or heritage, that past is not something that is "gone," but rather a source of possibilities that can be taken up and taken over in the present to create a shared destiny. When this occurs explicitly, it is through a process of deliberately "choosing a hero" or cultural exemplar to provide guidance for the conduct of one's own life. Such a choice involves, in Heidegger's words, "the struggle to loyally following in the footsteps of that which can be repeated" (BT, 437). Authentic Dasein recognizes the authority of the past—its "indebtedness" to a specific historical culture—and has reverence for this past as a source of repeatable possibilities.

What implications does this view of authenticity have for psychotherapy?

According to Guignon, Heidegger's concept of authenticity "can help us make sense of dimensions of therapeutic practice not fully accounted for in most forms of theorizing" (AMP, 237). The theories Guignon has in mind are those that presuppose that the self is an essentially isolated individual in a morally neutral, objectified universe. On Guignon's view, this presupposition is wrong on two accounts. First, the self in not an isolated individual. Second, the "universe," or world of the self, is not morally neutral.

For Guignon, Heidegger's analysis of *das Man* constitutes his (successful) counter to the presupposition that the self is an essentially isolated individual. "We can be human agents only against the backdrop of . . . a shared medium of intelligibility" (AMP, 226). Put in a narrativist mode, we can be human agents only against the backdrop of the "plot lines made accessible in the anecdotes, tales, and stories circulating in our public language" (AMP, 226). Further, this shared medium of intelligibility is not neutral. The anecdotes, tales, and stories that articulate and sustain our everyday practices transmit a sense of what is important that we inherit from our historical tradition. On Guignon's view, as we become initiated into the practices of our community, we take over shared commitments and ideals definitive of an historical people. We become "attuned" to the "shared quest for goods definitive of a community—such goods, for us, as fairness, honesty, dignity, benevolence, achievement, and so on" (AMP, 235).

Authenticity necessarily involves coming to grips with the normative dimension of existence: it includes an understanding that one's actions take up and project into the future certain moral commitments.[7] Such an understanding is also central to psychotherapy viewed as a "renarrativizing of a person's life story" (AMP, 236). Understood as renarrativizing, therapy involves the joint composition by the therapist and client of a more coherent and clear-sighted story about the client's life. It involves "emplotting events along the guidelines of a moral map of aspiration and evaluation that is rooted in the tacit background understanding of one's moral heritage" (AMP, 236).

Guignon presents therapy understood as self-narrativizing as an antidote to various "demoralization disorders" rooted in inauthentic life. It is significant that these demoralization disorders are viewed by Guignon as being at least partially a consequence of lacking the "steadfast resolve" required by authentic existence. When we fail to live "with a clear-sighted grasp of the temporal continuity and future-directedness of one's own life-happening," the present is trivialized as a succession of events lacking any cumulative significance or overriding purpose (AMP, 225). According to Guignon, this is one of the pernicious effects of one's involvement in public forms of life. In our everyday lives, we have a tendency to get bogged down in mundane activities, to drift along with the latest fads, to measure our actions by the lowest common denominator of what is acceptable and appropriate. Lacking any overarching sense of what makes life important, we become prey to the exigencies of life and the "its just one damn thing after another," "nothing makes sense," "nothing interests me" expressions of modern demoralization syndromes.

Conflictual Cultures, Oppressive Social Structures

Guignon's interpretation of Heidegger pivots on a contrast between an ontology that holds that human reality at its deepest level consists of self-encapsulated individuals in unavoidable conflict and one that holds that human reality at its deepest level consists of a "we" or co-Dasein "attuned to the shared quest for goods definitive of a community" (AMP, 235). On Guignon's view, the individualistic conflictual model is wrong, both as an interpretation of Heidegger and as an account of the fundamental nature of human reality.

But the "we" model can have conflictual elements that Guignon (following Heidegger) tends to ignore. Specifically, Guignon tends to homogenize the cultural and historical "we" and to downplay the existence of conflicting and oppositional narratives concerning fundamental matters such as what "goods" are to be taken as normative or what "moral maps of aspiration and evaluation" ought to prevail. Heidegger's language of "loyalty" and "reverence" (invoked by Guignon in his depiction of authenticity) is troublesome for precisely this reason: Heidegger doesn't make it clear enough that the hero or heroine one chooses may well exemplify a life that is disloyal to the dominant or prevailing cultural consensus and irreverent with respect to pervasive social norms.[8] The disloyalty and irreverence I have in mind has nothing to do with the rugged individualist, everything-is-possible, do-your-own-thing version of authenticity. Rather, it is based on a notion that historical cultures can have deeply divided "moral maps," even though only one or some of these maps prevail in dominant (hegemonic) institutions and practices.

Guignon is right to say that "our very ability to live coherent, meaningful lives presupposed that we operate within the range of possibilities opened up by a background of shared intelligibility" (AMP, 225). My quarrel is with the way in which this range of possibilities gets characterized. For example, historical cultures aren't "pure": through migration, conquest, and various forms of assimilation, different histories are mingled, and the resulting mixture is not always or even usually a homogeneous blend. Some of the paradigmatic stories, bedrock loyalties, and commitments of blended cultures are shared, but others are not. The assimilated Native American, for instance, quite likely has a tacit sense of what life is all about that is different in some important respects from mine because aspects of our histories do not overlap. Moreover, if she has difficulty in leading a "coherent, integrated life," this may be partially a function of the fact that the "sense of reality" built into the practices of the dominant, assimilating culture conflict with the sense of reality built into the historical practices of her native people. The dynamic here is not fallenness into the exigencies of the day, but rather the fragmentation that occurs when a person literally lives within multiple and incompatible cultural worlds.

Janet Campbell Hale's autobiographical work, *Bloodlines: Odyssey of a Native Daughter*, provides rich illustrations of this point.[9] Hale's father was a member of the Coeur d'Alene tribe who grew up on a northern Idaho reservation. Her mother was a "mixed blood" Irish and Kootenay who "spoke only English and was light-skinned and lived in white society all of her life" until she married Hale's father and made the Coeur d'Alene Reservation her home (ND, xvi). Among other things, Hale tells us this about the conversion of the Coeur d'Alene to Catholicism: "The conversion of the Coeur d'Alene was in response to an ancient prophecy that said three black ravens would come to them one day bringing the sacred word of the Creator. The ravens would only come when the people were ready to receive the new revelations. In time three Jesuit missionaries, or Black Robes, as they were called, did come, and they were welcomed and listened to. The tribe embraced Catholicism" (ND, 150). But the Catholicism practiced by the Coeur d'Alene was a "rather peculiar brand," taken over as an extension of their traditional religious beliefs (ND, 150). After the conquest of the Coeur d'Alene and the advent of the reservation system, the church functioned as an instrument of assimilation—committed to "civilizing" the Indian and making him or her as much like white people as possible. At the mission school, Hale's father was beaten by a priest for speaking his own language.

The fate of Hale's father reminds us of the fact that just as cultures aren't (or aren't typically) pure, they also are not (or not typically) egalitarian, by which I mean that prevailing institutions, practices, and norms don't embody the communal identifications, moral maps, and so on of every social grouping equally. The failure to acknowledge this is a weakness in the account of *das Man*, understood as the "shared medium of intelligibility . . . which first opens us onto a world and gives us the resources we need for being human" (AMP, 226). On Guignon's view, this shared medium of intelligibility articulates the sense of what is important, what is possible, and what is permissible that is definitive of a historical people. But prevailing media of intelligibility tend to express the interpretations of dominant social groups, and these interpretations can conflict with and even suppress alternative interpretations. Assimilation achieved through violence (for example, beating Hale's father for speaking his native tongue) provides just one example of how this can occur.

Because of this tendency to homogenize the historical and cultural "we," Guignon overlooks the "pernicious effect" that involvement in public forms of life can have for marginalized or oppressed people. According to Guignon, a person's involvement in public forms of life restricts "the possible options of choice to what lies within the range of the familiar, the attainable, the respectable-that which is fitting and proper" (AMP, 226). The result is a "leveling down" of possibilities, described by Guignon as the obliteration of "the kind of two-tiered sense of life that lets us distinguish higher from lower, crucial from trivial, central from peripheral" (AMP, 226). When inauthentic Dasein "falls into" public forms of life, it takes "the familiar demands of the public world as of consummate importance—as 'the only game in town'—and tends to become ensnared in its immediate concerns" and the "ordinary busy-ness of handling daily affairs" (AMP, 227).

But there is a kind of leveling down of possibilities that is not just an obliteration of the two-tiered sense of reality described by Guignon. When the norms articulated by *das Man* largely express the sense of what is important, what is possible, and what is permissible for dominant social groups, and when these norms conflict with or suppress alternative interpretations, leveling down also occurs as a suppression of alternatives expressed in marginalized stories and practices that contest the dominant culture.[10] For the Coeur d'Alene, conversion to Catholicism meant becoming more white, less Indian. Assimilation into the dominant white forms of life meant "falling away from" native culture. Stated in the narrativist mode, this assimilation involved obliterating the "folktales, stories, anecdotes, and histories" that articulated and sustained the practices of the Coeur d'Alene and replacing them with the "moral map" of the dominant white culture (AMP, 234).

Hale tells us that she never heard a creation myth from her own tribe and attributes this to the Coeur d'Alene's early conversion to Catholicism. But she notes, correctly, that "an Indian creation myth would contradict the one I was told about God creating Adam to live in the Garden of Eden and then, while he slept, taking one of his ribs and making Eve" (ND, 171). In the Americas, the (often forced) conversion of native populations from "pagan" to Christian beliefs and practices entailed superimposing one sense of reality over another, resulting in a form of "lostness" or "incoherence" far different from the "consumed by busy-ness" fate of Guignon's inauthentic Dasein.

This lostness or incoherence is often described in the narratives of immigrant and conquered populations. For example, in *Borderlands/La Frontera*, Gloria Anzaldúa uses "borderlands" as a metaphor for the condition of being caught between cultures—in her case, the dominant Anglo culture of the U.S. Southwest and the cultures of Mexico.[11] As seen by Anzaldúa, the borderland is both a physical and psychological space, where Mexican Americans are perceived as "aliens" in Anglo eyes and as aliens to themselves insofar as they also see themselves through these eyes, exiled from what is considered normal (what Anzaldúa calls "white-right"). The borderland is both a barrier and a passageway. "In between" Mexico and the United States, the borderland is a barrier to being either wholly Anglo or wholly Mexicana. But it is also an incessant passage back and forth between Anglo and Mexican culture. For those who reside in the borderland, there is no single "space of aspiration and evaluation," to use Guignon's language—no single set of shared practices, no single historical tradition. As Anzaldúa notes, while acculturating to Anglo ways may be necessary for economic survival, this does not mean that borderland people wholly identify with Anglo-American cultural values: "We don't identify with the Anglo-American cultural values and we don't identify with Mexican cultural values. We are a synergy of two cultures with various degrees of Mexicanness or Angloness. I have so internalized the borderland conflict that sometimes I feel like one cancels out the other and we are zero, nothing, no one. *A veces no soy nada ni nadie. Pero hasta cuando no lo soy, lo soy*" (B/F, 26). This struggle of identities is intrinsic to borderland existence. It is part of what it means to be there.

Anzaldúa's borderland is a good example of what I have called "conflictual culture." By conflictual culture I mean a culture in which there are fundamental divisions over what is important, possible, and permissible—in Guignon's terminology, conflicting "moral maps of aspiration." Note, however, that the conflictual nature of a culture does not entail that every member of the culture will experience the kind of struggle for identity that Anzaldúa describes. Immigrant populations and conquered populations are more likely to experience "fundamental divisions" than are people from assimilator and conquering groups. For these later populations, the state of "just drifting along" of Heidegger's inauthentic Dasein is easily achieved precisely because these groups are "at home" in the public world of the dominant culture in a way in which assimilated populations are not.

Conflictual cultures need not be the product of conquest, immigration, and assimilation. Traditional Marxism, to pursue another sort of example, holds that at least since the inception of class society, the prevailing "sense of reality" of a given society reflects the interests of the dominant class only. Slaves, for example, have a different "sense of reality" from that of their masters. Moreover, the slave's sense of reality harbors potentially subversive elements that the dominant class seeks to suppress. One way this has been done is by denying literacy and education to potentially subversive groups. Ostracism, censorship, and persecution are other means.

This analysis can be extended to Heidegger's account of *das Man* only by giving *das Man* a specific location in the social world. On the classical Marxist account, *das Man* would need to be (identifiable with) that social group in control of the means of production. But as sketched by Heidegger, *das Man* has no particular social location, even though the "They" is described as tyrannical and inquisitorial. On Guignon's interpretation, this lack of social location is irrelevant because *das Man* refers to Dasein's social nature per se. *Das Man* just is some shared "medium of intelligibility" that "opens us onto a world and gives us the resources we need for being human" (AMP, 227). We cannot be human and not participate in some "medium of intelligibility" or other—some set of historical practices and "the familiar folktales, stories, anecdotes, and histories that articulate and sustain those practices" (AMP, 234).

The problem with this view is not that it is wrong, but rather that it is too abstract as a starting point for conceptualizing the situatedness of *Dasein* within conflictual cultures. Granted, masters and slaves can only be masters and slaves given some "medium of intelligibility" that articulates master/slave as a possible social and economic relation. But it is quite another thing to suppose that master and slave have a common moral map or shared "space of aspirations and assessments." What Guignon fails to note is that being involved in a common set of historical practices does not entail that those practices involve us in the same way, with or within a common set of aspirations and assessments. Put in the narrativist mode, the folktales, anecdotes, and histories that articulate and sustain the practice of "being a master" may not be the same as the folktales, anecdote, and histories that articulate and sustain the practices of "being a slave." Indeed, history tells us that typically they are not.

Guignon, following Heidegger, is interested in the ontology of being human, and he is right to suppose that the social nature of human being does not entail conflict. But neither does it entail the broad sweep of commonality that he proposes. This presupposition of commonality leads Guignon to say, for instance, that "authentic historicity brings about a strong sense of our solidarity with others." Why? For Guignon, this sense of solidarity springs from "the recognition of our embeddedness in and indebtedness to the wider context of our culture" (AMP, 235). But if that culture is fundamentally conflictual, a sense of solidarity rooted merely in a recognition that we belong to this culture is not likely to be achieved. The master and the slave are cultural "cohorts," so to speak; yet the slave in rebellion is not likely to feel solidarity with her master based on their mutual cohort status.

We can see this more clearly by considering the notion of "choosing a hero," which Guignon correctly identifies as a practice of authentic existence. In choosing a hero, "authentic Dasein achieves self-focusing by articulating its existence in terms of the guidelines laid out be certain paradigmatic stories circulating in our cultural world—the stories of such heroes and heroines as Abraham Lincoln, Martin Luther King, Mother Teresa, Helen Keller, and Malcolm X. The lives of these cultural exemplars sketch out plot lines or mythoi for composing one's own life story—for 'following in the footsteps' of those who have come before" (AMP, 235). Suppose I chose Malcolm X as my hero.[12] This choice would heighten my sense of solidarity with oppressed African Americans but not with skinheads, neo-Nazi groups, or even the dominant white culture as a whole. It would also bring about a strong sense of being part of a generation of leaders working to change the oppressive practices and institutions that constitute part of the "fate" of an historical people. I would share with these leaders a "quest for goods," but these goods would not be a map of moral aspiration and assessment shared by all members of my culture. On the contrary, part of what would be involved in choosing Malcolm X as my hero would be a commitment to change the answer to the question, "Who are we?" as a people, a nation, and so on, articulated in dominant (racist) social institutions and practices. With this choice, I show reverence and loyalty to certain oppressed people, but not to the culture to which I belong or its history as a whole.

Authenticity in Situations of Oppression

In this essay, I have suggested that a failure to note that the social world in which we actually live is structured by relations of dominance and subordination may oversimplify and distort the complexities involved in authentic living for members of subordinate groups. More specifically, I have argued that for dominant and subordinate groups, the "pernicious effects" of involvement in public forms of life may be different. And I have shown that for these groups the authentic self-focusing that imparts narrative continuity to a life may emerge against a leveling process quite distinct from the banal conformism emphasized by Heidegger and Guignon.

What is authenticity to a person experiencing oppression? I have not answered this question. Instead I have skirted on its edges, nudging my reflection closer toward what this question might mean. What I do know, now, is that an adequate answer will not emerge in the absence of an exploration of the factical circumstances into which various oppressed groups have been "thrown" and the different ways in which possibilities can be "leveled down." If one follows Heidegger and Guignon in viewing authenticity as an ontical ideal, then one needs also to determine how this ideal can work itself out in those factical situations where it emerges as a concrete option.

Heidegger developed the ideal in terms of his own *Dasein* and historical situation. It stemmed from what Pierre Bourdieu has called the "*volkisch* mood" that affected the vision of the social world held by a generation of conservative German intellectuals during the early decades of the twentieth century.[13] And while one can rescue from Heidegger's analysis of *das Man* a less confused distinction between conformity and conformism than Heidegger was able to articulate, it is important not to lose sight of the understanding of the social world and the engagement with Christianity that the distinction *in its very confusions* reflects. In Heidegger's texts, *das Man* appears in the twin guises of a shared public world and as the "dictatorship" of a banalized form of life in which everything is reduced to the lowest common denominator. It was this latter manifestation—the shallow, irresolute, uprooted qualities that Heidegger perceived as dominating the *Dasein* of his present age—that motivated and framed his account of authenticity.

The question of how authenticity as an ontic ideal might work itself out for members of subordinate or oppressed social groups dislodges this framework. It displaces a focus simply on taking up and taking over the practices of an historical culture with a focus on the axes of domination and subordination that affect the construction of social identities and social groups and the production and circulation of social meanings within that culture. Moreover, it displaces talk of a monolithic cultural totality—the dominion of *das Man*—with talk of multiple and overlapping histories and practices. It provides conceptual space for competing moral maps, competing stories and interpretations. And it provides room for accounts of ways in which processes such as repression, suppression, or cultural hegemony dim or level down possibilities.

Reframed in this way, we can link authenticity to struggles over social meanings and see it as taking shape as part of a political practice.[14] For example, with this reframing, it becomes possible to conceptualize a political movement such as Black Nationalism as a resolve to combat the "demoralizing disorders" created by white racism—the lack of hope and self-worth and feeling that life has no meaning experienced by many black youth. This is accomplished by living one's life as part of the heritage of an "imagined community" of nation. As Patricia Hill Collins explains, "Reconstructing Black history by locating the mythic past and the origins of the nation or the people is intended to build pride and commitment to the nation. These elements allegedly can be use to organize the Black consciousness of people of African descent as a 'chosen people.' Identifying the unique and heroic elements of the national culture, in this case, Black culture, ideally enables members of the group to fight for the nation."[15] This mythic past, constructed from fragments of intersecting histories and their suppressed or marginalized meanings, heroes, and folktales, is intended to function for black people in the same way that the tradition valorized within the dominant white culture functions for white people—as a source of repeatable possibilities that one *wants* to be loyal to. To the extent that the narratives and practices of Black Nationalism take hold, they resituate black American *Dasein* as heir to a tradition capable of fostering pride, loyalty, and resolve rooted in the hope for futures more positive than the possibilities laid out by the dominant culture.

Identity politics such as Black Nationalism provide one kind of example in which authenticity might be said to work itself out for members of oppressed or marginalized groups. The struggle in such practices is to create a communal ground that can bind people together and create a culture of resistance. Such struggles are unintelligible if we assume, following Heidegger and Guignon, that a past viewed as a heritage of repeatable possibilities capable of engendering one's loyalty is equally available for everyone. In conflictual cultures, the cultural hegemony of dominant groups constructs social identities for oppressed groups that perpetuates their unequal status. Moreover, the dominant norms and practices that control "averageness" police alternative meanings through practices of deauthorization, suppression, surveillance, and appropriation. As a result, the competing stories and interpretations passed down within the complex of intersecting histories belonging to a conflictual culture are unequally available: the domination of some of these goes hand in hand with the dimming down or leveling off of others.

This brief analysis of how authenticity might work itself out in practices of identity politics is subject to multiple criticisms from Heidegger purists. For example, I have not situated the Black Nationalist movement on the backdrop of a story about "being-anxious" or fleeing from this anxiety. Nor have I situated the Black Nationalist movement against the backdrop of an account of why fleeing from anxiety into *das Man* is supposed to be "tranquilizing."

I have not done so because none of these stories seems centrally relevant. This is not to say that black American *Dasein* cannot or does not suddenly find itself in the grips of *Angst*. Rather, what seems more centrally relevant is the "unsettledness" or "not-at-homeness" that can spring from social relations of inequality. In "Black Women in Academia: A Statement from the Periphery," Linda Carty describes her own experience of this as follows:

> As a Black woman sitting in a classroom in a white, advanced capitalist country where privilege usually translates into 'white male,' it was hardly accidental that the world was presented to me from that perspective, that is, a perspective in which I was an object of domination. What caused my questioning, however, was that this world was presented as everyone's reality, with no recognition or validity given to the knowledge of others who experience the world differently, or from a different standpoint, regardless (or perhaps because) of the experiential nature of that knowledge.[16]

Carter's "not-at-homeness" in what the dominant culture takes for granted as *everyone's* reality is a function of the fact that from within her own social situatedness, alternative meanings, less embedded in prevailing paradigms, are available to her. Fleeing into this taken-for-granted reality cannot be thought of as "tranquilizing" for Carter. Perhaps she will "drift along" in her unsettledness. Perhaps, as other black feminists have done, she will resolutely take up the culturally marginalized place of her black womanhood as a source of creativity and power. Whatever she does, her resoluteness or irresoluteness will play itself out from within prevasive axes of dominance and subordination and the plurality of social sites that make up her facticity.

Notes

This essay incorporates parts of an earlier work, "Authenticity, Feminism, and Radical Psychotherapy," published in *Feminist Phenomenology*, ed. L. Fisher and L. Embree (Netherlands: Kluwer Academic Publishers, 2000), 237–49. Permission to reprint previously published sections has been granted by Kluwer Academic Publishers.

1. Charles Guignon, "Authenticity, Moral Values, and Psychotherapy," in *The Cambridge Companion to Heidegger*, ed. Charles Guignon (Cambridge: Cambridge University Press, 1993), 215–39. This work will hereafter be cited in the text as AMP, followed by page numbers.

2. See Hubert L. Dreyfus, *Being-in-the-World: A Commentary on Heidegger's Being and Time* (Cambridge: MIT Press, 1991). This work hereafter will be cited in the text as HD. Other members of the Berkeley school include William Blatner, John Haugeland, Harrison Hall, Robert Brandom, and Mark Okrent.

3. Charles B. Guignon, *Heidegger and the Problem of Knowledge* (Indianapolis: Hackett, 1983), 19.

4. Heidegger actually distinguishes between what he calls undifferentiated, authentic, and inauthentic modes of existence.

5. Heidegger does not refer to authenticity as a "higher" form of life. However, he does present it as an "ontical ideal" worth striving for.

6. Charles B. Guignon, introduction to the Heidegger chapter in *Existentialism: Basic Writings*, ed. C. Guignon and D. Pereboom (Indianapolis: Hackett, 1995), 200.

7. This does not mean that authenticity is a moral concept. Guignon's point is that moral reflection plays a crucial role in authentic living because moral understanding is built into the practices circulating in our culture.

8. The links between this language and Heidegger's later allegiance to National Socialism are also troublesome. But this important issue is beyond the scope of this essay.

9. Janet Campbell Hale, *Bloodlines: Odyssey of a Native Daughter* (New York: Random House, 1993). Hereafter cited in the text as ND.

10. Dreyfus points out that marginal practices, in other words, practices that were once central but that have now become rare and therefore are no longer what one normally does, can be retrieved by authentic Dasein, that is, taken up again in the present and projected into the future. See HD, 329. My analysis takes a different look at marginal practices by focusing on practices that are marginalized within structures of dominance and subordination.

11. Gloria Anzaldúa, *Borderlands/La Frontera: The New Mestiza* (San Francisco: Aunt Lute Books, 1987). References hereafter cited in the text as B/F.

12. The fact that I am a woman of Mexican, Polish, and Scottish heritage makes this example somewhat problematic. Certainly I can choose to live my life in accordance with the ideals of social justice laid out by Malcolm X. But I can never share his history as a man within the African-American community, which means that the concrete circumstances and consequences of this choice would be quite different for me from what they would be for someone who shares this history.

13. Pierre Bourdieu, *The Political Ontology of Martin Heidegger*, trans. Peter Collier (Stanford: Stanford University Press, 1991), 1–39.

14. This does not mean that for members of oppressed groups, authenticity always works itself out as part of a political practice.

15. Patricia Hill Collins, *Fighting Words: Black Women and the Search for Justice* (Minneapolis:

University of Minnesota Press, 1998), 160. Note that Collins is not uncritical of this movement; in particular, she objects to the gender ideology of Black nationalism.

16. Linda Carty, "Black Women in Academia: A Statement from the Periphery" in Bannerji et al., eds., *Unsettling Relations: The University as a Site of Feminist Struggle* (Boston: South End Press, 1991), 18.

4

"The Universe Is Made of Stories, Not of Atoms"

Heidegger and the Feminine They-Self

Nancy J. Holland

I

A man of about thirty seems a youthful, and, in a sense, an incompletely developed individual, of whom we expect that he will be able to make good use of the possibilities of development, which analysis lays open to him. But a woman of about the same age frequently staggers us by her psychological rigidity and unchangeability. . . . There are no paths open to her for further development; it is as if the whole process had been gone through, and remained inaccessible to influence for the future; as though, in fact, the difficult development which leads to femininity had exhausted all the possibilities of the individual.

—Sigmund Freud

Eric Berne was an American psychiatrist and "failed" psychoanalyst whose theoretical modification of classical Freudian theory met a rather bizarre fate. In a development of his earlier work on intuition, he intended what he called "transactional analysis" to help level the power differential in the psychotherapeutic relationship, so that the analyst would be forced to listen more carefully to what was said by the specific individual involved in the therapeutic transaction, rather than simply categorizing what was said, and too often the person who said it, in terms of fixed, identifiable symptoms and complexes. One way in which Berne sought to accomplish this was to democratize the vocabulary of psychoanalysis, substituting plain American English for the pseudomedical, Latinate terms such as ego, superego, and id that the American psychoanalytic establishment uses in place of Freud's own relatively straightforward German terms for what Berne called "ego states." Thus were born the terms that unfortunately evolved into a mass-market, pop culture phenomenon of the late 1960s and early 1970s—parent, child, adult, and "the games people play."[1]

As with Freud, however, the philosophically interesting aspect of Berne's work lies less in the ego states or games than in the larger-scale psychic structures offered to explain much of human behavior, which also raise serious questions about individual autonomy. Berne's word for these structures was "scripts." In transactional analysis, games are patterns of often self-defeating behavior that require other players to fill the reciprocal roles (for example, the popular game "Alcoholic" requires a persecutor and a rescuer); scripts are life-defining configurations of roles and behaviors, including characteristic games. Thus the Oedipus complex can be seen as a script that mandates conflict between its male protagonist and his father or other male authority figures in conjunction with an overattachment to his mother or other supportive female figures, with implications of unsatisfactory adult sexual relationships. The script analysis makes clearer, for instance, the role that the mother can play in maintaining the father-son conflict (crudely, by playing "Let's You and Him Fight"; a bit more subtly in the forms found, for example, in the work of D. H. Lawrence). It also clarifies the way in which this script can easily articulate with the father's own Oedipus script, with its concomitant self-loathing, inability to meet the wife/mother's sexual and emotional needs, and anxiety about close relationships with men. Thus what Berne and his follower were undertaking can be seen as fully compatible with orthodox psychoanalysis, while at the same time freeing up our intuitions through the use of a more commonsensical vocabulary.

The intuitions that flowed from this new paradigm generated whole new realms of scripts that went far beyond Oedipus. The game "Alcoholic" was best understood in the context of the corresponding life script, with its "spouse" games such as "Mother Hubbard" (the perpetual rescuer). In the same way, the script "Big Daddy" mates well, as it were, with the script "Cinderella" and correspondingly poorly with "Mother Hubbard." Thus perhaps the most common application of transactional analysis was in marital therapy and in the cognitive aspects of the treatment of addictions. Within transactional analysis, scripts are seen as inherently negative, even "banal" scripts that have no long-term tragic outcome, because "[s]cripting robs people of their autonomy."[2] They are patterns we learn as children that make us feel helpless to change our own behavior, but that can be eventually overcome by engaging our "adult" ego state (or superego) through the analytic process or in group therapy (which is where this process articulates with more recent forms of cognitive therapy): "Not everyone has a script, since not everyone is following a forced, premature, early-childhood decision."[3] As with the Freudian complexes that they closely resemble, scripts are things of which the client/patient is to be "cured."

Some philosophers, however, see the structures of traditional Freudian thought, such as the Oedipus complex, not as diseases of which the "normal" person is free and the "sick" person is to be cured, but rather as part of the existential condition of being human that must be incorporated into an "authentic" life, as what Simone de Beauvoir calls "the intermediate terrain between biology and psychology."[4] I would like to argue here that it is possible to adapt the neo-Freudian constructs of transactional analysis to the purposes of a feminist rereading of Martin Heidegger's existential analytic of Dasein. This can be done, as has been done with the Freud, by recognizing that, while the source of an individual's script can be traced to parental behavior in a nuclear family, the scripts available within a given social context will be to a large extent determined by the society as a whole, and thus are the creation, not of individual psyches or individual families, but of the they-self in which they are embedded. For instance, anthropologist Bronislaw Malinowski suggested that the sexualized Oedipus script as we know it may not be available in matrilineal societies such as those found in the Trobriand Islands, where young men are quite close to their fathers, but have a more antagonistic relationship with their maternal uncle, who controls their marital future.[5] By contrast, the script "Beauty and the Beast" (the model for much romantic literature) may be available only in strongly patrilocal societies, in which a new bride must marry and live among strangers to repay her father's marital debt.

In this way, scripts can be seen to come to us, not directly from individual family pathologies, but through them from the they-self of the social world in which we live. This is why Berne and his followers were immediately able to identify so many scripts that resonated with the life experience of vast numbers of people—they were the predominant scripts of American culture at midcentury. (Their historical relativity is perhaps best underscored by the disappearance of the game, and even the term, "Frigid Woman," if not necessarily of the phenomenon itself.) Our "helplessness" in the face of these preprogrammed roles and behaviors would then be a manifestation of the necessity of bad faith, that is, of our continued immersion in the they-self and failure to maintain complete authenticity. Seen in this way, the nature of scripts, and specifically the socially available scripts for women in any given tradition, may help us to understand the extent to which Heidegger's analysis of das Man and the they-self in Division One of *Being and Time* can provide useful tools for feminist analysis.[6] At the same time, Simone de Beauvoir's *The Second Sex*, which offers a classic listing of the scripts available to women in twentieth-century European culture (wife, mother, prostitute, lesbian, narcissist, mystic, "independent woman"), can also provide the feminist basis for an account of inauthenticity or "bad faith" that explains its differential moral weight in men and women, but without exonerating women completely from complicity in the perpetuation of the self-defeating scripts that they are compelled to live out.

II

[W]e frame the accounts of our cultural origins and our most cherished beliefs in story form, and it is not just the "content" of these stories that grip us, but their narrative artifice. Our immediate experience, what happened yesterday or the day before, is framed in the same storied way. Even more striking, we represent our lives (to ourselves as well as to others) in the form of narrative. It is not surprising that psychoanalysts now recognize that personhood implicates narrative, "neurosis" being a reflection of either an insufficient, incomplete, or inappropriate story about oneself.

—Jerome Bruner

Heidegger explains in the introduction to *Being and Time* that Dasein is to be investigated first "in its average *everydayness*" (BT, 16, his emphasis) because, as he explains later, "[a]t the outset of our analysis it is particularly important that Dasein should not be Interpreted with the differentiated character of some definite way of existing, but that it should be uncovered in the undifferentiated character which it has proximally and for the most part" (BT, 43). The outstanding phenomenal feature of this undifferentiated everydayness of Dasein is that it exists, not in individual consciousness, but in the impersonal they-self of das Man. This everyday immersion in the they-self is not intrinsically inauthentic. Rather, inauthenticity is derivatively linked to the they-self as a failure of the process of differentiation that would result in an authentic Self, "the Self which has been taken hold of in its own way." But such an authentic Self is always only partial and temporary, because it is primarily as a manifestation of the they-self that Dasein exists for others in the social world: "Proximally Dasein is 'they', and for the most part it remains so" (BT, 129). Inauthenticity or "bad faith" is, as Sartre suggests, to a certain extent inevitable.[7]

The they-self is the realm in which Dasein lives, and must live, "proximally and for the most part." As with the fairy tales and myths of script analysis, the character of any given they-self is relative to a specific social context. "We take pleasure and enjoy ourselves as *they* take pleasure; we read, see, and judge about literature and art as *they* see and judge; likewise we shrink back from the 'great mass' as *they* shrink back; we find 'shocking' what *they* find shocking" (BT, 126–27, his emphasis) But this goes far beyond mere social conformity or "leveling down." The publicness of das Man "controls every way in which the world and Dasein get interpreted and it is always right" (BT, 127). For this reason, "bad faith" can be seen as inevitable because only through the roles and meanings given by the they-self can individual Dasein encounter a world that is always already meaningful. Because the they-self has Dasein's existential character, it is not merely a sociological or anthropological aggregate or norm, but rather a genuine possibility of being a Self. "One may neither decree prematurely that this 'they' is 'really' nothing, nor profess the opinion that one can Interpret this phenomenon ontologically by somehow 'explaining' it as what results from taking the Being-present-at-hand-together of several subjects and then fitting them together" (BT, 128). Rather, das Man meets Dasein's need for meaning by prescribing "that way of interpreting the world and Being-in-the-world which lies closest" (BT, 129).

The they-self is necessary because it provides the terms in which we can engage with other Dasein in mutually meaningful social interactions. The Others we encounter in living out our scripts take on the appropriate reciprocal social roles, as understood in the overarching social narrative, and place us in the roles their scripts demand that we play. "Dasein's everyday possibilities of Being are for the Others to dispose of as they please. These Others, moreover, are not *definite* Others. On the contrary, any Other can represent them" (BT, 126, his emphasis). This is the full meaning of the existentiality of Dasein, a meaning that paradoxically undermines the radical freedom of which the existentialist made so much. People are what they do (BT, 126), that is, their identity lies in the roles that they enact in the social narratives in which they play their allotted roles. There might be some freedom within those roles to create new meanings, and there may be some freedom to step outside those roles under certain circumstances, but to live entirely outside the they-self, to make up one's own meanings in every case, would be one definition of madness. Not only must we live out a socially defined identity, but this identity is determined only within a specific social context. My identity as a "friendly colleague" entails behavior in the United States that my African-born colleague would interpret in his home county as quite rude. He has lived in this country long enough to be tolerant of me and correctly interpret my intentions, but our situation underscores the highly local definition of the social role I am adopting.

This existentiality means that Dasein is "*thrown possibility* through and through" (BT, 144, his emphasis). This thrown possibility does not belong in the first place to the individual Dasein who will enact it, but rather to the they-self of the social environment in which it will enact it. Moreover, the thrownness of Dasein means that this "projecting" is not an explicit plan, but rather "any Dasein has, as Dasein, already projected itself; and as long as it is, it is projecting" (BT, 145). This can be understood on a biological level, as in the necessary daily projects of getting enough food, enough rest, and so on, the lack of which can interfere with higher-order projects. It can also be understood on a socially defined level, both in terms of prosaic short-term projects (do we start the day with coffee or tea, eat cereal or rice and beans for breakfast?) and longer-term ones (as my students sometimes learn with dismay, there is virtually no way to become a professor of philosophy in the United States without a Ph.D.). Short-term projects that directly involve others are often eased by the availability of games or their lower-level equivalents, "pastimes": when forced into conversation with a casual acquaintance, we tend to fall back on something like "General Motors" (car talk, usually indulged in by men) or "PTA" (parenting talk, traditionally a female pastime).[8] Long-term projects, on the other hand, are shaped by life scripts: "Jock" is an American script that is now becoming available to women as well as to men.[9]

On the basis of these possibilities of the they-self, "Dasein can, proximally and for the most part, understand itself in terms of its world," but the existentiality of Dasein also opens another level of possibility, so that "[u]nderstanding is either authentic, arising out of own's own Self as such, or inauthentic." But because authenticity always remains an open possibility of Dasein, "authentic understanding, no less than that which is inauthentic, *can* be either genuine or not genuine" (BT, 146, his emphasis), that is, can be realized or remain an unfulfilled possibility. This existential openness even of authentic Dasein arises from its continued immersion in the public world of the they-self. "When, in our everyday Being-with-one-another, we encounter the sort of thing which is accessible to everyone, and about which anyone an say anything, it soon becomes impossible to decide what is disclosed in a genuine understanding and what is not" (BT, 217). When I discuss my children with others, it can be hard to tell whether I am authentically engaging in a meaningful sharing of common experience or simply playing "PTA." Conversely, if I refuse to join in the discussion to avoid inauthentic pastimes, I may find myself cast in the role of someone who does not have, or perhaps does not even like, children, due to the social meaning given to the interaction. Even authentic understanding remains a "thrown" possibility, that is, one over which the autonomous control of individual Dasein is necessarily limited because of Dasein's continual embeddedness in a particular social context.

The possibility of authentic Dasein is "thrown" in another sense, too. Authenticity is, to a certain extent at least, dependent on the particular possible configurations of the they-self available within a specific social world. I have already noted that insufficient nutrition or sleep can impede higher-order projects, including that of authenticity itself. Nor is this necessarily a gender-neutral consideration in a world where chronic undernourishment is far more prevalent among women than among men, or even in one where it is still overwhelmingly women whose sleep is interrupted by the nocturnal needs of infants and children.[10] At the level of socially determined scripts, gender disparities in how authenticity is facilitated can be far more overt. One could argue, for instance, that in the contemporary United States, anorexia and bulimia are primarily feminine scripts for not dealing with the existential anxieties of adolescence that young men are more often scripted to evade by sports, less socially acceptable forms of violence, or a premature fixation on making money. All are ways in which the they-self covers over the possibility of authenticity, but note that the script for young women not only requires an obsessive concern with their own bodies and biological processes, always the realm of the feminine, but also in fact hinders those processes in such a way as to impair not only their intellectual, but also their physical, capacity to attain authenticity. (The same is true, of course, of violence scripts for young men, but they carry their own overtones of racial and class oppression.)

We can see the tendency of das Man to cover over the avenues to authentic Dasein through what Heidegger calls "idle talk," "the kind of Being of everyday Dasein's understanding and interpreting" (BT, 167). This is the medium through which scripts are infused from the social environment into specific configurations of family life, from the media fascination with abnormally slender female bodies, for instance, into a family where emotional and physical control is valued above all else. "Proximally, and with certain limits, Dasein is constantly delivered over to this interpretedness, which controls and distributes the possibilities of average understanding" (BT, 167–68). Script analysis can include a short list of "Injunctions and Attributions" that echo the folk wisdom of our culture, such as the pair "Don't think" and "Be competitive" for "Jock."[11] For Heidegger, one of the main effects of idle talk is to keep even authentic Dasein from communicating its genuine understanding of Being. "The average understanding of the reader will *never be able* to decide what has been drawn from primordial sources with a struggle and how much is just gossip. The average understanding, moreover, will not want any such distinction, and does not need it, because, of course, it understands everything" (BT, 169, his emphasis). He even notes the importance of idle talk for individual psychology: "The 'they' prescribes one's state-of-mind, and determines what and how one 'sees'" (BT, 170). Some amount of absorption into the they-self, some amount of scripting, at least on this social level, remains inevitable.

Thus, we come to the quotation from Freud with which we began. A woman of thirty in the Viennese middle class of his day would seem rigid not necessarily, or not only, because of the effort of becoming "feminine," but also because quite literally "[t]here are no paths open to her for further development."¹² As Jane Austen knew already, the traditional upper- or middle-class script for women ends with marriage and motherhood. Once that happily-ever-after is accomplished, there is nothing more for a woman to do with her life. If scripts are essentially repeated patterns of behavior, the feminine they-self can express itself only through a script, even if not necessarily a tragic one, because once a woman is married, repetition is her only option: she can keep (in other words, constantly rewin) her husband's love, and she can raise new babies at regular intervals until menopause brings complete stasis. A man can retain at least the illusion of meaningful projects throughout most of his life in his work, but once married, the feminine they-self no longer has any new possibilities to be realized. And authentic Dasein will carry the same gender-specific burden because, as Heidegger reminds us, "[i]n the moment of vision, indeed, and often just 'for that moment,' existence can even gain the mastery over the 'everyday'; but it can never extinguish it" (BT, 371). Here lies, I would argue, the potential for a radical understanding of how, and how far, women can be understood to be complicit with the patriarchal scripts of their own oppression.

III

> Woman, we are told, envies man his penis and wishes to castrate him; but the childish desire for the penis is important in the life of the adult woman only if she feels her femininity is a mutilation; and then it is as a symbol of all the privileges of manhood that she wishes to appropriate the male organ. We may readily agree that her dream of castration has this symbolic significance: she wishes, it is thought, to deprive the male of his transcendence. But her goal, as we have seen, is much more ambiguous: she wishes, in a contradictory fashion, *to have* this transcendence.
>
> —Simone de Beauvoir

Like Freud, de Beauvoir renders an analysis of the situation of women in general that is, in fact, strongly tied to the European upper middle class of her time and place. Within this context, she finds a feminine they-self full of protopostmodernists, concerned with the complex interrelationships between truth, power, sexuality, and value in the discourse of the dominant group: "Woman does not entertain the positive belief that the truth is something *other* than men claim; she recognizes, rather, that there *is not* any fixed truth. . . . It is at the heart of the masculine world itself, it is in herself as belonging to this world that she comes upon the ambiguity of all principle, all value, of everything that exists. She knows that masculine morality as it concerns her, is a vast hoax."[13] Existential phenomenology provided de Beauvoir with the tools to understand, and to chart, the way in which her social environment created both a specifically feminine they-self and the illusion that this feminine self was actually the natural result of women's biology. As she says of the scripts for women catalogued in The Second Sex, "[T]he varieties of behavior reported are not dictated to women by her hormones nor predetermined in the structure of the female brain: they are shaped as in a mold by her situation" (SS, 562). This is now a familiar claim, if still a hotly debated one, but we must remember how radical it still was when de Beauvoir first pronounced it.

De Beauvoir in fact recognizes a certain ambiguity, or a certain opportunity, in the relationship between the feminine they-self and the masculine world in which it must survive. On the one hand, as noted above, women's scripts provide them with less opportunity for transcendence and existential growth; on the other hand, precisely the fact that women's scripts are banal and ultimately unrewarding can sometimes create a revealing distance between an individual woman's consciousness and the larger social world in which she is immersed: "she is not fully satisfied with ready-made forms and clichés; with the best will in the world, she has a sense of misgiving about them which is nearer to authenticity than is the self-important assurance of her husband." De Beauvoir goes on, however, to relativize even this possibility to class status by adding that "she will have these advantages over the male only on condition that she rejects the deceptions he offers" (SS, 590). For women from affluent and powerful groups, the rewards of complicity are high; conversely, for women from oppressed and impoverished groups, the costs of existential insight, or of acting on such insight, can be very high as well. The feminine they-self often carries with it special temptations to ignore the call of authenticity because of a woman's double dependency on acceptance and support both from the social environment as a whole and from the specific man to whom her life is traditionally supposed to be devoted.

It is in this context that de Beauvoir points out the necessary limitations of the concept of "woman" she has been invoking all along. "It is as absurd, then, to speak of 'woman' in general as of the 'eternal' man" (SS, 591). As she has noted earlier, the situation of women is in some ways not so different from that of other oppressed groups in society, despite the fact that most of the women to whom she refers have relative wealth and leisure. Even men of the middle class may in fact live lives no more transcendent, have scripts no more ultimately rewarding, than their wives' (SS, 588–89). But the one reward the scripts and social roles of men, no matter how banal, have always carried is the assurance of superiority and control over women. Thus, her focus is not on women or "woman," but on the differential between the situation of women in a given social context and that of men. And there her judgment is that men's life scripts give them a greater access to existential as well as material and intellectual freedom: "Under various forms, the snares of bad faith and the deceptions of overseriousness—temptations not to be genuine—await the one sex as much as the other; inner liberty is complete in both. But simply from the fact that liberty in woman is still abstract and empty, she can exercise it only in revolt, which is the only road open to those who have no opportunity of doing anything constructive" (SS, 591).

The impasse that de Beauvoir identified as blocking the way of women's gaining the same freedom that most men take for granted in the European social world corresponds to what a contemporary feminist might call the dilemma of becoming equal without becoming "male." The modern feminine they-self at midcentury, in de Beauvoir's view, wanted to take on male roles as equals, while also wanting to keep the privileges of traditional femininity. The masculine they-self, however, is reluctant to surrender its prerogatives while at the same time accusing women of wanting it both ways. "Want of authenticity does not pay: each blames the other for the unhappiness he or she has incurred in yielding to the temptations of the easy way; what man and woman loathe in each other is the shattering frustration of each one's own bad faith." Still, responsibility for the current situation, and the greater oppression that preceded it, is not evenly divided between the two sexes. Rather, the limited physical differences between men and women have been magnified, codified, universalized, ritualized, and eroticized by the masculine they-self for the material (economic, sexual) and existential benefit of men: "oppression is to be explained by the tendency of the existent to flee from himself by means of identification with the other, whom he oppresses to that end" (SS, 677). The feminine they-self, and the bodies and lives of individual women, thus become both a refuge from authenticity and a threat to self-identity that the masculine they-self perpetuates with all the force of his own existential anxiety.

Yet "[i]t must be admitted that the males find in woman more complicity than the oppressor usually finds in the oppressed." The feminine they-self has no recourse from its banal scripts in an alternative social environment that would offer other stories about one's life path, as might be the case for some oppressed groups. Moreover, the scripts of the feminine they-self offer precisely the most existentially reassuring path—denial of responsibility for one's own life. "[T]hroughout her life from childhood on, they damage and corrupt her by designating as her true vocation this submission, which is the temptation of every existent in the anxiety of liberty" (SS, 67–79). There is another level of temptation here, the more so the more a woman is aware of her situation: "she has good conscience because she in on the unprivileged side; she feels she is under no obligation to deal gently with the favored caste, and her only thought is to defend herself." But that neither exonerates the feminine they-self nor condemns it, because "justice can never be done in the midst of injustice" (SS, 681). Rather, authentic existence, even if necessarily partial and limited, always remains a possibility for all Dasein, and the responsibility for making that possibility a genuine one, for becoming a "Self which has been taken hold of in its own way" (BT, 129), always remains with the individual, male or female.

IV

As a matter of fact, man, like woman, is flesh, therefore passive, the plaything of his hormones and of the species, the restless prey of his desires. And she, like him, in the midst of the carnal fever, is a consenting, a voluntary gift, an activity; they live out in their several fashions the strange ambiguity of existence made body. In those combats where they think they confront one another, it is really against the self that each one struggles.

—Simone de Beauvoir.

Freud tells us that women have underdeveloped superegos or "exteropsyches," what Berne calls the parent ego state.[14] This is unlikely on the face of it, since women carry primary responsibility for the socialization of children, and hence for the creation of the superego, even if its force is often attributed to fear of the Father. What transactional analysis suggests is that women do often have an underdeveloped ego or adult, the ego state that mediates between the internal demands of their body/id/child, the social demands represented by the superego/parent, and the material demands of the physical world around them. De Beauvoir offers two kinds of explanation for this fact. She gives an account of how such a feminine they-self comes to be created, both historically and psychologically, but she also tells us how its creation benefits those who are liberated by women who can only be daughters and mothers to be only fathers and sons, that is, to retreat from the conflicted adult world of traditionally male responsibility and anxiety. But it is important to note that the vital bridge between Freud and de Beauvoir here lies in Heidegger, in the understanding of the social world of the they-self that gives us our scripts.

The significance of this bridge for contemporary feminist thought can be found in the problem of feminist transformation, or rather the problem of its apparently inherently partial nature and limitations. Ann Ferguson calls this dilemma, generalized to cover racial and other identities beyond gender, the "Determinism/Responsibility problem" and says that to avoid it, "no explanation of how systems of domination are supported by dominators and submitted to by subordinants can be deterministic in a way that implies that we cannot hold those who benefit from the system morally responsible nor understand how those who are victims of oppression can nonetheless resist oppression."[15] She takes explicit exception to psychoanalytic theories of gender formation as too deterministic/fatalistic, whereas she sees traditional liberal accounts of fully rational social choice-making as "thin" and unable, ultimately, to avoid blaming the victim for her "choosing" her oppression (a tendency found, paradoxically, in Freud as well).[16] The alternatives Ferguson finds in postmodern theorists such as Michel Foucault, Judith Butler, and Julia Kristeva and in earlier feminists such as Hannah Arendt and de Beauvoir can, however, all be traced back to Heidegger and ultimately to the delicate balance between the always open possibility of authenticity and Dasein's necessary immersion in the they-self.

Existential anxiety, as we have seen, provides a philosophical, rather than a material or psychological, motivation for both the efforts of the male-dominated das Man to create feminine scripts that suit male purposes, and the willingness of women to live out those scripts. This means that it may no longer be possible or necessary to have recourse only to family or biological explanations for, say, "female masochism." Women's gendered relationship to pain can be understood, rather, as mediated by the scripts of a they-self in which pain is expected and by which it is accepted as a normal, even an integral, part of female life. Pain can then safely be incorporated into men's lives as the sign of some specific disorder, so that this arrangement of complementary scripts, in which masochism can be seen to be, as Freud says, "truly feminine,"[17] allows men to avoid the fear of chronic or recurrent pain and maintain the illusion that male pain can be "cured." Similarly, the "normal" female bisexuality that so bothered Freud can be understood in part as resulting from the complex interactions between scripts of the feminine they-self that enforce heterosexuality, but at the same time normalize strong emotional bonds between women and also create vastly different male and female understandings of sexuality and love. Add to this the fact that any scripts that would allow women to act in the masculine world outside the home require them to do so only in roles usually reserved, and defined, for men, and the "bisexuality" of women is not mysterious but, if anything, overdetermined.

The commonsensical vocabulary of child, parent, adult, games, and scripts provided by transactional analysis allows us to see more clearly the relationship between individual psychology and the they-self, and so also to locate the nexus of responsibility and the possibility of feminist consciousness. At the same time, the reading presented here helps us to see the nexus between the concerns of psychology and those that are of primary philosophical interests, between the existentiell and the existential aspects of these phenomena, as the Heidegger of *Being and Time* might have said. This is why it is not the scripts themselves that are of interest for feminism philosophy, but the power differentials between them, the ways in which they structure privilege and oppression, the ways in which they may facilitate or impede the development of freedom and authenticity. All Dasein has the resources for authenticity and responsibility, to use Ferguson's term, as well as the motivation, and to some extent the need, for inauthenticity and the excuses of determinism. We cannot live as pure authenticity, as pure responsibility, not only because existentially we are necessarily immersed in a social world, but also because full responsibility is, I would venture to suggest, more than the human soul can bear.

V

Because one must avoid good conscience at all costs.

—Jacques Derrida

Heidegger has been criticized for insisting on the gender neutrality of Dasein and on the secondary nature of sexual difference.[18] If we see Dasein, however, as necessarily always already immersed in a they-self, a social world of meanings, roles, games, and scripts into which it has been thrown and from which it must draw its projects insofar as they are to be recognized and valued by those around it, then the fact that the scripts and roles of any possible social context will be heavily gender differentiated will mean that gender (and in certain circumstances, race or class) cannot be phenomenologically "secondary." We are "essentially" male or female because every possibility of the they-self is gendered in those ways, and it is the "essence" of Dasein to "be" its existence, that is, to be the roles and scripts it must live out in the social world in which it exists. In this way, gender might be seen to have the same status as language. Language is in some sense "essential" to Dasein; any given language is secondary, but not language itself. Heidegger tells us, first, that "[t]he *existential-ontological foundation of language is discourse or talk*" and then that "[a]s an existential state in which Dasein is disclosed, discourse is constitutive for Dasein's existence" (BT, 160–62, his emphasis). Similarly, all Dasein is gendered in a world in which the they-self is always already male or female. Even if Heidegger insists that Dasein is "a-sexual" (GA 26, 171), human existentiality dictates that gender is one of the most important facts about any possible life that any Dasein might in fact live.

We do not live our bodies or any other aspect of our lives as they would be "in themselves" but only as they are understood and interpreted within a specific social context, incorporated into a specific they-self for which body size, shape, or color may take on more or less social salience. Given the underlying biological salience of the sexual instinct, the social salience of sex-linked features of the body is not surprising. Given the kind of existential analysis hinted at above and developed in more depth by de Beauvoir, the elaboration of massive structures of inequality on this slim foundation should not surprise us. Among others, Joanna Russ's chilling futuristic novel *The Female Man* suggests that, in the absence of women, the same differentials would be created between men based on other physical or psychological differences.[19] Seen in this way, the reading we are pursuing here would offer a way to understand sexual difference in Heidegger that, while stepping outside limits of Heidegger's own thought, might reconfigure his ideas in ways that could be quite productive for feminist thinkers.

In the same text from which the preceding epigraph is drawn, Derrida points us to a second analogy for gender difference in Heidegger, based on a sentence from *On the Way to Language* that Derrida is investigating for reasons quite different from those here: "The essential relation between death and language flashes up before us, but remains still unthought"(US, 215/OWL, 107).[20] Death, like language, would be a "primary" fact about Dasein, but like the "secondariness" of which specific language Dasein speaks, and the "secondariness" of its particular gender, how one dies is highly dependent on both the scripts available for death in a specific social context and the limitations presented by a specific human body. Claude Steiner makes much of the timing of Eric Berne's death, reminding his readers that despite Berne's careful attention to his health, he died of heart disease at exactly the ago scripted by Berne's own father's death. In a sense, Steiner suggests, Berne could not help but die when and as he did, although Steiner hints that more thorough erasure of the relevant script might have given his "teacher, friend, father, brother" a few more years.[21] We might also, therefore, be able to say that the gender-specific scripts that Berne also lived were to a certain extent inevitable, given his social environment and his personal history, but also to a certain extent something he could have overcome, not entirely but more completely, in order to achieve the existential equivalent of longer life, greater authenticity.

We are not responsible for the language that we were born into, for the fact that we die, or for whether we are male or female in a society in which gender still yields huge disparities of power and freedom. But we are responsible for how we use language, what we create with it, how we harm or nurture others with our words. We are also responsible for how we die, in limited ways for the material cause of death (that we do or do not drive too fast, drink too much, or smoke in bed, to take just the most obvious cases), and in an unlimited way for the serenity and fortitude with which we deal with all the inevitabilities of life. Similarly, given the heavily gendered scripts available to us—which, like a disease that can cause either a slow, painful death or a quick, merciful one, can make authenticity almost easy for some us and almost impossibly hard for others—we are responsible for our own authenticity and through that for authentic Care for Others, for the effort to make the scripts that limit us less painful, less oppressive, less destructive of human life in all forms. But always remembering what Heidegger points out specifically in the context of Care: "When the 'I' talks in the 'natural' manner, this is performed by the they-self. What expresses itself in the 'I' is that Self which, proximally and for the most part, I am *not* authentically" (BT, 322, his emphasis). That is, remembering that authenticity, like the feminist consciousness that is its prerequisite for women today, is always a partial and limited achievement.

Notes

The title of this essay is from Muriel Rukeyser, "The Speed of Darkness," in *A Muriel Rukeyser Reader*, ed. Jan Heller Levi (New York: Norton, 1995), 231. Originally published in *The Speed of Darkness* (New York: Random House, 1968).

1. On this process see Claude M. Steiner, *Scripts People Live: Transactional Analysis of Life Scripts* (New York: Grove Press, 1974), 1–19. The scholarly version of Berne's project is *Transactional Analysis in Psychotherapy* (New York: Grove Press, 1961); the popular version is Eric Berne, *Games People Play* (New York: Grove Press, 1964). Disclaimer: I completed preliminary training as a lay practitioner of transactional analysis in 1971, while working in the social welfare system, and the Glen A. Holland referred to in Steiner's book was my father.

2. Steiner, *Scripts People Live By*, 146.

3. Steiner, *Scripts People Live By*, 103.

4. Simone de Beauvoir *Le deuxième sexe* (Paris: Gallimard, 1949/76), translated as *The Second Sex* by H. M. Parshley (New York: Bantam, 1953), 674 in the English edition. For other examples, see Jean-Paul Sartre, *Being and Nothingness*, trans. Hazel Barnes (New York: Washington Square Press, 1966), 590–93; and Richard Rorty, *Contingency, Irony, and Solidarity* (New York: Cambridge University Press, 1989), 30–39.

5. Bronislaw Malinowski, *The Sexual Life of Savages in Northwestern Melanesia* (London: N.p., 1929), cited in Claude Lévi-Strauss, *Structural Anthropology*, trans. Claire Jacobson and Brooke Grundfest Schoepf (New York: Basic Books, 1963), 41–42.

6. I will use the German term "das Man" without translation or italics throughout, as is commonly done with Dasein, due to the irresolvable complexity of any attempt to create a consistent and meaningful English equivalent to this singular, impersonal, and neuter construction. "They-self" is similarly awkward, but that is the case in German as well (*das Man-selbst*), so there would be no particular advantage to keeping the original language in that case (see Robinson and Macquarrie's footnote on page 167 of their translation of *Being and Time*).

7. Sartre, *Being and Nothingness*, 116.

8. Berne, *Games People Play*, 41–47.

9. Steiner, *Scripts People Live*, 201–2.

10. On the first point, see Amartya Sen, *Inequality Reexamined* (Cambridge: Harvard University Press, 1992), 122–25.

11. Steiner, *Scripts People Live By*, 202.

12. Sigmund Freud, *New Introductory Lectures on Psycho-Analysis*, trans. W. J. H. Sprott (New York: Norton, 1933), 184. (A nonstandard edition—the quotation is from the penultimate paragraph of Lecture XXXIII, "The Psychology of Women").

13. De Beauvoir, *The Second Sex*, 577, her emphasis. Hereafter cited in the text as SS.

14. Freud, *New Introductory Lectures*, 183–84 (penultimate paragraph of Lecture XXXIII); Berne, *Transactional Analysis in Psychotherapy*, 240–44.

15. Ann Ferguson, "Can I Choose Who I Am? And How Would That Empower Me? Gender, Race, Identities, and the Self," in *Women, Knowledge, and Reality: Explorations in Feminist Philosophy*, ed. Ann Garry and Marilyn Pearsall (New York: Routledge, 1996), 108.

16. Ferguson, "Can I Choose Who I Am?" 109–11.
17. Freud, *New Introductory Lectures*, 158 (fifth paragraph of Lecture XXXIII).
18. For one example of such criticism, see Jacques Derrida and Christie V. McDonald, "Choreographies: Interview," in *Feminist Interpretations of Jacques Derrida*, ed. Nancy J. Holland (University Park: Penn State Press, 1997), 35–37. The issue is also discussed by Elizabeth Grosz in her contribution to the same volume, "Ontology and Equivocation: Derrida's Ontology of Sexual Difference," 86–89, and in my introduction, 10–13.
19. Joanna Russ, *The Female Man* (Boston: Beacon Press, 1975), 165–84. A similar point was made in a lecture at the University of Minnesota several years ago by Andrea Dworkin.
20. Cited in Jacques Derrida, *Aporias*, trans. Thomas Dutoit (Stanford: Stanford University Press, 1993), 35.
21. Steiner, *Scripts People Live By*, 14–20. (The description of his relationship with Berne is from the dedication, v.)

Part Two

Poetics and the Body

5

The Absence of Monica

Heidegger, Derrida, and Augustine's *Confessions*

John D. Caputo

Heidegger's *Phenomenology of the Religious Life*, the text of the 1920–21 Freiburg lecture courses, is one of the most interesting documents published in the ongoing work of the *Gesamtausgabe*.[1] The text provides a remarkable insight into what, since Kisiel,[2] we all call the "genesis" of *Being and Time*, including one of the first discussions of the structure of "care." Indeed we learn from these lectures that this very term entered Heidegger's vocabulary as a translation of Augustine's *cura*, which Heidegger first rendered in 1921 as *Bekümmerung*. When later on, in *Being and Time*, *Bekümmerung* was replaced by *Sorge*, he added a note telling us that the analysis of care grew out of his study of Augustine in connection with Aristotle (BT, 492 n. vii). It is a very exciting Augustine indeed that we find in the summer 1921 lecture course "Augustine and Neoplatonism." (Perhaps too exciting.) For Heidegger, the *Confessions* recount the story of Augustine's mighty struggle with himself, of his trial and temptation (*tentatio*). The *Confessions* provide Heidegger with the first, and perhaps the principal, paradigm for what he called then "factical life," and later on in *Being and Time* the "Being of Dasein," which translates the deeply religious and biblical, very confessional and autobiographical figure of Augustine into the formal and quite Greek categories of a "fundamental ontology."

For Heidegger, in these years shortly after he returned from World War I, the *Confessions* are themselves a kind of war journal, a report from the front on the battle the soul wages with itself, which became for him the model of the being whose Being lies in taking up its Being. (It is interesting to note, too, that in the 1922 lectures on Aristotle's ethics he singles out the war experience of Socrates—he stood his post when all else fled—for our admiration.) (GA 61, 49–50) Following this Augustinian model, Dasein is called to take up the good fight and resist the pull (*Zug*) of fallenness, to gather itself together in the unity of resolute self-possession, lest its Being be dissipated amidst the curiosities of everyday pastimes. The range of this dissipation (*Zerstreuung*) of the self—the curiosity of the eyes, the concupiscence of the flesh, the pride of life—which is first catalogued by Augustine in Book X of the *Confessions*, following a New Testament text (1 John 2:16), is repeated in the existential analytic with an explicit citation of Augustine (BT, §35–38).

In the present context of a discussion of Heidegger and feminism, one of the most striking things about Heidegger's brilliant and provocative repetition of the *Confessions* is the complete absence of Monica from its pages. Monica does not make it into fundamental ontology. More precisely, the ontical and existentiell figure of Monica, or of Augustine's relation to Monica, is not transmuted or formalized into an existential-ontological structure, the way other features of Augustine's biography are. Monica does not provide a paradigm for a fundamental ontological structure of Dasein. As a matter of fact, she is not so much as mentioned, which reminds one of the complete absence of Antigone from Heidegger's discussion of the tragedy that bears her name in *An Introduction to Metaphysics*. When it comes to these women, Heidegger seems like a man reading a map who does not notice what country he examines, the name having been sprawled too widely across its surface. For Monica is a figure not of war but of weeping, not of manly *Entschlossenheit* but of *weiblich* tears that have nothing to do with Heidegger's virile Christian soldierism.

To be sure, the exclusion of Monica is to some extent a methodological one, a function of the decision to comment on Book X, not on the preceding autobiography in which Monica plays such an important part, but that decision is part of the problem, not of its solution; it does not resolve the problem but relocates it.

The absence of Monica is all the more striking when one compares Heidegger's commentary on the *Confessions* with Derrida's *Circumfession* (1991).[3] Derrida's highly autobiographical piece took the form not exactly of a commentary on the *Confessions*, but of a text that is cross-seminated with Augustine's text, in which entries from Derrida's journals are interwoven with citations of the Latin text of the *Confessions*. Derrida, a French-speaking Algerian and a "compatriot of Augustine" (Hippo is about one hundred miles from Algiers), raised on the rue Saint Augustin, keeps a journal of the death of his mother, Georgette (née Safar), in Nice, a city on the other side of the Mediterranean coast, that recalls for Derrida the death of Monica in Ostia Antiqua. If Monica is completely absent from "Augustine and Neoplatonism," everything in *Circumfession* is organized around the death of Georgette/Monica. If the figure of Monica prefigures absolutely nothing in "fundamental ontology," the figure of Monica/Georgette, the figure of the weeping woman, and her relation to Jacques/Augustine, the "son of these tears," prefigures the central operation of deconstruction.[4] For Jacques is himself, like Augustine (and Nietzsche), a man of tears, a phrase that for Heidegger would be a *contradictio in adjecto*, for there can be nothing manly about a man of tears. Weeping should be added to the list that Levinas has drawn—containing items such as getting hungry—that authentic Dasein does not do in *Being and Time*, while the author and the subject of *Circumfession* is bathed in tears.

To put all this in the massively Greek, austerely formal and ontological categories of *Being and Time*, Derrida's *Circumfession*, along with his *Memoirs of the Blind*,[5] published just the year before, might be somewhat amusingly construed as an inquiry into the Being of weeping. What is the Being of being-in-tears? What is the meaning of the Being of crying? When we are filled with grief—or with joy—when we are driven to extreme states of feeling and emotion, when *Befindlichkeit* and *Stimmung* are pushed to an extreme, why do our eyes fill up with tears? Why do these extreme states not find some other physiological expression? Why not some other sort of secretion of some other gland? These questions are no doubt too ludicrous, too *weiblich*, for fundamental ontology. The amusement, however, does not make tears look bad, but rather the fundamental ontology, and it calls for categories that are otherwise than Being and Dasein, for there is no crying in fundamental ontology. In terms of the present essay, the question is this: if Monica is missing, how does her omission affect our understanding of this "being which *we* ourselves are," we women and men? How can we understand who *we* are if *we* are not *all* there? That question is not amusing.

Let us regain our composure, wipe our eyes, and look into this matter more coolly.

Heidegger's Christian Soldier

The *Confessions*, Heidegger says, is not a speculative treatise but a work of confession (*confiteri*), that is, the self-examination that must be carried out by a being whose being has become a question to itself (*quaestio mihi factus sum*; *Confessions*, book X, 33), and the structure of whose life is to be a land of trouble and turmoil, a *terra difficultatis* (Book X, 16; cf. BT, 69). Factical life is *tentatio*, a trial, a test, a tribulation, a bit of trouble in which we are either victors or vanquished. *Vita . . . tota tentatio est* (Book X, 32): life is all trouble. A trouble (*molestia*) is not a physical obstacle, such as a tree blocking our path, but the pull of the world, the lure of everyday things. We are scattered abroad and disseminated into many thing (*in multa defleximus*) but we are to be gathered back into the unity of our being by the work of *continentia*, self-containment, self-possession. Factical life transpires in the distance between these possibilities, in the freedom either to give in to the fall, the pull of the world, or to pull oneself together. To regather the self is also to bring oneself back before God (*coram deo*) (GA 60, 249), for, as Kierkegaard points out, the sense of the self and the sense of God are directly proportionate to each other (GA 60, 248). The man who takes his measure from God is most himself, most a self. The possibility of falling is not a bit of bad luck the soul (self) suffers that it might have otherwise avoided, but its very structure, which prompts us to think of the soul not as a thing with properties but as a being of possibility and freedom (GA 60, 244).

The man who takes his measure from the world exposes himself to the pull of everyday temptations, which takes the form of the three threats or dangers to the soul with which it must wage "daily war" (*quotidianum bellum*). I am attacked on one front by the flesh, so that I take pleasure in pleasure instead of the good the pleasure means to facilitate (I eat in order to enjoy eating); and on another front by curiosity, so that I look for the pleasure of seeing. Finally, most seriously, I am assaulted by the pride of life (*ambitio saeculi*); I take delight in my own being and importance, my worldly validity or standing. I thus lose sight of my genuine freedom, which ought to be taken up with my autonomous and authentic selfhood instead of going about begging favor from the world.

Throughout the lectures, Heidegger differentiates the Neoplatonism that has worked its way into the *Confessions* from the structure of what he takes to be authentically Christian experience. In the preceding lecture course, on Paul's *Letters to the Thessalonians*, he sought out the factical experience of time in the earliest, most originary New Testament texts. Heidegger's passion for the *ursprünglich*, which was finally to settle on the Greeks to the exclusion of the Christian, was first exercised on the New Testament to the exclusion of the Greek, which is another of his notable reversals. The Neoplatonism to which Augustine is attached shows up in his metaphysics of glory and beauty, in his tendency to order everything to the Platonic and Neoplatonic contemplation of the divine being, in which God is taken as *summum bonum* and *summa pulchritudo*. This Neoplatonic thematic tends to undermine the genuinely "factical" thematic of setting our hands to the plow and not looking back, of fighting the good fight, of taking up the cross (GA 60, 277). For Christian Neoplatonism, "God" is given in the stillness and peace of vision and contemplation, while for the Christian, God is approached in anxious unrest (*inquietum est cor nostrum*), indeed, in fear and trembling. Just so, in his Neoplatonic moments, Augustine treats the self as a stable spiritual substance, but when he returns to the categories of Christian life, he thinks in terms of the restlessness of "factical life," the life of *tentatio*. Clearly then by the "Neoplatonism" of Augustine Heidegger has in mind the *theologia gloriae* condemned by Luther, while factical life is modeled after and formalizes what Luther called the *theologia crucis*, the way of the cross.[6]

Even so—and this is what interests us here—for this forms the point of contrast and pivot of the comparison with Derrida I am sketching here: In his "ontology of the cross" (*ontologia crucis*), as van Buren so felicitously describes it, Heidegger takes no note of the women weeping at the foot of the cross, even as he does not notice Monica in the *Confessions*. Yet those are exactly what draws Derrida's attention.

Derrida's Weeping Women

Let us begin with the eyes. Heidegger's Augustine is also interested in the eyes (*concupiscentia oculorum*), in eyes that are directed to their proper end, made to serve the ends of the soul, disciplined to do their duty dutifully, like good soldiers, as opposed to eyes that are wanton and undisciplined, distracted and led astray by every passing curiosity. Heidegger's Augustine does not take up blindness, the ab-ocular one (*aboculus, aveugle*), the wounded or diseased or disabled eye. Curiously, everybody in *Being and Time* is healthy, hale, and whole; they are either resolute or irresolute, self-possessed or dissipated, and they even die, but their bodies, if they have bodies, seem never to grow ill or lame, diseased or disabled, and when some *Stimmung* or other becomes too much for them, if it does, they never break out in tears!

But when Derrida is invited to serve as a guest curator for an exhibit at the Louvre, he chooses to bring together all the paintings in the Louvre that deal with *blindness*. One of the first things to strike Derrida by the collection he has assembled is that it seems to be governed by a law of sexual difference. These are largely paintings of blind *men*, he notices, and their blindness is always entered into a larger, usually sacrificial economy. The blindness of Saint Paul, for example, is a temporary block of his sensible vision that allows him to see with the eyes of faith. Sometimes these men are not really blind, but blindfolded, and always in such a way as to put their manly self-possession to the test. Among the Greeks, for whom seeing is the paradigm of the highest operation of the soul, blindness is either a freak defect of nature, or the blindness of the oracle, which signifies a higher spiritual vision, or the self-inflicted blindness of a tragic hero such as Oedipus. For the men, blindness is either sacrificial, in which case it returns a higher reward, or it is part of the manly price to be paid all-masterful fate.

Still, Derrida wonders, "if there are many great blind men, why so many weeping women?" (MdA, 128/MB, 127). The only blind women Derrida finds—apart from in a painting of Saint Lucy, the patron saint of the blind to whom the blind pray and weep—are women blinded by their tears. Toward the end of *Memoirs of the Blind* (MdA, 127/MB, 125, fig. 71) we find a reproduction of Daniele da Volterra's exquisite drawing *Woman at the Foot of the Cross*, her figure bent with grief, her face buried in her hands. All men, from Aristotle to the men of phenomenology, desire to see, even when, like Milton, they are blind. But the women are laid low by their blindness and they do not get a higher payback; their blindness is an expenditure, a loss or waste, without return. So the desire to see in these paintings is deeply phallocentric, centered upon a virile desire to see all and master all. But Derrida is interested in exploring *another desire*, nonphallocentric and signified by a blindness that is neither a defect of nature nor a sacrificial exchange, but a kind of signature of our condition, a sign of an imploration, a desire for something *tout autre*, for something we cannot see and for which we can only pray and weep.

Thus, if Heidegger's "Augustine and Neoplatonism" is modeled on the *theologia crucis*, on the manly virtue of taking up one's cross, Derrida writes from the point of view of the women weeping at the foot of the cross, of the wounded body. He associates Augustine's "confessional" (*confiteri*) mode not with the battle that freedom wages with the world but also with faith and flowing tears and blood. To confess one's faith (*cru*) is to pour out one's blood in a bottle like wine (*cru*) and to mix the blood and the tears (*Circ.*, 13/*Circum*, 10). An autobiography is "what mixes prayer and tears with blood" (*Circ.*, 22/*Circum*, 20). What does the body mean to say when we weep? Could we weep without tears? What if, instead of wiping away our tears, we learned to let them be? Suppose deep down the eye were meant to weep, not to see, and that being veiled with tears unveils the eyes for what they are (MdA, 125/MB, 126) When Derrida reads Augustine's *Confessions*, he finds there a "great book of tears" (MdA, 123/MB, 122), for tearful eyes are the organ of confession, of mourning and imploring, of misery and joy. Why are tears so sweet to us when we are in misery? Augustine asks (*Confessions*, Book IV, 5). Like Augustine, he writes, "I love only tears, I only love and speak through them (*Circ.*, 95/*Circum*, 98). (The *Confessions*, Derrida says in an interesting aside, might also be usefully compared to the "Dionysian counter-confessions of another blind man," that of Nietzsche's *Ecce Homo*.)

Derrida is searching for a desire that lies outside or breaks with the desire to see, the deeply Greek and primordially metaphysical, phallocentric desire of philosophy. The Heideggerian loyalists think that with his notion of *lethe* or concealment, Heidegger breaks the grip of seeing, vision, and light, but that I think is an optical illusion. For the dynamics of *lethe* and *a-letheia* belong together in a single movement, where *lethe* is the heart of *aletheia*, like the systole and diastole of the same heart (if it has a heart). *Lethe* is the deep well or reserve of *a-letheia*, from which the being emerges, however fleetingly and tenuously, into the *Lichtung*, the open light of day. As such, the hyphenation of *a-letheia* is still an economic operation, for *lethe* stands in reserve for and at the service of *aletheia* to draw upon.⁷ But the blindness of the woman weeping at the foot of the cross, the blindness of the women blinded by tears in the Louvre collection, is of a different order altogether, an-economic and otherwise than *lethe*, having to do with prayers and tears. The "truth" of the eyes is "to have imploration rather than vision in sight, to address prayer, love, joy, or sadness rather than a look or gaze" (MdA, 125/MB, 126). "To pronounce that which in the eyes, and thus in the drawing of men, in no way regards sight, has nothing to do with it. Nothing to do with the light of clairvoyance" (MdA, 128/MB, 127). This blindness belongs to a different order altogether, which has nothing to do with a phallocentric desire to see, which means to own and appropriate, which are deeply Heideggerian figures inscribed in the discourse of *Eigentlichkeit*, *Ereignis*, and *Er-aügen*.

That is why in the *Confessions* that Derrida is reading, Monica, the death of Monica, plays a central role. For Derrida, the *Confessions* are not a war journal, a report from the front in the *bellum quotidianum*, but a death watch over the dying Monica, which he grafts upon his own deathwatch over Georgette Safar Derrida. Heidegger too of course is famously interested in death, in a soldierly readiness for death that returns that anxiety-ready investment with anticipatory resoluteness. Like any good soldier, Dasein takes on death itself, or at least the menacing prospect of death. By making itself ready for death, death too becomes one of its possibilities, part of the repertoire of its *Seinkönnen*, the central part of that scene of mastery and self-possession which is *eigentliches Dasein*. Death in *Circumfession*, on the other hand, is a bedroom scene, a slow death, a scene of running bedsores, of trying to feed an aging woman while water runs down her chin. She who loved poker and played late into the night the day before her son was born, she whose once lively mind and beautiful and laughing face kept this weepy little boy safe from all the world, now lies helpless and does not so much as recognize her own son, the son of her tears. Death in *Circumfession* is not my death but the death of the (m)other (*Circ.*, 197–98/*Circum*, 211–12), and it is not a matter of self-mastery, but of mourning the other.

It is quite important to emphasize that the blood and tears, the blank stare, the running sores, the dying is not *only* that of Monica/Georgette, for everything about *Circumfession* speaks of the identity of "Jackie" and his mother. He favors his mother's side, was deeply attached to his mother, was a weepy child who ran to his mother for protection from the adults in the family and other children who loved to tease and provoke his tears. He, the son of these tears, is never sure whether these tears are his or his mother's (*Circ.*, 243/*Circum*, 263). He tells a touching story of feigning illness so that he could stay home from school with his mother, away from those "cruel mistresses," but she was not taken in by the ruse. When later in the day she came back to pick him up he reproaches her for leaving him "in the world, in the hands of others." When he sees her coming to the schoolyard, he writes, "She must have been as beautiful as a photograph" (*Circ.*, 250–52/*Circum*, 272).

That is why I think that Kelly Oliver is mistaken about *Circumfession*, which she regards as degrading portrait of women in terms of infirmity and ugliness, of menstrual blood and bedsores, of women whose bodies are "scarred, immodest, already dead."[8] For the point of these descriptions of the dying Georgette/Monica is Derrida's identification with them, with his mother, with her illness and mortality. He associates with her illness an attack of Lyme disease that he suffered and was for a while undiagnosed and seemed like a life-threatening attack; he associates with her scars his own scar of circumcision, which cuts him down to size; he wonders if he will die before her, if his weak and failing flesh will survive hers. *Circumfession* is his book of circumcision, of the cutting down of phallocentrism and virile mastery. Above all, Derrida identifies with Georgette's tears; and if tears are womanly, then he wants to be a womanly man, like weepy old Augustine himself, even as they were both a "mommy's boy." *Circumfession* is a confession that this feminine figure is his own. As he makes perfectly plain in "Choreographies," Derrida wants to multiply genders, to have as many genders as possible, not to divide them neatly into two, the one hierarchized over the other, while inhabiting himself the upper side. That would be the very opposite of what deconstruction tries to do.[9] He would multiply the steps in the dance of gender, which means that there would always be more moves to come when it comes to gender and a deep undecidability about one's gender. By identifying with his mother he sees to it that his own gender would never be identifiable and confined to a single side, thereby keeping the future of gender open, and so of everything else, if sexual difference is the fundamental problem of our time, instead of trapping us inside one role only.

Derrida regards da Volterra's portrait of the woman weeping at the foot of the cross as a portrait of us *all*, of "the beings which we ourselves are," *all* of us, men and women, a self-portrait of the blindness of the *human condition at large*. He is not saying, as Oliver seems to think, that we men, we fathers, are erect and straight, our flesh unscarred, our vision clear (which is perhaps what the *Aufklärers* think), while women are weepy, infirm, and blind. The figure of Monica/Georgette, the weeping mother, and of the woman weeping at the foot of the cross, blinded by her tears, the woman of prayers and tears, is the very figure of us all, and the figure of deconstruction itself, which we might best think of as lost in prayer, its face buried in its hands, or as groping blindly with its stick/stylus, writing in the dark. He remembers his mother praying and weeping each time he grew ill as a child—she had already lost one child—and when he recovered, when the temperature subsides, "I hear her say, 'grâce à Dieu, Dieu merci,' weeping in pronouncing your name . . . I'm mingling here the name of God with the origin of tears" (*Circ.*, 112–13/*Circum.*, 117–18). He associates the prayers and tears of Georgette with the name of God ("G," in English, happily standing for God, too, as well as Geoffrey), with *le désir de Dieu*, with that *other* desire, that *desire* for the coming of the other whom we cannot see.

This is not a phallocentric desire for the self-possession of the moment of truth, for the self-mastery of anticipatory resoluteness, but a desire that implores and prays for what it does not know or understand, for the *tout autre*. He makes Augustine's question his own: *quid ergo amo cum deum meum amo?* What do I love when I love my God? For what do I pray and weep? What is my desire? Unlike Heidegger, for whom the name of God spells the end of questioning, for Derrida and Augustine, the name of God makes everything questionable, for it is the name of our blindness. The blindness of the weeping woman is the *structural* condition of us all, not a weakness peculiarly affecting the weak flesh of women. For we are all, this is our condition and our passion, cut off (circumcised) from the secret, from the Truth, whether of unveiling or of correspondence, from *Eigentlichkeit* and *Ereignis*, sent out into a desert *khora* where nothing "gives." We live by a passion and a faith, praying and weeping for something to come, a justice to come, or a democracy, a hospitality, a gift to come. The weeping woman does not know the truth but desires it; she does not see it but confesses it; she does not know it but *does* it, as Augustine says (*veritatem facere*), bearing witness to it in the blind, her eyes veiled by tears.

Toward a Poetics of Prayers and Tears

However much one admires the extraordinary genius of the work that Heidegger did from 1919 to 1927 (and beyond, for that matter), one is struck—here and now, when faced with the question of Heidegger and feminism—by the deeply masculinist structure of Heidegger's Augustine, read Dasein. For Heidegger, the *Confessions* are a journal of the *bellum quotidianum*, of the daily *Kampf* in which a virile, hale, and healthy Christian soldier battles to remain erect and resolute, in unbending loyalty to God and self, *pro deo et patria*, to maintain himself in the moment of truth. For Derrida, it is the story of a very womanly man of prayers and tears, a weepy Augustine, his (her) eyes blinded by tears, a wo/man of faith, a being of flesh and blood, wounded and cut, praying and weeping over the coming of the *tout autre*.[10] These two readings and repetitions of the *Confessions* could hardly be more different. The "fundamental ontology" of Dasein, which was supposed to occupy a place of a priori neutrality, prior to the division between the genders (or between atheism and theism, good and evil, and so on), is deeply marked and inscribed by the traits of a very masculine subject, a knight of anticipatory resoluteness, ready for anxiety, a macho, virile figure out there all alone "without its mommy," as Drucilla Cornell once quipped. Without any women at all, as far as I can see, including the woman within, the womanliness within a man that saves men from themselves.

What are we to make of all this? For one thing, it makes sense, distressing, ominous sense, of the turn Heidegger next took toward a heroic voluntarism, beginning very likely in 1928–29. It makes sense of his affection in that unhappy time for Ernst Jünger, the bizarre World War I hero whose reading of Nietzsche's concept of the will to power captured Heidegger's fancy. It makes sense of Heidegger's militarism, in the literal and most political sense, which brooked no compromise with womanly pacifism, and of his ontological militarism in the Rectorial Address: his invocation of Prometheus, the first Greek god who was to come to save us; his citation of von Clausewitz's *Vom Krieg* and of his notion of Being itself as a *Kampf*.[11] True to his plan, Heidegger did indeed let the Being of Dasein, which was a *Kampf*, a *bellum*, be the clue to the meaning of Being. Irigaray thinks the violence at the root of sexism lies at the root of all violence.[12] Now it would certainly be too much to say that this militant masculinism led Heidegger down the road to fascism. But it quite clear that there was nothing in his of view of "man" (*sic*) in the 1920s to protect him from the violence that descended over Germany in 1933 and then engulfed the whole world, including Heidegger's own thought, career, and reputation.

By the same logic, the *next* turn Heidegger took, identifiable now in the *Beiträge*, the notebooks of 1936–38, constitutes a move beyond the militant voluntarism of the 1930s toward a philosophy, a thought, of *Gelassenheit*, and this must be seen as a movement beyond the virile militarism of erect and resolute Dasein. The thought of the "later" Heidegger is a deep and systematic break, not only with the "man of reason," the masculinist *Aufklärer* for whom the world is an object spread out before his mastering subjectivity, ready to be ravished by the system or the concept, but no less with the virile hero of resoluteness in *Being and Time* and the extremes to which resoluteness was pushed in the 1930s. "Letting-be" has renounced the posture of mastery, domination, and violence, in order to let the world, the gentle worlding of the world, come to pass. The figure of Dasein now is the rose that blossoms without why (PR, 32–49). In just the same way that Fred Dallmayr argues that the thought of *Gelassenheit* embraces a non-Western possibility that at least provides an opening for breaking the grip of Heidegger's Greco-Eurocentrism, so too it opens up a considerably more welcoming and receptive, more prayerful and less warrior-like relation to the world.[13] A great deal of the violence embedded in the *twin* paradigms of the "man of reason" and the knight of anticipatory resoluteness is disarmed by the surrender of thought to Being, to the world, to the Fourfold. Enlightenment rationality and existential resoluteness are siblings of the same subjectivism. What Heidegger calls "humanism" and "subjectism" are deeply masculinist models and *Gelassenheit*, by releasing their common grip, opens up the possibility of a nonphallocentric relationship to things, an "openness to the Mystery."

It is not an accident that the deep ecologists find inspiration in the later Heidegger and that there is and can be a ecofeminism that aligns itself with Heidegger. That, I think, is an insightful appropriation of a genuine possibility in Heidegger's later work. When Heidegger radically reconfigures *Entschlossenheit* as dis-closedness, openness, welcoming the world, as answering the call of the world, he has also radically altered the gender of Dasein, performing a bit of sex change on Dasein that has wonderfully scrambled its gender, throwing it into a most desirable undecidability and miscegenation. Of course, one could, if one wishes, actually believe what Heidegger says in "A Letter on Humanism," that this is what *Being and Time* really said all along, but no one but the most extreme Heideggerian loyalists, Heideggerians of the very strictest observance, can actually swallow that tall tale. One should instead view this as a salutary renunciation on Heidegger's part of the extreme voluntarism of the 1930s, of the virile militancy of Dasein, and an attempt on the part of Heidegger, who pulled his *Lederhosen* on one leg at a time, to think things through anew.

This is not to say that all is well with the later Heidegger and that the whole story has a happy ending. For if the later Heidegger found room for prayer, for thinking as thankfulness for the grace of Being, even for praying for a god to save us, he could never bring himself to tears. His thought remained resolutely hardened and indifferent to suffering and pain, to "flesh." When a prominent Heideggerian wrote a book called *Stone*, he said it all.[14] Dasein has stones, not flesh. For the later notion of *Gelassenheit* and of the worlding of the world, or the languaging of language, is dedicated to what I have called a "phainaesthetic" event, an event in which the subjectivism of aesthetics has been overcome, but not the aestheticism, which has been shifted from the aesthetic subject to Being. Everything in the later thought of the worlding of the world has to do with the splendor of Being, the shine of *Sein*, the shining *Schönheit* of *Sein*. Everything takes its measure from the fouring of the Fourfold, which leaves no room for the immeasurable misery of the masses, the suffering of the oppressed, the countless, untold tears of those who neither think nor poetize.

I will not attempt to repeat the argument that I have made at length in *Demythologizing Heidegger*, but simply to signal its principal critique.[15] There is an ominous and consistent tendency in Heidegger to mistreat pain, either by treating it as a test of manhood (from the early Freiburg lectures through the Nazi years) or to "essentialize" it in the manner of the later writings, which is perhaps even worse than the heroics of pain prior to the *Kehre*. The essentialization is at work in those tasteless declarations that appear with disturbing, lawlike regularity in the later writings. To the thousands of Germans (not to mention everyone else) made homeless by a war that Heidegger warmly supported and conducted by a criminal regime that Heidegger helped bring to power, he offered this insight: what really matters in homelessness, the really essential *Heimatlosigkeit*, is not being out in the cold, but the thoughtlessness that does not heed the house of Being. Speaking of Trakl's poetry, he says that the lifeless bodies that lay strewn across the battlefield of Grodek, and across the poem Trakl wrote about that battle, are not to taken as so many dead soldiers but as an event in the history of Being, which is something greater and more essential. Upon the victims of the Holocaust he broke his silence just long enough to make this stunning observation: the rule of *Gestell* in the mass murder of the concentration camps and modern agriculture are really essentially the same, *im Wesen dasselbe*. That is because what is essentially at stake, *das wesentlichste, das Wesen des Seins, das Sein des Wesens*, has nothing to do with suffering humanity, afflicted flesh, violence or murder, but rather with the shine of *Sein*, the glow of the Fourfold, with jugs and the old bridge at Heidelberg. Even after the Holocaust, after the war, after the ruins—not only ruined stones but also ruined flesh—left by the Nazis, Heidegger still did not get it. He still thought the violence lay in the technology, not the murder, that the truth of Being was defaced by the scarring of the earth, not by scarred flesh. The god who would come to save us would clean up the Rhein but he (*sic!*) was not coming to let justice flow like water over the land; the god would clear those power lines out of the *Schwarzwald* but he was not come to wipe away our tears.

Heidegger never saw the tears. With unfailing regularity, he missed the tears. And the women. He managed to read the New Testament very carefully in the early Freiburg years without ever noticing the blind and the beggars, the lame and the lepers, who are spread across its pages; and while he formalized the theology of the cross into a fundamental ontology, he never noticed the women weeping at the foot of the cross. Heidegger also read Augustine's *Confessions* with provocative originality and close scrutiny without ever noticing Monica, without noticing mother or son, not as such, not the weeping mother or the son of these tears, and without noticing Augustine's own tears, or his great book of tears, the praying and weeping on almost every page. Heidegger always was blind to the weeping woman, to the womanly man, the manly woman, of prayers and tears, who prays and weeps for the coming of the *tout autre*, the coming of mercy and justice. This was always too *weiblich* for him

The absence of Monica and of the women weeping at the foot of the cross represent a fateful omission, a fatal blindness about something that, as Irigaray says, "would allow us to check the many forms that destruction takes in our world" and that would make possible "the creation of a new *poetics*,"[16] what I might call a poetics of prayers and tears that would counter Heidegger's phainesthetics, his disturbing an-aesthetics, which never so much as noticed Monica or heard her constant weeping throughout the *Confessions*.

Notes

1. Heidegger's GA 60 or *Gesamtausgabe*, B. 60, *Phänomenologie des religiösen Lebens*, includes "Einführung in die Phänomenologie der Religion" (Wintersemester 1920/21), ed. Matthias Jung and Thomas Regehly; "Augustinus und der Neuplatonismus" (Sommersemester 1921); "Ausaurbeitung und Entwürfe," ed. Claudius Strube.
2. Theodore Kisiel, *The Genesis of Heidegger's Being and Time* (Berkeley and Los Angeles: University of California Press, 1993).
3. *Circon: Circonfession: Cinquante-neuf périodes et périphrases*, in Geoffrey Bennington and Jacques Derrida, *Jacques Derrida* (Paris: Éditions du Seuil, 1991); *Circum.*: in Geoffrey Bennington and Jacques Derrida, *Jacques Derrida* (Chicago: University of Chicago, Press, 1991).
4. I have made a detailed argument for such a reading of deconstruction in *The Prayers and Tears of Jacques Derrida: Religion Without Religion* (Bloomington: Indiana University Press, 1997).
5. Derrida, *Memoirs d'aveugle: L'autobiographie et autres ruines* (Paris: Éditions de la Réunion des musées nationaux, 1990), hereafter MdA; *Memoirs of the Blind: The Self-Portrait and Other Ruins*, trans. Pascale-Anne Brault and Michael Naas (Chicago: University of Chicago Press, 1993); hereafter MB.
6. See Alister E. McGrath, *Luther's Theology of the Cross* (Oxford: Blackwell, 1990), 148–75. For a groundbreaking commentary on this point in Heidegger, see John van Buren, *The Young Heidegger* (Bloomington: Indiana University Press, 1994), 144–202.
7. See John Sallis, "Deformatives: Essentially Other Than Truth," in *Reading Heidegger: Commemorations*, ed. John Sallis (Bloomington: Indiana University Press, 1993), 29–46.
8. See Kelly Oliver, *Womanizing Nietzsche: Philosophy's Relation to the Feminine* (New York: Routledge, 195), 56–64; and "The Maternal Operation: Circumscribing the Alliance," in *Derrida and Feminism: Recasting the Question of Woman*, ed. Ellen Feder, Mary C. Rawlinson, and Emily Zakin (New York: Routledge, 1997), 53–68. In "Fatherhood and the Promise of Ethics," *Diacritics* (Spring, 1997): 45–57, Oliver argues that in *The Gift of Death* Derrida advocates the "father's gift of the death of the mother that promises life to the son."
9. For a commentary on "Choreographies" see John D. Caputo, "Dreaming of the Innumerable: Derrida, Drucilla Cornell, and the Dance of Gender," in *Derrida and Feminism: Recasting the Question of Woman*, ed. Feder, Rawlinson, and Zakin, 141–60.
10. Derrida associates himself with certain things in the *Confessions*, not with everything. He is not submitting *Circumfession* as a work of Augustine scholarship. His reservations about Augustine would be massive—not the least being reservations about Augustine's politics and about the *other woman* who goes unnamed, the woman Augustine loved and lived with for fourteen years, the mother of Adeodatus, their child. Of course, the same proviso could hold for Heidegger, too, who is trying to extract a formal ontological structure from the *Confessions*. True enough. The disturbing thing would be not the selectiveness of Heidegger's and Derrida's readings, but the contrast in what they have selected.
11. Heidegger, *Die Selbstbehauptung der deutschen Universität: Das Rektorat 1933/34*; see SdDU; English trans., "The Self-Assertion of the German University" (SA).

12. Luce Irigaray, *An Ethics of Sexual Difference*, trans. Carolyn Burke and Gillian C. Gill (Ithaca: Cornell University Press, 1993), 5.

13. Fred Dallmayr, *The Other Heidegger* (Ithaca: Cornell University Press, 1993), 200ff.

14. John Sallis, *Stone* (Bloomington: Indiana University Press, 1994).

15. John D. Caputo, *Demythologizing Heidegger* (Bloomington: Indiana University Press, 1993); see especially, chaps. 6–8.

16. Irigaray, *An Ethics of Sexual Difference*, 5.

6

Sappho

The She-Greek Heidegger Forgot

Carol Bigwood

Crossing-Over

Heidegger and she? At first sight, they seem to be as unpaired and awkward as two left shoes. The "and" holds the two in an incompatible, or at least unrelated, indifferent, pairing. As Derrida notes, the appearances of women in Heidegger's texts are "discreet, furtive, almost unnoticed."[1] Women in Heidegger's corpus are disappointingly trivial and stereotypical, offered up as inconsequential examples that could just as easily be dropped.[2]

And yet. There is the Thracian servant girl whose laughter takes Heidegger on an unusual pathway of thought and leads him, despite himself, to a rather uncanny place and situation.

This "maid's" laughter prompts Heidegger in an early lecture to think that "the question 'What is a thing?' must always be rated as one with which one can do nothing and which causes housemaids to laugh" (WIT, 3). "And genuine housemaids," Heidegger adds, "must have something to laugh about" (WIT, 3). It is from this same jesting housemaid that Heidegger even learns a little something:

"As we ask 'What is a thing?' we now mean the things around us. We take in view what is most immediate, most capable of being grasped by the hand. By observing such, we reveal that we have learned something from the laughter of the housemaid. She thinks we should first look around thoroughly in this round-about-us (*Um-uns-herum*)" (WIT, 7).

Like Zarathustra learning a little truth from an old woman, Heidegger appears to be learning something from a housemaid. Who is this servant woman whose mere laughter can teach Heidegger something? If we are to believe philosophical rumor, this maid (*therapaina*) was there at the very inception of Western philosophy. Her archaic laugh was heard around 600 B.C. by Thales, our first philosopher. The story comes to us through Plato, two hundred years or so after the supposed incident: "The story is that Thales, while occupied in studying the heavens above and looking up, fell into a well. A good-looking and whimsical maid from Thrace laughed at him and told him that while he might passionately want to know all things in the universe, the things in front of his very nose and feet were unseen by him" (*Theaetetus* 174b, quoted in WIT, 3).

Plato remarks that this jest fits all those who become involved in philosophy. Heidegger, at the other far end of our philosophical tradition, is prompted by her philosophical jest to define philosophy itself as "that thinking with which one can start nothing and about which housemaids necessarily laugh" (WIT, 3). "Such a definition of philosophy," Heidegger continues, "is not a mere joke but is something to think over" (WIT, 3).

Indeed. How seriously are we to take this laughter that Heidegger says comes of necessity (*notwendig*) from the mouths of housemaids when confronted with the thinking called philosophy? If this necessity of Heidegger's holds the weight of the Parmenidean "necessity" that Heidegger analyzes in *What is Called Thinking?* then it is needful and useful for philosophy that housemaids laugh.[3] Philosophy needs the laughter of housemaids? That is a most serious thought.

Yet Heidegger does not take his own definition of philosophy and her joke seriously enough. At first he understands her jest to be advising philosophers to turn to immediacy in their search for the nature of a thing.

They should turn to that which is most capable of being grasped by the hand. But when he takes up her hint, he immediately falls into "embarrassment" because, he says, these things have been settled long ago by the scientist (WIT, 7). He escapes his own embarrassment by dismissing this charming maid's way as common opinion and the scientific attitude that, he says, are outside a genuine philosophical approach to things. Like the path of *doxa* that Parmenides says fills the ear with noise and the tongue with chatter, this maid's way of ordinary experience turns out to be the wrong way for philosophical thinking. Heidegger tells us that everyday experience is "not at all sufficient" because it needs further grounding that philosophy must attempt to offer (WIT, 12, 14). Thus, this maid's wanting Heidegger to "stick to the facts and their exact observations to find out what things are" is inadequate (WIT, 8), he says.

Heidegger, like other philosophers before him, relegates "her" to the outside of philosophy, serving as the other. But hints, as Heidegger well knows, can be ambiguous in meaning, and her archaic mockery appears to confuse him here. For, of the two, the maid and the philosopher, surely Thales is the more adequate representative of both practical sense and the scientific attitude. Thales was renowned not only for his accurate observations and calculations as an astronomer and geometer, but precisely for practically applying his discoveries.[4] Of course, Heidegger would not associate Thales with the scientific attitude because for Heidegger the scientific attitude properly belongs to modern science and Thales belongs to the great beginnings before concepts such as subjective and objective existed (IM, 101).

But she, too, is ancient Greek. She, too, existed well before the "workshops and research laboratories" to which Heidegger says she is confining his investigation (WIT, 8). She, too, existed at a time when "Being" disclosed itself as *phusis* (nature), as an emerging, abiding, shining appearing. But Heidegger forgets that the Greek can be "she." The "clever and witty (*chariessa* and *emmeles*)" Thracian "handmaid (*therapaina*)" is stripped of all attributes to become only "housemaid" or "servant maid" (*Dienstmagde*) (FD, 5) for Heidegger, a woman whose workliness is emphasized, like the peasant woman in "The Origin of a Work of Art."

Philosophers gaze up at the immensity of the heavens; maids look down, "trapped" in immediacy, hauling water from the well in earthen jugs. The rumor of one maid's wisdom at the very beginning of philosophy happens to slip into the margins of the philosophical tradition. Could this little contribution that managed to survive, this tiny joke, give feminist philosophers food for thought? Certainly there is a sense of rebellion and freedom in her jest, for this charming slave mocked one of the most famous, influential, and revered men of her time.[5] Laughter can escape repression by "stealing thorough" boundaries. Those in archaic Greece who heard the anecdote may well have associated her mockery with Aphrodite, whose cult was popular among slaves and women. Operating at the crossroads of recognized and accepted structures, Aphrodite was a goddess who could deny, contradict, or challenge the basic categories and ethical norms of society.[6] Homer's most common epithet for Aphrodite is "laughter-loving." Aphrodite is mistress of multiple deceits, wiles, persuasion, and other arts to bring about amorous relations.[7] Her laughter is tender, charming, and innocent, but it can also be dangerous.

Could a witty maid's little laugh bring philosophy to its essential nature as Heidegger intimates? One thing for sure: her laughter not only unsettles our first philosopher, but also beguiles Heidegger himself, who, in some sense, can be called a "last" philosopher, given that he understood his work as a thinking toward the "end" of philosophy. For Heidegger not only forgets that "she" can be ancient Greek, but he also curiously multiplies this charming maid. She even greatly expands to become a veritable "horizon of housemaids" (WIT, 10). The "one" becomes "many" housemaids for Heidegger and their laughter continues to haunt him.

Heidegger is quite aware that laughter can be dangerous. Being "exposed to the laughter of housemaids," he says, "is one of the risks philosophers must recognise" (WIT, 3, 10).[8] Given that his philosophical work attempts to prepare us for an untraditional leap of thinking out of representational thought that relies on certain grounds, and into a nonmetaphysical way of thinking, Heidegger understands that he is especially vulnerable to such hazards as falling down wells or into the abyss. He is exposed to criticisms, for example, that his ideas are "farfetched and one-sided" (IM, 176).

Like the tightrope walker in *Thus Spoke Zarathustra* who attempts to go between man and the overman and, as he is overtaken by a jester, falls to his death, so in attempting to leap out of metaphysics—a leap that requires long preparation—Heidegger's concentration and balance may be disrupted by a sudden laugh. He realizes that he may fall into a well where he might not hit bottom for some time (WIT, 3, 8): "Where are we to get a foothold? The ground slips away under us. Perhaps we are already close to falling into the well. At any rate the housemaids are already laughing" (WIT, 27).

Heidegger, with the laughter of his housemaids in his ear, loses his nerve for the leap and reveals to his readers a curious fear: "And what if only we ourselves are these housemaids, i.e., if we have secretly discovered that all this talk of the "this," as well as similar discussions, is fantasy and empty!" (WIT, 27).

"What if only we ourselves are these housemaids?" asks Heidegger and in so asking sees himself as his housemaids. Heidegger here places himself in between the truth of the serious philosopher and the fantasy of the laughing other. He has left that place on the inside of philosophy with its firm male tradition to a space somewhere in between. He is in-between, neither fully inside nor outside metaphysics, preparing a way for a leap out. He is attempting to cross over, laughing at himself, echoing she who laughed at the first philosopher. Is he leaping out of philosophy or falling down a well as Thales did? He is, in either case, in midair. He puts himself in the conditional. He is in the air philosophers have forgotten, wondering if philosophy is fantasy and emptiness, cross-dressed as his housemaid.[9]

One has to admit that Heidegger in an Archaic Greek woman's dress would look more awkward than if he were wearing two left shoes. Heidegger himself admits that he is in a "bad situation," but he says it would be worse to try to escape by stealing away on some clandestine path (WIT, 27).

But I must be joking! Did that maid's joke for philosophers really draw Heidegger into this embarrassing situation? It would seem so. But then, is this "deconstruction" of Heidegger (namely, tugging at a thread of his work to unravel his corpus) mere feminist mockery of a philosopher of some importance? No, because for me laughter and mockery is a feminist way of salvaging what I find thought provoking in his work. Heidegger, with a little coaxing, has put himself where I want him: in that place where philosophers might hear the laughter of women. He is up in the air and in the feminine, and it will be my attempt to keep him there, against himself, in the following pages.

As a practitioner of fundamental philosophy, Heidegger is a most serious philosopher. Yet he himself tells the grandest and most fundamental philosophical joke of all: that philosophy *begins* by letting what is most thought provoking remain forgotten! The task of thinking, he says, is to think the unthought, and this is why he returns to the pre-Socratic Greek philosophers and poets to uncover what was left behind in philosophy's beginnings. But he forgets that the pre-Socratic Greeks includes women and thereby does not think through the implications of that Thracian maid's laugh fully enough. More important, he thereby overlooks the work of Sappho, the earliest of poet-thinkers and one who would have brought him to think on Being and sex. Heidegger meditates on the ontological difference (the relationship of beings with Being) but ignores sexual difference. By ignoring sexual difference he remains bound to the body-denying, animal-denying, and elemental-denying tradition of Western metaphysics, despite his groundbreaking efforts to release ontological thinking from that tradition.

I am playfully placing Heidegger in the feminine here against himself in the attempt to prepare for his encounter with this significant Greek of antiquity whose sweet-winged logos does not subordinate erotics and the body to metaphysics. A Greek whose logos might have called Heidegger to think sexuality and Being, to think on the "drawing pull" of Being as inclusive of a sexual sense. I cannot hope to do justice to even a single one of her fragments here, but will only sketch out a meeting place for Heidegger and Sappho in the neighborhood of grace and remembrance. By focusing on Heidegger in the feminine, I am also hoping to help prepare an inviting place, even if in only the most preliminary manner, for Sappho's reception in philosophy.[10] For I am not merely reprimanding Heidegger for forgetting her, but more important, attempting to confront our own philosophical forgetfulness of she whose words are gold for contemporary thought.

In my thinking here I am concurring with Heidegger that the task of philosophy is to think its unthought, but also with Irigaray that the unthought of philosophy centrally involves sexual difference. As Krell puts it (speaking of Irigaray's thoughts on Heidegger), the task of thinking is not "a matter of merely drawing a parallel between ontological and sexual difference" but rather "to think sexuality and being or sexuality and the granting [*Es gibt*, one of Heidegger's later names for Being] in one and the same breath."[11] I am suggesting that the regioning of Aphrodite is one place to attempt this. Aphrodite compels us to think sexual and ontological difference at the same time, for she is the divinity of sexuality. She draws us to think in between the spiritual and the carnal, for she embodies the sexual instincts we share with animals and divinities.

Aphrodite is often neglected by specialists of Greek myth and religion, being categorized as foreign and "oriental." Her cult came to the Aegean from Cyprus, but there are traces of her back to Old European, Indo-European, Semetic, Sumerian, and Egyptian sources. Her name comes from the sea foam. She encourages the dew that permits fertilizing unions. In her more ancient sources, Aphrodite is a bird goddess, associated with the dove, swan, and fecund sparrows. She is also a water goddess, a patron of navigation. Through the ages she became reduced to an insignificant divinity, known best as patron of prostitutes, yet at one time she may have been more important in popular cult than any of the other goddesses.[12]

The key way of understanding Aphrodite in a nonmetaphysical way is through the work of Sappho, who is our earliest and most important authority on Aphrodite. But I am already ahead of myself and do not want to forget that charming Thracian maid whose laughter began this essay.

Who was she? Perhaps she was only a story told at dinner parties for the entertainment of men, although the fact that the rumor lasted for hundreds of years is telling. I did come across evidence of a most famous Thracian slave woman who lived at the time of Thales. Her name was Doricha.[13] She was so renowned for her beauty, charm, and wit that there were stories surrounding her for centuries after her death. They even say a pyramid was built for her, her name being confused with that of an Egyptian queen. Doricha, it turns out, married Sappho's brother, although the marriage didn't last. So maybe the woman who mocked our first philosopher was Sappho's sister-in-law. In any case, we can be sure that when this famous woman's laugh brought philosophy into its essential nature (as Heidegger would have us believe), Sappho was nearby.

Air Is Nearest

Air, that which brings us together and separates us. Which unites us and leaves a space for us between us. In which we love each other but which also belongs to the earth. Which at times we share in a few inspired words.

—Luce Irigaray, *I Love to You*

Now if philosophy "begins" with a servant woman laughing at what the first philosopher forgot and "ends" with this woman's laughter still haunting the very philosopher who tried so hard to remember what philosophers had forgotten, it would seem prudent to give some attention to her advice. Despite his initial dismissal of that maid's advice, Heidegger doggedly pursues it, for in his later writings he insists that we turn to our immediate surroundings and what is nearest at hand in order to understand the ontological significance of a thing. In his later writings he does not dismiss immediacy as he did in that early lecture. The concept of immediacy in fact becomes highly significant, for through it we may encounter the "uncanny" out of which all that is ordinary emerges and is suspended and into which it falls back (Pa, 102). The "uncanny," says Heidegger, "appears in advance in all that is ordinary; shining through it and around it" (Pa, 106) and is a name for Being itself: "What shines into beings, though can never be explained on the basis of beings, nor constructed out of beings, is Being itself" (Pa, 106).

Heidegger takes the concept of "immediacy" (a concept with which women have been traditionally associated) and raises it to the highest significance. In the process he teases the concept out from its associations with dichotomies such as the mind/body and the abstract/concrete and renames "immediacy" "nearness (*Nahe*)." Could the concept of nearness that describes an ontological relation for Heidegger be thought within the regioning of Aphrodite, goddess of the proximity of touch? My attempt to let Heidegger meet Sappho in the final sections of this essay is at the same time an attempt to think the concept of nearness within the region of sexual love. I understand the concept of nearness as an avenue to thinking sexuality and Being in one breath.

For the later Heidegger, more dangerous than our overlooking what is under our feet and falling down wells because of a passion for observing the remote heavens is our own modern constant rushing ahead of what is most near. All distances in time and space are shrinking, and merging into a distanceless uniformity. In such a place and time where everything is equally near and far, indifferent and available for use, nearness as well as remoteness is absent (OWL, 129). This absence of nearness and remoteness is not mere emptiness, he says, but is the concealment or withdrawal of "Being" together with our own "refusal" of nearness (OWL, 120).

Nearness cannot be encountered directly, says Heidegger, but we may reach it by attending to the things that are at hand and around us (PLT, 166). As though he were still reflecting beside that same well where a woman stood laughing at the first philosopher, Heidegger, in his later meditation on the thing, encounters nearness by attending to the inner recesses of a clay jug. The jug's "thingness," says Heidegger, "does not lie in the material of which it consists, but in the void that holds" (PLT, 169).

By attempting to encounter what is near, Heidegger in fact pays tribute here to the air that Irigaray says he forgot. For it is not so much the earth that contributes to the thingliness of the jug, but the seemingly empty air inside the jug. The jug's void holds by receiving and keeping what is poured in. Its essential character lies in this concealed airy space where there is a "sheltering" and "holding."

Now, inside the intimate space of this jug, I feel free to confess what these endless preparations have been hiding. Sappho! Her name trembles me to wordlessness. My fear? That my thinking will bludgeon the beauty of her words. How to prepare a soft enough bed for this almost divine woman's reception? If only my thoughts could receive her words as simply as my breath receives the fragrance of these peonies beside my laptop. How to begin to touch her?

When I turned to her tattered remains for the occurrence of the word "logos," I found it accompanied by the adjective "sweet."[14] *Sweet logos? How to approach words that taste sweet on the tongue?*

Heidegger could not have chosen a more femininely encoded place than inside a jug's dark recesses. By describing that airy inner space as actively sheltering and holding, he overturns the traditional dichotomy of active and passive. These feminine encoded concepts of sheltering and holding are crucial to Heidegger's ontology, not only to what he calls the "self-concealment" of Being but also to the "gathering" of logos. Heidegger's descriptions of the gush of the outpouring in this later essay on the thing are sensual, even somewhat sexual. The very passage where Heidegger remembers air stirs with erotic overtones.[15] Irigaray suggests that oblivion of air is oblivion of the sexual character of Being but she leaves this thought as a question.[16] Might remembering to remember that element that appears so empty for thinking bring remembrance of the sexual character of Being?

Sappho Begins with Words of Air

Sappho! In antiquity, she was so renowned they simply called her "the Poetess," as they called Homer "the Poet." Plato, two hundred years after her death, calls her "the tenth Muse" and Aristotle notes she was honored "though she was a woman."[17] The first line of her first book of poems likely reads:

May the Gods show their favor. With words of air I begin but beneficial.[18]

Irigaray's words at a great distance from Sappho's resonate with hers: "As we move farther away from our condition as living beings, we tend to forget the most indispensable element in life: *air*. The air we breathe, in which we live, speak, appear; the air in which everything 'enters into presence' and can come into being."[19] To think Sappho we are confronted with thinking about the nourishing air in which we dwell, that background support that Irigaray says lets itself be forgotten.

Sappho's words are of air because hers is already a singing logos. Her lyric poems were meant to be committed to memory and sung for oral performance accompanied by the music of the lyre and performed with or without a chorus of her *hetairia* dancing or singing. Sappho gives measure to air with both her breath and the vibrating strings of her lyre.[20] She is a musician and poet, a master of meter and rhythm. She improvised on the Homeric meter, the only significant available literary source at the time, and invented her own poetic meter, which was named after her and imitated by poets for centuries after. She writes in many meters. She pays attention to rhythm and tone, to sounds that alliterate, rhyme, and echo one another, weaving her stanzas together with a delicate phonic texture. Sappho's words sing and vibrate, respectful of breath, the bearer of life. Her breath is sweet, passionate, rhythmic, and measured by a most graceful restraint.

She lived during the transition from an oral culture to a literate one, from an audiotactile way of saying to visual writing. Orality is not only speaking words but includes the tactility of breath. To think with Sappho we must pay attention to this relationship of breath to word.

But to think about breath and word will be difficult because we tend to forget the relationship of air to voice: it is as if "the less we breathe, the nearer we come to correct thinking," says Irigaray.[21] In our tradition we use breath and speech in almost inverse proportions and subordinate breath to speech. "Speech, instead of bearing breath, replaces it."[22] "In the transition from those traditions which respect breath to one subordinate(d) to speech, to the Word, heedless of breath, the manner of speaking has changed from poetic telling, hymns and chants, prayers of praise, and dialogue into pre-written discourses or texts, often resorting to the imperative . . . the very use of words, the circulation of breath in and through language, has therefore changed."[23]

Heidegger recalls this relationship of breath to words when he says, "It is just as much a property of language to sound and ring and vibrate, to hover and to tremble as it is for the spoken words of language to carry a meaning. But our experience of this property is exceedingly clumsy, because the metaphysical-technological explanation gets everywhere in the way, and keeps us from considering the matter properly" (OWL, 98). How to let her words sound and ring and vibrate when we live in a culture that stifles breath?

In antiquity the resonance between words and the breath was well established because spoken words were understood to be carried through the air as though on wings.[24] Both Sappho and Homer call their poems "winged words." Words are winged when they are spoken, and unwinged when they are kept unspoken in the *phrenes*. The *phrenes*, which are located in the chest or midriff, are the organs of breath and mind. They receive and produce words, thoughts and understanding. For the Greeks, breath is consciousness, perception and emotion.[25]

Sappho's sweet words begin with air. Her words come from the *phrenes* and move through the air on wings, but not even the fragments of her words can be heard by us as she would have wanted. We encounter Sappho's words, rigid and flat on the page, divorced from the element in which they rang and vibrated, hovered and trembled. To encounter Sappho we first encounter the absence of air.

Sappho: Beginning Again?

... for the instant I look upon you
I cannot anymore speak one word,
But in silence my tongue is broken ...

—Sappho (31, V)

How to even say one word with Sappho? How to begin to translate ourselves to her way of thinking two thousand six hundred years ago? Sappho's tongue is broken. We can no longer hear her ancient Archaic Greek language with its Aeolian dialect. It is impossible to reach across that great chasm of time and place without assumptions even when we stay close to her fragmented texts. No amount of preparation would seem to be enough for the leap.

And why even attempt the leap back? In this lateral postmodern world, going back to beginning stories is regarded with suspicion of nostalgia, grand narratives, and traditional needs for firm foundations. I will not argue these points here but simply affirm the need to go back to beginning stories in order to honor our unthought ancestral mothers who may help us think through the fundamental traits of the present age and into the times ahead.

Sappho! Who is she? She is a bridge between mythos and logos. She is the last to directly look back to the older Goddess cults and sing with authority, and the first female writer of the Western tradition whose works have survived in any quantity.[26] Sappho is as ephemerous as air. She is what any century wanted her to be. Stories abound about her life, but facts are few. Sappho is a "beginning" poet-philosopher whose story is as variegated, fragmented, and contradictory as one could expect "her" beginning to be.

As one might also expect of a woman who managed to make it into our earliest history's books, sex has been central to the centuries of her debate. Was she a prostitute or priestess? Probably neither. Sappho was part of an early pan-Hellenic women's culture of poetry. She taught young women who would come to her from around the Aegean to be instructed in poetry, music, dance, and singing, and likely knowledge of sex and motherhood, preparing them for marriage. The fact that she wrote of love for women evoked neither praise nor blame from her readers in antiquity, but her works were banned and burned for this reason by the Christians so that by the ninth century she became almost unknown. Whatever her personal sex life (she was likely married and had a daughter, and likely had sexual relationships with her female companions), what is important and undeniable is that in her poetry she sings of love and of women's active desire.

The woman-centered love and desire of which Sappho sings presents an appropriate model for any love relationship. She was the first to use the same words to designate love between women, love between men and women, and love between mother and child. Sapphic passion is based on eroticism and reciprocity. It cultivates grace, gentleness, and beauty. Her description of love, however, is not simply between mortals but also expresses a reciprocal divine love between mortals and immortals since love for Sappho always brings us in contact with Aphrodite. Her poetry offers a premetaphysical understanding of the ontological difference. In some sense, All is Love for Sappho, where Love is not simply intersubjective human love, but is already in some way inclusive of All, or "Being" (a concept that was nonexistent in her day). If we could think through Sapphic love, it might bring us closer to the postmetaphysical understanding of the ontological difference that Heidegger articulated through his descriptions of the vibratory drawing pull and the active reciprocity involved in this difference. Heidegger's work offers a preparatory way for approaching the thought of Being and Love, even though wedding Sapphic-Aphroditic thoughts with Heidegger's might end up displacing his thought altogether.[27]

What is love for Sappho? Sapphic desire and love offers an alternative to Western desire and love that, mainly through Plato and Freud, has been based on Eros, Aphrodite's son.[28] Our culture has masculinized the divine figure of love. In the majority of early Greek myths, Eros is a young god, submissive to his mother's power. That the divinity's son takes over his mother's sphere of activity is a typical story in the development of our myths. Eros was unimportant in Homer but became prominent by Plato's time as the patron of male homosexuality.[29] The philosophers of classical Greece honored principally Apollo and Eros, and not Aphrodite, whose cult was associated with women and slaves. They considered love between males philosophically superior to heterosexual love and love between women not worth mentioning. As the myth of Eros takes precedence over that of Aphrodite and love is dissociated from its corporeal aspect, a woman's body is no longer regarded as a pathway to the sacred but rather as an obstacle to it. Much later, Freud takes the myth of the primordial Eros from Hesiod's very brief description to develop his model of the libido when there were many other more prominent myths of Aphrodite that he could have chosen.

Both Aphrodite and Dionysus accord a central position to the spontaneity of the body and sexuality and offer the power of transmuting physical experience to divine ecstacy. But philosophers, such as Nietzsche, who think on the body and sexuality ignore Aphrodite, goddess of rapture, and turn to Dionysius, whose erotic desire is associated with Eros. Dionysus's sexual approach is rough and impetuous, and in this he is akin to the satyr who hustles the nymph or to the frenzied women of the Bacchanals who throw themselves upon their prey.[30]

Aphrodite's sexual approach, by contrast, pays more attention to the drawing pull and the preparation of the way to the joining. She creates the fragrant space in which erotic desire can be fulfilled. She teaches the refinements of delay, the artistic subtleties of delightful adornment and the language of courtship. She is goddess of the art of lovemaking, including various positions, the use of perfumed oils and cosmetics, the lore of aphrodisiac drinks and foods, singing and dancing, and all the wiles and charms of amorous relations. Her arts are ephemeral rather than lasting and need constant renewal. In antiquity, under the guidance of Aphrodite, these skills, attitudes, and moral and aesthetic values were passed down through mother to daughter, and transmitted between women.

Why do feminist philosophers turn to Plato speaking Diotima's words on Eros for the words of a woman on love and desire, and not turn directly to Sappho's Aphrodisian love? Sappho's logos is poetic, but this does not mean that her word is not relevant to philosophy. Heidegger readily confirms that poetry and thinking have a close relationship (that was already evident to the Greeks). Thinking and poetry are "neighbors," he says. Thinking is "primordial poetry," and "all poetizing is in its ground a thinking" (EGT, 19).[31]

But even though Heidegger turns to Greek poetry and German lyric poetry for philosophical hints of a way out of metaphysics, he ignores Sappho, who was one of the most famous and accomplished poets in the art of Aeolian lyric poetry that for a time was in the foreground of Greek literature. He mentions Sappho only to forget her: "Homer, Sappho, Pindar, Sophocles are they literature? No! . . . if by literature we mean what has been literally written down and copied with the intent that it be available to a reading public" (WT, 134).

Heidegger will turn to Homer, Pindar, and Sophocles, but not Sappho. He turns to Homer, who celebrates valor and remembers victories on the battlefield; not to Sappho, who celebrates lovers and remembers pleasures on soft beds. He turns to Pindar, who looks west to Attica; not to Sappho, who looks east to Lydia and Sardis.[32] Her poetry reflects the undeniable refreshing influence of Asia Minor and offers an alternative to a certain Eurocentric classical tradition.[33]

Heidegger also turns to Sophocles of classical Greece. Much of our information on the Greeks focuses on fifth-century Athens, a time and place where a woman poet such as Sappho would have been unthinkable. A hundred years earlier on the island of Lesbos, women had an unusual degree of freedom, mixing freely with male society.[34] Sappho disrupts the typical view of our ancestors as the classical pedimental Attic Greeks dwelling in an austere, balanced, and exclusively masculine domain.[35]

Grace: A Hint

O immortal Aphrodite of the many-colored throne,
child of Zeus, weaver of wiles, I beseech you,
do not overwhelm me in my heart with anguish and pain,
O Mistress,
But come hither, if ever at another time
hearing my cries from afar you heeded them,

—Sappho 1.1–6, V.

The only goddess who made it into the history of Western philosophy is the goddess of truth who appears in Parmenides' work as guide. Could Aphrodite—this laughing, contradictory, excessively "feminine" goddess of sex, love, grace, and beauty—ever guide a philosopher's thinking?

As goddess of love and procreation, she is associated with the sweetness, fragrance, and bright colors of fruits and flowers, particularly apples and roses. She is known as kind and tender, fond of children and softness, sheltering all that flourishes and flowers. Aphrodite conjoins the carnal and divine, nature and culture.[36] Her star hugs the horizon between earth and sky. The rose color that marks the moment of day-joining-night belongs to her, as does the dark rose of tender fleshy lips and inner lips. She is a near and mobile divinity, operating and influencing not in a direct material sense, but through the *thumos*, the mind-heart, causing psychophysical states of desire and longing. Already under your skin, she comes even nearer than the things around us.

Aphrodite is present in Heidegger's *What Is Called Thinking?* (a work that he considered in his last public interview the most important and least read) when he speaks of what is most thought provoking:

> What is thought-provoking, so understood, need in no way be what causes us worry or even perturb us. Joyful things, too, and beautiful and mysterious and gracious things gives us food for thought. These things may even be more thought-provoking than all the rest which we otherwise, and usually without much thought, call "thought-provoking." These things will give us food for thought, if only we do not reject the gift by regarding everything that is joyful, beautiful, and gracious as the kind of thing that should be left to feeling and experience and kept out of the winds of thought. (WT, 31)

Heidegger fully leaps into the fragrant neighborhood of Aphrodite when, in his search for the unthought of philosophy, he leaps outside the realm of both science and philosophy and finds himself standing in a meadow "face to face" with a blossoming tree in all its "radiance and fragrance" (WT, 41).

"Let us stop here for a moment," he says, "as we would to catch our breath before and after a leap" (WT, 41). Heidegger is thinking flowers when he notes that the word "blossoming" sounds and speaks like the word "being." As a participle "blossoming" can be used in a verbal sense to mean "the act of blossoming" and it can also mean "the given something that is blossoming—the rosebush or apple tree" (WT, 221). He directs us to think the blossoming tree as the unthought of philosophy: "Judged scientifically, of course, it remains the most inconsequential thing on earth that each of us has at some time stood facing a tree in bloom" (WT, 42). However, "[t]he thing that matters first and foremost, and finally," he says, "is not to drop the tree in bloom, but for once let it stand where it stands" because "to this day, thought has never let the tree stand where it stands" (WT, 44). To think the rosebush or apple tree in bloom would certainly bring us to think Aphrodite.

Heidegger also thinks in the neighbourhood of Aphrodite when he attempts to understand grace and the gracious (*Iki* in Japanese) in his "A Dialogue on Language" as a bridge linking Eastern thought on the nature of art and language to the unthought of Western metaphysics. Grace, in this East-West dialogue, is central to Heidegger's attempt to think art beyond aesthetics, and to think language and presence beyond metaphysics. The interlocutors find their common ground in their thinking on grace through the ancient Greek word for grace, *charis*, which they associate with poetry. Sappho would confirm this connection between grace and poetry, but she would emphasize the strong erotic connotations of *charis*, for the Graces attend Aphrodite, goddess of sexuality, and grant erotic attractiveness.

"[All] presence [has] its source in grace," says the Inquirer in Heidegger's dialogue. Grace then would seem to be an important hint. Grace, for Heidegger, is a "delight" that "ensnares us and carries us away" (OWL, 44). Sappho might well agree, but she would have sexualized Heidegger's understanding of the "ensnaring delight."

For Sappho, the sexed body is the site of grace. The sensual connotations of grace have a deep history, since the cognates of *charis* derive from a common Indo-European root, *gher*, meaning "pleasure." In Hesiod, the Graces (Radiance, Joy, and Bloom) are born with *eros* dripping from their eyes.[37] The frequent use of *charis* in Sappho's poetry confirms the reciprocal nature of presencing that Heidegger insists upon, for she often uses this word to put into relief a reciprocal sensual flow between giver and receiver of delight.[38] Grace for Sappho is the gift of Aphrodite. It is a gift of gracious manner before *aesthesis*. Grace is a gesture as soft and delightful as the shifting drapery of Gongula's dress that Sappho says sets Abanthis's heart aflutter (22, V).

Grace for Heidegger is "a hint that beckons on and beckons to and fro" (OWL, 44), but Sappho could have offered him her own thought on the nature of grace:

> O Dika, put lovely garlands on your tresses,
> binding together shoots of dill in your tender hands,
> For the blessed Graces favor more the well-flowered,
> but turn away the ungarlanded.
>
> Fragment 81 (V)

How to approach such soft tender hints that "need the widest sphere in which to swing" (OWL, 27)? How to garland thinking with flowers so that the Graces do not turn thinkers away? In order not to reject Aphrodite's gift of grace but stay in the fragrant draft of her beauty, it would seem that we must imbue our way with some of the gentleness and grace of our guide. Our thinking would need the "vigorous fragrance" of which Nietzsche speaks, and that Heidegger recalls but immediately laments: "How many of us today still have the senses for that fragrance?" (OWL, 70).[39] How to regain a lost sense? How to think fragrant air?

Grace may be a way for thinking sexuality and Being in one breath, but hints are "enigmatic" (OWL, 26). "They beckon to us," says Heidegger. "They beckon away. They beckon us toward that from which they unexpectedly bear themselves toward us" (OWL, 26).

Heidegger, the Obscure. This pathway of thought is vanishing into thin but fragrant air. I feel there is something here to be thought but I can't quite reach it. Hints are so annoying, for they tempt the thinker onward and then seem to dematerialize. Hints can also be misinterpreted. Even before this: how to recognize when a hint is a hint and not merely a joke?

The Japanese in Heidegger's dialogue speaks of adopting a comportment of "shy reverence" in the face of hints (OWL, 28). In Sappho's day, the word for this gesture would be *aidos* (shamefastness). Heidegger has interest in this word because of the pull back inherent in it (EGT, 107; PA 74–76). For Heidegger, *aidos* is "awe." More than a disposition, *aidos* is the "disposing that determines the relation of Being to man" (Pa, 75). Might *aidos* help us think toward Aphrodite? For Sappho and the love poetry of her day, *aidos* is "a sort of voltage of decorum" between two approaching the other for the crisis of contact, "an instinctive and mutual sensitivity to the boundary between them."[40] In Archaic Greek love poetry, *aidos* is said to reside upon the sensitive eyelids. This "is a way of saying that *aidos* exploits the power of the glance by withholding it, and also that one must watch one's feet to avoid the misstep called *hybris*."[41]

Grace and *aidos* may be hints for a way of thinking Aphrodite. The gesture of *aidos* might at least help me as I finally bring Heidegger to meet Sappho in the following two sections. The respectful look down will at least keep me mindful of that other graceful (*chariessa*—as Plato describes her) woman's hint for philosophers to watch our step.

Forgetting (Almost)

just like a sweet-apple (*glukumalon*) that ripens on the uppermost bough,
on the top of the topmost;
but the apple-gatherers (*malodropees*) have forgotton it (*lelathonto*),
or rather, they haven't altogether forgotten it (*eklelathonto'*),
but they could not reach it.

—Sappho (105a, V)

One of Heidegger's most important contributions to philosophy is his reinterpretation of truth according to the Greek word for truth, *aletheia*, which he contrasts with the traditional understanding of truth as correctness. *A-letheia* derives from the Greek word *lanthanein*, which means to remain concealed or forgotten. *Lanthanein* is indicative of *aletheia*'s original and most telling meaning. It is the "counterword" to *aletheia*, but not in the sense of a mere opposite of unconcealment or truth, for its meaning is not "falsehood," just as truth's is not "correctness" (Pa, 22). Heidegger attempts to think through the meaning of *lanthanein* in its various modes in order to gain insight into the present coming to pass of concealment and forgetfulness. To explore the meaning of *lanthanein* he often turns to the poets of Archaic Greece. If Heidegger had turned to Sappho, for the occurrence of *lanthanein*, he would have discovered the preceding fragment.

Perhaps Heidegger and Sappho can meet in the airy space of this fragmented metaphor. The poem is incomplete as will be this tentative meeting. Someone or something is being compared to a sweet apple out of reach. The fragment enacts the Sapphic reach for what is most worthy of desire and appears to describe Heidegger's own reach for the highest thought. Being for Heidegger is out of reach of thinkers as this apple is out of reach of gatherers.⁴² The reddening pulpy fruit (melon) is ripening, is even overripe, sweetening in the sun, biding its time, ready to fall, but our reach falls short. If Being in metaphysics is like an apple, it is because, as Parmenides' first epithets say, it is full, well rounded, and stable. But the primary attribute of Sappho's apple is its sweetness. Could Being (the granting) be sweet? For Heidegger, it remains the highest of the high, almost forgotten, yet not quite, for it still entices this thinker. Could the drawing pull of what is most thought-worthy consist of its barely noticed and still unthought shine and beauty, and therewith its promise of unsurpassed delightful sweetness? Heidegger warns us that thinking on truth, beauty, and grace may be dangerous: "What is most thought-provoking—especially when it is man's highest concern may well be also what is most dangerous. Or do we imagine that a man could even in small ways encounter the essence of truth, the essence of beauty, the essence of grace—without danger?" (WT, 31).[43]

The apple in this poem is not the sinful apple of knowledge that Eve offered to Adam, casting them both out of paradise, but rather belongs to Aphrodite. Aphrodite is divine existence made flesh, but in delight, not sorrow. As divine existence made incarnate, she is almost the opposite of Eve, who brings forth in agony.[44] The reach for the sweet apple is nonetheless not without risks. This fragment of Sappho's enacts the aporia of erotic desire.[45] The reach takes place in an erotic space where there is no final consummation. "The word *epi* (motion to, toward, for, in quest of, reaching after) thoroughly shapes the poem, and the action in the present indicative verbs attain, with the last word, infinite disappointment."[46] One yearns to dissolve the boundary between self and other, hand and apple, tongue and taste, but realizes in the final moment that one never can. Desire for Sappho is this paradoxical touch of difference and presents a bittersweet dilemma for the body and senses. The inevitable pain of separation is latent in the pleasure of union. The beautiful and endless reach of desire is a longing to be as one love forever with another, but this reach can never be brought to ultimate closure, for then two would be one.

Heidegger and Sappho are thinkers of sameness in difference and work at the intersection of gathering and differing. As Sappho brings the crisis of contact between lovers to poetic word, so Heidegger brings the crisis of contact that occurs in the ontological difference to philosophical word. These differings are not separate, for our emotional-sexual being is already involved in every encounter. I think that Sappho would concur with Heidegger that "pain is the joining agent in the rending that divides and gathers," that "pain is the dif-ference itself" (PLT, 204), and that "the greatest joy withdraws, halts in its withdrawal and holds itself in reserve" (OWL, 66). But unlike Heidegger, Sappho emphasizes the sweetness of the ache. She says love is "sweetbitter (*glukopikron*)" (130, V). For Sappho, as we shall see, the tonality of differing and of remembering is ultimately sweet.

Sappho's metaphor of the reach intimately speaks to Heidegger because, as a practitioner of the craft of thinking, he is especially attentive to the "way" in which thinking reaches for, and attempts to touch, the highest thought.[47] Way, for Heidegger, "means melody, the ring and tone" "from which and to which what is said is attuned" (WT, 37). Thinking for him is a "way-making" movement that is already "underway" despite our still not-thinking (WT, 45–46). The "way" is that "by which we reach" (OWL, 91). The way "lets us reach what reaches out for us by touching us, by being our concern" (OWL, 91).

Thinking is a "handicraft" that he describes by way of the reach of the hand (WT, 16–17).[48] For Heidegger, the grasp of the thinker is not a centralized focal grabbing in the sense of grasping a concept (*Begriff*) (WT, 211). Nor is thinking an amassing of information. The reach of the thinker is like that of the gatherer of fruits in Sappho's poem. Gatherers are those who bring in the harvest with sheltering care. The harvest gatherer does not amass and store in the manner of challenging-out because gatherers in their approach have a concern that shelters (EGT, 61–62). Without this caring gathering, says Heidegger, we could not read a single word, for gathering (*lesen*) is already included in the *legein* (saying) of logos (WT, 208).[49]

But what is most thought-worthy is out of the reach of thinking.[50] Heidegger's thinking, like Sapphic desire, is a reaching that refrains from closure. It reaches out for the highest apple to where philosophers before him did not reach, but it never arrives. He never leaps clearly out of metaphysics or gives a final master word for Being. Readers on Heidegger thinking pathway will ultimately find themselves frustrated when they encounter that point where he follows Being into its withdrawal, where his thinking on concealment seems to fold into itself and disappear.

Both Sappho and Heidegger are thinkers on nearness, yet their thought could be characterized by the Greek word *pothos*, a yearning for something absent, elsewhere, too high to reach. For Sappho what is nearest and most thought-worthy is love. For Heidegger what is nearest is

Being itself. But Sappho thinks love as "Being," for love achieved is an initiation into Aphrodite's sphere, bringing us in momentary contact with a divine principle.[51]

What is near for both Sappho and Heidegger does not have to do with proximity. They reach for what is uppermost, for what is most worthy, but not in order to bring it to the closest proximity to what is present and thereby gain complete accessibility. For both Sappho and Heidegger, yearning puts distance and unattainability into relief.

It has been well noted that Sappho often re-creates the time of love at a distance. We are so captured and enraptured by her poetic rendering of immediate intimacy that we are often at first unaware that she has distanced lover from beloved by way of remembered desire.[52] In Fragment 16 (V), love in recollection is the most beautiful thing for Sappho because such love is not possessive and domineering. Remembered love is not caught up in the immediate gratification of desire. Memory is a reminder of what we don't have and also of what we cannot control or measure. For example, in contrast to the male valuation of "the most beautiful thing" of her day (Lydian chariots, full-armed infantry, a fleet of ships), Sappho says the most beautiful thing is "what one loves" (16.4, V). She then *recalls* the dancing step and glancing eye of her beloved Anactoria, those aspects of the young woman that were beyond possession even when she was near. For Sappho, erotic love is a divine gift that cannot be possessed, quantified, or measured. It resides neither in the subjective eye of the beholder nor the material beloved's flesh, but rather within the space of desire enacted through the lover's memory.

But the erotic experience, which is at the same time contact with the divinity of beauty and love, occurs in the fleeting perishable moment. Love is paradoxically fleeting and enduring, divine and destructible; but through memory, beauty, love, and desire endure and are sheltered in their absence. Remembering, for Sappho, is a way of sheltering the gifts of Aphrodite. For Sappho, love seems to be even nearer when it has to be remembered and brought to poetic word.

Heidegger also puts distance into relief in his search for what is nearest (OWL, 102). The current danger, as he sees it, is that the intimate connection between all things is being thoroughly converted into a calculable uniformity that obliterates nearness (*das Nahe*) and farness (*das Ferne*). He turns to the thing and attempts to let it be as thing rather than as object, product, or standing-reserve. "Thinging," he says, "is the nearing of the world" (PLT, 181). He emphasizes, however, that in bringing the thing near, remoteness (*das Ferne*) is not canceled out, but rather "preserved" (*wahrt*). Preserving remoteness brings the most intimate nearness: "Bringing near in this way, nearness conceals its own self and remains, in its own way, nearest of all" (PLT, 178).

Like the apple in this poem, the location of that to which we are drawn in Sappho and Heidegger is remote and sometimes doubly remote. Sappho's apple is on the outermost edge of the top of the topmost branch. Each poetic line launches an initial impression that we are locating the apple, but this is at once modified, and then launched again.[53] One gets the sense of a gradually imposed restraint and withdrawal of that to which we are drawn. So too there is a certain hesitation and shift of distance as Heidegger follows Being in its withdrawal. It occurs, for example, when we realize that Heidegger is concerned not so much with concealment as with the concealment *of* concealment. For Heidegger, such doubling of distance reminds us that forgetting is not only the result our own poor attention and distraction, but proceeds from Being, which withdraws itself and hides (Pa, 28). Heidegger and Sappho reach out and long for that highest provoking something that has been forgotten, but no, not quite forgotten. Forgetting that we have forgotten would no longer be forgetting (*lanthanein*), but "oblivion," says Heidegger. Oblivion is concealment where the concealment is itself concealed (Pa, 71). Yearning keeps alive our forgetting. To forget that we have even forgotten would be oblivion of desire, collapse of the drawing pull. The act of remembering for both Heidegger and Sappho it would seem keeps open a vibrating space for that which is most worthy.

Remembering (Again)

I say that even later someone will remember us.

—Sappho (147, V)

As Sappho's poetic word teaches love as remembrance, so Heidegger teaches thought as remembrance. These two can meet at the outermost ends of the philosophical tradition as patrons of Mnemosyne (Memory), mother of the Muses. Sappho was inspired by the Muses and honored as a Muse herself. She describes her house as a place where the "Muses are served" (150, V). The Muses were so important in Sappho's day because she lived in a predominately oral society where poetry, song, and dance, often in ritual form, were the basic media for transmitting historical knowledge and cultural values.

For Heidegger, remembering is a way of coming near. The first step toward the "vigilance" that can preserve nearness and remoteness, he says, is "to step back from the thinking that merely represents—that is, explains—to the thinking that responds and recalls" (PLT, 181). But remembering is "something else than merely the psychologically demonstrable ability to retain a mental representation, an idea, of something which is past" (WT, 11). "Memory is the gathering and convergence of thought upon what everywhere demands to be thought about first of all" (WT, 11). The key movements of memory for Heidegger are "[h]olding, embracing, gathering, and bestowing or gift-giving."[54] He turns to Mnemosyne, the mother of the Muses and the creative source and ground of poetry.[55] Poetry is crucial for the later Heidegger. *Poiesis*, for him is "our basic capacity for human dwelling" (PLT, 228) that is almost forgotten. He counterpoises the forgotten bringing-forth of *poiesis* to that of the modern challenging-out of *Gestell* (the essencing of technology).

I think that Sappho would concur with Heidegger that "poetry is what really lets us dwell" (PLT, 215) and that remembering is a thinking back that safely keeps and shelters what is most worthy, but she will have none of the mourning that tinges Heideggerean remembering and longing.[56] In what may have been her last note, addressed from her deathbed to her daughter, Cleis, Sappho says: "For it is not right (*themis*) for there to be lamentation in the house of those who serve the Muses (*en moisopolon [domoi]*). That would not be suitable for us" (150, V). The Muses are often depicted in the art of antiquity with lyre in hand. Their immortal music and poetry brings rest and relief from pain. They grant sweet voice and inspiration. The dwelling that invites their gift of healing air cannot be in sorrow. It would not be in keeping with Themis.[57]

Sappho does not remember with the sentiment of nostalgia, but with a courageous joy. In one poem she says to her beloved girlfriend, who is being forced to leave her, "Go rejoicing as you remember" (94.7, V).[58] The pain of separation was an inevitable aspect of Sappho's circle, for the young women who were sent to her by their families from around the Aegean would eventually have to leave the freedom and intimacy they experienced with their female companions on Lesbos.[59] The time would come when they would leave that island, enter marriage, and assume their social position in a society that subordinated and segregated women. Sappho offers her companions the memory of an almost mythical time of music, passion, and beauty. In another poem, she reminds her departing girlfriend of the beautiful erotic ritual that she and their companions had shared over and over again:

> Close by my side you put around yourself
> [many wreaths] of violets and roses and saffron . . .
> And many woven garlands made from flowers . . .
> around your neck,
> And . . . with costly royal myrrh . . .
> you anointed . . . ,
> And on a soft bed
> . . . tender . . .
> you satisfied your desire. . . .
> Nor was there any . . .
> nor any holy . . .
> from which we were away,
> . . . nor grove . . .
>
> (94.13–23, V)

Sappho's words, fragmented by the winds of history, completely break off into silence here. But the words "temple" and "grove" that occur in the badly damaged two last stanzas of this poem suggest that the pleasure consummated on soft beds continued into an experience that was enjoyed by a circle of celebrants.[60] The time of pleasure is removed from personal narrative. The "you" evoked in the poem is only a presence called up by the gestures—the touch of petals, the odor of perfume, and the sheen of soft skin. The remembering of gestures is not an attempt to regain a lost time of fusion or wholeness when the beloved was a part of Sappho's circle, for the past that Sappho wants her companions to remember is not a lost original. Ritualized song and dance connects the community of girls and women to an even deeper past of cultural experience. Singing the song of love gathers and holds a knowledge of female ancestries that bind them through transitions. There is to be no sadness in this gathering where Sappho "sings beautifully to please her companions" (160, V). The beloved girlfriend was brought into a rite that is never rendered futile by one particular completion. The remembered ritual enables their intimacy to be rekindled and repeated, though not in the sense of duplication, since it will be different in every enactment. There is no mourning in Sapphic remembering, because the nature of love is such that it can be renewed and come again in ritual. The incantatory quality of Sappho's vibratory poetic word and music can work a connective magic among participants that will evoke love again. With the appropriate respect and preparation, Aphrodite could come again and heal the suffering caused by her absence:

> you, O Blessed Lady,
> with a smile on your immortal face,
> asked what I had suffered again (*deute*)
> and why I was calling again (*deute*)
> And what I was most wanting to happen for me
> in my frenzied heart: "Whom again (*deute*)
> shall I persuade to come back into friendship (*philotata*) with you?
> Who, O Sappho, does you injustice (*adikesi*)?
>
> ("Hymn to Aphrodite" l.V.13–21)

I find it uncanny that these words directly from Aphrodite to Sappho were given at about the same time as Anaximander spoke of the injustice (*adikia*) of time in the oldest extant fragment of philosophy. Heidegger interprets Anaximander's fragment to be speaking of time's "stiffening."[61] While Anaximander's *adikia* of time is the beginning of time's stiffening for Heidegger, Nietzsche's eternal recurrence is the setting in of rigor mortis. What for Neitzsche is the final liberation from metaphysic's ill will against time marks, for Heidegger, a final expression of the temporality of the Being of metaphysics. Heidegger searches for an understanding of time beyond metaphysics (to which he understood Niezsche as still bound).

Could Aphrodite guide us here? Love and time?[62] I cannot give this topic or the words of the Goddess that we hear directly through Sappho any justice here, but will only mark a small word, *deute*, repeated above in Sappho's "Hymn to Aphrodite."

This adverb, *deute*, meaning "again" or "now," is a crasis, or mingling of two words that have been contracted into one. *Deute* combines the particle *de* with the adverb *aute*. The particle *de* signifies vividly that something is actually taking place at the moment, whereas the adverb *aute* means "again, once again, or over again." "Each of the two words that make up *deute* has a different vantage point on time."[63] Their intersection creates a paradox. "*De* places you in time and emphasizes that placement: now. *Aute* intercepts now and binds it into a history of 'thens.'" It peers past the present moment to a pattern of repeated actions stretching behind it. *Deute* is a word "on which the eyes open wide in sudden perception, then narrow in understanding."[64] Love—here it goes again! *Deute* suggests a timing, a rhythmic stroke, that is a throwing open rather than a stiffening of time, and hints at a premetaphysical understanding of "again" that is not the "again" of eternal recurrence.

"Now" is the moment when change erupts, when desire begins, when one is completely invested in a moment that is open to risk. Now is the instant of desire when the world is enhanced in its beauty, time is fully present, and you feel really alive as the gods are. Now is love for the first time. But the remarkable feelings and gestures of love have been experienced innumerable times before. The present moment of love is intersected by echoes from the past. Sappho lets "now" include "then" without ceasing to be "now." Her poetic words calls desire forth "here" from the past to "now" while leaving it "there." It does not wrest the past away from the remoteness in which it is kept. She brings the absent to presence without collapsing the difference.

Sapphic remembering is a way of temporal care, a way of gathering time without revenge or mourning. When we lose heart, time stiffens. Remembering for Sappho is a fluid movement of sweet pleasure. Intimacy again. Sapphic remembering eroticizes time, shelters and holds love, as in the way a jug holds the space inside open for liquid.

Air again? Sapphic remembering? Fantasy and emptiness! For how could we ever remember as Sappho remembers? The ground is slipping under my feet. I hear a charming laugh. My thought yearns to honor her, yet it reaches for her sweet words like "a small and graceless child," and those words I manage to touch are crushed like hyacinths in the mountains that the shepherd men trample with their feet.[65] I remain longing to remember Sappho!

> Greetings wherever you are, lady, greetings as to a god:
> for your songs, your immortal daughters, are with us still
>
> (Dioscorides, *Greek Anthology* 7.407)[66]

Notes

1. Jacques Derrida, *Truth in Painting*, trans. Geoff Bennington and Ian McLeod (Chicago: University of Chicago Press, 1987), 307.

2. The most significant mentioning is the peasant woman in "The Origin of the Work of Art" to whom the shoes in Van Gogh's painting may belong. As Derrida points out, these shoes in Heidegger's own text only belong to a woman when the shoes are considered "outside" the painting (*The Truth in Painting*, 305–7). When Heidegger discusses the shoes inside the painting as an exemplary product (in other words, an equipmental thing), he neutralizes the shoes. They are simply *"ein Paar Bauernschuhe"*—a pair of peasant shoes. It is only when he looks for the shoes in their actual use that Heidegger attaches sex to the shoes. Just as the painting by Van Gogh is brought in to "facilitate the visual realization" of the shoes (Heidegger, PLT, 33), so a woman is brought in to facilitate the visual realization of the shoes in movement. She models the shoes for Heidegger as a worker in the fields. When Heidegger returns to the painting itself, the peasant woman disappears as easily and fortuitously as she had appeared.

3. Her laughter turns philosophy to use by "handling" it, for as Heidegger points out, the Greek *chre* (necessity) is from *he cheir*, meaning "the hand" (WT, 186). This handling of philosophy by her laughter is not using it up but turning it according to its nature, thereby letting philosophy's nature become manifest through the handling (WT, 195).

4. For example, Thales' response to those who mocked him for doing philosophy "with which one can do nothing" was not to philosophically defend philosophy as Heidegger does, but to immediately go out and use his knowledge of the heavens to make a small fortune. Even scholars are puzzled why Thales is the brunt of the slave woman's laughter, since it would have had more point if it applied to someone not "so notoriously practical in his interest as Thales" (G. S. Kirk, J. E. Raven, and M. Schofield, *The Presocratic Philosophers*, 2d ed. [Cambridge: Cambridge University Press, 1987], 81).

5. Thales is the most often first mentioned in antiquity on their list of the great Seven Sages. The Sages were known by their "sayings." "Thales used to say that he thanked Fortune for three things in particular: that he was born a human and not an animal, a Greek and not a foreigner, a man and not a woman" (Arthur Weigall, *Sappho of Lesbos* [New York: Frederick A. Stokes, 1932], 256). Thales was friends with Solon, another of the Seven Sages, whose restrictive laws greatly subjugated women. Upon hearing Sappho's poetry recited at a dinner party, Solon was so enthralled that he said he wanted to "learn it and die" (Weigall, *Sappho of Lesbos*, 255–61).

6. For example, Aphrodite patronizes sex both inside and outside of marriage. Aphrodite is a "liminal" or intersititial divinity, acting between boundaries. *Liminel* is from the Latin *limen*, "threshold." This forms the basis of Paul Friedrich's thesis on Aphrodite, which he argues convincingly through a historical and structural study in *The Meaning of Aphrodite* (Chicago: University of Chicago Press, 1978). In cult worship she was often associated with Hermes, the winged messenger god of communication and interpretation, from whence we get our word *hermeneutics*, and from whose association we get the word *hermaphrodite*.

7. Sappho calls Aphrodite "weaver of wiles" (*doloploke*) and as having a "many-colored throne" (*poikilothron*). *Poikilia* (variegated, intricate, subtle) suggests the shimmering and sparking of a rainbow and *throna* may suggest the herbs Aphrodite uses as drugs or magic charms (Jane McIntosh Synder, *Lesbian Desire in the Lyrics of Sappho* [New York: Columbia University Press, 1997], 10 and 91–95).

8. Zarathustra, Nietzsche's creation based on the Persian prophet Zoroaster, who happens to be a contemporary of Thales, is also plagued by a woman's laughter. He hears the laughter of a woman when he is in his stillest hour. It surrounds him, tearing at his entrails, slitting open his heart, and leaving him with a double stillness. See *Thus Spoke Zarathustra: A Book for All and None*, trans. Walter Kaufmann (New York: Penguin Books, 1978), 147.

192   Poetics and the Body

9. "This air that we never think of has been borrowed from a birth, a growth, a *phusis* and a *phuein* that the philosopher forgets" (Luce Irigaray, *An Ethics of Sexual Difference* [Ithaca: Cornell University Press, 1993], 127).

10. There has been excellent recent feminist literary and classical scholarship on Sappho. See especially Anne Carson, *Eros the Bittersweet* (Princeton: Princeton University Press, 1986); Page duBois, *Sappho Is Burning* (Chicago: University of Chicago Press, 1995); Ellen Greene, ed., *Reading Sappho: Contemporary Approaches* (Berkeley and Los Angeles: University of California Press, 1996); Ellen Greene, ed., *Re-Reading Sappho: Reception and Transmission* (Berkeley and Los Angeles: University of California Press, 1996); and Snyder, *Lesbian Desire*. Both Carson and duBois look at her work from a more philosophical angle.

11. David Farrell Krell, *Daimon Life: Heidegger and Life-Philosophy* (Bloomington: Indiana University Press, 1992), 308.

12. Friedrich, *The Meaning of Aphrodite*, 2. The preceding description of Aphrodite has been gathered from his extensive analysis.

13. Doricha had the same owner as a fellow slave, Aesop, author of the *Fables*. Sappho's brother spent a fortune paying for her freedom and married her, but shortly after she left him and resumed her career as a courtesan and in so doing accumulated vast wealth. See Weigall, *Sappho of Lesbos*, 244–47.

14. The adjective *dulogoi* is from Fragment 73 (V). Her poetic word had such a reputation for being sweet and beautiful that there was a debate in antiquity over which of her words is the most beautiful. One answer was her word "honey-voiced," (*melisophon*) (185, V).

15. As Derrida says, "Of sex, one can readily remark, yes, Heidegger speaks as little as possible, perhaps he has never spoken of it" (Jacques Derrida, "Geschlecht: Sexual Difference, Ontological Difference," in *A Derrida Reader Between the Blinds*, ed. Peggy Kamuf [New York: Columbia University Press, 1991], 380). Heidegger does in fact come close to thinking on the sexed body in his discussions with Fink on Heraclitus. Heidegger admits that bodily understanding is something that metaphysics has not touched upon and that we need to turn to the body by way of Nietzsche. Fink even brings up the importance of Eros for understanding the body, but Heidegger doesn't take him up on the issue (HS, 145).

16. Luce Irigaray, *L'oubli de l'air chez Martin Heidegger* (Paris: Éditions de Minuit, 1983), 94. She leaves this thought as a question.

17. See Miller and Robinson, *Songs of Sappho*, 69, and 330–31.

18. *Theoi, aerion epeon archomai all' onaton* (Sappho [Fragment 1AE]). These words may have been the first lines of her first book of poems. They are found on a red-figure vase of about 430 B.C. in Athens. Sappho, with her name inscribed, is depicted seated, reading from a scroll to three women. One of the women holds a wreath over Sappho, another a lyre. The title on the scroll is "Winged Words." See Marion Mills Miller and David M. Robinson, *The Songs of Sappho* (Lexington, Ky.: Maxwelton, 1925), 43–44, 178, and 220, whose translation I use here. This fragment is 1A in the Loeb Classical Library edition John Maxwell Edmonds, *Lyra Graeca* 1 (New York: G. P. Putnam's Sons, 1922). Hereafter I will cite Sappho in the main text using the Greek text and numbering from Eva-Maria Voigt, *Sappho et Alcaeus: Fragmenta* (Amsterdam: Athenaeum-Polak and Van Gennep, 1971) and translations from Snyder, *Lesbian Desire*, unless otherwise indicated.

19. Irigaray, *An Ethics of Sexual Difference*, 127.

20. Sappho is said to have invented a modification of the lyre called the *pekstis*. The Lesbians made the lyre and lyric poetry peculiarly their own. See Miller and Robinson, *The Songs of Sappho*, 74–75. Coins of Eresus and Mytilene with her image engraved in relief on one side have the lyre depicted on the reverse.

21. Irigaray, *I Love to You: Sketch for a Felicity Within History*, trans. Alison Martin (New York: Routledge, 1996), 121.

22. Irigaray, *I Love to You*, 122–23.

Sappho   193

23. Irigaray, *I Love to You*, 122.

24. Derrida ignores this when, in contrast to Heidegger and Irigaray, he understands the oral itself to be in fact privileged by metaphysics over the written word. In his "Plato's *Pharmakon*," he rebukes Plato for privileging the oral over the written because of speech's proximity to consciousness (Jacques Derrida, "Plato's Pharmacy," in *Dissemination*, trans. Barbara Johnson [Chicago: University of Chicago Press], 1981, 61–173). However, it is not speech's proximity to consciousness, but its proximity to breath and its analogous relationship to living love that is central to Plato's argument here. Derrida misinterprets the *Phaedrus* because he surprisingly ignores its prominent erotic content which is central to Plato's preference of the oral to the written word. That the *Phaedrus* is equally a discourse on love is well recognized by scholars. Plato even makes a passing reference to "the beautiful" Sappho (235c) as one of the "wise men and women of old (235bc)" who might be consulted on the matter of love. According to Carson's analysis in *Eros the Bittersweet* (123–73), Socrates' disagreement with the written word and possessive love advocated by Lysias essentially involves Socrates' view that both logos and love are best lived out freely in real time, rather than manifesting themselves in a controlling attitude that freezes the beloved and word. Plato's privileging of orality, she argues, centrally involves the correspondence between words and love that was well established in antiquity.

25. Carson, *Eros the Bittersweet*, 48. Heidegger points to the connection between thinking and the heart in his translation of *noein* as taking something to heart (WT, 202–4). *Noos* is also linked to the heart in a number of Greek idioms.

26. Greek scholars at Alexandria collected her songs and arranged them into nine books based on the meter of the songs. The first book was composed in the Sapphic meter. Out of a rough total of perhaps three hundred songs, we have one complete song, along with substantial glimpses of a dozen others and hints of others. See Snyder, *Lesbian Desire*, 2–3. The fragments of Sappho consist of quotations of her works cited by ancient grammarians or literary critics, and scraps of ancient papyri found in the dry sands of Egypt, laboriously deciphered by paprologists and most of them written long after her time. Her poetry enjoyed great popularity and was still being copied and circulated as late as the third century B.C.

27. Empedocles, of course, would also be of help.

28. This is Ginette Paris's thesis, which she develops in *Pagan Meditations: The Worlds of Aphrodite, Artemis, and Hestis*, trans. Gwendolyn Moore (Dallas, Tex.: Spring, 1987) 40–42, 90–100. The following depends on her analysis.

29. Sappho speaks often of Eros, perhaps because she was aware of his growing patronage in Athens. Sappho emphasizes his position as young son of Aphrodite. He is a powerful, even dangerous, force that cannot be resisted but that can be creatively channeled and enjoyed with the help of his mother.

30. Paris, *Pagan Meditations*, 19.

31. See also OWL, 69, 74, 82–87; and PLT, 89–143, 211–29.

32. So, too, Heidegger selectively turns to Anaximander, Heraclitus, and Parmenides and leaves out Empedocles and Pythagoras, who reflect an Asian influence. For a full argument on Sappho's Asian influence, see duBois, *Sappho Is Burning*, 168–94.

33. DuBois notes that classical studies in the eighteenth and nineteenth centuries was constituted in an atmosphere of anxiety about origins for the Aryan beginnings of Western civilization and supported an erasure of the African and Semitic influences on Greek culture. We cannot confront Sappho's poetry, she argues, without gaining an awareness of how Greek culture was an admixture of the Orient and Occident, of the North and South (*Sappho is Burning*, 164–68).

34. In Homer, the women of Lesbos have a reputation for being both beautiful and masters of feminine arts (*Iliad* 9.128–30).

35. DuBois rebukes Foucault for forgetting Sappho, for starting a certain narrative trajectory in his *History of Sexuality* with a beginning that is originally devoted to misogyny and the control of women, and to a program of philosophical self-mastery. See *Sappho Is Burning*, 26.

36. For a fuller analysis of Aphrodite's conjoining of nature and culture, see Friedrich, *The Meaning of Aphrodite*, 143–46.

37. Hesiod, *Theogeny*, 910–11, cited in Synder, *Lesbian Desire*, 81.

38. Synder, *Lesbian Desire*, 81. I am here merely sketching out her much fuller analysis of *charis*.

39. "Our thinking should have a vigorous fragrance, like a wheatfield on a summer's night" (Nietzsche [*Grossoktav* WW XI, 20] cited in Heidegger [OWL, 70]).

40. Carson, *Eros the Bittersweet*, 20. *Aidos*, she continues is "the shame suitably felt by a suppliant at the hearth (e.g., *Odyssey* 17.578), a guest before his host (e.g., *Odyessey* 8.544), youth making way for old age (e.g., Sophocles OC 247), as well as the shared shyness that radiates between lover and beloved (e.g., Pindar, *Pythian* 9.9–13).

41. Carson, *Eros the Bittersweet*, 20–21.

42. Heidegger does use the metaphor of the apple to describe thinking: thinking has not yet "ripened so that it drops like a fruit from the tree " (OWL, 27).

43. It was well known in antiquity that Aphrodite's gifts of grace and beauty could bring devastation. Only the three virgin goddesses Artemis, Athena, and Hestia, were immune to her. She could create states of mind that might become the cause of murder, interfamily feuds, and wars between nations. The Trojan war that split the Greek world in two was initiated by her winning a beauty contest.

44. Luce Irigaray, *Thinking the Difference for a Peaceful Revolution*, trans. Karin Montin (New York: Routledge, 1994), 95.

45. This is Carson's thesis, which she develops in *Eros the Bittersweet*. The following depends on her analysis.

46. Carson, *Eros the Bittersweet*, 27.

47. In "The Principle of Identity" he even advises us to "pay attention to the path of thought rather than to its content" (ID, 23).

48. Thinking relates to what is to be thought not like the hand that manipulates machinery but as a craftperson's hand relates to its materials. When we grasp something with the hand, our hand must fit the thing. Proper use implies fitting response bringing the used thing to its essential nature and keeping it there. See also Pa, 80–87 for the importance of hand and an analysis of the handwritten in contrast to the typed word.

49. *Legein* "simply tries to let what of itself lies together here before us, as what lies before, into its protection, a protection in which it remains laid down" (EGT, 62–62).

50. Whether "we can attain relatedness to what is most thought-provoking, is something altogether out of the hands of those who practice the craft of thinking" (WT, 25).

51. Anne Pippin Burnett, *Three Archaic Poets: Archilochus, Alcaeus, Sappho* (Cambridge: Harvard University Press, 1983), 277. This analysis of remembrance in Sappho is inspired by hers.

52. She will also separate lover from beloved through various love triangles.

53. Carson, *Eros the Bittersweet*, 27. The following analysis is inspired by hers.

54. David Farrell Krell, *Of Memory, Reminiscence, and Writing: On the Verge* (Bloomington: Indiana University Press, 1990), 264.

55. Mnemosyne is mother of nine Muses: Kalliope, the Muse of epic poetry; Klio, of history; Euterpe, of lyric poetry; Melpomene, of tragedy; Terpsichore, of choral dances; Erato, of love poetry; Polymnia, of sacred hymns; Urania, of astronomy; and Thalia, of light or comic poetry.

56. "Longing is the agony of the nearness of what lies afar" (N2, 217), says Heidegger in reference to Zarathustra's longing for deliverance from revenge against time.

57. Themis is mother of the Horai (including Dike), who attend Aphrodite. She calls the gods to council. She is the gathering of ordinances of what must be done, what society compels. Because what must be will be, she holds the prophecies of what shall be in the future. She is the oracular power of the earth. At Delphi, Themis comes next in order after Gaia. See Jane Harrison, *Themis: A Study of the Social Origins of Greek Religion* (London: Merlin Press, 1977).

58. [C]hairois ercheo damethen memnais (Burnett, *Three Archaic Poets*, 292). I am using her translation here. She argues that there is "clearly happy pleasure in the word" (*chairois*) despite the fact that rejoicing seems out of place for us.

59. There is much debate over what sort of "education" the young women received. We know it involved music, poetry, and dance. I agree with Judith P. Hallett that her poems likely served as a "social vehicle for imparting sensual awareness, and sexual self-esteem, to women on the threshold of marriage and maturity" ("Sappho and Her Social Context: Sense and Sensuality," in *Signs* [Spring 1979]: 456).

60. Burnett, *Three Archaic Poets*, 299.

61. Heidegger understands Anaximander's *adike* to mean that time is out of joint, that what has arrived insists on staying and "strikes the willful pose of persistence, no longer concerning itself with whatever else is present. It stiffens—as if this were the way to linger—and aims solely for continuance and subsistence" (EGT, 42). The *adikia* of time that is noted by Anaximander in the beginning movement of metaphysics would seem to culminate, for Heidegger, in Nietzsche's thought on eternal recurrence.

62. Certainly Nietzsche could speak here on love and time, for Eternal recurrence is Zarathustra's "great longing" and his "nuptial ring of rings" (*Thus Spoke Zarathustra*, 228).

63. Carson, *Eros the Bittersweet*, 118–19. The following analysis of *deute* is from her.

64. Carson, *Eros the Bittersweet*, 119.

65. From Fragments 49 (V) and 105b (V).

66. Test. 58, cited in Margaret Williamson, *Sappho's Immortal Daughters* (Cambridge: Harvard University Press, 1995), 13.

7

Feminine Figures in Heidegger's Theory of Poetic Language

Jennifer Anna Gosetti

Heidegger's philosophy involves a radical critique of the modern subject,[1] and, after *Being and Time*, of the anthropocentrism and humanism of an existential self (BW, 208–9, 222). Concordant with this critique, Heidegger's elucidation of poetic language eschews all traces of poetic-lyrical subjectivism.[2] This is particularly evident in the illumination of the notion of *Andenken* that informs Heidegger's account of the poet's role as the remembrance of the sending-withdrawal of Being in its historical dimensions.[3] If Heidegger in these interpretations refers to an "essential abode of the self" (*Wesensort des Selbst*) (GA 4, 129), this is to be understood in a unique sense. For the self's abode has little to do with a speaking subject in any traditional account; for it is, in Heidegger's ontological account, language that speaks, Being that speaks through language, and the poet is thought to assist language by bringing its truth into unconcealment without reference to his own 'I' or 'person' (GA 4, 129).[4]

The most compelling feminist[5] analysis of poetic language offered in the wake of Heidegger's theory is that by Kristeva in *Revolution in Poetic Language*.[6] For Kristeva, poetic language reveals both the self or subject in process in any utterance, and the feminine, maternal (and therefore social-bodily) grounds seen to inhabit the sphere of meaning theretofore reserved for the traditional subject or the paternal law.[7] While the paternal law (to use Freud's term) denotes entrance into the sphere of symbolic meaning, uttered by a neutral, transparent speaker whose subjectivity is severed from the truths uttered or meanings intended, a feminine "logic" remains tethered to the social-bodily, interdependent grounds of speaking and suggests that truth is less univocal. If there are moments in which Heidegger's theory of poetic language involves a notion of the feminine, as I shall show in this essay, the transparency afforded the "essential abode of the self"—Heidegger's only capitulation to the self's element in essential poetic Saying—is curious in light of Kristeva's analysis and in light of the possible factical dimensions of that feminine. For Kristeva poetic language in particular reveals that every utterance, and thus every account of language, explicitly or not, implies—in fact discloses—a subject. In some sense offering an inverse of Heidegger's critique of metaphysics, Kristeva argues that poetic language in particular reveals the intersocial process of subjectivity in formation at the grounds of saying, even as utterance points to what Heidegger calls the 'uncanniness', or the unsaid that underlies it. Poetic language involves a subject distressed from the point of view of a speaker's possession of meaning and truth, wherein truth is pluralized and the subject is opened to alterity. Heidegger's *Gelassenheit*, as a letting-be of things and a letting-go of such possession and thus of knowledge that confines and defines its object, or represents, binds, reduces it, might then be found at the site (*Ort*) of a subject; this is to challenge the view—to which Heidegger provides no alternative—that *any* kind of subject is opposed to *Gelassenheit*.

To put the subject into question is to claim that subjects cannot master language. Yet how we experience language—whether or not language, even for the poet, is transparently ontological—remains a question to be asked. The problem of the subject or self, and the recent challenge to Heidegger's "disqualification" thereof,[8] arises in reading Heidegger's analysis of poetic language, which oscillates between the ontological-historical founding and phenomenological disclosure offered by the poetic word.

Examining some figures of the feminine in Heidegger's elucidation of poetic language—Hölderlin's Germania, Sophocles' Antigone, and the 'mother tongue' to which Heidegger claims language, as bound to earth or home,[9] gives expression—I will suggest that Heidegger symbolizes the ontological disclosure of language in terms of femininity, but also that he does so in a way that overlooks its social dimensions. While Heidegger comes to reject the will to power that, he argues, characterizes subjectivity and its technological domination of the earth, he maintains the logic of mastery for the 'subject' by not taking into account the social and cultural, even 'semiotic' dimensions of language that compromise the subject's transparency as well as hold over the sphere of meaning. Thus his feminine figures do not offer the corrective that they might and remain within the egological ethos Heidegger aimed to criticize. An abode of the self as an abode in language must be a more radical critique of subjectivity, which, I argue, is helped along by an examination of Kristeva's analysis.

From the Figure of Germania to the Thinking of *Gelassenheit*

It is necessary, first of all, to trace a crucial shift in Heidegger's thinking of language from his treatments following *Being and Time* to his later works. Heidegger's theory of poetic language is issued in a critique of the subject that takes several forms throughout Heidegger's path of thinking and that finds some of its first expressions in the "Origin of the Work of Art" and the lecture course text *Hölderlins Hymnen "Germanien" und "Der Rhein"* that precedes it (GA 39). In the 1930s, in these texts and in the *Introduction to Metaphysics*, overcoming the subject or the existential self involves, it has been argued,[10] the attribution of resolute, founding properties (which had belonged to the subject or genius in traditional aesthetics) to the work of art itself, to poetic language as the essence of art and of work, or to the concealing-revealing movement of Being, as history "confirmed in works" (IM, 137).[11] In this moment in Heidegger's thinking, poetic language is decidedly not "feminine" as he makes clear in the lecture course on "Germanien," to which I will turn shortly. Poetic language is, rather, illuminated in (somewhat phallic) terms of erecting, founding, striving, setting-up, and setting-into-work; poetry demands a people's decision or their resoluteness as a historical response to destiny (*Schicksal*) (PLT, 43). The disclosure of poetic language "wrests" that which is out of concealment, and this wresting involves power, "belligerence," and conflict (PLT, 55).[12] In *Introduction to Metaphysics*, Heidegger calls this power an "overpowering" and links it with historical founding (IM, 137).

This "violence of poetic speech," the "violent act" (*Gewalttat*) of the creative work (IM, 132), is not the act of the subject. The human being is, rather, in a term Heidegger will later use, a "vessel" (DI, 79) for the power of the work, and as such requires an heroic resoluteness. This being-vessel is not a 'feminine' maternity or even a Socratic midwifery but a transparent heroism; creation is found "not in the form of 'psychic' experiences in which the soul of the creative human being wallows . . . but wholly in terms of the accomplishment itself, the putting-into-work" (IM, 137). Resoluteness and decision are no longer linked to the resolute acts of authentic Dasein who has recovered its self, who has retrieved *itself* in totality to be freed for *Schicksal* (BT, §74), but rather belong to language itself as put-into-work by the creative human being. Poetic language is the institution (*stiften*) of Being as historical destiny (GA 52, 91; DI, 124). The human being who belongs to this founding is the resolute but selfless, which is to say transparent, hero or even soldier—for the work "lies in ambush" for Being—and is decidedly not feminine despite Heidegger's critique of (presumably masculine) egocentricity. While Heidegger has overcome the egoism he ascribes to the modern transcendental subject, his poet-founder is to participate in the movements of historical Being in such a way as to preserve that subject's power, will, and aggressiveness even if these are responses to or issue from Being rather than determining Being as object for the subject's transcendental gaze. In other words, the transparency Heidegger ascribes to the subject in order to uproot its egological foundations undermines Heidegger's effort to move away from a more masculine logic to a more feminine one.

In Heidegger's reading of "Germanien," creative response to Being is put in explicitly gendered terms when the 'feminine' is explicitly rejected and implicitly opposed to destinal-historical founding. For Heidegger, Hölderlin's poem tells of the historical German destiny and is not to be confused with the 'worldview' ('*Weltanschauung*') the poet himself might have had (GA 39, 17). Beyond entanglement in subjectivity, the poem speaks of something more essential, speaks of "the origin, the farthest and most difficult" (GA 39, 4). Hölderlin's poem is read according to the logic of historical destiny, and yet his own figure of Germania—the image (*Bild*) which appears in the poem—is, Heidegger claims, "too 'feminine' " for such a task. Hölderlin's image is that of a "dreaming girl 'hidden in the forest with blooming poppies' " (GA 39, 17). Heidegger contends that this image is too "unheroic" (*unheroisch*), too "romantic" (*romantisch*), too " 'feminine' " (*zu 'feminine'*). Heidegger replaces this Germania with one not too feminine, with one far more heroic, more masculine. Heidegger offers, then, the image of a terrible Germania, the "*Mordsweib* with flying hair and a gigantic sword," such as that found on the Niederwald monument (GA 39, 17), which symbolizes a resolute and nationalist defender of the *Vaterland*. Not only is Hölderlin's image, and what Heidegger calls the 'worldview' precipitating it, explicitly replaced by Heidegger; Hölderlin's own 'femininity' is rejected as "apparently a 'pacifist' " stance "bordering on treason" (*Landesverrat*). Heidegger claims that Hölderlin himself, his "character," is "untimely for our hard times." Hölderlin himself is treated as a *Bild* of the feminine, uncompetetive and incompetent (*könnte sich nirgendswo durchsetzen*). Hölderlin's worldview is likewise suspect, for he apparently favors the "one-sided disarmament" of Germany, rendering the nation defenseless (GA 39, 17).

While Heidegger clearly rejects references to Hölderlin's own biography and subjective intentions as inessential to the poem, Heidegger is pressed nevertheless to salvage Hölderlin, his most essential poet, against this 'feminine' *Bild*. Thus Heidegger makes reference to two letters written by Hölderlin in reference to the French Revolution in which a "call to action" might be demanded (GA 39, 18–19). The dreaminess of the girl is transformed thus into the "sword" of heroism; yet while Hölderlin writes to his brother that they might "go where we are most needed," violence or taking up arms is nowhere mentioned or defended. Heidegger does not mention, further, the "clarity and tenderness" for which Hölderlin asks in the same paragraph—"arranging . . . everything human" in an "increasingly free and intimate relation."[13]

In later works, Heidegger's account of poetic language shifts from an aim for resolute, heroic founding—from the Germania *Bild* he presents in the aforementioned lecture course and to which he attaches a specifically gendered demand—to a different kind of alternative to metaphysical subjectivity and humanism. This is the thinking of *Gelassenheit* as a quiet sheltering of beings, essential origin, or both[14]—a decidedly more 'feminine' task insofar as that no longer involves erecting and instituting, but rather sheltering and letting-be—a task, it must be noted, no less difficult. The gentle aiding of truths into unconcealment indeed appears as a more feminine task, insofar as that recalls the gentleness attributed to femininity in many moments of the Western tradition or invokes the notion of maternity that Kristeva considers an apprenticeship in a gentle kind of self-forgetting. If Heidegger earlier rejected the subject or self as 'inessential' (*unwesentlich*) to its destinal-historical relevance, his rejection of subjectivity here now amounts to a rejection of the will to power that characterized his earlier view of poetic language as an "overpowering" force (IM, 137) and by which Heidegger now characterizes the modern subject. In the 1950s, Heidegger's reading of poetic language tends increasingly toward a *Gelassenheit* thinking and away from the 'resoluteness' or heroism demanded in the "Germanien" lecture course. Subjectivity is now not merely the femininity of wallowing in the (inessential) sphere of the subjective, but is indicted in a radical critique of humanism, in its traditional sense, as anthropocentric and technological.[15] Subjectivity is now opposed to *Gelassenheit*; but Heidegger, moving away from the entanglement in "the pressing throng of beings unthought in their essence" that characterizes subjectivity's fallenness (*Verfallen*) (BW, 212), does not take pains to develop the notion of a self that might take the place of the rejected *ego* of metaphysics.[16]

Yet even in reading Hölderlin, Heidegger admits that the self cannot be removed from the sphere of poetic language entirely, and that there is an essential "abode of the self," which Heidegger relates to the reception of Being's sending (GA 4, 129). If this abode is determined now more in terms of *Gelassenheit* than of resolute heroism, it is still understood as a transparent relation between poet and language. This abode admits no essential intersocial dependence, or even significant bodily or emotional experience, that might compromise the clarity of the poet's interception of the revealing-concealing, and now presencing-withdrawing, movement of historical Being.[17] If the gendered determination of Germania seems to give way to a more *gelassen* stance, the transparency of the self in service of poetic language remains, even if that self is in joy or pain— unless joy or pain is purely a form of Being's presencing or withdrawal. In a reading of Trakl and the intense, even subjective-lyrical pain expressed in "The Wandering Stranger" and "To One Who Died Young," Heidegger claims that "the troubled, hampered, dismal, and diseased, all the distress of disintegrating, is in truth nothing else than the single semblance in which truth—truly—conceals itself" (OWL, 183). No longer resolute, this self is transparent in its memorializing recollection of Being's essential origin and in its preparation for a new arrival; this self wanders and loses itself, which means "to loosen one's bonds" and to "slowly slip away" (OWL, 171), but is recovered, in the case of the most essential poetry, in a gathering (*versammelnde*) recollection of origin.

Speaking (*sprechen*), Saying (*sagen*), and the "Mother Tongue"

Heidegger's understanding of language is both phenomenological and ontological, though this phenomenological ontology does not, as in Husserlian phenomenology, admit the primacy of a subject who speaks. Heidegger has shown that in order to understand language we must "be careful not to regard utterance, let alone expression, as the decisive element of human speech" (PLT, 209). For Heidegger language is not expression (*Ausdruck*), as in Husserl, that, when given over to a sign, raises sense (*Sinn*) to meaning (*Bedeutung*) in communication from one subject (*ego*) to another. Language cannot be reduced to expression because expression does not account for the physical character of language and for the fact of its "Showing" or its relation to Being itself. Heidegger argues that if we "listen" properly to language as saying (rather than as the speaking of a subject or what is thereby meant), language is disclosed as self-revealing and is intimately linked to *physis* (QCT, 10). For Heidegger, language is defined by its role in ontological disclosure (OWL, 63), a role that is irreducible to the intentions of speaking subjects. While Kristeva likewise shows that language is not merely the expression of self-possessed subjects and their intended meanings, it is still tethered in its essence to speaking subjects; for Heidegger, "language . . . is not a mere human faculty" (OWL, 107). The capacity "to sound and ring and vibrate, to hover and tremble" is just as much a property of language itself "as it is for spoken words of language to carry a meaning" (OWL, 98). And in words—in their sensuous element, their vibrations in the organ of the mouth—"the landscape, and that means the earth, speaks in them, differently each time" (OWL, 98). These elements of language are close to what Kristeva calls its 'semiotic' dimension—which denotes the material, rhythmic, bodily origins of langauge in its traces and signs that prefigure meaning. What the classical theory of expression neglects, according to Heidegger, is that the sensuality of language is our connection to the earth, which Heidegger links, particularly in the interpretations of Johann Peter Hebel, to the "mother tongue," that is, to dialect and the speaking that occurs in a region or landscape (see GA 13, 133–50; 155–80). Heidegger seems to approach the bodily and physical elements of language and employs a gendered determination thereof. Here I will suggest that Heidegger's ontology of language is made richer by drawing it out in its resonances with what Kristeva calls the semiotic.

In the lecture course text *Hölderlin's Hymnen "Der Ister,"* Heidegger writes about that named river, which becomes a model for "poetic time" (DI, 9)—the lingering-whiling he also describes as the *Ereignis*. Hölderlin's reference to the "womb" of the holy that the river "imitates" is interpreted by Heidegger as "what it does as a son of the mother" (DI, 162–63). In this context Heidegger writes explicitly of "mother" earth (DI, 160). Remembrance itself is the "womb and origin of poetizing" (DI, 152). The "night" into which the poet wanders is the "mother" of the day (DI, 149) and, therefore, of the lighting-clearing that presences. In keeping with Hölderlin's poem, Heidegger writes here not of the *Vaterland* but of the "motherland" (DI, 131). Hertha is named here, according to Heidegger reading Tacitus, as the Germanic "mother earth" (DI, 158). This emphasis on the maternal gives one expression to Heidegger's development of the notion of 'earth', which has overtaken his earlier world-earth opposition in "The Origin of the Work of Art." Yet the mother earth is here not the mere organic; if "history is nothing other than . . . a return to the hearth" (DI, 125), "everything merely 'organic' in nature is foreign to the law of history" (DI, 143). The 'motherland' is destinal-historical according to the law of history and is thus not essentially distinct from the theme of the *Vaterland* that runs throughout the "Germanien" lecture course, and to which Heidegger refers in the lecture course on "Der Ister" (DI, 164).

In reference to the mother, Heidegger nevertheless undermines the relation of possession implied by subjectivistic theories of language that speak not out of an 'essential' relation to earth but of the presumed autonomy of the 'I' in Enlightenment philosophy. This undermining is a displacement of "speaking" (*sprechen*) in favor of a "Saying" (*sagen*)— that "announces itself" in the poem (OWL, 9). In this vein, Heidegger argues that poetry, which makes this relation of words to earth and to Being apparent, is 'essential' language and that the language of speaking subjects is derivative of an ontologically (though not ontically) prior Saying on the part of Being, a Saying in which the poet who listens to

Being engages. Heidegger claims that "language speaks" (OWL, 124). "Language" thus, for Heidegger, refers to the revealing and concealing that belongs to the Being of things as their relation to presence and absence; language, as the name for this process that precedes predication or postulation, is indeed not *directed by* speaking subjects even if it is related to human speaking. As Heidegger puts it, "[S]peaking must have speakers, but not merely in the same way as an effect must have a cause" (OWL 120). Yet if this undermines the traditional, 'masculine' logic of intentionality, the mother is no actual, speaking, maternal voice nor even an organic relationship to material being, but a figure of poetic Saying that recalls *physis*—in this account nearly identical, if not identical, to Being itself. The 'tongue' of the mother does not speak, because, as Heidegger writes of the human body, it is not organic in the sense of an "animal organism" (BW, 204). We might engage in revealing things by virtue of our speaking, but the fact of revealing itself—that things can be revealed and also concealed in and by language—does not belong to us as speakers (OWL, 125). In this sense, poetry is more 'essential' in that it makes obvious its own process of revealing, and its own relation to the sensual—or to the emerging-into-appearance of nature—whereas other kinds of speaking or discourse do not. The word does not essentially exhaust or possess the thing to which it refers, that which it reveals, but brings it to presence or "nearness" (OWL, 86). Thus "the essential Being of language is Saying as Showing" (OWL, 123).

Kristeva's theory follows Heidegger in criticizing the view that language is the expression of meaning on the part of a self-possessed, intentional subject; and she lingers upon the fact that poetry does indeed illuminate the musicality and sensuality of language that exceed and precede categories of "meaning" and the "contents" of subjective intention. In Kristeva's terms, poetry contains within it a "heterogeneousness" to meaning and signification that characterize the "disposition" of other kinds of discourse.[18] While Heidegger grants primacy and primordiality to the fact that language has an ontological function—as he argues, that it founds things in their Being (OWL, 86–87) and that "the word alone gives Being to the thing" (OWL, 62)—Kristeva's language structures social reality and holds that only in accounting for the subject can this fact be understood. What underlies 'speaking' is not to be set aside in favor of essential 'Saying', for speaking involves the social and bodily interdependence of the subject upon others, recalls the initial dependence of the infant on the mother as well as the social origins of learning to speak, and involves the maternal, semiotic inscription into the process of subject-formation preceding the symbolic sphere along with the induction of the subject.

Kristeva's theory marks its ground, in the wake of Freud and Lacan, between structuralist and Husserlian theories of language. Contrary to Heidegger's own radical critique of the transcendental ego, Husserl is credited in Kristeva's account with both maintaining a subject and locating judgment within language via the act of expression (DL, 130). We must "first acknowledge, with Husserl" that "it is impossible to treat problems of signification seriously . . . without including in these considerations *the subject thus formulated as operating consciousness*" (DL, 131). Theories of language—Heidegger's or that of structural linguistics and its signifier/signified distinction—that "eliminate the speaking subject" ignore that a "subject of enunciation takes shape within [that] gap that admits both structure and interplay . . . structural linguistics ignores such a subject" (DL, 127–28). Yet if Kristeva maintains Husserl's speaking subject, Husserl's account is problematic, too; for this subject is always an "act of expressing meaning, constituted by a judgment on something" (DL, 129). Husserl supposes the ego and its capacity to express meanings—its "thetic" capacities to articulate categorically (RPL, 92)—without accounting for the construction of that ego; Kristeva argues that we must "search for that which produces, shapes, and exceeds the operating consciousness," and that "this will be our purpose when confronting poetic language" (DL, 131). Poetic language is seen to disclose the subject in formation at the grounds of speaking, and thus puts the subject "in process/on trial."

Thus Kristeva's analysis diverges from Heidegger's ontological-historical account—though in conclusion we will ask again about the 'unsayable' that for Kristeva, as for Heidegger, underlies all saying. In accounting for the subject, Kristeva's theory must include the organic bodily and social grounds of speaking which she relates to the 'semiotic' that I will discuss shortly. Heidegger attributes to poetic language an originality, an "originary knowing" (DI, 163) or knowledge of origin, but does not abandon altogether the claim that language is connected to speakers of a region or landscape; yet there is in Heidegger little account of the social, communal, or formative dimensions of such speaking. The 'mother tongue' indeed points to the handing over of traditional (*überlieferte*) language from one generation of speakers to another; but Heidegger is silent about the relationality that makes this handing-over possible—

the relation to the 'tongue' and to the 'mother', the way in which being able to speak is not only conditioned by Being as withdrawing disclosure but also by a carnal, phenomenologically disclosable, dependence, a play of proximity and distance between speakers. In ignoring the social dimensions of language, I will argue, Heidegger misconstrues the nature of human freedom that he sees as operative in creative speech. Even celebration, which Heidegger takes up as a Hölderlinian emblem of social historicity, requires a kind of phenomenology of social proximity and distance, an account of the way in which human beings 'shelter' the emergence by bearing witness to it. Witness must be related not only to poetic works themselves but also to the facts of maternity, natality, and the subtleties of shared existence that are their preconditions. Kristeva attempts to explain why discourse is not solely the 'play' of signification, nor the logical/mathematical structures hidden in language (as in theories of generative grammar), nor even the process of ontological disclosure that Heidegger has shown language to be, but also the legislation and structure of social relations, which illuminate the political, cultural, social sphere underlying speaking. Including the semiotic in an account of language—which Heidegger does in part by acknowledging the materiality and rhythm of words and their relation to the speaking body—nevertheless brings Heidegger's account closer to the humanism he hoped to avoid. Yet it also opens up a way to rethink the social element of Saying, even as Saying continues to refer to the emergence and withdrawal of presence. I want to show that *Gelassenheit* can be understood as including, rather than being opposed to, a bodily, social, organic, and not exclusively ontohistorical, abode of the self.

The views of both Heidegger and Kristeva rely upon a contrast between different kinds of discourse—scientific and poetic. According to Kristeva, scientific discourse "tends to reduce as much as possible the semiotic component," in "aspiring to the status of a metalanguage" (DL, 134), just as everyday speech ignores, in Valéry's terms, the "strange resistance" of words to the transparent function of meanings. Similarly, Heidegger suggests that in poetry, when the word loses its communicative clarity, its essence (*Wesen*) becomes apparent. What for Valéry is the "true nature" of words revealed in poetry—their capacity to name and carry meanings but also to slide in and out of ambiguity, adjusting themselves to new contexts and to each other—belongs for Heidegger to the essence of language as "showing." If this showing—to which the poet or dweller or thinker, listening to poetry, answers with *Gelassenheit*—puts the subject of utterance into question, for Kristeva it brings up the question of the nature of the maternalness and materiality that Heidegger (in an essential sense) attributes to poetic language.

If in the lecture course on "Der Ister" Heidegger rejects 'organic' nature, in the essays of *On the Way to Language* Heidegger claims that it is the 'earthiness' of language that lets language be experienced properly, that unties it from a fixed meaning and thereby makes apparent how meaning comes to occur. As Heidegger writes, "[O]nly because in everyday speaking language does not bring itself to language but holds back, are we able to simply go ahead and speak a language, and so to deal with something and negotiate something by speaking" (OWL, 59). Yet in poetry the "physical element of language, its vocal and written character, is more adequately expressed" (OWL, 98). The materiality of language comes to the fore only when our speaking as expression is called into question; and yet for Kristeva this questioning involves the irreducibly factual—perhaps 'organic', certainly biological and psychic—maternal element. For Heidegger the "kinship between song and speech" (OWL, 98) is its relation to earth, which again becomes apparent especially when language becomes 'foreign'; yet for Kristeva this element of alterity is already found within the 'mother tongue' and its materiality. For Kristeva this materiality cannot be 'earthiness' understood in an exclusively historical-ontological sense, but would be associated with the organicity Heidegger rejects as ahistorical. It is always made apparent when the semiotic element of language is revealed; language must be associated with "the archaisms of the semiotic body" and therefore always co-gives the speaker with the 'Saying' (DL, 136).

For Kristeva, the semiotic processes are what Heidegger calls the ringing, hovering, trembling, tracing of language; they are the drives of the psychic-social body, involving the materiality, emotionality, and interdependence associated in much of the Western philosophical tradition with the realm of the 'feminine'. These elements are released in poetic language and its "unsettled and questionable subject." The semiotic processes in poetic language do not trail off into nonsense, are "far from being set adrift" (DL, 134–35). Rather, they are the "never-finished undefined production of a new space of significance. Husserl's 'thetic function' of the signifying act is thus re-assumed, but in different form." Poetry "unsettles" the signifying ego, unsettles the signified; but it "nevertheless posits a thesis, not of a particular being or meaning, but . . . [of] its own process as an undecidable process between sense and nonsense, between *language* and *rhythm*, between the semiotic and the symbolic" (DL, 135). It is as this undecidability, this showing process as process—as Heidegger would say, language revealing itself and invoking the rhythm of presencing withdrawal, but for Kristeva untetherable to Being's narrative or history—that poetry gains a revolutionary character. Poetry transgresses the thetic in "crossing the boundary between true and false." It tends, as Kristeva puts it, "to prevent the thetic from becoming theological," which means that it prevents the (paternal) law, the universal, the transcendental signified in its fixation and stasis, from 'hiding' its origins in the fluctuating semiotic which produces them. Poetry thus bars the thetic "from inducing the subject . . . to function solely within the systems of science and monotheistic religion" (RPL, 110), escaping the metaphysics of "onto-theology" that Heidegger has deconstructed. In being exposed as the in-process source of an utterance, the subject can no longer hide itself in the supposed ('masculine') transparency of the signified. If Being cannot be formulated as the content of a 'said', poetic language illuminates its unsayability by disclosing what language is for the one who speaks, even for the poet called by that alterity that radically exceeds him.

The transcendental ego—and I would add the transparent poet of resoluteness and decision who is for Heidegger beyond subjectivity—is, in poetic language, decentered (RPL, 30) precisely by the 'earthiness' of language. Illuminated by poetic practices, the subject or speaker can no longer maintain its stability and identity or its essentialness vis-à-vis a likewise stable and identified transcendent 'object' of reference—mathematics, logic, God, or Being. Because, as Husserl shows, judgment is dependent upon language, and, as Kristeva shows, language issues from the semiotic economy as well as from the symbolic, the knowledge of the speaking subject is itself guaranteed no autonomy from the semiotic, maternal elements—from the 'mother tongue'—that precede and inhabit speaking or 'Saying'. This very dismantling of subjective autonomy affords another kind of freedom; it is in Heidegger both a radical *Geworfenheit* and a *Gelassenheit* openness to the otherness of Being. The "abode of the self" of poetic language is nothing less than this freedom. What Kristeva calls the subject is, in poetic language, returned to the semiotic (maternal) elements of language as such, to its materiality; the symbolic maintains its presence, but without totalitarian rule, without the (paternal) logic of possession. This is the freedom of creativity and response grounded in admittedly social foundations, in heteronomy. The illumination of the semiotic in language, according to Kristeva, shows that all language, like the identity of the subject itself, is not static but is rather a process. One might call this a strange, even estranged, *Gelassenheit*, one belonging to what Heidegger names the "uncanny" (*das Unheimische*) (DI, 84, 103) and to what both Kristeva and Heidegger call 'risk' (DI, 89).[19]

The Figure of Antigone and the Law of Uncanniness

What does it mean to suggest that alterity is released into language as a necessary correlative to the subject's abandonment or loss of legislative power vis-à-vis a world received or a meaning uttered? Is alterity an accomplice to the 'self' of *Gelassenheit*? Heidegger illuminates the problem of alterity in reading another 'figure' of the 'feminine', namely Sophocles' character Antigone, who illustrates Heidegger's notion of the 'between' (*Zwischen*), the uncanniness (*Unheimlichkeit*) that belongs to the human being endowed with language. For Heidegger, the interstice that is Antigone reaches all the way down to the 'not' between Being and beings, defined throughout Heidegger's transformations of thinking as the ontological difference. In Heidegger's lecture course, the river we saw in Hölderlin's poem "Der Ister"—as the 'son of the mother' earth—becomes for Heidegger not only the model for tarrying in the abode but also for the "law of becoming unhomely" (*unheimisch*)—which Heidegger thinks is the condition for return to "home," for becoming "homely." If the river and its lingering-whiling is the 'son', Antigone is the 'daughter', and as such is still more uncanny.

As uncanny, an 'unnamable' inhabits the "essential abode of the self" to which Heidegger has referred in reading poetic language. Antigone becomes this self of the abode, which is shown to be precisely not at home, or a state of being at home only in wandering. This 'unnamable' is ontological and governs for the human being the 'law of uncanniness' as such. Hölderlin's hymn and its river constitute a model for ecstatic, meandering time; they are likened by Heidegger to the 'uncanniness' of Antigone as she wanders 'outside' the polis, but who, Heidegger further claims, *is* the polis. We learn that for Heidegger uncanniness is the 'essence' of the polis itself, which he argues here is nothing explicitly political. Heidegger treats the river poem and Antigone, further, as models of "uncanniness" in the context of the relation between the "foreign" (*das Fremde*) and the "proper" (*das Eigene*).

Heidegger's reading of Antigone names this rift which is the human being—as mortal or conscious—an uncanny wandering, a 'law of becoming unhomely'; explicit here is the relation between familiarity and unfamiliarity, between nearness and distance. For Heidegger it is the *Ereignis* that, as an event of appropriation, gathers the familiar and strange into a proper relation. For Heidegger the relation of the *Ereignis* and the mortal is a linguistic relation. In language, we are cast out into the "foreign" as well as finding the way to the "proper." Heidegger writes: "That which is unhomely [*das Unheimische*] is not merely the non-homely [*das Nicht-Heimische*], but rather that homely [*das Heimische*] that seeks and does not yet find itself, because it seeks by way of a distancing and alienation from itself" (DI, 84). Language is the seeking alienation, which recalls the "askew perspective" of which Hölderlin writes in "Remarks on Antigone."[20] In *Being and Time* Dasein undergoes such a wandering, that is lost in *Verfallen*—or resolved in *Entschlossenheit*. While Dasein is thrown into existence and flees from itself (BT, 295), anticipatory resoluteness (*vorlaufende Entschlossenheit*) affords Dasein a finding of itself. Dasein "finds itself in the very depths of its uncanniness" by acknowledging finitude (BT, 321). Dasein, thrown into the world, recognizes itself not in the particularity of any given project but as "not-at-home" in the "nothing of the world" (BT, 321). Just as the anticipatory resoluteness with regard to death is Dasein's mode of coming home to itself, in Heidegger's reading of Antigone "dying is her becoming homely" (DI, 104). Antigone is most uncanny in being expelled from the polis, and in reaching that limit that is itself the limit of sayability. For Heidegger, "Antigone is the supreme uncanny" (DI, 104). And yet the uncanniness of Antigone as the self's abode is far uncannier than the self of Dasein, grounded in the unity of ecstasis, a unity Heidegger calls *Sorge*.

For Heidegger's Antigone the law of uncanniness is the "becoming homely within and out of such being unhomely." Home, which Heidegger has defined according to Hertha and thus to the 'mother earth' is, then, linked to death as the freedom of the "not" between Being and beings, to which the human being is alone privy. But it is also the proper relation to "earth" as the abode or "hearth" (DI, 105–6). Uncanniness is "an essential trait of Being itself." (DI, 78) Yet Being, as we have seen in Heidegger's reading of the river poems, "returns to the source," involves the "inwardly counter-turning essence" away from unhomeliness—just as Dasein is afforded the possibility of turning toward (*Ankehr*) itself, into its own thrownness, the "nothing of the world."

In Heidegger's reading, Antigone's polis is the "pole" to which the human being turns in becoming homely through unhomeliness (DI, 82)—finding the proper (*das Eigene*) through the foreign, as the *Eignen des Ereignis*. Antigone cannot become homely merely in the realm of beings, an attempt that always "turns in itself . . . counter to what humans are fundamentally seeking from it" (DI, 84). In order to become "homely" amidst beings Antigone must relinquish the familiar, or beings, to embrace uncanniness itself; in embracing the law that demands the burial of her dead brother, Antigone is released from familiarity—the familiar law—into the sphere of unfamiliarity. Only as such can a "return" home—no longer into the mere familiar but the uncanny familiar—be effected. In terms of Kristeva's analysis this would be just such a return to the familiar abode of the maternal-semiotic, and thus the 'uncanniness' of that which precedes and cannot be accounted for by the transcendental ego. For Heidegger becoming homely requires the appropriation of the proper through the appropriation of the foreign, much the way Kristeva suggests that the poet does not abandon the symbolic realm but ruptures its boundaries, appropriating the semiotic rhythms and traces that had been excluded from the sphere of meaning. For Heidegger the law of being unhomely, itself a "counteressence" (DI, 84), is the path of this return. Heidegger claims that this must be humans' appropriation of "the essential site of their history" (DI, 87), whereas for Kristeva poetic language returns the speaker to the 'essential'—that is, 'original', sphere of formation, the organicity that underlies the history of subjects, and even places a monumental history of works into radical question. The subject itself is thus risked. If for Heidegger in *Being and Time* Dasein must "pass under the eyes of death" in order to authentically repeat (*Wiederholen*) the inheritance (*Erbe*) of history, in the "Der Ister" lectures only a "relation of risk . . . places human beings and them alone in the open site in the midst of beings" (DI, 89). Antigone is likewise risked.

Yet if the 'mother tongue' and 'mother earth' are not merely organic but rather the essentially historical, this risk is likewise "no blind recklessness," but a risking of the human being in its essence (DI, 95).[21] Such risk involves another kind of "knowing that belongs to those who are expelled." Antigone's is a "poetizing knowing" (DI, 111), one that is involved in the naming of the gods or of beings as a whole, and that Heidegger locates in Plato's *Phaedrus*. Although Plato refuses the poet's capacity to "unveil beings . . . and to place them in a pure light," and thereby demotes poets to "an entirely subordinate rank within the polis" (DI, 114), we learn from Plato's lines in the *Phaedrus* something of the "homestead" of the gods and of Hestia, who is "earth," as the home for human beings (DI, 113). In this other kind of knowing, "becoming homely, being unhomely,"—or having a relationship to Being as *Ereignis*—"is first accomplished." (DI, 115). Thus Antigone, the one expelled, is unhomely only in an "ambiguous" sense (DI, 115)—"to be sheltered within and to become homely in what is thus unconcealed" is Antigone's wandering journey. Only in tragedy is the "decision" made about the "proper" kind—or path—of unhomeliness (DI, 117). Heidegger links this to "belonging to death and blood" (as in the blood relation of Antigone to her brother) (DI, 118).

Antigone, Heidegger reminds us, serves as the model for the poet, which Heidegger nearly identifies with Hölderlin—who translated the play into German—and with Sophocles as Antigone's author (DI, 117). If uncanniness seemed to have been granted a femininity, a wandering— the rhythms of which Kristeva would ascribe to the maternal-semiotic underlying language and released radically into poetic language— Antigone's gender, in the absence of an account of the paternal-avuncular law she transgresses, is ambiguous. Antigone, moreover, ceases to be a 'figure' at all, but is literalized as the *Ereignis* or the "event" itself: she is "the singular thing" that is to be poeticized—"becoming homely in being unhomely" (DI, 121). Absent from Heidegger's discussion is the social context in which Antigone finds herself, the conflict of aims that each character faces, and that which Hölderlin, in the "Remarks on Antigone" to which Heidegger makes reference, names the "relativity of the moral law." Antigone's tragic situation is the subversion of avuncular-paternal law for the higher law of particularity—the problem of wholeness and separation that is for Hölderlin explicitly "religious, political, and moral."[22]

In view of this, it is not surprising that Heidegger repeats the move he made in the "Germanien" lecture course insofar as a 'feminine' figure assumes a symbolic role in depicting a 'masculine' kind of heroism. For Heidegger ascribes to Antigone resoluteness; she is not described as caught between the paternal-symbolic and the particular, the domination of human law (Creon) and duty or care (her brother's burial) for the infinite. Nor is she portrayed, as for Hölderlin, as pressing against the limits of human knowing. Her exile is not read according to the usurpation of paternal-avuncular law, a wandering inscribed by in fact *not* being the source of the logic of the polis. Her uncanniness is to face death: "she will not flinch in her resolve" (DI, 102). Just as Heidegger replaced Hölderlin's "dreaming girl" with a terrible Germania, and gave her a sword in exchange for "blooming poppies," so too does Heidegger give Antigone a sword as well. In elucidating the discussion of Antigone with Ismene, Heidegger claims that "the words and the counter-words of the two sisters are like an encounter between two swords whose sharpness, gleam, and power we must experience in order to apprehend something of the lightning that flashes when they strike" (DI, 98). Ismene "pronounces the essence of Antigone" when "pursuit" is mentioned in the "first antistrophe of the choral ode" (DI, 102). In concluding his discussion of Antigone, Heidegger returns to the Böhlendorff letter and argues that "the law of becoming homely" involves what Hölderlin named as the German and the Greek (DI, 125, 123). Here exile has found for Heidegger its locale of return and is thought as a meditation on German destiny (DI, 124).[23] For Heidegger, this law of encounter (*Auseinandersetzung*) between the foreign and one's own is the law of history. Yet historical process might need to be understood in a way that admits a more radical alterity, or demands a less transparent destiny.

For Kristeva, whose analysis of poetic language maintains a subject returned to the (maternal) semiotic—to the 'feminine', to what she calls a feminine kind of temporality[24]—this law of history must be deconstructed along with the subject itself. Such a law would be linked, despite the 'play' Heidegger in moments ascribes to the logic of epochal transformations of the *Seinsgeschichte*, to a Hegelian and, for Kristeva, "paternal" law. Such a law is dismantled by poetic practice, "since writing breaks the 'subject' apart into multiple doers, into possible places of retention or loss of meaning within 'discourse' and 'history', it inscribes, not the original-paternal law, but *other* laws that can enunciate themselves differently beginning with these pronomial, transsubstantive agencies. Its legitimacy is illegal, paradoxical, heteronymic" (DL, 113). To acknowledge that we can never transgress the history of meanings in a pristine manner is to examine the operation of these other laws, and to suggests a view both of exile and of home more radical than Heidegger is able to provide.

A Feminine Abode of the Self?

Heidegger's understanding of the foreign seems then to be guided, as Derrida suggests,[25] by the return home in a way that belies a paradoxical anxiety[26] about the equivocity of uncanniness (DI, 104, 166). Uncanniness must be seen to follow a law (DI, 125) that does not get lost; thus the uncanniness of Heidegger's Antigone, never feminine enough, is perhaps never truly exiled. Even Hölderlin's encounter with the figure of Antigone is "removed from any arbitrariness" (DI, 49): "thought in terms of historical reflection, translation is an encounter with the foreign for the sake of appropriating one's own." Germans, Heidegger argues, "may learn Greek only when we must learn it out of an historical necessity for the sake of our own German language" (DI, 66). This radically differs from Kristeva's reading of Hölderlin's translations, which involves exile in a much more radical sense, and to which she relates his line on the foreign (*das Fremde*): "[W]e have almost lost our language" (*wir haben fast . . . unsere Sprache verloren*).

Heidegger inscribes a 'gathering' into Antigone's wandering—a wandering that we might now loosely call a 'feminine' one—in an essential movement toward or appropriation of 'home'. Likewise, the 'mother earth' and 'mother tongue' are themselves gathered essentially, for they are nothing organic but belong exclusively to an essential relation to history. Listening to the essential saying of the mother tongue is thus to be spared from the realm of ('actual') maternal speakers, as the 'dreaming girl' is transformed into a nonfeminine defender of the "home port,"[27] and as Antigone, the most uncanny of Heidegger's figures, is pulled against arbitrariness into the direction of arrival, of hitting the mark. Yet Kristeva's analysis of poetic language suggests that uncanniness involves a far more radical sense of *Geworfenheit* than Heidegger allows here, and the "essential abode of the self" that Heidegger admits poetic language involves is entangled in this *Geworfenheit*, even if this compromises the essentialness of the abode. If the "abode of the self" is Antigone herself, she is a figure of uncanniness, one whose logic of arrival is upset by the carnality, the 'earthiness' Heidegger has shown language is. For the rhythm, the singing, hovering, humming of language as song—Kristeva would say the rhythms of the semiotic, of the body inscribed by the 'traces' of the maternal—knows no direction, follows no strict law of 'gathering'. A 'feminine'-poetic account of the 'self' would conform to Heidegger's own critique of the metaphysical subject as Kristeva, too, dismantles it. Yet such a 'poetic self' then makes room both for a *Gelassenheit* that draws no swords, that in fact celebrates Hölderlin's "pacifism," and for a *Geworfenheit*, a 'thrown' wandering, which then complicates the transparency—and, we can now say, the 'masculine' or paternal neutrality, of the self poetic language is admitted to indicate. If the 'earthiness' of language is an index to 'mother earth' and the 'mother tongue', this involves much more the wandering 'dreaminess' of the hidden girl Germania and the 'wandering' of Antigone as 'uncanny' and 'exiled' than it does the 'essential' navigation toward home, or the drawing of swords over such essentialness. Heidegger's domesticity, the Heimat that language indexes, is drawn into the logic of 'masculine' determination—a 'masculine', essential, 'gathered' domesticity; but this is then challenged by the tensions Heidegger's 'feminine' figures pose to the question of the "abode of the self."

To rethink the 'self' of poetic language according to this view is to extricate that 'self' from the law of return that characterizes Heidegger's Antigone; but it is also to begin to reelaborate the notion of the 'self' or subject in the wake of Heidegger's critique. For the Gelassenheit precariousness of poetic language, when not spared from the 'feminine' elements it encounters, might admit the very equivocality that Heidegger in the "Der Ister" lecture course attempts to avoid, the very attachment to feeling and mood, inessential dreaminess, carnal Being, and personal biography that Heidegger's reading of poetic language eschews.[28] Kristeva has shown that poetic language does not leave aside the 'abode' of the speaker of an utterance and the intersocial grounds of the speaker's formation, that it reveals a fundamental lack of *telos*, an alterity that cannot be rendered according to the strict destiny of appropriation by the proper. As wandering and exile, a 'feminine self' of poetic language would not arrive at the abode of an essential, destinal, nonorganic gathering of history, nor at a resolute, transparent founding (*stiften*) thereof. This 'self', formed and in formation, forever in 'process' within language, is set on a course that arrives only in *not* arriving at a totalized, unambiguous site of eventhood. It is in not arriving—as Heidegger writes of Dasein, being "not-at-home," being uncanny—that the return to "poetic dwelling" is perhaps accomplished and, at the same time, incessantly in process as the oscillating rhythms of language are.

For Kristeva, the rhythm of language is the unsaid, unsayable, even uncanniness, of the semiotic body. If from Heidegger's point of view this is not thought ontologically enough—as that otherness in and that precedes, but exceeds, even human corporeality, psychic and social life—her view nevertheless opens Heidegger's discussion to an alterity obviated in favor of the determination and logic of the essence of home. Joined with a Kristevan account of the subject-in-process, Heidegger's insights into poetic language are granted, too, an access to the body and to the social which have been neglected in his account. Thus the 'mother tongue' is given a voice, the maternalness of 'earth' is granted carnality and organicity not exiled from the sphere of essential historicality. Released from the destiny of return, the 'tongue' of poetic language—its hovering, ringing, trembling—is given flesh and sociality in a postmetaphysical self and is opened to an *Ereignis* that, recalling no singular origin, brings poetic language into a more radical, and perhaps more radically poetic, sphere of thinking.

Notes

1. See François Raffoul, *Heidegger and the Subject*, trans. David Pettigrew and Gregory Recco (Atlantic Highlands, N.J.: Humanities Press International, 1998).

2. Heidegger rejects the notions of 'feeling' (*Gefühl*), experience (*Erlebnis*), the lyrical tone of the 'I' and 'self' in the poem, the poet's (subjective) mood and intention, and so forth, in his elucidations of Hölderlin in particular. Heidegger aims to read Hölderlin outside of 'metaphysical,' subjective determinations, outside a theory of expression as articulated in traditional aesthetics. See Heidegger, GA 52, 5–6, 22–24, 28–29, 36, 50, 54, 58, 61, 71; GA 39, 42; GA 4, 51, 129. Heidegger rejects an "entanglement in subjectivity" in reading Hölderlin and, in the same lecture course, Sophocles' Antigone, in *Hölderlin's Hymn "The Ister"* (DI, 165). A reference to expression and experience in poetic language in general is made in "A Dialogue on Language," in OWL, 36, wherein Heidegger explicitly criticizes Dilthey's notion of 'experience' in illuminating poetry. See also Heidegger's discussion of Trakl in the same volume of essays. It is worth noting, however, that in *Being and Time*, where Heidegger maintains the notion of a self (*Selbst*), albeit radically other than the subject of metaphysics, poetic language is linked with *Befindlichkeit*: "Die Mitteilung der existenzialen Möglichkeiten der Befindlichkeit, das heißt das Erschließen von Existenz, kann eigenes Ziel der 'dichtenden' Rede werden." GA 2, 162. See the discussion of this passage by Friedrich-Wilhelm von Hermann, *Subjekt und Dasein: Interpretationen zu "Sein und Zeit."* 2. *Auflage* (Frankfurt am Main: Vittorio Klostermann, 1984) 179–80. All translations from the "Der Ister" and "Germanien" lecture courses, as well as from *Erläuterungen zu Hölderlins Dichtung*, are my own.

3. For a critical discussion of Heidegger's elucidation of "Andenken," see Verónique M. Fóti, *Heidegger and the Poets* (Atlantic Highlands, N.J.: Humanities Press International, 1992) and "Textuality, Totalization, and the Question of Origin in Heidegger's Elucidation of 'Andenken,' " *Research in Phenomenology* 19 (1989): 43–58; Dieter Henrich, "The Course of Remembrance" in *The Course of Remembrance and Other Essays on Hölderlin* (Stanford: Stanford University Press, 1997); Christoph Jamme, "Hölderlin und das Problem der Metaphysik. Zur Discussion um 'Andenken' " in *Zeitung für philosophische Forschung* 42 (1988): 645–65.

4. The masculine possessive pronoun is used here deliberately, not only insofar as Heidegger's poets are all men, but, as I shall argue below, insofar as a 'masculinity' is granted to the poet's role either in the 'belligerent,' striving 'founding' of the poetic word, and thus of historical destiny, or in being transparent in terms of 'subjective' feelings, moods, personal relations, and so forth (see above, n. 2). We encounter the 'feminine' in 'figures' employed by Heidegger, such as Hölderlin's Germania or Sophocles' Antigone, in which case I will use the feminine pronouns.

5. I use the term *feminist* loosely, to indicate neither a political or intellectual doctrine, nor any particular brand of feminism, but a critical sensitivity and revaluation of traditional accounts or neglect of the 'feminine', the maternal, women, or the notion of 'woman', and so forth. In this essay I am taking up the 'feminine' in a literally figurative sense, for I am examining moments in which the notion of the 'feminine', by way of figures thereof (such as that of Germania or Antigone, or the 'mother tongue'), appears in Heidegger's account of poetic language. Kristeva's relationship to what can be called 'feminism' is complicated and critical, and yet her analysis centers on the maternal in the dialectic of semiotic-symbolic subject-formation, and outlines the liberation or release of the former into and by poetic language practices. Thus outside of this qualification I view her account as 'feminist.'

6. Julia Kristeva, *Revolution in Poetic Language,* trans. Margaret Waller (New York: Columbia University Press, 1984). Hereafter cited in text as RPL.

7. I use the terms *self* and *subject* to some degree interchangeably in this essay; yet the term *subject* generally refers to the structure of experience in the first person, whereas *self* generally refers to the site of this experience and the accumulation of a history of experiences, as well as the various dimensions of this experience in, among others, social, bodily, phenomenal, and emotional, terms.

I use the term *paternal law* as laid out by Freud's account of subject formation, wherein entrance into the symbolic order of speech requires the absence of subjective presence in favor of objectivity. The subject is supposedly neutral in referring to a signified that transcends subjectivity. Kristeva's *Revolution in Poetic Language* analyzes, via poetic language, the subject in its process of formation all the way into saying or speaking; the division between the maternal (semiotic) and paternal (symbolic) is radically compromised, and thus what I call here the 'feminine' is released into language with poetic language.

8. Jacques Derrida calls for a reelaboration rather than Heidegger's "disqualification of the concept of the 'subject'" in *Points . . . Interviews 1974–1994,* ed. Elizabeth Weber, trans. ed. Peggy Kamuf et al. (Stanford: Stanford University Press, 1995), 321.

9. The relation between language and 'home' is articulated in many of Heidegger's writings, but is made no more explicit than in the essay "Sprache und Heimat," GA 13.

10. See J. M. Bernstein, "The Genius of Being," in *The Fate of Art: Aesthetic Alienation from Kant to Derrida* (University Park: Penn State Press, 1992).

11. I have altered the translation in some citations of IM.

12. Michel Haar provides a discussion of this power and its Nietzschean overtones in Heidegger's theory. See his *The Song of the Earth: Heidegger and the Grounds of the History of Being,* trans. Reginald Lilly (Bloomington: Indiana University Press, 1993), 106–7. On the violent element of the notion of creativity here, see Werner Marx, *Heidegger and the Tradition,* trans. Theodore Kisiel and Murray Greene (Evanston: Northwestern University Press, 1971), 234.

13. This letter can be found in Friedrich Hölderlin, *Essays and Letters on Theory,* trans. Thomas Pfau (Albany: State University of New York Press, 1988), 138–40. Here I am citing 140.

14. While a defense of this claim is beyond the bounds of this essay, I would argue parenthetically that there is here a tension between phenomenological ontology—as an account of the disclosure of beings—and the *seinsgeschichtliche* ontology that aims, in these decades, toward a thinking of *Ereignis,* of the origin and the withdrawal that makes possible the sending (*Geschick*) of Being, a thinking of history in which Being is the "sole occurrence." See TB, 1–24. There Heidegger attempts to think Being "without beings," 24. See also Heidegger's account of his relation to phenomenology in "My Way to Phenomenology," in TB, 74–82. See Joan Stambaugh's introduction, x–xi.

15. See "Letter on Humanism" in BW, 193–42; and QCT, 27–28.

16. Werner Marx, in addition to Derrida as cited above, calls for an account of the fact that the human being finds itself in the world not only exposed to Being but as a self. See *Heidegger and the Tradition.*

17. In the "Letter on Humanism," Heidegger treats the human body both as a derivative ele-

ment, grounded in ek-sistence, and as "something essentially other than an animal organism" (BW, 204).

18. Kristeva, *Desire in Language*, ed. Leon S. Roudiez, trans. Gora, Jardine, and Roudiez (New York: Columbia University Press, 1980), 133. Hereafter DL.

19. For Kristeva this 'risk' is linked to psychosis and suicide, which she takes up in *Revolution in Poetic Language*, among other texts, and which is, in the later text *Powers of Horror*, linked to the notion of 'abject' literature. A discussion of this is, however, must be left aside in favor of my principal aim here, which concerns the illumination of Heidegger's theory of language through some insights found in Kristeva's analysis.

20. Hölderlin, *Essays and Letters on Theory*, 116.

21. One wonders if Heidegger is not referring to his own 'expulsion' or turn away from politics. Heidegger here implicitly criticizes the "arbitrary willfullness of dictators" in a discussion of the political, which is evidence of his distance from the reign of National Socialism in what Otto Pöggeler called its "externalized" form; this despite Heidegger's troubling reference in this lecture course to National Socialism's "historical uniqueness" (DI, 86).

22. Hölderlin, *Essays and Letters on Theory*, 115.

23. Heidegger's interpretation relies on Hölderlin's suggestion to Böhlendorff (upon whose play "Fernando," sent to Hölderlin, Hölderlin is commenting) that "what is familiar must be learned as well as what is foreign." Hölderlin argues that Greek and German poetry, rather than sharing common traits, have "reverse" strengths (*Essays and Letters on Theory*, 150). The occasion of Hölderlin's letter is then also disclosed as Hölderlin's departure from Germany, "perhaps forever" (*Essays and Letters on Theory*, 151). There is no explicit mention of history in Hölderlin's letter, while for Heidegger history is "nothing other than such a return to hearth." The hearth is Being (DI, 108–9). Heidegger writes: "Whether or not, in determining the historical interrelation between Greek and German historicality, Hölderlin has already hit upon what belongs to the commencement, is something we may ask only at that time when Hölderlin's word has truly been heard and when, as the poetizing that it is, it has awakened an appropriate obedience to it" (DI, 124).

24. See Kristeva's essay "Women's Time," in *The Kristeva Reader*, 187–213.

25. Derrida, *Points* . . . , 324.

26. See Michel Haar, *The Song of the Earth*, 142.

27. Derrida, *Points* . . . , 324.

28. See above, n. 2.

Part Three

Ethics, Home, and Play

8

Heidegger and Ecofeminism

Trish Glazebrook

> Die φύσις ist sogar ποίησις im höchsten Sinne.
> (Nature is in fact poetry in the highest sense.)
> —Martin Heidegger, *Vorträge und Aufsätze*

Michael Zimmerman, a forerunner in applying Heidegger to the environmentalist cause, recanted in 1993 because of recent disclosures concerning Heidegger and National Socialism. He feared that an Heideggerian ecology may be prone to ecofascism.[1] Yet John Llewellyn argues that Heidegger's notion of ontological responsibility is a basis for ecological conscience.[2] I intend to develop Llewellyn's vision through an ecofeminist lens. For ecofeminist strategies of multiplicity, diversity, and reciprocity preclude fascism. Furthermore, Heidegger offers ecofeminism philosophical grounding for an alternative conception of nature, and ecofeminism can recognize in Heidegger a gynocentric epistemology.

Heidegger can be situated in ecofeminist discourse in three movements. First, historical analyses of the oppression of both women and nature have exposed two ideological sources: ancient philosophy and modern science. Heidegger's archaeology of science renders these accounts complementary by uncovering the bedrock of modern science in ancient philosophy. Second, ecofeminists have charged deep ecologists with gender blindness. Heidegger is explicitly gender blind in 1928. His claim that transcendent Dasein is prior to gender difference can displace the debate between ecofeminists and deep ecologists without naively reproducing androcentrism. A gynocentric logic can be put in place of the phallocentric logic of modernity. The second movement in which Heidegger is located with respect to ecofeminism thus treats androcentrism, gender blindness, and the role of anthropocentrism in a phallic logic of objectivity. Third, Heidegger argues in the 1930s that the pre-Socratic experience of nature decayed into a nihilistic metaphysics, and in 1940 he listens for an echo of the pre-Socratic insight in Aristotle's *Physics*. In the 1950s, he argues that a Western metaphysics of subjectivity has overrun the globe in technological domination, and he breathes new life, that is, alternative possibility for dwelling, into the homelessness of human being in modernity. That notion of dwelling can be filled out by means of a gynologic that is at home in nature. In conclusion, this Heideggerian account can be used to respond to criticisms of ecofeminism.

Ecofeminism

It was Simone de Beauvoir who first saw that in the logic of patriarchy, both women and nature appear as other.[3] In 1974, Francoise d'Eaubonne coined the term *l'eco-féminisme* to point to the necessity for women to bring about ecological revolution.[4] She argued that human being faces two threats: overpopulation and the destruction of resources. Both have their source, she suggested, in the phallic order. The exploitation of female reproductive power has led to overpopulation, an excess of births, as exploitation of resources has led to their destruction in an excess of production. D'Eaubonne warned that human being will not survive the ecological consequences of patriarchy. That the phallic order is an origin of the exploitation both of women and of nature makes ecology a feminist issue.

Rosemary Radford Ruether argued for the connection of feminism and ecology for reasons much the same as d'Eaubonne's: a common source and shared goals. "Women," Ruether said, "must see that there can be no liberation for them and no solution to ecological crisis within a society whose fundamental model of relationships continues to be one of domination."[5] She set her goal as the transfiguration of society from values of possession, conquest, and accumulation to those of reciprocity, harmony, and mutual interdependence.

Since the 1970s, ecofeminists have uncovered and corroborated new facts about the exploitation and domination of women and nature and their common source in the phallic order in a burgeoning research program that is truly progressive in Lakatos's fullest sense.[6] This research program is philosophical, but also political, social, theoretical, and practical. Vandana Shiva argues that Western development of emerging nations fosters a distribution of resources and policies that directly and negatively affects women's lives and their ability to feed and care for their children.[7] Irene Diamond shows that environmental health risks are borne disproportionately by women.[8] Val Plumwood establishes that environmental philosophy consists not just in ethics, but in a political exploration of the dichotomy between what is nature and what is human.[9] Others argue for a politics of women's spirituality, that is, a renewed spirituality manifest in the ties of women in indigenous populations, particularly Native American, to the earth.[10] Carol Adams argues that the abuse of animals is tied to patriarchal concepts.[11] Douglas Buege applies Lorraine Code's responsibilist ethics to environmentalism, while Ariel Kay Salleh uses the critical theory of Horkheimer and Adorno.[12] Karen Warren raises questions of ethical practice, as she does also with Jim Cheney.[13] There is not one single, unified ecofeminist ethic. Westra's is an ethic of respect, while Curtin's is an ethic of care.[14] Nor are speculations confined to theory. Chris Cuomo and Stephanie Lahar consider activism and grassroots politics in order that theory might guide yet be grounded squarely in praxis.[15]

These resistance writers can be seen as a shattered mirror of social and political critique, whose diverse interests in ecology, gender, class, and race fragment into competing and dwindling interests, that is, into *Holzwege*, dwindling forest paths, in this case, paths of thinking upon which the thinker becomes lost and can find no way to proceed. Or ecofeminism can be taken as a clearing, an open space in which each of those who resist oppression and exploitation in their many forms and instances has a place. This is precisely the spirit in which ecofeminism is best understood: not in totalitarian terms that homogenize through synthesis, but in an intellectual climate of solidarity, connection and intersection. As diversity promotes health and stability in an ecosystem, so monoculture in ecology diseases, excludes, and hegemonizes. As a first step against reproducing a phallogocentrism of domination within ecofeminism itself, the τόπος (*topos*) is mapped as an ἦθος (*ēthos*) of inclusivity that seeks introduction over reduction, emergent growth over confining and common denominators.

Form and Matter: Ancient Greeks and Modern Scientists

Ruether and Griffin argue that Greek philosophy, particularly in its dualisms, is the ideological source of oppression for both woman and nature.[16] Merchant and Shiva point rather to modern science as the origin of the logic of domination of Western rationality.[17] Heidegger's analysis of the genesis and development of modern science from classical roots can show how these two critiques of the rationality of modernity are complementary. For Heidegger shows how the modern scientific conception of nature is grounded in Aristotle's metaphysics.

Aristotle is for Heidegger a pivotal thinker. Although his account of nature is, in its echo of pre-Socratic thought, a basis for an alternative vision to the modern scientific and technological reduction of nature to object and resource respectively, which vision I will elucidate below, his distinction between matter and form was for Heidgger decisive for subsequent metaphysics in its laying of the ground for those reductions. Heidegger argues in "On the Being and Conception of φύσις in Aristotle's *Physics* B.1" that Aristotle made possible the reduction of nature to artifact by interpreting things as formed matter. In *Physics* B.1, Aristotle asks what nature is. He comes up with two answers: it is the "ultimately underlying material of all things," and it is "its form, that is . . . the 'kind' of thing it is by definition."[18] He gives priority to form in determining a thing's being, for it is only when the form is present that a thing is actually what the matter otherwise is only potentially. Furthermore, says Aristotle, in growing, a thing attains its nature by attaining its form.[19]

In this account, notes Heidegger, Aristotle has separated form and matter such that a thing is understood as formed matter. This is of course the case for production (τέχνη), in which the artist imposes a form upon matter. That the artist begins production with a conception beforehand of what is to be made was, in fact, definitive of τέχνη (*technē*) for Aristotle.[20] To understand all beings in this way, however, is to reduce nature to artifact by analogy. Subsequent to Aristotle's analysis of form and matter, argues Heidegger, nature is understood as the self-produced artifact (BCP, 234/GA 9, 255; BCP, 262/GA 9, 292). Nature is thus interpreted according to the ancient model of production. Natural things are analogous to artifacts, only divinely or self-produced.

In "The Question Concerning Technology," Heidegger names the essence of technology *Ge-stell*. The essence of technology is not for Heidegger a piece of equipment. Rather it is a way of revealing, a logic of production, that underwrites the modern experience of nature. He characterizes *Ge-stell* explicitly as a logic of domination. It is a "setting-upon [*stellen*]," an "ordering [*bestellen*]," a "challenging revealing [*herausfordern den Entbergen*]" (QCT, 17/VA, 25). The representational thinking of technology is an assault upon nature that has already been set up as object by modern science.

For Heidegger holds that modern science is ideologically grounded not in ancient science, but in τέχνη. In *Die Frage nach dem Ding*, he analyses the difference between Newton's physics and Aristotle's (BW, 286–88/FD, 67–68). Examining Newton's first axiom of motion, that "every body continues in its state of rest or of uniform motion in a right line unless it is compelled to change that state by forces impressed upon it,"[21] Heidegger concludes that Newton questions nature differently from Aristotle because his concept of nature is different. It is homogenized. Motions are only locomotions for Newton, and locomotions are no longer distinguished as earthly versus celestial, rectilinear versus circular, and violent versus natural. Place itself is now a matter of indifference. Whereas for Aristotle, things had a proper place, for example, the earthly belongs at the center and the fiery at the periphery, for Newton any body can in principle occupy any place.

Thus Newton reduces nature to homogenized bodies in locomotion and thereby substitutes a mechanical universe for Aristotle's teleological conception of nature. In "The Question Concerning Technology," Heidegger attempts precisely to retrieve causality from its shrinking into the efficient cause (QCT, 6–11/VA, 15–19). In Heidegger's reading, then, Newton excludes the final cause from physics and brings into focus instead the efficient cause. Should this account seem an unfair reading of Newton, since in his day his account was subject to the controversy of appealing to mysterious and magical action at a distance, one should consider Newton's response to Richard Bentley's inquiries wherein Newton appeals to "divine power," and says he knows of no power in nature to cause the circular revolution of the earth about the sun "without the divine arm," and that gravity "must be caused by an agent."[22] He on occasion denies knowing the cause of gravity,[23] but when pushed he describes the divine as its efficient cause.

In "Der Zeitbegriff in der Geschichtswissenschaft," Heidegger distinguished Galileo from Aristotle in similar terms. He found homogenization to be definitive of modern science, and he argued that it consists in idealism. Whereas Aristotle drew conclusions on the basis of observations, Galileo formulated a universal law a priori and then looked to nature for evidence of it. In Aristotle's account, the artist began with an a priori conception of what was to be made, but in modernity, it is science that begins with an object it has constructed a priori and then projected onto the things it encounters in experience. Modern science "pursues and entraps nature as a calculable coherence of forces . . . physics, indeed already as pure theory, sets nature up to exhibit itself as a coherence of forces calculable in advance" (QCT, 21/VA, 29), and orders its experiments accordingly. Modern science is the herald of its quintessence in technology, which in turn sets nature up as resource, as standing-reserve (*Bestand*) to be organized, reckoned, and stockpiled.

Likewise in *Die Frage nach dem Ding*, Heidegger finds the metaphysical origin of modern science in idealism. He pinpoints Descartes's metaphysics of subjectivity as the place where reason positions itself prior to being: "With the *cogito—sum*, reason now becomes *explicitly* posited according to its own demand as the first ground of all knowledge and the guideline of the determination of things" (BW, 304/FD, 82). The grounding moment of science is, according to Heidegger, the self-assertion of the thinking subject, which projects its ideas onto nature.

This was for Aristotle definitive not of the inquiry into τὰ φυσικά (*ta physika*) but of τέχνη (*technē*). The artist begins with a conception of what is to be produced and then brings the thing into being in production. Accordingly, Aristotle's distinction between form and matter, as uncovered by Heidegger, sets the stage for interpreting nature according to the logic of domination that underwrites modern science and technology. For Aristotle's interpretation of artifacts as passive matter upon which an actualizing form is imposed evolves into the representational thinking of modernity in which idealized conditions are imposed upon nature by the scientist. Representational thinking, the logic of the dichotomy between subject and object, has its roots in Greek thinking and flourishes in modern science. It comes to its most devastating and destructive formulation in technology. Heidegger's critique of the logic of domination that informs modernity has much in common with the feminist critique of both ancient metaphysics and modern science, for it shows how they belong together. What the ecofeminists have pointed out, beyond Heidegger, is that this logic is gendered: it is phallic.

And indeed, the Aristotelian distinction between form and matter is complicit in a logic of gender domination, for it aligns activity with form and passivity with matter. Given what Caroline Whitbeck has called Aristotle's "flower pot theory of pregnancy,"[24] that man supplies form and woman matter, this simplistic alignment has turned the social and sexual domination of women into an apparent consequence of biology. Likewise, the inert passivity with which Newton informs nature when he reduces it to bodies subject to impressed force, and Bacon's plan for the inquisition of nature, "that the mind may exercise over the nature of things the authority which properly belongs to it,"[25] can be traced back to a false dualism between form and matter, which, though Aristotle found them inseparable in experience, he was well prepared to make separable in thought. Heidegger resists the interpretation of ὕλη (hylē) as matter, arguing instead that "in the ordinary sense [ὕλη] means 'forest', 'copse', the 'woods' in which the hunter hunts. But it likewise means the woods which yield wood as construction material. From that ὕλη comes to mean material for any and every kind of building and 'production'" (BCP, 249/GA 9, 274). Matter is not just a passive receptor for form. Rather it has a nature that persists throughout production and that properly belongs to it regardless of its appropriation for production. Under an Heideggerian ecofeminist account, then, nature is not just passive (female) matter which provides the material for human enterprise. Aristotle's separation of form and matter is anthropocentric, and androcentric.

Androcentrism

Heidegger's analysis of modern science is already, then, insightful insofar as it diagnoses anthropocentrism. If modern science has its ideological roots in Aristotle's conception of production, then *homo faber* is at the center of nature for the thinker in modernity. If Heidegger is right that modern science has reduced causality to the efficient cause, then things in nature are no longer taken as Aristotle took them in opposition to production: to have their own end, purpose, τέλος (*telos*) toward which they are busy propelling themselves. Once final causes are eliminated from nature, then nature is purposeless and hence readily available *for the imposition of human purposes*. According to Heidegger's account in 1935, modern science, in grounding knowledge on the Cartesian subject, converts ὑποκείμενον (*hypokeimenon*) to *subjectum*, (BW, 301/FD, 80), such that being is not the underlying substratum (ὑποκείμενον) upon which thought moves, but rather the thinking subject underlies all experience and is the absolute fundament on the basis of which things receive their thinghood, that is, objectivity. Science determines nature as object, underwritten by human subjectivity, and hence human being feels free to dominate and use nature in technology. This Heideggerian tale about the modern ideological and technological exploitation of nature is consistent with the deep ecologist's diagnosis of anthropocentrism as causal rather than merely symptomatic of contemporary environmental crises.

In the 1980s, a conflict developed between deep ecology and ecofeminism. Arne Naess argued against the anthropocentrism of human attitudes toward nature, and for what he called the intrinsic value of nature.[26] In 1973, he characterized two kind of ecologists. Shallow ecologists fight pollution and resource depletion toward the central objective of promoting the health and affluence of people in developed nations. Deep ecologists, on the other hand, practice what Naess names ecosophy: ecological egalitarianism, based on principles of diversity and symbiosis in which organisms are understood in terms of their relation to other organisms, not just to people. In 1985, Bill Devall and George Sessions published a statement of the deep ecologist platform.[27] Deep ecology is a political movement, promoting local autonomy and decentralization while supporting an anti-class posture, and Naess argues that struggle against oppression permeates deep ecology as well as any other resistance to exploitation. A year later, in 1974, ecofeminists too were making the claim that environmental problems do not stand alone, and that remedy must be sought not for isolated issues, but in the conjunction of questions of value into a new social vision.

Deep ecology and ecofeminism accordingly have much in common. They both connect ecology with other forms of oppression, and their healing vision for nature and human beings rings of common values, strategies, and goals. In 1987, however, Janet Biehl criticized deep ecologists for their concept of anthropocentrism.[28] Deep ecologists argue that human-centered thinking lies at the root of environmental crises, but women should not be implicated in that assumption of mastery over nature, argues Biehl. Likewise, Michael Zimmerman argues that ecofeminism challenges *andro*centrism rather than *anthropo*centrism.[29] Cheney makes the stronger claim that deep ecology is itself androcentric.[30] Ariel Salleh articulates this charge in her claim that "deep ecology brings little social analysis to its environmental ethic . . . [because] deep ecology is constrained by political attitudes meaningful to white-male, middle-class professionals whose thought is not grounded in the labor of daily maintenance and survival."[31] Evidence for her claim she finds in the deep ecologist's defensive response to ecofeminism. A year earlier, she argued that deep ecologists fail "to grasp both the epistemological challenge offered by ecofeminism and the practical labor involved in bringing about social change."[32] Deborah Slicer has further suggested that until deep ecologists "take time to study feminism and ecofeminist analyses, only disputes—not genuine debate—will occur between these two parties."[33] It seems, then, that deep ecology simply reproduces a patriarchal logic of exclusion, of oppressive theory over liberating practice.

Nonetheless, if the ecofeminist premise holds true, that women and nature are oppressed by the same logic of domination such that the goals of feminism and environmentalism cannot but together be solved, then by this very founding assumption, gender oppression and the exploitation of nature are two sides of the same coin. If deep ecologists were to achieve their goals, then the goals of ecofeminism would be met too. The deep ecologist's social vision is one in which no kind of oppression has a place. Either ecofeminists must give up the claim that they can end women's oppression by healing environmental wounds and the ongoing processes that cause them, or ecofeminists must show how their social vision is different from the deep ecologist's vision. What they clearly have in common is that they both oppose the phallic order. Accordingly, I suggest that deep ecology itself operates on the basis of a gynocentric logic, which could be called a yonic logic in distinction from the phallic logic that underwrites modernity. Of course, if Arne Naess and other deep ecologists acknowledged and accepted the ecofeminist point, the relation between ecofeminism and deep ecology would readily become one of both/and rather than either/or. Indeed, ecofeminists and deep ecologists can work together effectively.

The collaborations in 1991 and 1993 between Karen Warren and Jim Cheney on ecosystem ecology exemplify exactly such cooperative work. Drawing upon O'Neill,[34] they argue that hierarchy theory is "the most viable attempt to provide an inclusive theoretical framework for the wide variety of extant ecosystem analyses."[35] Hierarchy theory is an integrative approach to ecosystems that attempts to reconcile the population-community approach with the process-functional approach. It promotes the layering of different approaches because ecosystem complexity conduces analytic multiplicity. The central idea in hierarchy theory is "that ecosystems are organized into levels of organization which result from differences in process frequency rates."[36] Ecologists need to understand organization within particular levels, and of different levels with respect to each other. Warren and Cheney's suggestion, that different analytic strategies not only can but also should be applied to an ecosystem if it is to be understood, is a helpful model for an inclusive ecologism. The ecofeminist's critique of the logic of domination and the deep ecologist's assertion of intrinsic value are precisely such differing strategies that belong together and between which one should not have to choose.

Gender Blindness

Toward this end, it is helpful to look again at the question of gender blindness and gender neutrality. Virginia Woolf and W. E. B. Du Bois both speak of a sense in which gender and race, respectively, can be transcended. They can be laid against an argument of Heidegger's in order to show that, although there is no such thing as a gender-neutral perspective, preoccupation with gender is unhelpful to ecologism, and hence also to ecofeminism. In 1928, Virginia Woolf wrote *A Room of One's Own*, published the following year.[37] Looking at male and female writers, she argues that "it is fatal for any one who writes to think of their sex."[38] When it comes to a certain kind of bad literature, she argues, "all who have brought about a state of sex-consciousness are to blame."[39] Writing is impeded by the intrusion of the self into the work, for this compromises what Woolf calls "integrity,"[40] and gender is a moment of the self. Hence Woolf praises Mary Carmichael: "[S]he wrote as a woman, but as a woman who has forgotten that she is a woman."[41] A woman need not become a man to write, but nor need gender be an issue in the text.

Of course, a problem for a woman writer in a context dominated by male authors is that the woman's (male) critics need not forget that she is a woman. One is criticized as a woman, even when one does not write about being a woman. There is a tension in Woolf's work: how can a woman write unconsciously of gender when she writes in patriarchy? Woolf herself writes A Room of One's Own absolutely self-consciously as a woman, and as a woman who will also be heard by men. On the one hand, Woolf advises the woman writer to forget about gender. On the other hand, such blindness seems possible only for men who write within the phallic order.

W. E. B. Du Bois, writing as a black man, describes what he call "the veil,"[42] in which the marginalized must always live in terms of how they are perceived within hegemony. He first recognized racial difference when a girl at school refused his visiting card.[43] That event taught him that the color of his skin informs his experience through the other's awareness of his difference, even when he is not conscious of it himself. His only escape from the veil comes through literature. Something in that intellectual experience transcends and is irreducible to racial difference: "I sit with Shakespeare and he winces not. Across the color line I move arm in arm with Balzac and Dumas, where smiling men and welcoming women glide in gilded halls. From out of the caves of evening that swing between the strong-limbed earth and the tracery of the stars, I summon Aristotle and Aurelius and what soul I will, and they come all graciously with no scorn or condescension. So, wed with Truth, I dwell above the Veil."[44] Du Bois can transcend color, but only in the solitary space of his reading of literature, as Woolf could forget gender in a room of her own. As soon as Du Bois returns to the public realm, ἀγορά (agora) or πόλις, (polis) he is again within the veil, as Woolf is confined within gender by her critics.

In Heidegger's account, Dasein is likewise transcendent. When he takes up the question of Dasein and gender, he argues that transcendence is prior to gender. In the summer of 1928 (as Woolf wrote A Room of One's Own perhaps), Heidegger gave a lecture course titled "Logik." In §10 of this text, published as The Metaphysical Foundations of Logic, he argues, presumably in response to a question that could have come from Helene Weiss, that Dasein is a gender-neutral term. It is in the part of Heidegger's lecture constructed from the notes of Weiss that his comments on the neutrality of the term Dasein, in particular, on its gender-neutrality, appear.

One approaches these comments warily. The gender neutrality of rational subjectivity has long been suspect insofar as the history of philosophy has barely concealed misogyny beneath its apparent neutrality. Paula Ruth Boddington has shown that a philosophy "impregnated with maleness" is falsely influential if it is "putting about as universal and absolute what is only male and relative."[45] Geraldine Finn has argued that philosophy is itself oppressive of women, and she cites enough sexist material from the canon to silence any claim that philosophy has been historically gender neutral.[46] Rather, it has engaged and continues to engage, she argues, in exclusionary ideology and practice. Jane Flax treats the sexism of philosophy psychoanalytically. She argues that the patriarchal unconscious glimpsed in political philosophy is "partially rooted in a need to deny the power and autonomy of women."[47] Following Kittay, one could similarly read the history of philosophy psychoanalytically as a response to what she calls "womb envy."[48] Heidegger's claims in 1928 must be read against the feminist claim that gender-neutral transcendent thinking is precluded in the public realm, the ἀγορά (agora), and the academy, as long as the πόλις (polis) is determined by a patriarchal ἦθος (ēthos).

Heidegger argues that Dasein's sexlessness is "not the indifference of an empty void, the weak negativity of an indifferent ontic nothing," nor is Dasein "the indifferent nobody and everybody . . . the voidness of an abstraction" (FL, 136–37/GA 26, 172). Rather, Dasein in its neutrality is "the primordial positivity and potency of the essence . . . the potency of the *origin* [*des Ursprunges*], which bears in itself the intrinsic possibility of every concrete factual humanity" (FL, 137/GA 26, 172). He further suggests that Dasein never exists as neutral, but neutral Dasein is rather the condition for the possibility of Dasein's existence. Dasein is not the egocentric individual, whose factual, existentiell isolation Heidegger denies here in favor of what he calls "the *metaphysical isolation* of the human being" (FL, 137/GA 26, 172). This could be read as Woolf's isolation in a room of her own, or as Du Bois's in his solitary reading. Yet Heidegger's metaphysical isolation is not so clear. It entails that transcendent Dasein exist in some sense prior to its world. This is not practically possible, nor consistent with Heidegger's general thesis in *Being and Time* that Dasein is constituted first and foremost as being-in-the-world (BT, 78–90/GA 2, 78–62).

Dasein can be dispersed factically into bodiliness and therefore sexuality, Heidegger argues, because it harbors this possibility in its neutrality. Dasein is disseminated in gender, likewise space, Heidegger argues, because its essence "already contains a primordial *bestrewal* [*Streuung*], which is in a quite definite respect a *dissemination* [*Zerstreuung*]" (FL, 138/ GA 26, 173). Heidegger claims that this dissemination of Dasein is what makes being-with other Dasein possible in a "species-like unification" (FL, 139/GA 26, 175). The language of bestrewal and dissemination here is not overly helpful, and certainly the claims to potency and origin beg a womanly metaphoric, however unintended by Heidegger. Can sense be made of these claims such that a useful notion of gender transcendence can be developed, one that does not transcend gender as a prelude to misogyny, that does not erase gender in order to reduce the other to the self in a logic of the same that Irigaray has diagnosed as phallic?

Heidegger suggests that Dasein is not indifferent to gender, but that it is logically prior to any gendering. It contains the possibility of gender, which is therefore not yet determined. Were gender determined, it should be so in confinement to a gender at the exclusion of the opposite gender. Heidegger holds that Dasein always lives factically, that is, in its existence it is always of a determined gender. In other words, Dasein's possibility for gender is always disseminated into an existent gender. But insofar as Dasein is the questioner, for whom its own existence is an issue, it is not yet reduced to a gender. Hence "it" rather than "she" or "he." Heidegger is suggesting that Dasein's existence can be an issue for it prior to its gender being an issue.

Dasein always thinks from a concrete historical situation; as Heidegger has shown incontrovertibly in *Being and Time,* Dasein is first and foremost being-in-a-world. This world is *very much informed* by gender. To think transcendently, then, in a gender-neutral way, would be precisely to transcend the world, to be worldless. This is, in Heidegger's own terms from *Being and Time,* impossible. In 1928, Heidegger has not yet overcome the metaphysics of subjectivity that informs his own thinking. He struggles with Kant over a series of texts from 1925 to 1935 in exactly that overcoming of idealism. The implications of his insight into Dasein's worldliness have not been thought through in 1928: there in no transcendence in the sense of worldlessness. Hence there can be no Dasein that is not always already situated in a world, and subsequently there can be no gender-neutral thinker, and no thinking that is not either phallological or gynological. Thinking is first and foremost in a world, and therefore it *must be* gendered.

Yet both Woolf and Du Bois describe a freedom in which gender or race is a confinement that has in a sense been left behind. To borrow from Du Bois, women live within a veil they cannot escape in patriarchy. As Du Bois's reading of literature is not an experience wherein he has lost his color, but an experience wherein he is no longer confined and limited by his color, so Woolf seeks such a release for women's writing. One can write as a woman without gender being intrusive or reductive to one's writing. A woman cannot but write self-consciously of her gender when she writes in patriarchy. She writes from the margins. Yet marginalia, rather than being trivial, is in fact a standpoint location for critique of the dominant order.

Ecofeminists can write most effectively by writing as women, from women's perspective, without hijacking the ecological issues to the politics of gender in the discipline of ecology itself. They can write from and toward a gynologic that subverts the phallologic of domination without becoming bogged down in the issue of women's role and reception in ecology. For indeed, if ecofeminists are right that ecology and feminism set their sights on the same social vision, then ecologists are always already feminists (however adequately or poorly), whether they realize it or not. The ecofeminist insight that ecology and feminism both seek to subvert the phallic order and its logic of domination implies that ecologists, regardless of their gender, are already thinking gynologically.

Anthropocentrism and Objectivity

The first premise of feminism is that women are an oppressed group. Yet oppression is not peculiar to women. Is there anyone who has never felt some form of oppression? Likewise, can anyone say they have never oppressed? Women have demonstrated their complicity in patriarchy, as well as an ability to support institutions and structures horribly oppressive of other women, and of nature. Contrary to Biehl's claim, women are implicated in the mastery of nature.[49] The cosmetics industry stands as an incriminating example. Pleasant though it would be to see in a straightforward and easy way who is oppressing, who oppressed, we live in matrices and constellations of power in which each and everyone is implicated as both oppressor and oppressed in varying and different combinations. We are all located in what Maria Lugones has analysed as a geography of oppression. If the task is to establish an ἦθος (ēthos) of inclusivity and reciprocity in order to replace the green-washing treatment of symptoms that characterizes our social response to a diseased phallologic, then ecofeminism can envision itself according to the transcendence I have drawn out of Woolf, Du Bois, and Heidegger. Women can think and write *as* women, but that does not confine them to thinking and writing *about* gender.

Ecofeminists suggest that women have something valuable and unique to bring to ecology: a woman's logic of reciprocity and care. This logic may be grounded in biology, in social construction, in the perspectival standpoint of marginalization, or in the fact that woman's body is a political site. The task of thinking through the ἀρχή (*archē*) of woman's logic remains; it is only just incipient, neonatal in, for example, Irigaray's *Speculum*.[50] This murkiness of source should not, however, stand in the way of recognizing that this logic is a politics of the social order, an order in which nature has a crucial part to play. Woman's logic can build itself a home in patriarchal diaspora by reforming that ἦθος (*ēthos*), by deforming a phallologic and informing an ecologic. Women can bring a gynologic to bear when they do ecology. Ecofeminists who are women work as women, but they can work most effectively when they forget that they are women, and when deep ecologists resist both androcentrism and anthropocentrism.

Accordingly, the debate between ecofeminists and deep ecologists over anthropocentrism and androcentrism is helpful to neither. It invites the antifeminist, backlash suspicion that feminism is an old record, and a whining one at that. In response to Cheney's claim that deep ecology is androcentric,[51] it is true that deep ecology is not explicitly gynocentric. Its central proponents have certainly been men. It is in the nature of thinking to be perspectival, and deeply informed assumptions are difficult to make thematic. Gender is not the deep ecologist's issue. Yet, as Woolf refers to Coleridge on the androgyny of the writer, such that one can write in a man-womanly or a woman-manly way,[52] and Cixous describes *l'écriture féminine* for which she cites Jean Genet as an example,[53] so the deep ecologist can think gynologically. The deep ecologist's and the ecofeminist's social vision overlap fundamentally. Both movements support reciprocity, diversity, nurturance, and egalitarianism in human dealings with others and with nature. Both resist the logic of domination embedded in the history of the West, which feminists have diagnosed as phallic. Ecologic, whether ecofeminist or deep ecologist, can therefore be called yonic, gynological. Ecofeminists need much more that deep ecologists continue to think gynologically, than that they acknowledge the gender blindness of deep ecology. As long as deep ecologists think gynologically, what does it matter that they see that they do? In fact, why tell them? Heidegger has shown in his critique of modernity that our most powerful assumptions are the ones to which we are blind.

The Heideggerian perspective on gender transcendence has something further to contribute to the ecofeminist concern that history is androcentric, for Heidegger's argument that existent Dasein is embedded in facticity goes beyond Woolf's suggestion that women write as women who have forgotten they are women. What does it mean to be embedded in facticity? It means that the veil of gender may always be present in a reader's perception, but also that one thinks, that is, writes, from a location, a location informed by history in the Heideggerian account, race in Du Bois's account, and gender in Woolf's account. Yet Heidegger argues that thrownness into one's location is not insurmountably confining.

In §74 of *Being and Time*, Heidegger distinguishes fate (*Schicksal*) from destiny (*Geschick*). Fate is one's giving oneself over to a tradition, that is, one's interpreting oneself in terms into which one has been thrown. Destiny is a larger vision that transcends fate such that it guides fate. Destiny constructs historical possibilities that can be lived out as fate, or exceeded, as Woolf exceeds fate with her five hundred pounds a year, which allows her to be an intellectual in a world that defines academic turf as male. The ecofeminist thinker can "take over its own thrownness and be in the moment of vision for 'its time' " (BT, 437/GA 2, 385). Ecofeminists can best make real their ecologic vision by thinking like women about ecology, not gender.

Furthermore, there is a sense in which anthropocentrism can be rethought that is grounded in Heidegger's account of truth. Elizabeth Harlow argues for anthropocentrism on the basis of what she identifies as "post-Wittgensteinian epistemology." She finds "paradoxically that this kind of anthropocentrism can ground a genuine sense in which nature is valuable in its own right, yet as part of human good."[54] She is not the only one to reject nonanthropocentric environmental philosophy. Bryan Norton argues that theories of inherent value set the impossible task of providing "a single, ontological unification of ethics under nonanthropocentric holism to capture the fine nuances of ethical obligations as experienced in varied communities,"[55] while Judith Green seeks to retrieve the human place in nature.[56] There are two issues that herein need to be addressed from Heidegger's thought. The first is anthropocentrism; the second is intrinsic value.

Anthropocentrism is inevitable in the sense that any understanding of nature entails necessarily the one who understands. In Heidegger's account of modernity, in representational thinking, the object is constructed reductively on the basis of the self-assertion of the subject. Hence Heidegger critiques Descartes in *Die Frage nach dem Ding* for establishing a metaphysics of subjectivity (BW, 296–305/FD, 76–83) in which the "I" becomes a special subject. It is "the foundation of all knowledge," hence "the essential definition of man," and hence "the guideline for the determinations of Being" (BW, 304/FD, 82). The modern subject figures not just as an element of reality, but as its ground. Some twenty years later, in "The Question Concerning Technology," Heidegger points to the threat of modern technology in the delusion that "it seems as if man everywhere and always encounters only himself" (QCT, 27/VA, 35). In representational thinking, the coming together of subject and object, the object is reduced to being only what it appears as to the subject. Heidegger holds an alternative conception of truth, that truth is ἀλήθεια (*alētheia*), unconcealment, an openness, a "sheltering that clears [*lichtendes Bergen*]" (BW, 137/GA 9, 201), in which a subject can encounter objects, the thinker what is thought. Truth is possible because thinker and thing come together in "the open region [*das Offene*]" (BW, 125–26/GA 9, 189) that Heidegger later calls "the clearing [*die Lichtung*]" (TB, 65/SD, 71) in which the event (*Ereignis*) of being takes place. Accordingly, a Heideggerian ecofeminist holds that there is something to an object of thought that does not reduce to its objectivity, while acknowledging that the very thing at stake in ecology is human being.

For in Heidegger's analysis, truth cannot occur without a thinker. Dasein's encounter with beings calls for Dasein's presence. Yet the open region is logically prior in the encounter to both Dasein and the beings it understands. Under this account, truth is epochal. Worlds open in different ways, and how a world is opened is informative and definitive of an historical epoch. This view cannot avoid being anthropocentric: human being is always present in the account it gives of nature, for it is human being giving the account. Furthermore, human being must figure in ecology, since it is the survival of the human species that is ultimately threatened in modernity's logic of domination of nature. Hence the idea of an account of nature that is entirely independent of human being is nonsensical. The notion of a noumenal, inaccessible nature is incoherent. Yet this does not mean that human accounts of nature need necessarily reduce it entirely to its value for human being.

For, second, there is a Heideggerian move that captures the intent of arguments from intrinsic value without appealing to the noumenal dead-end entailed by a nonsensical nonanthropocentrism. The notion of intrinsic value figures in ecological debate as an attempt to argue that there is more to nature than human being can conceive or say. One such conception and account is, for example, modern science. Those who appeal to intrinsic value do so to resist the idea that science is an exhaustive account of nature, that things in nature can be reduced to entirely human values, and therefore uses, by science and its application in technology. Arne Naess argues that things in nature have a value in their own right. He names this value "intrinsic value," which he claims is synonymous with "inherent value."[57] Baird Callicott had drawn a distinction between these two kinds of value, however, precisely in order to avoid nonsensical nonanthropocentrism. He argued that something can be said to have intrinsic value "if its value is objective and independent of all valuing consciousness," while it has inherent value if "it is valued for itself and not only merely because it serves as a means to satisfy the desires, further the interests, or occasion the preferred experience of the valuers."[58] Heidegger's account of truth is a philosophical basis for inherent value. It does not reduce nature nonsensically to value for no valuer, that is, to intrinsic value. Yet nor does it give itself over immediately to a logic of domination, wherein all things have a value for human being to exploit. Heidegger's account of truth can support an ecofeminist ethic in alliance with deep ecology by taking advantage of the deep ecologist's argument against anthropocentric value without interpreting the argument as philosophically naive.

Heidegger argues throughout his life that the modern scientific account of nature is reductive. In 1916, he argues that whereas Aristotle's method was to generalize over several observations, Galileo begins with a general assumption, an hypothesis (GA 1, 419). In §69(b) of *Being and Time*, Heidegger argues likewise that the theoretical attitude replaces what is ready-to-hand with what is present-at-hand. He repeats the claim from 1916, that modern science homogenizes time and space, and therefore also bodies. In *Die Frage nach dem Ding*, the claim is again explicit: "All determinations of bodies have one basic blueprint, according to which the natural process is nothing but the space-time determination of the motion of points of mass" (BW, 267/FD, 71). In the *Beiträge*, Heidegger suggests again that the ordering principle in modern science does not come from observation (GA 65, 161). Rather, reason orders nature on the basis of a priori laws. It is this intent on a rule that determines objectivity (GA 65, 162). His concern is not the realist worry expressed in analytic philosophy of science that science may be constructing elaborate fantasies such that theoretical entities could turn out to be fictitious. Rather, Heidegger is expressing a deeper concern: modern science reduces nature to object.

In *What Is Called Thinking?* Heidegger argues that "only by such objectivity do [beings] become available to the ideas and propositions in the positing and disposing of nature by which we constantly take inventory of the energies we can wrest from nature" (WT, 234/WD, 142). Shortly after the lecture course that is this text, Heidegger argued in "The Question Concerning Technology" that technology is "a way of revealing [*eine Weise des Entbergens*]" (QCT,12/VA, 20). In other words, it is for Heidegger a truth. It is a clearing, a lighting, an opening up of a world. And it is a way of revealing beings as "standing-reserve [*Bestand*]" (QCT, 17/VA, 24), that is, as resource, available for human use and appropriation. Heidegger's critique of technology is an analysis, worked out over some forty years, in which he comes to the conclusion that there are other ways to think about nature than its reduction to value in terms of human use. Indeed, *What Is Called Thinking?* is an argument that there is more to thinking than representational thinking, the logic of objectivity that is characteristic of modernity in which subjects represent objects. Toward the end of his life, Heidegger questions the possibility of another way of thinking than representational thinking. At the end of philosophy, that is, at the end of the metaphysics of subjectivity that is representational thinking, a task remains for another kind of thinking. Ecofeminism has taken up that task of thinking beyond the reductive confines of objectivity.

Thinking is precisely the relation that is at stake in ecofeminism: how can human being stand in a thinking relation to nature that is not a logic of domination? Heidegger has shown that technology, understood not as a collection of equipment, but as a truth, a way of revealing and experiencing things, is precisely a logic of domination. Human being is a necessary part of the equation and must take responsibility for its intervention and appropriation of nature rather than hiding behind the incoherent discourse of independence from human relation or value. Human being has carved out for itself a special role among beings: no other creature is capable of realizing such wide-scale manipulation of its environment. Acknowledging how human being, though itself part of nature, has singled itself out as steward is the first step in re-establishing that role ethically rather than in the domineering destruction and exploitation that are characteristic of the West. For if human being has a privileged role in the knowing of nature, the Heideggerian account also points out that this human role is made possible by something larger, the very ground upon which human being stands. According to Heidegger, being is that place. Obscure though the question of being may be, it is nonetheless clear that according to Heidegger, being, at least in its historically first unconcealment, that of the pre-Socratics, is nature (IM, 61, cf. Index under being as φύσις [physis] [GA 40, 47]). I retrieve this point as a Heideggerian ecofeminist: the place of human being is nature.

Heidegger can, then, speak to anthropocentrism at several levels. There is a Heideggerian response to the ecofeminist demand that deep ecologists reformulate their charge from anthropocentrism to include androcentrism. Heidegger argues in 1928 that human questioning, though always undertaken from a concrete and therefore gendered perspective, is transcendent of gender. Rather than dismissing this view as simply another androcentric denial of gender, ecofeminists do well to take under advisement the Heideggerian/Woolfian suggestion that gender issues may obscure rather than conduce their project. Furthermore, Heidegger's account of truth is a basis for an anthropocentrism that grounds an ethical rather than an exploitative relation to nature.

For in Heidegger's view, nature is in fact the primary ἦθος (ēthos) in which human being dwells. Will McNeill has argued that "the home for Heidegger has always returned as a *question*, perhaps even *the* question."[59] I pose the question of the home as the question of the meaning of being as it stays with Heidegger throughout his life: what would it mean for human being to safeguard its home in nature? I will defend this interpetation of Heidegger, previously unarticulated by his critics, and put the Heideggerian vision that this interpretation makes possible to work in ecofeminism.

Visionary Dwelling

When he renamed the open region he associated with truth "the clearing [*die Lichtung*]" (TB, 65/SD, 71), Heidegger talked of it as a forest clearing into which the light may come. He traces *opening* etymologically through the French *clairière* to the older words *Waldung* and *Feldung*, translated by Stambaugh as "foresting" and "fielding" respectively. The metaphor of a forest clearing for truth is not incidental to Heidegger's account. He argued in 1930 that what makes truth possible is the *Da* of Dasein (BW, 126/GA 9, 189), the place where thinker and thought come into encounter. Such unconcealment was experienced for the first time, he argues, when being revealed itself as φύσις (*physis*), nature, where " 'nature' . . . does not yet mean a particular sphere of beings, but rather beings as such as a whole" (BW, 126/GA 9, 189–90). Heidegger develops this novel reading of Greek philosophy into an account of the ontological priority of nature with respect to truth.

In 1935, in *Introduction to Metaphysics*, he argues that being was φύσις (*physis*) for the pre-Socratics. He resists translating the Greek term in order to forestall its quick interpretation according to the modern concept of nature already informed by science and technology. Rather, he calls it self-blossoming emergence, for example, the blossoming of a rose (IM, 14/GA 40, 11), and suggests that it means "the emerging and arising, the spontaneous unfolding that lingers" (IM, 61/GA 40, 47). The implications for a philosophy of nature of this insight into pre-Socratic experience become explicit in 1940 in Heidegger's painstaking reading of Aristotle's *Physics* B.1, and indeed his earlier work on being, truth, and φύσις (*physis*) can be used to read that difficult text. For example, that being was for the pre-Socratics φύσις (*physis*) makes sense of the enigmatic claim that "meta-physics is 'physics'—i.e. knowledge of φύσις" (BCP, 223/GA 9, 241). Understanding being as nature is not peculiar to the pre-Socratics, but informative also of modern metaphysics in that modernity is determined in Heidegger's analysis by an interpretation of nature as scientific object, and likewise postmodernity by nature as technological resource. The history of being is the history of interpretations of, as Heidegger puts it in the *Nietzsche* volumes, "what Goethe experiences as 'nature' and Heraclitus as κόσμος [*kosmos*]" (N4, 237/NII, 346). To use an anglicized version of Heidegger's later claims about the event of being, nature is what gives. The expression "what gives?" captures nicely the complexity and dual function of Heidegger's phrase "Es gibt" in that the question "what gives?" asks not just what is given, but also what is doing the giving in the matrix of truth and being. Nature, as self-placing in unconcealment, is the given, the giving, and hence indeed the full constellation of the event of being.

In the 1940 lecture course, Heidegger retrieves from Aristotle another possibility for φύσις (*physis*), other to its devolution into object and resource, by listening for the echo of the pre-Socratic experience of nature. Aristotle argues at *Physics*, B.1 that everything in nature "has within itself a principle of motion and of stationariness (in respect of place, or of growth and decrease, or by way of alteration)."[60] Artifacts have no such internal impulse to change, except insofar as they are made from some natural material in which the principle of internal impulse persists. Aristotle borrows from Antiphon: if one planted a wooden bed, and anything grew, it would be wood and not a bed. Heidegger argues that therefore nature is not like an artifact, which requires an artist. Nature cannot be understood by analogy to artifact. Such an analogy, argues Heidegger, "fails *from ever conceivable point of view*. That means: we must understand the being of φύσις entirely from itself, and we should not detract from the astonishing fact of φύσις . . . by overhasty analogies and explanations" (BCP, 262–63/GA 9, 292). Nature is something about which to be amazed.

This sense of wonder in the face of nature is useful for the ecofeminists' disruption of phallic logic. Heidegger previously pointed to wonder in 1929, where he made it the beginning of real, philosophical enquiry in opposition to the mere chasing after the real that characterizes science for him (BW, 109/GA 9, 121). He argues there that science serves merely "to amass and classify bits of knowledge" (BW, 111/GA 9, 121). In subsequent years he describes scientific enquiry as "the mere advancement of knowledge" (SA, 32/SdDU, 13), a preoccupation with the superficial, with a blind reckoning and frenzy of explanations,[61] as "mere busyness . . . [that] simply chases after such results and calculations" (QCT, 138/GA 5, 97). This bland reduction of nature to object is a bad infinite, an eternal return of trite repetition that Kuhn called "normal science." Its mechanism is representational thinking, which Heidegger denigrates in *What Is Called Thinking?* "[T]hought in the sense of logical-rational representations turns out to be a reduction and an impoverishment of the word that beggar the imagination" (WT, 139/WD, 92). In the last of the *Nietzsche* volumes, he argues explicitly that representational thinking is a logic of domination "which must bring every stockpile . . . into its own possession and must secure this possession" (N4, 242/NII, 351). Representational thinking is scientific and technological mastery. Hence Heidegger shares the ecofeminist insight, articulated repeatedly by Karen Warren from 1987 onward, that science and technology are informed by a logic of domination.[62] This logic can be ruptured only by a new logic, one that resists domineering sameness and reductivity and that comes to nature inspired by love and wonder. Such an interruption of phallic logic would be gynological, and I articulate and support this claim through Heidegger's call for *Denken* and *Besinnung*.

In *What Is Called Thinking?* Heidegger envisions an alternative to representational thinking that he calls *Denken*, which he traces to "*Danken*." Thinking in this sense is thanking in that it recognizes "the thanks owed for being [*das Sichverdanken*] . . . with which the inmost meditation of the heart turns toward all that is in being" (WT, 141/WD, 93). He first articulated *Besinnung* in 1938 in a text by that name published in 1997 as volume 66 of the *Gesamtausgabe*. *Besinnung* is an overcoming of reason through a revolutionary struggle with the history of philosophy (GA 66, 49).[63] *Besinnung* does not reduce itself to objectivity, but is "the beholding that watches over truth" (QCT, 165/VA, 53). The truth originally experienced by the pre-Socratics, the truth of modern science, and the truth of technology are ways in which human being knows nature. But *Denken* and *Besinnung* are thoughtful, respectful, and thankful relations to nature, rather than its reduction to object and resource. Heidegger's vision is an ethic of reciprocity and care, the very vision for which ecofeminists call, that stands in marked contrast to what has been diagnosed and rejected as a logic of domination by both.

Ecofeminists can learn from Heidegger that such a logic cannot come from the sciences themselves. Objectivity has as its standard truth and falsity. But theories must also be judged, as Lugones and Spelman have pointed out, according to whether or not they are "useless, arrogant, disrespectful, ignorant, ethnocentric, imperialistic."[64] This judgment can only come from outside science, since it considers science according to criteria that do not figure within it. This is not to say that scientists cannot engage in such reflection, just that to do so would be an interruption of their scientific practice. These criteria are precisely the ones ecofeminists wish to use to reflect on the sciences. The claim is not that truth and falsity are irrelevant, but that they are insufficient. Ethical criteria are also requisite. In fact, the deeper truth of science lies not in the correctness of its facts, but in the way that it opens an ἦθος (*ēthos*) for human being to make its home. The future of human being depends on scientists also being able to step outside their science in order to evaluate it on ethical terms that go far beyond its accuracy and correctness.

Such an ecoethics that is thinking as thanking recognizes that mastery and control of nature are at worst illusory, at best shortsighted goals. This is not a normative claim, but the Aristotelian insight that nature moves of its own accord, driven by a teleology from which technology can at most borrow but neither underwrite nor overpower. Nature is the very ground upon which human being stands, upon which all human machinations and lives take place. Hence my project is to read this Aristotelian conception of nature by means of dwelling, in Heidegger's fullest sense of the word. In *Being and Time*, Dasein's "uncanniness" (BT, 233/GA 2, 189), literally *Unheimlichkeit*, un-home-liness, is its anxiety at not being at home in the world. In *Basic Problems of Phenomenology*, Heidegger is already analyzing being-in-the-world in terms of what it means to be at home, "*zu Hause*," by means of Rilke's writing (BP, 172–73/GA 24, 244–46). In *The Notebooks of Malte Laurids Brigge*, the speaker stands before a half-torn-down house and is overwhelmed by the terrible recognition of self in the tenacious life that still announces itself in the filthy ruins: "I recognized it . . . it's at home in me." Home is appealed to here not in an idyllic nostalgia, but in recognition that the self is not an isolated Cartesian subject . Rather, self and world are mutually constitutive.

Hence in subsequent analyses, Heidegger dissociates homelessness from existential *Angst*, and recognizes it as the human condition of alienation from nature and itself in modernity. In "Letter on Humanism," he uses the word *Heimat*, which means home not just in the sense of one's house, but also homeland, or hometown, that place of which we say "where the heart is," "with the intention of thinking the homelessness of contemporary man from the essence of Being's history" (BW, 241/GA 9, 338). In the *Nietzsche* volumes, he diagnoses "the organized global conquest of the earth" (N4, 248/NII, 358) as symptomatic of and indeed causally active in human being's homelessness. Will McNeill has shown that the "extreme possibility of unhomeliness does *not*, then, simply belong to Dasein's ownmost being: it is rather the opening up of the very possibility . . . of any belonging or non-belonging whatsoever."[65] In 1950 and 1951, in three essays, "The Thing," "Building, Dwelling, Thinking," and ". . . Poetically Man Dwells . . . ," Heidegger explores this possibility for human belonging: dwelling.

For Heidegger, dwelling is a play of what he calls the fourfold: earth and sky, mortals and gods. Ruether has argued that "Mother and nature religion traditionally have seen heaven and earth, gods and humans, as dialectical components within the primal matrix of being."[66] She hears the call of being in the same matrix as Heidegger, and I suggest that her ecofeminist vision meets Heidegger's outside the phallic logic of modernity. In a reading of Hölderlin, Heidegger calls *Heimat* "the power of the earth" (GA 39, 88). In "The Thing" he says of earth that it is "the building bearer, nourishing with its fruits, tending water and rock, plant and animal" (PLT, 178/VA, 176), "the serving bearer, blossoming and fruiting, spreading out in rock and water, rising up into plant and animal" (PLT, 149/VA, 149). In the following year, he says, "Dwelling is the manner in which mortals are on earth" (PLT, 148/VA, 148), and he explains dwelling in terms of peace, preservation and safeguarding, sparing and preserving. Human beings "dwell in that they save the earth. . . . To save the earth is more than to exploit it or even wear it out. Saving the earth does not master the earth and does not subjugate it, which is merely one step from spoilation" (PLT, 150/VA, 150). As McNeill puts it, "Dwelling means protecting the fourfold, saving the earth and heavens in letting them be."[67] This is the force of both Heidegger's argument for freedom in "On the Essence of Truth" and for *Gelassenheit* in *Discourse on Thinking*. Human thinking can assault its object or give it the freedom to speak for itself, that is, let it be what it is without appropriating and reducing it to object and resource. McNeill articulates this idea in terms of love: "the desire that the beloved remain the one that it is."[68] This is precisely the deep ecologist's argument for intrinsic value: nature should not be confined to its use-value. Rather, Heidegger, ecofeminists and deep ecologists each hold to the Aristotelian point that nature has its own ends. When Heidegger calls dwelling "cultivating and caring [*Pflegen und Hegen*]" (PLT, 217/VA, 191) in "The Origin of the Work of Art," he means exactly that nature's teleology can be respected rather than ransacked.

In order to express this vision of dwelling as an alternative to global, ecological destruction, Heidegger borrows from Hölderlin the phrase that ". . . poetically man dwells . . ." (PLT, 213–29/VA, 181–98). His claim that the "poetic is the basic capacity for human dwelling" (PLT, 228/VA, 203), is an appeal to the Greek ποίησις (*poiēsis*). The following year Heidegger binds together Aristotle's four causes with this notion of the poetic. Aristotle conceives of causes as material, formal, efficient and final. These causes are all ways things are brought into appearance, brought forth as the things that they are, argues Heidegger. And "φύσις [*physis*] also, the arising of something from out of itself, is a bringing-forth, ποίησις [*poiēsis*]" (QCT, 10/VA, 19). In fact, "φύσις [*physis*] is indeed ποίησις [*poiēsis*] in the highest sense" (QCT, 10/VA, 19). For if poetry in the original Greek sense is the bringing of something into appearance, nature is the self-placing into appearance of what comes into being without an artisan. Hence the human power to create is dependent upon and secondary to nature's power as origin. All human creations take their materials from the earth and build upon it. Indeed, the very capacity to produce is, as Aristotle saw, in the nature of human being. To recognize that human being can never separate itself from nature, which separation is the condition for the possibility of mastery, but that human being is always already part of nature, is to leap onto the ground upon which we already stand. Heidegger's argument that human being dwells poetically is the claim that human being can dwell in nature thoughtfully, creatively, and symbiotically rather than exploitatively and destructively.

Karen Warren has shown that "there are important connections between how one conceives and treats women and how one conceives and treats our ultimate home, the planet earth."[69] Indeed, Sherry Ortner has argued convincingly that female is to male as nature is to culture,[70] and women's identification with nature has been complicit in a dialectic of devaluation in which both nature and earth are known as "mother." Historically, woman has been identified with her body, whose functions are known as "lower," and this has been the basis of her exclusion from the public realm and the academy. Women are literally not at home in the public realm, and likewise the home is undervalued in its social and political function. Woman has not been truly at home in her home, when property rights in the phallic order have historically delegated ownership of and final authority in the home to the patriarch. It is not surprising, then, that Warren describes a longing for home: it is "a troubling, nagging, uncomfortable feeling,"[71] particularly discomforted by science and technology. Likewise from *Being and Time* through to the *Nietzsche* volumes, Heidegger describes human being's homelessness in modernity in similar terms of alienation and displacement. As Warren subverts a logic of domination in order "to honor, cherish, and respect the value of earth as our home," so Heidegger thinks *Denken* and *Besinnung* as just such an alternative logic of dwelling on earth. Both rely on memory, desire and respect for all beings (cf. WT 11, 141/WD 7, 93) in order to think a visionary dwelling in nature in which one can also be at home with oneself.[72]

Conclusion

From a Heideggerian perspective, Janet Biehl's charge that ecofeminism has "become a force for irrationalism" misses the point.[73] To mistake any suggestion of a way of thinking outside phallic logic for irrationalism is to foreclose on the possibility of change that both Heidegger and ecofeminists seek. Heidegger offers ecofeminists the promise of a new way of thinking. Only those deeply entrenched in and unwilling to give up representational thinking, the logic of the phallic order, could see that promise of ways of thinking that dwell rather than assault as irrational. That Heidegger and ecofeminists explore ways of thinking that do not succumb to rationality's logic of domination does not mean that they are thoughtless or make no sense. This is new sense, not nonsense; and it is in fact eminently sensible, unless one holds that ecological crises are a conspiracy of scientists and philosophers.

Simone de Beauvoir offers a deeper criticism. She was irritated by the equation of ecology and feminism, for she saw in the feminist appeal to "traditional feminine values, such as woman and her rapport with nature, . . . [a] renewed attempt to pin women down to their traditional role."[74] Indeed, the Heideggerian support I have drawn for ecofeminism is very much an argument for traditionally female values, particularly in its claim that a gynocentric logic recognizes nature as the home of human being. This is preceisely why I have named this alternative epistemology gynologic, and unhesitatingly associated it with the home. What my argument suggests is the reinvestment of value in the qualities associated with woman, a retrieval of these values from their devaluation in patriarchy. Acknowledgment of gynocentric values, of gynologic, is not essentialism. Gynologic and gynocentric values are not a consequence of biology alone, but also of woman's standpoint, her othering in marginalization, the fact that her body is a political site. The distinction between nature and nurture has become obsolete here. Both biology and social construction figure in woman's experience. Her destiny plays out in her body, and her body grounds her otherness as well as her (de)nurtured experiences of menstruation, sexuality, motherhood (or not), and menopause. Yet in the end, the source of gynological values is irrelevant. Whatever their origin, they inform a logic of dwelling: nurturance, interdependence and care, multiplicity and being-with over isolating individualism. The argument is not that women belong in the home, but that the qualities of a functional home are long overdue in the public realm. Phallocentric logic has produced social structures of domination and alienation. Gynologic shelters.

Heidegger has much to offer ecofeminism. He concurs with both the ecofeminist critique of the logic of domination that underwrites modernity, and the suggestion that this logic has its roots in ancient Greek thinking. He provides a context to think through the problem of anthropocentrism. This issue is currently pivotal in environmental philosophy because arguments that human being is part of nature, not elevated above it, are foundering on the fact that human being has the ability to manipulate its environment on a scale much larger than that of any other creature. Heidegger's account of human thinking locates human being squarely within nature, and hence opens up a place for thinking honestly and ethically about the possibility of human working with rather than against nature. What, for example, is the difference between leaving a field fallow every third year and flooding it yearly with fertilizers? What will it take to heal the wounds caused to women and nature by a phallic logic of domination, which reduces both to object and resource? Heidegger's vision of thinking as thanking and nature as dwelling is precisely a gynologic for building a home in the patriarchal diaspora.

Notes

1. Michael Zimmerman, "Rethinking the Heidegger-Deep Ecology Relationship" *Environmental Ethics* 15, no. 3 (1993): 195–224, 205.

2. John Llewellyn, *The Middle Voice of Ecological Conscience* (New York: St. Martin's Press, 1991), 355.

3. Simone de Beauvoir, *The Second Sex*, trans. H. M. Parshley (New York: Vintage Books, 1952), 144.

4. Francois d'Eaubonne, *Le Féminisme ou la mort* (Paris: Pierre Horay, 1974).

5. Rosemary Radford Ruether, *New Woman/New Earth: Sexist Ideologies and Human Liberation* (New York: Seabury Press, 1975), 204.

6. Imre Lakatos, "Falsification and the Methodology of Scientific Research Programmes" in *Criticism and the Growth of Knowledge*, ed. Imre Lakatos and Alan Musgrave (Cambridge: Cambridge University Press, 1970), 118.

7. Vandana Shiva, *Staying Alive: Women, Ecology, and Survival in India* (London: Zed Books, 1988).

8. Irene Diamond, "Babies, Heroic Experts, and a Poisoned Earth," in *Reweaving the World: The Emergence of Ecofeminism*, ed. Irene Diamond and Gloria Feman Orenstein (San Francisco: Sierra Club Books, 1990).

9. Val Plumwood, "Nature, Self and Gender: Feminism, Environmental Philosophy, and the Critique Of Rationalism," *Hypatia* 6, no. 1 (1991): 3–27.

10. Paula Gunn Allen, *The Sacred Hoop: Recovering the Feminine in American Indian Tradition* (Boston: Beacon Press, 1986), and "The Woman I Love Is a Planet; the Planet I Love Is a Tree," in Diamond and Orenstein, *Reweaving the World*; Sharon Doubiago, "Mama Coyote Talks to the Boys," in *Healing the Wounds: The Promise of Ecofeminism*, ed. Judith Plant (Santa Cruz: New Society, 1989); and Annie L. Booth and Harvey L. Jacobs, "Ties That Bind: Native American Beliefs as a Foundation for Environmental Consciousness," *Environmental Ethics* 12, no. 1 (1990): 27–44.

11. Carol Adams, *The Sexual Politics of Meat: A Feminist-Vegetarian Critical Theory* (New York: Continuum, 1990); and "Ecofeminism and the Eating of Animals," *Hypatia* 6, no. 1 (1991), 125–45.

12. Lorraine Code, *Epistemic Responsibility* (Hanover: University Press of New England, 1987); Douglas Buege, "Epistemic Responsibility to the Natural: Toward a Feminist Epistemology for Environmental Philosophy," *American Philosophical Association Newsletter* 9, no. 1 (1991): 73–78; Ariel Kay Salleh, "Epistemology and the Metaphors of Production: An Ecofeminist Reading of Critical Theory," *Studies in the Humanities* 5, no. 2 (1988): 130–39.

13. Karen J. Warren, "The Power and Promise of Ecological Feminism," *Environmental Ethics* 12, no. 2 (1990): 125–46; Karen J. Warren and Jim Cheney, "Ecofeminism and Ecosystem Ecology," *Hypatia* 6, no. 1 (1991): 179–97, and "Ecosystem Ecology and Metaphysical Ecology: A Case Study," *Environmental Ethics* 15, no. 2 (1993): 99–116.

14. Laura Westra, "Ecology and Animals: Is There a Joint Ethics of Respect?" *Environmental Ethics* 11, no. 3 (1989): 215–30; Deane Curtin, "Toward an Ecological Ethic of Care," in *Ecological Feminist Perspectives*, ed. Karen J. Warren (Bloomington: Indiana University Press, 1996).

15. Chris Cuomo, "Toward Thoughtful Ecofeminist Activism" in Warren, *Ecological Feminist Perspectives*; and Stephanie Lahar, "Ecofeminist Theory and Grassroots Politics," *Hypatia* 6, no. 1 (1991): 28–45.

16. Ruether, *New Woman/New Earth*, and Susan Griffin, *Woman and Nature; The Roaring Inside Her* (San Francisco: Harper & Row, 1978).

17. Carolyn Merchant, *The Death of Nature: Women, Ecology, and the Scientific Revolution* (San Francisco: Harper & Row, 1980); and Shiva, *Staying Alive*.

18. Aristotle, *Physics*, books 1–4, trans. P. H. Wicksteed and F. M. Cornford, Loeb Classical Edition (Cambridge: Harvard University Press, 1929), 1.193a29, 1.193a30.

19. Aristotle, *Physics*, 1.193b1 and 193b7.

20. Aristotle, "Parts of Animals," in *The Basic Works of Aristotle*, ed. Richard McKeon (New York: Random House, 1941), 640a32, and *Nicomachean Ethics*, in *The Basic Works of Aristotle*, 1140a13.

21. H. S. Thayer, *Newton's Philosophy of Nature: Selections from His Writings* (New York: Macmillan, Hafner Press, 1953), 25.

22. Thayer, *Newton's Philosophy of Nature*, 51, 29, 54.

23. Thayer, *Newton's Philosophy of Nature*, 53.

24. Caroline Whitbeck, "Theories of Sex Difference" in *Women and Values: Readings in Recent Feminist Philosophy*, ed. Marilyn Pearsall, 2d ed. (Belmont, Calif.: Wadsworth, 1992), 35.

25. Francis Bacon, *The Great Instauration and New Atlantis*, ed. J. Weinberger (Arlington Heights, Ill.: Harlan Davidson, 1980), 7.

26. Arne Naess, "The Shallow and the Deep, Long-Range Ecology Movement: A Summary," *Inquiry* 16, no. 1 (1973): 95–100; and "The Deep Ecological Movement: Some Philosophical Aspects," *Philosophical Inquiry* 8, no. 1–2 (1986): 10–31.

27. Bill Devall and George Sessions. *Deep Ecology: Living As If Nature Mattered* (Salt Lake City: Peregrine Smith Books, 1985).

28. Janet Biehl, "It's Deep, but Is It Broad? An Eco-Feminist Looks at Deep Ecology," *Kick It Over*, special supplement, Winter 1987, 2A.

29. Michael Zimmerman, "Feminism, Deep Ecology and Environmental Ethics," *Environmental Ethics* 9, no. 1 (1987): 21–44, 37. See also Marti Kheel, "Ecofeminism and Deep Ecology," *Elmwood Newsletter* (Winter, 1988): 7, and "Ecofeminism and Deep Ecology: Reflections on Identity and Difference," in Diamond and Orenstein, *Reweaving the World*, 129; and Charlene Spretnak, "Ecofeminism: Our Roots and Flowering," also in Diamond and Orenstein, *Reweaving the World*, 11.

30. Jim Cheney, "Ecofeminism and Deep Ecology," *Environmental Ethics* 9, no. 2 (1987), 115–45: 129.

31. Ariel Kay Salleh, "Class, Race, and Gender Discourse in the Ecofeminism/Deep Ecology Debate," *Environmental Ethics* 15, no. 3 (1993): 225–44, 225.

32. Ariel Kay Salleh, "The Ecofeminist/Deep Ecology Debate: A Reply to Patriarchal Reason," *Environmental Ethics* 14, no. 3 (1992): 195–216, 195.

33. Deborah Slicer, "Is There an Ecofeminism–Deep Ecology 'Debate'?" *Environmental Ethics* 17, no. 2 (1995): 151–69, 151.

34. R. V. O'Neill, D. L. DeAngelis, J. B. Waide, and T. F. H. Allen, *A Hierarchical Concept of Ecosystems* (Princeton: Princeton University Press, 1986), and R. V. O'Neill, "Perspectives in Hierarchy and Scale," in *Perspectives in Ecological Theory*, ed. J. Roughgarden, R. M. May, and S. A. Levin (Princeton: Princeton University Press, 1988).

35. Warren and Cheney, "Ecosystem Ecology and Metaphysical Ecology," 99.

36. Warren and Cheney, "Ecosystem Ecology and Metaphysical Ecology," 103.

37. Virginia Woolf, *A Room of One's Own* (London: Harcourt and Brace, 1929).

38. Woolf, *A Room of One's Own*, 104.

39. Woolf, *A Room of One's Own*, 103.

40. Woolf, *A Room of One's Own*, 72.

41. Woolf, *A Room of One's Own*, 93.

42. W. E. B. DuBois, *The Souls of Black Folk* (New York: Penguin Books, Signet Classic, 1969), 45; see 102, 122.

43. DuBois, *The Souls of Black Folk*, 44.

44. DuBois, *The Souls of Black Folk*, 139.

45. Paula Ruth Boddington, "The Issue of Women's Philosophy," *Feminist Perspectives in Philosophy*, ed. Morwenna Griffiths and Margaret Whitford (Bloomington: Indiana University Press, 1988), 205, 206.

46. Geraldine Finn, "On the Oppression of Women in Philosophy—Or, Whatever Happened to Objectivity?" in *Feminism in Canada: From Pressure to Politics* (Montreal: Black Rose Books, 1982).

47. Jane Flax, "Political Philosophy and the Patriarchal Unconscious: A Psychoanalytic Perspective on Epistemology and Metaphysics," in *Discovering Reality: Feminist Perspectives on Epistemology, Metaphysics, Methodology, and Philosophy of Science*, ed. Sandra Harding and Merrill Hintikka (London: D. Reidel, 1983), 245.

48. Eva Feder Kittay, "Womb Envy: An Explanatory Concept," in *Mothering: Essays in Feminist Thought*, ed. Joyce Trebilcot (Totowa, N.J.: Rowman and Allanheld, 1984).

49. Biehl, "It's Deep, but Is It Broad?" 2A.

50. Luce Irigaray, *Speculum of the Other Woman*, trans. Gillian C. Gill (Ithaca: Cornell University Press, 1985); *Speculum de·l'autre femme* (Paris: Les Éditions de Minuit, 1974).

51. Cheney, "Ecofeminism and Deep Ecology," 129.

52. Woolf, *A Room of One's Own*, 98.

53. Hélène Cixous, "The Laugh of the Medusa," trans. Paula Cohen and Keith Cohen, in *Women and Values*, 79 and 85.

54. Elizabeth M. Harlow, "The Human Face of Nature: Environmental Values and the Limits of Nonanthropocentrism," *Environmental Ethics* 14, no. 1 (1992): 27–42, 27.

55. Bryan G. Norton, "Why I Am Not a Nonanthropocentrist: Callicott and the Failure of Monistic Inherentism," *Environmental Ethics* 17, no. 4 (1995): 341–58, 341.

56. Judith M. Green, "Retrieving the Human Place in Nature," *Environmental Ethics* 17, no. 4 (1995): 381–96.
57. Naess, "The Deep Ecological Movement," 14.
58. Baird Callicott, "Intrinsic Value, Quantum Theory, and Environmental Ethics," *Environmental Ethics* 7 (1985): 257–75, 262.
59. Will McNeill, "*Heimat*: Heidegger on the Threshold," in *Heidegger Toward the Turn: Essays on the Work of the 1930s*, ed. James Risser (Albany: State University of New York Press, 1999), 347.
60. Aristotle, *Physics* 1.192b14–16.
61. Martin Heidegger, "Die Bedrohung der Wissenschaft," in *Zur philosophischen Aktualität Heideggers*, Band 1, ed. Dietrich Papenfuss und Otto Pöggler (Frankfurt am Main: Vittorio Klostermann, 1991), 16.
62. Karen Warren, "Feminism and Ecology: Making Connections," *Environmental Ethics* 9, no. 3 (1987): 3–20, esp. 6.
63. See GA 66, 15.
64. María Lugones and Elizabeth Spelman, "Have We Got a Theory for You! Feminist Theory, Cultural Imperialism, and the Demand for 'The Woman's Voice,' " in *Women and Values*, 24.
65. McNeill, "*Heimat*," 321.
66. Ruether, *New Woman/New Earth*, 194.
67. McNeill, "*Heimat*," 326.
68. McNeill, "*Heimat*," 344. Cf. GA 53, 175–76: "In guest-friendship, however, there also lies the resolve . . . to let the foreigner be the one he is."
69. Karen J. Warren, "Ecofeminism and the Longing for Home," *The Longing for Home*, ed. Leroy S. Rouner (Notre Dame: University of Notre Dame Press, 1996), 228.
70. Sherry B. Ortner, "Is Female to Male as Nature Is to Culture?" *Women and Values*, 59–72.
71. Warren, "Ecofeminism and the Longing for Home," 227.
72. Warren, "Ecofeminism and the Longing for Home," 226.
73. Janet Biehl, *Rethinking Ecofeminist Politics* (Boston: South End Press, 1991), 2–4.
74. Simone de Beauvoir, *After the Second Sex: Interviews with Simone de Beauvoir*, ed. Alice Schwarzer (New York: Pantheon Books, 1984), 103.

9

House and Home

Feminist Variations on a Theme

Iris Marion Young

For millennia the image of Penelope sitting by the hearth and weaving, saving and preserving the home while her man roams the earth in daring adventures, has defined one of Western culture's basic ideas of womanhood. Many other cultures historically and today equate women with home, expecting women to serve men at home and sometimes preventing them from leaving the house. If house and home mean the confinement of women for the sake of nourishing male projects, then feminists have good reason to reject home as a value. But it is difficult even for feminists to exorcise a positive valence to the idea of home. We often look forward to going home and invite others to make themselves at home. House and home are deeply ambivalent values.

In this essay I sort through this ambivalence. On the one hand, I agree with feminist critics such as Luce Irigaray and Simone de Beauvoir that the comforts and supports of house and home historically come at women's expense. Women serve, nurture, and maintain so that the bodies and souls of men and children gain confidence and expansive subjectivity to make their mark on the world. This homey role deprives women of support for their own identity and projects. Along with several feminist critics, furthermore, I question the yearning for a whole and stable identity that the idea of home often represents. Unlike these critics, however, I am not ready to toss the idea of home out of the larder of feminist values. Despite the oppressions and privileges the idea historically carries, the idea of home also carries critical liberating potential because it expresses uniquely human values. Some of these can be uncovered by exploring the meaning-making activity most typical of women in domestic work.

Instead of following one line of argument, I aim here to weave together several thematic threads. All of them wind around meanings of subjectivity or identity. I begin by noting Martin Heidegger's equation of dwelling with the way of being that is human, and note his division of dwelling into moments of building and preservation. Despite his claim that these moments are equally important, Heidegger nevertheless seems to privilege building as the world-founding of an active subject, and I suggest that this privileging is male-biased.

Luce Irigaray makes explicit the maleness of Heidegger's allegedly universal ontology. Man can build and dwell in the world in patriarchal culture, she suggests, only on the basis of the materiality and nurturance of women. In the idea of "home," man projects onto woman the nostalgic longing for the lost wholeness of the original mother. To fix and keep hold of his identity man makes a house, puts things in it, and confines there his woman who reflects his identity to him. The price she pays for supporting his subjectivity, however, is dereliction, having no self of her own.

Irigaray writes about the association of house and home with a male longing for fixed identity in a timeless tone. The property acquisition she describes men as engaging in as a means of substituting for the lost mother, however, is probably best thought of as characteristic of bourgeois society, whose values became hegemonic in the twentieth century in the West, and increasingly in the world. Thus I explore the specific attachment of personal identity to commodified houses and their contents, in order to find another angle of critique of the longing for home.

Before entering a critique of Simone de Beauvoir's devaluation of housework, I digress to tell the story of one bad housekeeper: my mother. The purpose of this gesture is to commemorate, but also to describe in concrete terms how disciplinary standards of orderly housework and PTA motherhood continue to oppress women, especially single mothers.

Like Irigaray, Beauvoir describes women's existence as deprived of active subjectivity because their activity concentrates on serving and supporting men in the home. Unlike Irigaray, however, Beauvoir materializes this account by reflecting on the sexual division of labor. Because she accepts a dichotomy between immanence and transcendence and identifies all of women's domestic labor with immanence, however, Beauvoir misses the creatively human aspects of women's traditional household work, in activities I call preservation.

That aspect of dwelling which Heidegger devalues thus provides a turning point for revaluing home. Preservation makes and remakes home as a support for personal identity without accumulation, certainty, or fixity. While preservation, a typically feminine activity, is traditionally devaluated at least in Western conceptions of history and identity, it has crucial human value.

I next challenge a group of feminist texts whose writers all reject the idea of home as inappropriately totalizing and imperialist. Essays by Biddy Martin and Chandra Mohanty, Teresa de Lauretis, and Bonnie Honig all argue that longing for home expresses an oppressive search for certainty and attachment to privilege. Although I accept much of their analysis, I question the wholesale rejection of an ideal of home for feminism. While values of home do indeed signal privilege today, analysis of those values and commitment to their democratic enactment for all can have enormous critical political potential in today's world. In addition to preservation, those values include safety, individuation, and privacy.

Dwelling and Building

Dwelling, says Martin Heidegger, is man's mode of being. Habitual human activity reveals things as meaningful, and through dwelling among the meaningful things people have a place for themselves. Dwelling and building, Heidegger says, stand in a circular relation. Humans attain to dwelling only by means of building. We dwell by making the places and things that structure and house our activities. These places and things establish relations among each other, between themselves and dwellers, and between dwellers and the surrounding environment. But we only build on the basis of already dwelling as the beings whose mode of being is to let things be, to think and reveal them.[1]

Building has two aspects, according to Heidegger: cultivating and constructing. One mode of building consists in cherishing, protecting, preserving, and caring for, whose paradigm is agriculture, the cultivation of the soil. "Building in the sense of preserving and nurturing is not making anything" (BDT, 147). Thus to remain, to stay in place, is an important meaning of dwelling. "To dwell, to be set at peace, means to remain at peace within the free, the preserve, the free sphere that safeguards each thing in its nature. The fundamental character of dwelling is this sparing and preserving" (BDT, 149).

After introducing this duality of building, as preservation and construction, Heidegger's text leaves preservation behind to focus on construction. A curious abandonment, in light of the above claim that preservation is fundamental to dwelling. To describe the human mode of being in the world, Heidegger dwells on the heroic moment of place through creative activity that gathers the environment into a meaningful presence.

We can dwell only in a place. Edifices enclose areas with walls and link areas by planes, thus creating locations. Walls, roofs, columns, stairs, fences, bridges, towers, roads, and squares found the human world by making place.[2] Through building, man establishes a world and his place in the world, according to Heidegger, establishes himself as somebody, with an identity and history. People inhabit the world by erecting material supports for their routines and rituals and then see the specificity of their lives reflected in the environment, the materiality of things gathered together with historical meaning.[3] If building in this way is basic to the emergence of subjectivity, to dwelling in the world with identity and history, then it would appear that only men are subjects. On the whole, women do not build.

Even today, when women have moved into so many typically male activities, building houses and other structures remains largely a male activity in most parts of the world.[4] In building industries, a woman with a hard hat is still a rare sight. Nowhere in the world do women participate in the building trades in more than very small numbers. Perhaps even more significantly, men dominate the ranks of those who make building decisions—corporate boards of directors, architects, planners, engineers.

Even in some of the most egalitarian households, the work of building and structural maintenance falls most often to men.

In many traditional societies of Africa and Asia, women were the home builders. But peasants all over the world have migrated to cities and towns because capitalism and environmental destruction have made it nearly impossible in many places to live off the land in traditional ways. Many rural and urban development projects include programs where people build the houses in which they will live. Despite the fact that poorer households in developing countries are very often headed by women, they rarely participate in these house-building projects. Either they do not have title to land on which to build because of male biases in property laws; or the development project has simply assumed that men are more natural builders and thus have designed construction projects with men in mind. Frequently women's income and assets are so low that they cannot qualify for the credit necessary to participate in building projects.[5]

If building establishes a world, if building is the means by which a person emerges as a subject who dwells in that world, then not to build is a deprivation. Those excluded from building, who do not think of themselves as builders, perhaps have a more limited relation to the world, which they do not think of themselves as founding. Those who build dwell in the world in a different way from those who occupy the structures already built, and from those who preserve what is constructed. If building establishes a world, then it is still very much a man's world.

Women as a group are still largely excluded from the activities that erect structures to gather and reveal a meaningful world. It will be women's world as much as men's only when women participate as much in their design and founding. But the male bias of building also appears in the devaluation of that other aspect of building Heidegger discusses, preservation, a devaluation to which his own philosophy tends. For a distinction between constructing and preserving, as two aspects of building and dwelling, is implicitly gendered. Later I will pick up the thread of this concept of preservation, to argue that much of the unnoticed labor of women is this basic activity of meaning maintenance. First we shall explore further the masculinism implicit in a philosophy of existence that takes building as world founding, by way of a bridge from Heidegger to his feminist follower and critic, Luce Irigaray.

Building, says Heidegger, gathers together dispersed surroundings, which have no center apart from the artifice around which they are oriented. The house in the woods gives to the trees and lakes a placement.

The bridge across the river gathers the shores, revealing a nexus of relationships, a context. But man's building, Heidegger points out, occurs on the foundation of already dwelling. Man is enveloped by being, finds himself as already having been at home in nature, which building reveals as already surrounding. This revealing of the world itself depends on a prior ground that sustains and nurtures.

With such a move Heidegger believes himself to be sublating modern Western philosophy, and its specifically technological orientation. Descartes and those who come after him have the hubris to think of man as self-originating, the thinking subject as the master and representor of being. They have forgotten the humility of the ancients, who understand better the placement of mortals in a nature on which they depend, whose thoughtful tending and preserving is the lot of mortals. Man builds for the sake of dwelling, to make himself at home, in respect to the prior elements that envelop and nourish him, which his building gathers and reveals.

Woman as Nostalgic Home

Luce Irigaray names the gendering already present in Heidegger's worlding of the world: Man builds for the sake of dwelling, to make himself at home, on the basis of Woman as already always positioned as the enveloping nurturing presence of nature. For man, woman is always mother, from whose dark womb he emerges to build solid structures in the light of day, with whose light he returns to look in the caverns with the speculum. In lovemaking he seeks to return to the enclosing warmth of the original union with the mother. The patriarchal gender system allows man a subjectivity that depends on woman's objectification and dereliction; he has a home at the expense of her homelessness, as she serves as the ground on which he builds.

Everyone is born in loss. Ejected from the dark comfort of the mother's body, we are thrown into a world without walls, with no foundation to our fragile and open-ended existence. Speaking mortals must come to terms with this separation from the mother, to find and form meaning and identity for ourselves, without foundation or certainty. In patriarchal culture, according to Irigaray, the gender system of masculinity and femininity makes it possible for man to come to terms with his loss by never really dealing with it; instead, he attempts to return to the lost home of the womb by means of woman.

Man deals with the loss by building, in order that he may recover his dwelling. He seeks to make himself a home to stand in for the lost home. Through building he gathers the amorphous and fluid elements into solid structure. Through projecting outward he makes objective works where he can see himself reflected. He makes and affirms himself as subject through building and making. In this objectifying self-reflection woman serves as material both on which to stand and out of which to build, and women likewise serve as a primary object for reflecting himself, his mirror.

> Man's love is teleological. It aims for a target outside them. It moves toward the outside and the constitution, on the outside, within that which is outside themselves, of a home. Outside of the self, the tension, the intention, aims for a dwelling, a thing, a production. Which also serves men as a third part and stake.
>
> To *inhabit* is the fundamental trait of man's being. Even if this trait remains unconscious, unfulfilled, especially in its ethical dimension, man is forever searching for, building, creating homes for himself everywhere: caves, huts, women, cities, language, concepts, theory, and so on.[6]

Building is for the sake of dwelling, gathering together natural material and element into a determinate place. In the patriarchal gender scheme, woman serves as the construction material (ESD, 103–107), and as the *place* within which man dwells. His self-affirming subjectivity is possible because she supports and complements his existence as both an origin of his creativity and the product in which he can see his self reflected. She serves as the material envelope and container of his existence. "She is assigned to be place without occupying place. Through her, place would be set up for man's use but not hers. Her jouissance is meant to 'resemble' the flow of whatever is in the place that she is when she contains, contains herself" (ESD, 52).

The form of man's self-affirmation in this gender system is *nostalgia*, a longing for the return to a lost home. Man puts woman in her place, so that he can return to the original maternal home. Nostalgia is this recurrent desire for return, which is unsatisfiable because the loss is separation, birth, mortality, itself. Nostalgia is a flight from having to come to terms with this loss, by means of constant seach for a symbolic substitute for lost home. Man yearns nostalgically for an original union with the mother within safe walls of warmth. In women men look nostalgically to return to their own lost home; thus they fail to face women as subjects with their own identities and need of covering.

> He arrests his growth and repeats, endlessly, searching for the moment when the separation of memory and forgetting was lost to him. But, the more he repeats, the more he surrounds himself with envelops, containers, "houses" which prevent him from finding either the other or himself. His nostalgia for the first and last dwelling prevents him from meeting and living with the other. (ESD, 142)

Man seeks nostalgically to return to the lost home by making buildings and putting things in them that will substitute for that original home. He creates property, things he owns and controls. But because the property doesn't satisfy the longing for lost home, he is launched on an acquisitive quest for more property. In this acquisitive economy women serve as raw materials, caretakers, and goods themselves to be traded. Her role is to be the home by being at home. Her being home gives him comfort and allows him to open on the expanse of the world to build and create. For her, however, the placement is an imprisonment.

> Centuries will perhaps have been needed for man to interpret the meaning of his work(s): the endless construction of a number of substitutes for his parental home. From the depths of the earth to the highest skies? Again and again, taking from the feminine the issue or textures of spatiality. In exchange—but it isn't a real one—he buys her a house, even shuts her up in it, places limits on her that are the opposite of the unlimited site in which he unwillingly situates her. He contains or envelopes her with walls while enveloping himself and his things in her flesh. The nature of these envelopes is not the same: on the one hand, invisibly alive, but with barely visible limits; on the other, visibly limiting or sheltering, but at the risk of being prison-like or murderous if the threshold is not left open. (ESD, 11)

Since woman functions for man as the ground of his subjectivity, she has no support for her own self. She is derelict. She too must deal with the same loss as he, with the abandonment of mortality, radical freedom, and groundlessness, and the expulsion from warmth and security of the mother's body. By means of her, man makes for himself a home to substitute for this loss. He creates by holding her as his muse, he rests by having her serve his needs at home. Her only comfort is to try to derive her satisfaction from being in the home, the Other. She tries to take her subjectivity from her being-for-him. She tries to envelop herself with decoration. She covers herself with jewelry, makeup, clothing, in the attempt to make an envelope, to give herself a place. But in the end she is left homeless, derelict, with no room of her own, since he makes room for himself by using her as his envelope.

If building establishes a world, if building is the means by which a person emerges as a subject who dwells in that world, then not to build is a deprivation. In the patriarchal gender system, men are the builders and women the nurturers of builders and the ornaments placed within their creations. As homeless themselves, women are deprived of the chance to be subjects for themselves. Language, says Heidegger, is the house of being. Men not only build material shelters, temples, bridges to gather the environment into a place. Masculine subjects are also the founders of civilization itself, those who name things and construct the theories and epics in which their meanings are preserved over generations. According to Irigaray, woman's place in language is a sign of her dereliction, of her inability to attain to the position of subject for herself.

The question for postmodern living is whether an end to such exploitation requries rejecting entirely the project of supporting identity and subjectivity embodied in the patriarchal ideology of home. The feminist writers with whom I engage in Section VI answer this question affirmatively. While I accept many of their reasons for leaving home, I wish to explore another possibility. Is it possible to retain an idea of home as supporting the individual subjectivity of the person, where the subject is understood as fluid, partial, shifting, and in relations of reciprocal support with others? This is the direciton in which I find Irigaray pointing to an alternative to the desire for fixed identity that historically imprisons women. Before thematizing an alternative concept of house and home, however, I want to explore more of its questionable aspects.

Commodified Home

Iragaray's rhetoric invokes a (patriarchal) universality. Her images of women's enclosure in the house, a house in which man arranges his possessions to satisfy his desire to substitute for the lost security of the womb, presuppose a specifically modern, bourgeois conception of home. The subject that fills its existential lack of seeing itself in objects, by owning and possessing and accumulating property, is a historically specific subject of modern capitalism. Economic and psychosocial processes collude in the twentieth century in particular to encourage the expression of a subject that fulfills its desire by commodity consumption.[7] While this consumer subject is best realized in advanced industrial societies, its allure has spread around the globe. House and home occupy central places in this consumer consciousness as the core of personal property and a specific commodity-based identity.[8] Radical critics of the allure of home rightly find this link of home and identity to be a source of quietism and privilege. The commodified concept of home ties identity to a withdrawl from the public world and to the amount and status of one's belongings.

In many societies, both historically and today, people do not "live" solely in a house. There are huts and cottages reserved for certain life activities, such as sleeping, making love, and giving birth, but dwelling in a wider sense occurs outdoors and/or in collective spaces, both sheltered and not. In rural Botswana, for example, this individual private "home" is outdoor space enclosed by a fence, within which stand small houses for different family members and different activities. When the family grows they build another little house. Preparing food, cooking, eating, washing, child's and adult's amusements all usually occur outdoors. If these families move to a small apartment in the city, they often have difficulty adjusting their lives.[9]

In many societies "home" refers to the village or square, together with its houses, and dwelling takes place both in and out of doors. While few societies fail to distinguish status partly by the size and artfulness of the individual houses, in many societies houses are rather small and plain and do not function very much as status symbols. They and their contents are only minor sources of identity. In many of these societies people take their personal pride more from collective buildings, such as churches or meeting houses. They invest creative energy into erecting and decorating these buildings with carvings, columns, statues, paintings, and fine furnishing. The celebrated carvings of the Maori people, for example, belong for the most part to the collective meeting houses on the *marae* of each clan. Even in modern capitalist cities some people "live" more in their neighborhood or on their block than in their houses. They sit in squares, on stoops, in bars and coffee houses, going to their houses mostly to sleep. The bourgeois sensibility of civic privatism, however, finds such street living disorderly and threatening. In "better" neighborhoods and communities people discretely and privately sit behind their houses, leaving the streets to teenagers.

Under these modern circumstances, home tends to be restricted to the living space of house or apartment. Personal identity is linked to commodified home in specific ways. The house is the primary place of consumption itself. Freedom consists in release from work and public responsibility in activities of leisure, pleasure, and consumption. The house or apartment is the site of many of these activities, filled with comfortable furnishings and gadgets.

Commodified home supports identity not only as the site of consumer freedom, but as the mark of one's social status. The size, style, and especially the location of the house, along with its landscaping and furnishing, establish the individual's location in the social hierarchy. Everyone knows which are the better houses or apartments, better streets, better neighborhoods, better communities, and the aspiration for upward mobility is often expressed in the desire to move house from one neighborhood or community to another.

Attachment to home as status symbol and investment opportunity creates and perpetuates a market competition in which most people are losers. The project of maintaining good "property values," and not simply a comfortable living space, produces or exacerbates racial and class exclusion, which condemns a majority to inferior housing while a few reap windfall profits. To the extent that housing status is also associated with lot size and building size, attachment to house as status also maldistributes land and living space, giving too much to some people and wrongly crowding others. The social and economic organization of commodified housing thus makes the value of home a privilege, and constructs many as relatively or absolutely deprived.

In this commodified construction of personal achievement and lifestyle, the house often becomes an end in itself. The goal of a dream house sets workers working and keeps workers working, fearing job loss, working overtime. The consumer-driven desire of civic privatism tends to produce political quietism because people invest their commitment into their private life, which needs even greater income to fuel it.[10] Women have entered the labor force in mass numbers partly because one person's income is no longer sufficient to pay for the house; ironically, all the adults now stay away from the house for most hours of the week in order to earn the money for the house in which they invest their sense of self.[11]

Fantasy feeds consumer desire that fuels this privatist identity attached to house and home. Whatever our actual living conditions, we can buy the dream of a beautiful home in magazines. Along with sex, sports, and clothes, house and home are million-dollar magazine subjects. The magazines offer countless sets on which one can imagine one's life staged. Dining rooms, airy and light, diaphanous curtains revealing a sunny garden beyond the French doors. Solid living rooms, tasteful painting on the walls, a grand piano in the corner, massive leather couches. Cozy bedrooms, fluffed with pillows, lace, and comforters. A kitchen for grand cuisine, with a double-door refrigerator, forty feet of smooth, uncluttered wooden counter, and copper cookware hanging from the ceiling. The rooms in house magazines are nearly always empty of people, thus enabling us to step into their spaces.

The house magazines often sing with nostalgia. Rustic house in the woods, old wood, antique furniture, leaded glass windows. New tiles and floorings are reminiscent of the turn of the century. The dream house often evokes the image of the cozy traditional cottage.[12] Even when the images do not explicitly evoke the past, they often are calculated to produce a longing for a way of life gone by or which might have been as nostalgic. These home images also whisper of stillness, rest.

The attachment of personal identity of commodified home is not specifically gendered. Men and women are equally prone to assess their status and self-worth according to the things they have. The commodified home does have some specific consequences for women, however. The reduction of home to living space can confine women even more than before, especially when suburban development reduces whole townships to living space. Making the house and its furnishings an indicator of personal and family status, moreover, can increase the pressure on women to be good housekeepers, not for the sake of nurturance, efficiency, or hygiene, but for the sake of appearances.

Interlude: My Mother's Story

The dream of a house in the suburbs became my mother's nightmare.

My daddy left our Flushing apartment each morning in one of his three slightly different grey flannel suits and took the subway to midtown Manhattan. An aspiring novelist turned insurance underwriter, he was moving slowly but steadily up the corporate ladder. I imagined his office as Dagwood's, and his boss as Mr. Dithers.

My sister and I tripped out to school each morning, in the horrid saddle shoes our mommy made us wear, and she stayed home with the little baby boy. A perfect picture of '50's family bliss, with one flaw: my mother didn't clean the house.

Our two-bedroom apartment was always dirty, cluttered, things all over the floors and piled on surfaces, clothes strewn around the bedroom, dust in the covers, in the rugs, on the bookcases; the kitchen stove wore cooked-on food. I never invited my friends into my house. If they came to the door and peered in I told them we were getting ready to move. Mostly my friends did not care, since we played in the alleys and hallways, and not in each other's houses.

My mother spent her days at home reading books, taking a correspondence course in Russian, filling papers with codes and calculations. She seemed to me an inscrutable intellectual. But she also played with us— authors, rummy, twenty-questions, with gusto—and sang and sang, teaching us hymns and old army songs. Sometimes on a Saturday she hauled out the oils and sat her little girls down to model, and then let us make our own oil paintings. From my mommy I learned to value books and song and art and games, and to think that housework is not important.

It was 1958. My mother had to stay home with her children even though she had worked happily in a Manhattan magazine office before we were born, even though she spoke three languages and had a Master's degree. I was mortified then by her weirdness, sitting in her chair reading and writing, instead of cooking, cleaning and ironing and mending like a real mom. Later, after she died in 1978, I read her refusal to do housework as passive resistance.

Like most of the Joneses (well, more likely the Cohens) on our block, my mommy and daddy dreamed of owning a house in the suburbs. They dragged us three kids all over the state of New Jersey looking at model homes in new developments. Back in Flushing, they pored over houseplan sketches, looked at paint samples, calculated mortgage costs. Finally we settled on one of the many mid-Jersey developments built on filled-in wetlands (called swamps at that time). From the four models available my parents chose the mid-priced split-level. My sister and I chose the blue for our room and my three-year-old brother pointed to the green patch on the sample chart. Many Sundays we drove the more than hour-long trip to watch the progress of the house: foundation, frame, walls, grass.

Finally we moved. This was happiness. We were the Cleavers. We bought a ping-pong table for the game room. My sister and I went careening on the streets on our bikes. Then my daddy died—quickly, quietly, of a brain tumor.

My mother was devastated. She relied on us for what comfort there could be in this wasteland of strangers in four types of model homes. At first the neighbors were solicitous, bringing over covered dishes, then they withdrew. The folks at church were more helpful, offering rides to the insurance office or church. My mommy drank, but never on Sunday morning. My sister and I went to school sad, my brother stayed home with our mother, who had less motive than ever to clean the house. We were not poor once the insurance and social security money came, just messy.

But one spring day a uniformed man came into my class and called my name. He escorted me to a police car where my brother and sister were already waiting. Without explanation, they drove us to a teen-reform home. No word from or about our mommy, where she was, why we were being taken away. Slowly I learned or inferred that she had been thrown in jail for child neglect. Daughters do not always defend their mothers accused of crimes. Being one to please authorities, and at eleven wanting to be knowing and adult, I believe that I told stories to confirm their self-righteousness, of how I did most of the cooking and how my mother did not keep house.

A woman alone with her children in this development of perfectly new squeaky clean suburban houses. She is traumatized by grief, and the neighbors look from behind their shutters, people talk about the disheveled way she arrives at church, her eyes red from crying. Do they help this family, needy not for food or clothes, but for support in a very hard time? A woman alone with her children is no longer a whole family, deserving like others of respectful distance. From my mother's point of view there was no difference between child-welfare agents and police. A woman alone with her children is liable to punishment, including the worst of all for her: having her children taken from her.

Neglect. The primary evidence of neglect was drinking and a messy house. We ate well enough, had clean enough clothes, and a mother's steady love, given the way she gave it: playing ping-pong, telling bible stories, playing twenty-questions. We were a family in need of support, but we children were not neglected.

After two months we were reunited, moved back to our grey split-level. My sister and I rode our bikes on the street again, played kickball and croquet with the neighbor kids. My mother was determined to prove she could manage a household by suburban standards, so she did what she thought she had to—called an agency for live-in maids.

One day a thin fourteen-year-old black girl arrived at the door, fresh from North Carolina. We gave her my brother's room and he moved in with my mommy. I felt a strange affinity with this shy and frightened person, who sobbed so quietly in her room. She was not prepared for the work of housekeeping. She and I worked together to prepare the packaged macaroni and cheese. We sorted laundry, silently sitting across from each other, for she did not know whose things were whose. We hardly talked; she told me the barest facts about her life. I see her standing on the landing in a cotton summer dress, a Cinderella figure holding a broom and wistfully sweeping. She quit within two weeks, and the house was not any cleaner.

So we glided through the summer, playing punch ball and tag with the kids in the terrace. My mother went to the city frequently to look for work. In August she took us out to buy three pairs of new shoes, for my brother would start kindergarten. School began, my mother was off to work, my twelve-year-old life seemed rosy enough.

Until one day in early fall I came home from school to find a police sign nailed to my door. A fire. A smoldering ember in my mother's slipper chair had ignited and sent out flames, the neighbors had summoned the fire department. I used their phone to call a family friend to come and get us kids—I wasn't going to any reform school again. There was not much damage to the house, they had caught the fire early, but when breaking in to douse it they had seen the papers strewn about and dust on the floor and beer cans. My mother was arrested again.

We lived with those family friends for a year. Every three months a box of clothes arrived for us from the Department of Social Services—I loved the discovery of what they thought we ought to be wearing. After they let my mommy out of jail and rehab we visited her every couple of months in an impersonal office for an hour or so. She hugged us and cried, and told us of her job in the city and the new cleaning lady, Odessa. As I plummeted into adolescence and my brother entered his seventh year, there was a crisis in our foster home: our foster father died suddenly of pneumonia. Headed now only by a woman, our foster family instantly became a bad environment for us; they shipped us back to my mother without warning. Her family reunited again, my mother wasted no time packing up and moving us all back to the safe indifference of New York City.

Waves of grief rolled up from my gut when, ten years after my mother died, I saw the movie *Housekeeping*.

Historicity, Preservation, and Identity

Beauvoir on Housework

Simone de Beauvoir's *The Second Sex* still stands as one of the most important works documenting women's oppression, because it describes the typical life and dilemmas of women so graphically. One cannot read Beauvoir's descriptions of domestic labor without appreciating how endless the work is, how oppressive.

> Such work has a negative basis: cleaning is getting rid of dirt, tidying up is eliminating disorder. And under impoverished conditions no satisfaction is possible; the hovel remains a hovel in spite of women's sweat and tears: "nothing in the world can make it pretty." Legions of women have only this endless struggle without victory over the dirt. And for even the most privileged the victory is never final.
>
> Few tasks are more like the torture of Sisyphus than housework, with its endless repetition. The clean becomes soiled, the soiled is made clean, over and over, day after day. The housewife wears herself out marking time: she makes nothing, simply perpetuates the present.[13]

Beauvoir's account of the oppressions of domestic work fits in the frame of her general account of women's situation as confined to immanence, whereas man exists as transcendence.

> The fact is that every human existence involves transcendence and immanence at the same time; to go forward, each esistence

> must be maintained, for it to expand toward the future it must integrate the past, and while intercommunicating with others it would find self-confirmation. These two elements—maintenance and progression—are implied in any living activity, and for *man* marriage permits precisely a happy synthesis of the two. In his occupation and in his political life he encounters change and progress, he senses his extension through time and the universe; and when he is tired of such roaming, he gets himself a home, where his wife takes care of his furnishings and children and guards the things of the past that she keeps in store. But she has no other job than to maintain and provide for life in pure unvarying generality; she perpetuates the species without change, she ensures the even rhythm of the days and the continuity of the home, seeing to it that the doors are locked. (430)

In the existentialist framework Beauvoir uses, transcendence is the expression of individual subjectivity. The subject expresses and realizes his individuality through taking on projects—building a house, organizing a strike, writing a book, winning a battle. These projects, which may be individual or collective, are determinate and particular contributions to the world of human affairs. Transcendence also expresses a mode of temporality. The living subject is future oriented; the future is open with possibility, which generates anxiety at the same time as its openness and possibility restructure the meaning of the present and the past. Human existence is historical in this framework, in that it is structured by creative deed and always must be structured by future deeds.

In Beauvoir's scheme, immanence expresses the movement of life rather than history. Life is necessary and very demanding. Without getting food and shelter and caring for the sick and saving babies from harm there is no possibility for transcendence and history. The activities of sustaining life, however, according to Beauvoir, cannot be expressions of individuality. They are anonymous and general, as the species is general. Thus if a person's existence consists entirely or largely of activities of sustaining life, then she or he cannot be an individual subject. Women's work is largely confined to life maintenance for the sake of supporting the transcending individual projects of men and children. As in Irigaray's account, for Beauvoir man's subjectivity draws on the material support of women's work, and this work deprives her of a subjectivity of her own.

The temporality of immanence is cyclical, repetitive. As the movement of life it moves in species time unpunctuated by events of individual meaning. The cycles go around, from spring to summer to fall to winter, from birth to death and birth to death. Beauvoir describes the activity of housework as living out this cyclical time, a time with no future and no goals.

Beauvoir has an entirely negative valuation of what she constructs as women's situation, a negative valuation of the activity of giving meaning to and maintaining home. She is surely right that much of what we call housework is drudgery, necessary but tedious, and also right that a life confined to such activity is slavery. But such a completely negative valuation flies in the face of the experience of many women, who devote themselves to care for house and children as an meaningful human project. If Irigaray is correct, of course, many women pour their soul into the house because they have no other envelope for the self. But it seems too dismissive of women's own voices to deny entirely the value many give to "homemaking." Following Irigaray, we can reconstruct core values from the silenced meanings of traditional female activity. Because she relies on the dichotomy of transcendence and immanence to conceptualize women's oppression, Beauvoir misses the historical and individualizing character of some of the activity associated with the traditional feminine role, which in the above quotation she calls "guarding the things of the past that she keeps in store." Giving meaning to individual lives through the arrangement and preservation of things is an intrisically valuable and irreplaceable aspect of homemaking.

Homemaking

Beauvoir is surely right that the bare acts of cleaning bathrooms, sweeping floors, and changing diapers are merely instrumental; though necessary, they cannot be invested with creativity or individuality. She is wrong, however, to reduce all or even most domestic work to immanence. Not all homemaking is housework. To understand the difference we need to reconsider the idea of home, and its relation to a person's sense of identity. Home enacts a specific mode of subjectivity and historicity that is distinct both from the creative-destructive idea of transcendence and from the ahistorical repetition of immanence.

D. J. Van Lennep suggests that we can learn what it means to inhabit a space as "home" by thinking about forms of shelter that are not home;

he suggests that we consider why a hotel room is not a home. A hotel room has all the comforts one needs—heat, hot water, a comfortable bed, food and drink a phone call away. Why, then, does not not feel at home in a hotel room? Because there is nothing of one's self, one's life habits and history, that one sees displayed around the room. The arrangement is anonymous and neutral, for anyone and one no one in particular.[14]

A home, on the other hand, is *personal* in a visible, spatial sense. No matter how small a room or apartment, the home displays the things among which a person lives, that support his or her life activities and reflect in matter the events and values of his or her life. There are two levels in the process of the materialization of identity in the home: (1) my belongings are arranged in space as an extension of my bodily habits and as support for my routines, and (2) many of the things in the home, as well as the space itself, carry sedimented personal meaning as retainers of personal narrative.

(1) Home is the space where I keep and use the material belongings of my life. They are mine—or ours, when I live together with others—because I/we have chosen or made them, and they thus reflect my needs and tastes. Or they have found their way into my home as inheritance or gifts or perhaps even by accident, but then I have appropriated them. The home is not simply the things, however, but their arrangement in space in a way that supports the body habits and routines of those who dwell there. The arrangement of furniture in space provides pathways for habits—the reading lamp placed just here, the television just here, the particular spices on the rack placed just so in relation to this person's taste and cooking habits. Dwelling, says Lennep,

> is the continuous unfolding of ourselves in space because it is our unbroken relation with things surrounding us. It is human existence itself which constitutes space. We simply cannot do otherwise. The things which surround us present themselves in a quality of space which we ourselves are as those who live in space. The pronoun "my" in the expression "my room" does not express my possession of it, but precisely a relation between me and the room, which means that my spatial existence has come about.[15]

Edward Casey carries this insight further in his idea of the body forming "habit memories" in the process of coming to dwell in a place. One comes to feel settled at home in a place through the process of interaction between the living body's movement to enact aims and purposes and the material things among which such activities occur. The things and their arrangement bear witness to the sedimentation of lives lived there. The home is an extension of and mirror for the living body in its everyday activity. This is the first sense in which home is the materialization of identity.

> But more than comfort is at issue in the elective affinity between houses and bodies: *our very identity is at stake*. For we tend to identify ourselves by—and with—the places in which we reside. Since a significant part of our personal identity depends on our exact bodily configuration, it is only to be expected that dwelling places, themselves physical in structure, will resemble our own material bodies in certain quite basic respect.[16]

(2) The process of sedimentation through which physical surroundings become home as an extension and reflection of routines also deposits meaning onto things. Material things and spaces themselves become layered with meaning and personal value as the material markers of events and relationship that make the narrative of a person or group. The meaningful things in my home often have stories, or they are characters and props in stories. I was a little boy in Japan and I picked out that statuette on my own. Those gashes in the top of the chest show the time I got mad at my mother and went at the chest with a pair of scissors. There's our son's room, still with the trophies he won and the books he read in high school. The things among which I live acquired their meaning through events and travels of my life, layered through stories, and the wordless memories of smells, rhythms, and interactions. Their value is priceless: often worthless even on the yard sale market, the arrangement of these things in rooms is what I would mourn with the deepest grief if they were destroyed by fire or theft.

The activities of homemaking thus give material support to the identity of those whose home it is. Personal identity in this sense is not at all fixed, but always in process. We are not the same from one moment to the next, one day to the next, one year to the next, because we dwell in the flux of interaction and history. We are not the same from one day to the next because our selves are constituted by differing relations with others. Home as the materialization of identity does not fix identity, but anchors it in physical being that makes a continuity between past and present. Without such anchoring of ourselves in things, we are, literally, lost.

Preservation

Homemaking consists in the activities of endowing things with living meaning, arranging them in space in order to facilitate the life activities of those to whom they belong, and preserving them, along with their meaning. Things are made or chosen for the house—furniture, pictures, draperies. Traditionally and today women furnish and decorate houses more than men. Often a home reflects a woman's taste and sensibility, often, the style and image she projects of herself and her family. The decor of a poor or modest home usually reflects this meaning-giving impulse as much as the homes of more wealthy people—she bought fabric for the window curtains that she made by hand, she painted or covered the chairs.

That is the photograph of my grandmother, who died before I was born, and it hung over the piano in every apartment and house we lived in while I was growing up; when my mother died it was the first thing I took home. The history embodied in the meaningful things of the home is often intergenerational. Traditionally women are the primary preservers of family as well as individual histories. Women trace the family lines and keep safe the trinkets, china cups, jewelry, pins, and photos of the departed ancestors, ready to tell stories about each of them. I am suggesting that a main dimension for understanding home is time and history.

Beauvoir, like Sartre, tends to associate historicity with futurity. So she considers the oppression of women to consist in our being inhibited from the creative activity of bringing new things into being.

> The male is called upon for action, his vocation is to produce, fight, create progress, to transcend himself toward the totality of the universe and the infinity of the future. But marriage does not invite the woman to transcend herself with him—it confines her to immanence, shuts her up within the circle of herself. (448)

This focus on futurity, on the unique moment when the human actor brings something new into the world, makes Beauvoir ignore the specifically human value of activities that, as she puts it, guard the things of the past and keep them in store. She implicitly collapses the activities that consist in preserving the living meanings of past history into her category of immanence. This conflation prevents her from seeing the world-making meaning in domestic work. The particular human meanings enacted in the historicality of human existence depend as much on the projection of a past as of a future.

Hannah Arendt's distinction between labor and work is similar to Beauvoir's distinction between immanence and transcendence. Labor consists in the grinding activity of doing what is necessary to meet needs and maintain life. Its temporality is repetitive and cyclical because the products of labor are always consumed by the needs of life, and thus they leave no lasting monuments. Work, on the other hand, is that individualizing activity that makes a world of permanent historical objects—temples, squares, great books, lasting political constitutions. For Arendt too, a quintessential moment of human meaning and individuality is that of *founding*—erecting the city, establishing the republic.[17] But as soon as the deeds of founding are accomplished, as soon as the heroic work of the artist, statesman, or planner are recognized and celebrated, a new task comes into play: preservation.[18]

Earlier I cited Heidegger's claim that building has a dual aspect: constructing and preserving. But even his discussion of the correlation of dwelling with building drops the thread of preservation and concentrates on the creative moment of constructing. It is time to pick up the threads of preservation in order to understand the activities of homemaking. Traditional female domestic activity, which many women continue today, partly consists in preserving the objects and meanings of a home.

Homemaking consists in the activities of endowing things with living meaning, arranging them in space in order to facilitate the life activities of those to whom they belong, and preserving them, along with their meaning. Dwelling in the world means we are located among objects, artifacts, rituals, and practices that configure who we are in our particularity. Meaningful historical works that embody the particular spirit of a person or a people must be protected from the constant threat of elemental disorganization. They must be cleaned, dusted, repaired, restored; the stories of their founding and continued meaningful use must be told and retold, interpreted and reinterpreted. They must also be protected from the careless neglect or accidental damage caused by those who dwell among and use them, often hardly noticing their meaning as support for their lives. The work of preservation entails not only keeping the physical objects of particular people intact, but renewing their meaning in their lives. Thus preservation involves preparing and staging commemorations and celebrations, where those who dwell together among the things tell and retell stories of their particular lives, and give and receive gifts that add to the dwelling world. The work of preservation also importantly involves teaching the children the meanings of things among which one dwells, teaching the children the stories, practices, and celebrations that keep the particular meanings alive. The preservation of the things among which one dwells gives people a context for their lives, individuates their histories, gives them items to use in making new projects, and makes them comfortable. When things and works are maintained against destruction, but not in the context of life activity, they become museum pieces.

The temporality of preservation is distinct from that of construction. As a founding construction, making, is a rupture in the continuity of history. But recurrence is the temporality of preservation. Over and over the things must be dusted and cleaned. Over and over the special objects must be arranged after a move. Over and over the dirt from winter snows must be swept away from the temples and statues, the twigs and leaves removed, the winter cracks repaired. The stories must be told and retold to each new generation to keep a living, meaningful history.

It would be a mistake, however, to conceive of the identity supported through this preservation of meaning in things as fixed. There are no fixed identities, events, interactions, and the material changes of age and environment make lives fluid and shifting. The activities of preservation give some enclosing fabric to this ever-changing subject by knitting together today and yesterday, integrating the new events and relationships into the narrative of a life, the biography of a person, a family, a people.

Preserving the meaningful identity of a household or family by means of the loving care of its mementos is simply a different order of activity from washing the unhealthy bacteria out of the bathroom. As Beauvoir rightly says, the latter is general, the abstract maintenance of species life. The former, however, is specific and individuated: the homemaker acts to preserve the particular meaning that these objects have in the lives of these particular people. The confusion between these acts and the level of immanence is perhaps understandable, because so many activities of domestic work are both simultaneously. The homemaker dusts the pieces in order to keep away the molds and dirts that might annoy her sinuses, but at the same time she keeps present to herself and those with whom she lives the moments in their lives or those of their forebears that the objects remember. She prepares the sauce according to her mother's recipe in order physically to nourish her children, but at the same time she keeps alive an old cuisine in a new country.

Thus the activity of preservation should be distinguished from the nostalgia accompanying fantasies of a lost home from which the subject is separated and to which he seeks to return. Preservation entails rememberance, which is quite different from nostalgia. Where nostalgia can be constructed as a longing flight from the ambiguities and disappointments of everyday life, remembrance faces the open negativity of the future by knitting a steady confidence in who one is from the pains and joys of the past retained in the things among which one dwells. Nostalgic longing is always for an elsewhere. Remembrance is the affirmation of what brought us here.[19]

We should not romanticize this activity. Preservation is ambiguous; it can be either conservative or reinterpretive. The same material things sometimes carry the valences of unique personal identity and status privilege. By using my grandmother's china I both carry the material memory of childhood dinners and display the class position of my family history. I spoke once to a woman committed to restoring and preserving her grandmother's Victorian southwestern ranch house, fully mindful of her grandmother's passive participation in the displacement of Native Americans from the land. The house has the history whether she chooses to live in it or not. The moral and political question for her is how she constructs her own identity and tells the stories of her family to her children. Homemaking consists in preserving the things and their meaning as anchor to shifting personal and group identity. But the narratives of the history of what brought us here are not fixed, and part of the creative and moral task of preservation is to reconstruct the connection of the past to the present in light of new events, relationships, and political understandings.

Given the cruelties of the histories of persons and peoples, remembrance and preservation often consists in the renewal of grief or rage. A Jewish survivor of the Holocaust keeps safe the small and tattered mementos of her long-dead parents. A city debates whether to demolish or preserve the two-hundred-year-old slave auction block that once stood in its center; after much political struggle in which many African Americans, among others, demand its preservation, the city decides to leave it as a painful memorial of slavery. Some of the meaning preserved in things that anchor identity can be summed in the words "never again."

Preservation of the history that supports a person's identity by means of caring for and arranging things in space is the activity of homemaking still carried out primarily by women in the West, and in many other cultures as well. Such homemaking is not done exclusively by women, but to the degree that women more than men attend more to family and community ties in everyday life, the activities of presevation tend to be gender specific. Through these same activities, moreover, as I have already begun to indicate, the identity of groups and peoples is preserved. Especially in this late modern world where public administration and corporate standardization tend to drain individualized meaning from politics, schooling, and work, home and neighborhood retain meaningful importance as primary bearers of cultural identity and differentiation. For many migrants who wish to succeed in their new land, for example, their home is the primary place of the expression of cultural identity and continuity with their native lands.[20]

In many premodern or non-Western societies, I pointed out earlier, home is not confined to houses. Often the spaces of village squares, meeting halls, or mountaintops are more the home of the people in a group than are their individual shelters. The activities of preservation of the meaningful things that constitute home are important here as public acts of the group: maintaining collective spaces, guarding and caring for statues and monuments. For some traditional societies this preservative work is highly regarded, the responsibility of priests and elders. Modern Western societies also perform such public acts of preservation, but they are less often noticed or valued.

Such collective preservative activities continue in the interstices of modern urban societies today in the activities of civic clubs, neighborhood organizations, and religious institutions. When cities commemorate buildings as historic landmarks and stage periodic historically tinged festivals, they are also often performing the self-sustaining actions of preservation. These projects of keeping the meaning of past events and characters by maintaining material thus are not confined to things with positive feeling. In modern Western societies these public activities of preservation are also often coded as feminine, the devalued responsibility of "preservation ladies" who drink tea and look through moldy records, and often it is women in fact who seek to maintain or recover, interpret and reinterpret the historical meaning of places.[21]

Beauvoir is right to link her account of women's oppression with domestic work, but not entirely for the reasons she has. A sexual division of labor that removes women from participation in society's most valued and creative activities, excludes women from access to power and resources, and confines women primarily to domestic work is indeed a source of oppression. Much of typically women's work, however, is at least as fundamentally world-making and meaning-giving as typically men's work. Especially modern, future-oriented societies devalue this work, at the same time that they depend on its continued performance for the nurturance of their subjectivity and their sense of historical continuity. We should not romanticize this activity. Like the other aspects of home that I have discussed, preservation is ambiguous; it can be both conservative and reinterpretive, rigid and fluid. To the extent that it falls to women to perform this work for men and children, just as they perform the work of cooking and washing for them, without men's reciprocation, then women continue to serve as material for the subjectivities of men without receiving the like support for themselves. Equality for women, then, requires revaluation of the private and public work of the preservation of meaningful things, and degendering these activities.

Contemporary Feminist Rejection of Home

I have been arguing that the value of home is ambiguous, and that feminists should try to disengage a positive from an oppressive meaning of home. If women are expected to confine themselves to the house and serve as selfless nurturers, and as those who automatically expand their domestic tasks when economic retrenchment rebounds on families,[22] then house and home remain oppressive patriarchal values. To the extent that both men and women seek in their homes and in the women who make them a lost unity and undisturbed comfort, moreover, the idea of home fuels a wrongful escapism. Values of homemaking, however, underlie the affirmation of personal and cultural idenetity, which requires material expression in meaningful objects arranged in space that must be preserved.

A chain of recent interlinked essays elaborates an argument that feminists should reject any affirmation of the value of home. Biddy Martin and Chandra Mohanty launched this discussion in their reading of Minnie Bruce Pratt's reflections on growing up as a privileged white woman in the American South.[23] Teresa de Lauretis then commented on Martin and Mohanty, enlarging their insights about the connection between home and identity.[24] Most recently Bonnie Honig criticizes what she perceives as a privileged position of withdrawal from politics that the idea of home affords, and she enlarges de Lauretis's ideas about decentered identity and feminist politics.[25]

All these essays express a deep distrust of the idea of home for feminist politics and conclude that we should give up a longing for home. Although I agree with much in their critiques, in this section I argue that while politics should not succumb to a longing for comfort and unity, the material values of home can nevertheless provide leverage for radical social critique. Following bell hooks, I shall suggest that "home" can have a political meaning as a site of dignity and resistance. To the extent that having home is currently a privilege, I argue, the values of home should be democratized rather than rejected.

All of these writers suspect a tendency they perceive among feminists to seek a home in a sisterhood with women. Home is a concept and desire that expresses a bounded and secure identity. Home is where a person can be "herself"; one is "at home" when she feels that she is with others who understand her in her particularity. The longing for home is just this longing for a settled, safe, affirmative, and bounded identity. Thus home is often a metaphor for mutually affirming, exclusive community defined by gender, class, or race.[26]

Feminist analysis reveals that this feeling of having a home as a bounded identity is a matter of privilege. Recall Irigaray's claim: man's ability to have a home, to return to his original identity, is achieved by means of the dereliction of woman as she provides the material nurturance of the self-same identity and the envelope that gives him his sense of boundary. In the feminist texts I am exploring here, the privilege of home the writers refer to is less a specifically gender privilege, and more of a class and race privilege. Martin and Mohanty interpret Pratt's text as revealing how the sense of security and comfort that Pratt experienced as a child was predicated on the exclusion of blacks and lower-class whites at the same time that they were invisibly present as workers producing the comforts of home. Bonnie Honig argues that the sense of home as a place where one is confident who one is and can fall back on a sense of integrity depends on a vast institutional structure that allows such a luxury of withdrawal, safety, and reflection for some at the expense of many others who lose out in the global transfer of benefits. Home is here constructed in opposition to the uncertainties and dangers of streets and foreign territories where various riff-raff hang out in less than homey conditions.

> "Being home" refers to the place where one lives within familiar, safe, protected boundaries, "not being home" is a matter of realizing that home was an illusion of coherence and safety based on the exclusion of specific histories of oppression and resistance, the repression of differences, even within oneself.[27]

In his study of the construction of modern Western imperialist culture through interaction with the culture of the places constructed as colonies, Edward Said similarly suggests that the material comfort of bourgeois home derives from the material and discursive exploitation of distant colonies. Through a reading of Jane Austen's *Mansfield Park*, Said argues that a British sense of settled bourgeois home depended quite specifically on the nationalist enterprise of empire. Austen makes it plain, says Said,

> that the values associated with such higher things as ordination, law, and property must be grounded firmly in actual rule over and possession of territory. She sees clearly that to hold and rule Mansfield Park is to hold and rule an imperial estate in close, not to say inevitable, association with it. What assures that domestic tranquility and attractive harmony of one is the productivity and regulated discipline of the other.[28]

The women writers we are examining all conclude from these considerations that feminist politics should reject the idea of home. In giving up the idea of home, feminism is consistently postcolonial, exposing the illusion of a coherent stable self or a unified movement of women. A more honest and open attitude toward the world recognizes the plural identities of each of us and that a politics that recognizes and affirms differences cannot draw safe borders for the self.

> When the alternatives would seem to be either the enclosing, encircling, constraining circle of home, or nowhere to go, the risk is enormous. The assumption of, or desire for, another safe place like "home" is challenged by the realization that "unity"—interpersonal and well as political—is itself necessarily fragmentary, itself that which is struggled for, chosen, and hence unstable by definition; it is not based on "sameness," and there is no perfect fit.[29]

According to de Lauretis, feminism must make a shift in historical consciousness that entails

> a dis-placement and self-displacement: leaving or giving up a place that is safe, that is "home"—physically, emotionally, linguistically, epistemologically—for another place that is unknown and risky, that is not only emotionally but conceptually other; a place of discourse from which speaking and thinking are at best tentative, uncertain, unguaranteed.[30]

Bonnie Honig argues specificaly against the use of "home" as a means of withdrawing from politics into a place of more certain principle and integrity. Feminist politics should be prepared to face dilemmas to which there are no simple responses. Longing for home is the effort to retreat into a solid unified identity at the expense of those projected and excluded as Other.

> The dream of home is dangerous, particularly in postcolonial setting, because it animates and exacerbates the inability of constituted subjects—or nations—to accept their own internal divisions, and it engenders zealotry, the will to bring the dream of unitariness or home into being. It leads the subject to project its internal differences onto external Others and then to rage against them for standing in the way of its dream—both at home and elsewhere.[31]

Martin and Mohanty, de Lauretis, and Honig are right to criticize the bourgeois-dominative meaning of home, and earlier sections of this essay have explicated why. They are also right to fear the nostalgic seductions of home as a fantasy of wholeness and certainty. Through a reading of

Irigaray, I have also elaborated on this claim. They are right, finally, to suggest that the attempt to protect the personal from the political through boundaries of home more likely protects privilege from self-consciousness, and that the personal identities embodied in home inevitably have political implications. I have also explored this undecidable difference between the personal and the political in preserving the meaning of things. These writers make persuasive analyses of the depoliticizing, essentialist, and exploitative implications that the idea of home often carries.

While agreeing with much of this critique, I have also argued that home carries a core positive meaning as the material anchor for a sense of agency and a shifting and fluid identity. This concept of home does not oppose the personal and the political, but instead describes conditions that make the political possible. The identity-supporting material of home can be sources of resistance as well as privilege. To the extent that home functions today as a privilege, I will argue later, the proper response is not to reject home, but to extend its positive values to everyone.

bell hooks expresses a positive meaning of "home" for feminism. She agrees with Martin and Mohanty, de Lauretis, and Honig, that "home" is associated with safety and the making of identity. She gives a positive and political meaning, however, to these functions of "home." Appealing to the historic experience of African American women, she argues that "homeplace" is the site of resistance to dominating and exploiting social structures. The ability to resist dominant social structures requires a space beyond the full reach of those structures, where different, more humane social relations can be lived and imagined. On hooks's view, homeplace uniquely provides such safe visionary space. The mutual caring and meaningful specificity provided by homeplace, moreover, enables the development of a sense of self-worth and humanity partially autonomous from dominating, exploiting, commercial or bureaucratic social structures. Thus hooks agrees with the feminist critics of "home" that home is a site of identity; whereas they criticize a search for pregiven, whole, and apolitical identity, however, hooks finds homeplace to be the site for a self-conscious *constructed* identity as a political project of criticism and transformation of unjust institutions and practices.

> Historically, African American people believed that the construction of a homeplace, however, fragile and tenuous (the slave hut,

> the wooden shack), had a radical political dimension. Despite the brutal reality of racial apartheid, of domination, one's homeplace was the one site where one could freely confront the issue of humanization, where one could resist.[32]

Thus hooks reverses the claim that having "home" is a matter of privilege. "Home" is a more universal value in her vision, one that the oppressed in particular can and have used as a vehicle for developing resistance to oppression. As long as there is a minimal freedom of homeplace, there is a place to assemble apart from the privileged and talk of organizing; there is a place to preserve the specific culture of the oppressed people. The personal sense of identity supported in the site and things of a homeplace thus enables political agency.

hooks emphasizes this political value of homeplace as the place of the preservation of the history and culture of a people, in the face of colonizing forces of the larger society. This project of preservation and remembrance, I have argued, above, is very different from the nostalgic longing for home that Martin and Mohanty, de Lauretis, and Honig rightly suspect. Preservation and remembrance are historical. Colonized people can project an alternative future partly on the basis of a place beyond dominance that is preserved in everyday life. hooks herself seeks in her essay to remember the African American mothers and grandmothers who have preserved generations of homeplace, distinct African American cultural meanings in stories, foods, songs, and artifacts.

> I want to remember these black women today. The act of remembrance is a conscious gesture honoring their struggle, their effort to keep something for their own. I want us to respect and understand that this effort has been and continues to be a radically subversive political gesture. For those who dominate and oppress us benefit most when we have nothing to give our own, when they have so taken from us our dignity, our humanness that we have nothing left, no "homeplace" where we can recover ourselves.[33]

Home as a Critical Value

The criticisms of the idea of home I have reviewed dwell primarily on a temptation to reject or reconstruct conflict and social difference by creating safe spaces in politics. Nationalism is an important and dangerous manifestation of this temptation, in romanticizing "homeland." The positive idea of home I have advocated is attached to a particular locale as an extension and expression of bodily routines. Nationalism attempts to project such a local feeling of belonging onto a huge territory and "imagined community" of millions,[34] and in so doing creates rigid distinctions between "us" and "them" and suppresses the differences within "us." Other attempts to project an ideal of home onto large political units are just as damaging. A useful response to such idealizations of politics as a search for home, however, is to emphasize the radical potential of values that attend to the concrete localized experience of home, and the existential meaning of being deprived of that experience.

Having the stability and comfort of concrete home is certainly a privilege. Many millions of people in the world today do not have sufficient space of their own to live by themselves or with others in peace. They do not have the time or space to preserve much of the history and culture of their family and community, though only refugees and the most desperately destitute are unable to try. With upwards of 500 million refugees and other homeless people in the world, that deprivation is serious indeed. Even if people have minimal shelter of their own, moreover, they need a certain level of material confort in their home for it to serve as a place of identity-construction and the development of the spirit of resistance that hooks discusses. In this way having a home is indeed today having a privilege.

The appropriate response to this fact of privilege is not to reject the values of home, but instead to claim those values for everyone. Feminists should criticize the nostalgic use of home that offers a permanent respite from politics and conflict, and which continues to require of women that they make men and children comfortable. But at the same time, feminist politics calls for conceptualizing the positive values of home and criticizing a global society that is unable or unwilling to extend those values to everyone. There are at least four normative values of home that should be thought of as minimally accessible to all people. These stand as regulative ideals by which societies should be criticized.

(1) Safety—Everyone needs a place where they can go to be safe. Ideally, home means a safe place, where one can retreat from the dangers and hassles of collective life. It is too much to ask, perhaps even in the ideal, that everyone can be safe anywhere. The potential for violence and conflict cannot be eradicated from the world. But it is not too much to

ask that everyone have a home in which they can feel physically safe and secure.

Today we are frighteningly, horrible far from this simple goal. For too many women and children, their houses do not enclose them safely, but threaten them with violence from the men who live there with them. Too many poor peasants and barrio dwellers in the world cannot sleep peacefully in their homes without fear that paramilitary squads will rouse them, rape them, shoot them, or carry them away in the dark. If anything is a basic need and a basic liberty, it is personal safety and a place to be safe. Yet ensuring such safety at home is an arduous and complex matter, one that seems too daunting for the will of the late twentieth century. We must be ashamed of a world in which safety at home is a privilege, and express outrage at any stated or implied suggestion that such a need and liberty is too expensive for any society to meet.

(2) Individuation—A person without a home is quite literally deprived of individual existence.[35] However minimal, home is an extension of the person's body, the space that he or she takes up, and performs the basic activities of life—eating, sleeping, bathing, making love. These need not all be done in the same place or behind closed doors, in a house. But the individual is not allowed to be if she does not have places to live and to perform the activities of life, with basic routine and security. As I have already outlined in the concept of homemaking, moreover, people's existences entail having some space of their own in which they array around them the things that belong to them, that reflect their particular identity back to them in a material mirror. Thus basic to the idea of home is a certain meaning of ownership, not as private property in exchangeable goods, but in the sense of meaningful use and reuse for life. Even the monk has a cell of his own in the collective life of the monastery; even in crowded families with little space there is usually an effort to allocate each person a corner of his own where he can sleep and put the things he calls his own. Where this is not possible it nevertheless remains as an ideal.[36]

(3) Connected with the value of individuation is privacy. A person does not have a place of her own and things of her own if anyone can have access to them. To own a space is to have autonomy over admission to the space and its contents. Some feminists doubt the value of privacy, because they associate this idea with the "private sphere," to which women have been historically confined. But there are crucial differences in the two concepts. Privacy refers to the autonomy and control a person

has to allow or not allow access to her person, information about her, and the things that are meaningfully associated with her person. The traditional "private sphere," on the other hand, confines some persons to certain realm of activity and excludes them from others. As a value, privacy says nothing about opportunities for the person to engage in activity. It only says that whatever her social activities, a person should have control over access to her living space, her meaningful things, and information about herself.[37]

Feminists have been suspicious of a value of privacy also because traditional law has sometimes appealed to a right of privacy to justify not interfering with autocratic male power in the family. Because of a supposed right of privacy, the law should turn a blind eye to marital rape or battering. But perhaps the most important defense against this legitimation of patriarchal power is an insistence that privacy is a value for individuals, not simply or primarily for households. Anita Allen argues that if we insist on privacy as a value for all persons as individuals, then the extent to which women deserve privacy at home and elsewhere, and do not have it, becomes apparent.[38] The appeal to privacy as a value thus enables social criticism.

Some might claim that appeal to a value of privacy is ethnocentric, because the idea of privacy is a Western idea. Scholars disagree on the question of whether non-Western societies both historically and today have held a value of privacy. My cursory reading of that literature leads me to conclude that there is often, if not always, a form of respect for the physical person of another and for some kind of spaces associated with the person. In stratified societies, such respect may be restricted to those in the upper strata. This does not mean that such a value does not exist in the society, but rather that it is held as a privilege. I am arguing here that certain values associated with home, among them control over access to one's person and personal space, be made available everyone: to the degree that non-Western and premodern societies, as well as modern societies, do not democratize privacy, then I am indeed criticizing them.

Thus while it seems to me that an ideal of respect for the personal space of others is not restricted to Western societies, one can argue that conceptualizing this idea in terms that we call privacy is Western. The concept of privacy is a relatively recent development of positive law based in rights. The concept of rights to privacy extends law to relations of interaction among private individuals or between private agents, as well as between the state and individuals. Thus I wish to suggest that there are long-standing ideas and practices analogous to privacy in many societies, and that to the degree that positive law and social policy have evolved in those societies, it is not a mistake today to appeal to a value of privacy.

(4) The final value of "home" that should be available to everyone I have already explicated at length in an earlier section: preservation. Home is the site of the construction and reconstruction of one's self. Crucial to that process is the activity of safeguarding the meaningful things in which one sees the stories of one's self embodied, and rituals of remembrance that reiterate those stories. I have argued that preservation in this sense is an important aspect of both individual and collective identity.

Home is a complex ideal, I have argued, with an ambiguous connection to identity and subjectivity. I agree with those critics of home who see it as a nostalgic longing for an impossible security and comfort, a longing bought at the expense of women and of those constructed as Others, strangers, not-home, in order to secure this fantasy of a unified identity. But I have also argued that the idea of home and the practices of home-making support personal and collective identity in a more fluid and material sense, and that recognizing this value entails also recognizing the creative value to the often unnoticed work that many women do. Despite the real dangers of romanticizing home, I think that there are also dangers in turning our backs on home.

Notes

I am grateful to David Alexander, Robert Beauregard, Edward Casey, Delores Hayden, Dorothea Olkowski, and Geraldine Pratt for helpful comments on earlier versions of this paper. I also benefited from a discussion of the paper at the University of Pittsburgh women's writing group, including Jean Carr, Nancy Glazener, Paula Kane, Margaret Marshall, and Marianne Novy.

    1. Martin Heidegger, "Building, Dwelling, Thinking," in *Poetry, Language, Thought,* trans. Albert Hofstadter (New York: Harper and Row, 1971). Hereafter cited as BDT.

    2. Compare Edward Casey, *Getting Back into Place: Toward a Renewed Understanding of the Place-World* (Bloomington: Indiana University Press, 1993), 112. Casey also notes (176–77) that Heidegger slides into identifying dwelling with construction even though he begins with a wider scope for building.

    3. Hannah Arendt also theorized building as a fundamental aspect of human meaning. She distinguishes between labor, activity useful for production and consumption of the means of living, and work, the construction of artifacts that transcend mere life because they are made to be perma-

nent. Thus for Arendt the moment of founding is the primordial moment of action. Through the construction of edifices people create a built environment, a civilization, by means of which they emerge as thinking and speaking subjects. See Hannah Arendt, *The Human Condition* (Chicago: University of Chicago Press, 1958).

4. Aliye Pekin Celik, "Women's Participation in the Production of Shelter," and Victoria Basolo and Michelle Moraln, "Women and the Production of Housing: An Overview," both in Hemalata C. Dandekar, *Shelter, Women, and Development: First and Third World Perspectives* (Ann Arbor: George Wahr Publishing Co., 1993).

5. Caroline O. N. Moser, "Women, Human Settlements, and Housing: A Conceptual Framework for Analysis and Policy-Making," in Caroline O. N. Moser and Linda Peake, eds., *Women, Human Settlements, and Housing* (London: Tavistock Publications, 1987); Irene Tinker, "Beyond Economics: Sheltering the Whole Woman," in Blumberg, Rakowski, Tinker, and Maneton, eds., *Engendering Wealth and Well-Being* (Boulder: Westview Press, 1995), 261–84.

6. Luce Irigaray, *Ethics of Sexual Difference* (Ithaca: Cornell University Press, 1992), 101. Hereafter cited as ESD.

7. One of the classic statements of this idea is Herbert Marcuse's *One Dimensional Man* (Boston: Beacon Press, 1964); see also Stuart Ewen, *Captains of Consciousness* (New York: McGraw-Hill, 1976).

8. See James S. Duncan, "From Container of Women to Status Symbol: The Impact of Social Structure on the Meaning of the House," in James S. Duncan, ed., *Housing and Identity: Cross-Cultural Perspectives* (New York: Holmes and Meier Publishers, 1982).

9. Anita Larsson, "The Importance of Housing in the Lives of Women: The Case of Botswana," in Dandekar, *Shelter, Women, and Development*, 106–15.

10. See Jurgen Habermas, *Legitimation Crisis* (Boston: Beacon Press, 1975).

11. See Sophie Watson, *Accommodating Inequality: Gender and Housing* (Sydney: Allen and Unwin, 1988).

12. Delores Hayden compares the suburban desire for the detached single-family home as a nostalgia for the cottage in the woods; see *Redesigning the American Dream* (New York: W. W. Norton, 1983). Carole Despres discusses how the design of homes in contemporary Quebec suburbs nostalgically aims to evoke the traditional Quebequois cottage. Despres, "De la maison bourgeoisie a la maison moderne. Univer domestique, esthetique et sensibilite feminine," *Recherches Feministes* 2, 1 (1989): 3–18.

13. Simone de Beauvoir, *The Second Sex*, trans. H. M. Parshley (New York: Random House, 1952), 451.

14. D. J. Van Lennep, "The Hotel Room," in Joseph J. Kockelmans, ed., *Phenomenological Psychology: The Dutch School* (Dordrecht: Martinus Nijhoff, 1987), 209–15.

15. Ibid., 211.

16. Casey, *Getting Back into Place*, 120.

17. Arendt, *The Human Condition*.

18. See Sara Ruddick, "Preservative Love," in *Maternal Thinking: Toward a Politics of Peace* (New York: BallantineBooks, 1989), 65–81; Joan Tronto, *Moral Boundaries* (New York: Routledge, 1992). Both theorists focus on the preserving and protecting actions of caring persons, but both also talk about the caring for things that supports this activity. In this essay I focus on preserving meanings through things partly because this has been a less noticed aspect of domestic work than material and emotional caring for people. The two are deeply intertwined, of course.

19. On the distinction between nostalgia and memory, see Gayle Greene, "Feminist Fiction and the Uses of Memory," *Signs* 16, 2 (Winter 1991), 290–321.

20. See Keya Ganguly, "Migrant Identities: Personal Memory and the Construction of Selfhood," *Cultural Studies* 6, 1 (January 1992): 27–49; Susan Thomason, "Suburbs of Opportunity: The Power of Home for Migrant Women," Proceedings of the Postmodern City Conference, Sydney University, 1993.

21. See Delores Hayden, *The Power of Place* (Cambridge: MIT Press, 1995).

22. Governments all over the world, in both developed and developing countries, have been cutting social services and allowing prices for basic foodstuffs to rise. The result is usually more domestic work for women. See Haleh Afshar and Carolyne Dennis, *Women and Adjustment Politices in the Third World* (New York: St. Martin's Press, 1993).

23. Biddy Martin and Chandra Talpade Mohanty, "Feminist Politics: What's Home Got to Do with It?" in Teresa de Lauretis, ed., *Feminist Studies/Cultural Studies* (Bloomington: Indiana University Press, 1986), 191–212.

24. Teresa de Lauretis, "Eccentric Subjects: Feminist Theory and Historical Consciousness," *Feminist Studies* 16, 1 (Spring 1990): 115–50.

25. Bonnie Honig, "Difference, Dilemmas, and the Politics of Home," *Social Research* 61, 3 (Fall 1994): 563–97.

26. See Benice Johnson Reagon, "Coalition Politics: Turning the Century," in Barbara Smith, ed., *Home Girls: A Black Feminist Anthology* (Kitchen Table: Women of Color Press, 1983), 356–69. Reagon criticizes the attempt to seek the comforts of home in politics, but as I read her she does not reject the values of home.

27. Martin and Mohanty, "Feminist Politics," 196.

28. Edward Said, *Culture and Imperialism* (New York: Vintage Books, 1993), 87.

29. Martin and Mohanty, "Feminist Politics," 209.

30. De Lauretis, "Eccentric Subjects," 138.

31. Honig, "Difference," 585.

32. bell hooks, "Homeplace: A Site of Resistance," in *Yearning: Race, Gender, and Cultural Politics* (Boston: South End Press, 1990), 42.

33. Ibid., 43.

34. Benedict Anderson, *Imagined Communities: Reflections on the Origin and Spread of Nationalism* (London: New Left Books, 1983).

35. Compare Jeremy Waldron, "Homelessness and the Issue of Freedom," in *Liberal Rights: Collected Papers 1981–1991* (Cambridge: Cambridge University Press, 1993), 309–38.

36. Seyla Benhabib affirms this individuating function of home and privacy in her discussion of the need for feminists to retain a certain meaning to a distinction between public and private. See Benhabib, *The Reluctant Modernism of Hannah Arendt* (London: Sage, 1996), 213.

37. For a feminist defense of privacy as the right to inviolate personality, see Jean L. Cohen, "Democracy, Difference, and the Right of Privacy," in Seyla Benhabib, ed., *Democracy and Difference: Contesting the Boundaries of the Political* (Princeton: Princeton University Press, 1996).

38. Anita Allen, *Uneasy Access* (Totowa, N.J.: Rowman and Allenheld, 1988).

10

Thrownness, Playing-in-the-World, and the Question of Authenticity

Mechthild Nagel

Prelude

In his seminal work *Truth and Method,* Hans-Georg Gadamer oddly uses the notion of play (*Spiel*) as his methodological thread to hermeneutic explication. Hermeneutics, simply put, is the art of rendering something, whether it is a sacred text, a human experience, or an artwork, intelligible—in other words, it is about the "business of interpretation."[1] Gadamer suggests that aesthetic experience has affinity with play. He notes that play has ontological primacy, not the (human) players. When a player has entered the game or the horizon of the game (*Spielraum*), familiarizing herself with the rules, casting the dice, and becoming absorbed in the activity, the game gains authority over the player. This is the case even though the player freely engages in the game's rules and objectives and thus actualizes the game.[2] Gadamer's philosophical play draws on the epistemological and aesthetic "play tradition" from Kant to Nietzsche, Heidegger, and Eugen Fink. The philosophical deployment of play, whether as play of the imagination (Kant) or as Dionysian free spirits (Nietzsche), seems to signal one's metaphysical commitment to—or critique of—the philosophy of the subject. Gadamer shares with Heidegger the desire to critique and to overcome the subjectivist and foundationalist tendencies in Western philosophy, and he expands on Heidegger's novel analysis of the hermeneutic circle.[3]

In this essay, I wish to present a feminist critique of Heidegger's discussion of play in *Being and Time*. While the notion of play is not conceptually laid out as forcefully as in Gadamer's work, I argue that Heidegger's use of play is very instructive for a feminist play discourse. First, Heidegger notes the prevalence of agonistic play in rational discourse, and second, his notions of thrownness and attunement bring to light that the self already is in tune with her cultural background or tradition and need not rely on expertly objective interpretation in order to become conversant. Both insights are useful for an antifoundational feminist play theory that wishes to critique the hegemonic agonistic subjectivism in modern, Western play discourse, which suggests that the self qua genius establishes rules against the cultural norms. Heidegger's notion of thrownness might also be helpful in rallying against the problematic binary and hierarchical structure of Apollonian rational (good) play versus Dionysian violent (bad) play insofar as Heidegger does not appear to take sides in this debate over the proper use of play, which has troubled play theory perhaps ever since Plato's famous mimesis critique in the *Republic*.[4] Yet, to a great extent, Heidegger reinscribes the traditional ontological tradition he wishes to 'destruct' (*Destruktion*, GA 2, 22). I will problematize Heidegger's analyses of projection, the fore-structure of interpretation, and authenticity. The agonism prevalent in the process of conceptualization (*Vorgriff*) remains insufficiently theorized and, arguably, his analysis of projection makes it clear why discursive agonism is not explored and critiqued further. Dasein's authentic play with its possibilities in the hermeneutic horizon takes on agonistic proportions of a masculinist and thanatological nature.

My focus on play intends to highlight how ultimately—despite disavowals—Heidegger remains committed to the Cartesian ontological tradition that he attempts to 'destruct' by suggesting that the self is historically situated and coexists meaningfully with others. Dasein's concern for mineness displays an image of a radically isolated, monologically positioned player whose ultimate game is projection of possibilities toward anxiety and death. Such an image that celebrates the solitary (male) hero is quite at odds with a feminist perspective of play. The kind of play I would like to advocate may have some of the following features: it is a social, communicative, and creative endeavor, where one is playfully engaged with others in jesting, imitation, and masquerade. Such serious play may be performed in excess or moderation; defying rationalist hierarchies it troubles the conceptual borderlines of the Dionysian (wild, chaotic) and Apollonian (orderly, rational) aesthetic elements. Feminist play eludes foundational tendencies yet seeks to be life-affirming; it grasps that there is violence in conceptualization yet does not worship violence, rather it strives for nonagonistic play where there are no winners or losers. Fond of masquerade, it may toy with tricksterlike ambiguity and is wary of gestures that espouse claims of authenticity. I will suggest that this vision of feminist play is at odds with fundamental ontology. Yet I think that feminist play theorists can draw important lessons from Heidegger's analysis of Dasein and its playful, albeit agonistic, encounter with the world. In the next section I will look at agonism as a primordial mode of playing in *Being and Time*.

Agonistic Play: Interpretation as Projection

Projection of Understanding

The notions of thrownness and attunement (*Befindlichkeit*) seem particularly useful for a nonfoundational play theory. In section 31 of BT, Heidegger introduces understanding as co-primordial with *Befindlichkeit*. He does not suggest that there is a good or better way of being in the world. One simply is, and actually Dasein is already in tune, already understands itself and its surroundings by virtue of being thrown into its environment and taking its cultural background for granted. Take, for example, a violinist who knows how to play a note without having to remap the fingering every time she picks up the instrument; however, this has not yet anything to do with being an expert or even competent; competence and skill are displayed by playing a melody in a way that it meets the musical expectations of the player and her audience. For Heidegger, understanding means to already understand well. Analogously, one could hold that playing, too, is about playing well—*pace* Aristotle, a child does not need a lesson in pretend play, enacting a scene.

However, understanding as the projection of Dasein's possibilities is emphatically agentic and agonistic. Section 32 opens with the assertion that understanding thrusts back onto Dasein—presumably the vehemence of the return of a hit[5] (*Rückschlag*) is necessary in order to counter the effect of thrownness (*Geworfenheit*). Dasein has to develop its own critical capacities in opposition to—not in intersubjective cooperation with—its environment; it is thrown into projection and gets its room for maneuver vis-à-vis Dasein's potentiality. So projection resolutely lays out possibilities qua possibilities—within a certain leeway (*Spielraum*) (BT, 145). Such is the explication of understanding as interpretation (*Auslegung*). "As projecting, understanding is the kind of Being of Dasein in which it *is* its possibilities as possibilities" (BT, 145). How is Dasein's world to be interpreted? Before I devote more space to the notion of *Spielraum*, I wish to turn to a discussion of the fore-structure of interpretation and the hermeneutic circle.

Fore-structure of Interpretation

Heidegger outlines a three-part stage theory for the concept of interpretation: fore-having, fore-sight, and fore-conception (BT, 150). First, fore-having fleshes out the idea hinted at with the notion of *Befindlichkeit*: one has already understood one's environment and takes it for granted in an unreflected way.[6] Once something is put into one's perceptual horizon, one begins to view or appropriate it in process which is called fore-sight. "This fore-sight 'takes the first cut' out of what has been taken into our fore-having" (BT, 150). Last, after fore-sight has viewed the entity, fore-conception comes into play forcing the entity into a formal concept. I would like to use the example of language acquisition as a way to illustrate this tripartite temporal process: a newborn baby (or a cyborg)[7] learns to differentiate the overwhelming 'noise' that inundates her senses at first, and after a while she begins to make sense of her environment in its totality (fore-having). She may then focus on a particular object and discern its meaning from others (fore-sight). After the entity can be perceived (seen, tasted, smelled, and so forth) and singled out, she can finally put a concept to it, for example, mother's milk, voice, and so on (fore-conception).

Let me focus here on the notion of fore-conception. Note first that fore-conception (*Vorgriff*) is not simply about randomly picking and choosing from a menu of linguistic vocabulary. Fore-having, one's cultural background, in other words, one's native language, limits one's choices. One grabs unfailingly a particular term and holds on to it. Thus, in the process of meaning creation (through interpretation) one latches onto a concept (a category or an *existentiale*) that is not a nebulous, ambiguous, multifaceted metaphor but already a limiting, excluding conception that will contribute to and enrich a particular horizon of meaning. In other words, we rely on 'legitimate prejudices' which mark our engagement with thrownness.[8]

Second, with his neologism of *Vorgriff*, Heidegger clearly plays upon the meaning of *Begriff* (*greifen* = grabbing, grasping) and also remarks on the agonistic activity, not captured in English translations of the term as 'anticipation' or 'grasp'. The literal meaning of *Begriff* is made more explicit by turning 'concept' into *Vorgriff* (in German, the latter conveys better the notion of literally grabbing something than the former) so that the notion of making an indelible (albeit cognitive) mark is fore-grounded. The activity of bringing entities into concepts, Heidegger says, can be violent (compare the expression "*in Begriffe zwängen*," GA 2, 150) because entities may resist identification. I find this remark rather noteworthy, and it may have interesting consequences for play theory. It has been claimed, after all, from Plato to Kant, that reason bestows meaning onto things or subjects in a rational, in other words, nonviolent manner. Similarly, it is said that Apollonian play is rational, orderly, and harmonious, not tainted with cacophony, erratic leaps in thought, nor violence— characteristics, to be sure, only of Dionysian playfulness. Rational conceptualization thus is not simply an "innocent" weaving of the incoherent, colorful manifold into a temporal order and a formalizing of it into an abstract category, but it is a forceful gathering up and binding of entities into concepts. Concepts do not exist in isolation. They are context-bound, historically specific, in other words, they are intelligible against a specific cultural background. Heidegger's notion of *Vorgriff* thus problematizes the traditional dichotomy of the Apollonian (rational) and the Dionysian (irrational, violent) by indicating that violence in fact can be rational!

In the Spielraum *of the Hermeneutic Circle*

As mentioned above, a key insight in Heidegger's approach to understanding is that it is already vested with presuppositions and prejudgments. We already understand Being before we begin to interpret Dasein in order to understand the meaning of Being: "[a]ny interpretation which is to contribute understanding, must already have understood what is to be interpreted" (BT, 152). In conventional logic, Heidegger acknowledges, such an assertion runs the risk of becoming a vicious circle. But what is needed is a different way of seeing, or a different room for maneuver, which is the hermeneutic circle. Heidegger says surprisingly little about the significance of this peculiar circle, given that it is "the expression of the existential *fore-structure* of Dasein itself." This circle is the realm for ascertaining the meaning of human existence. He says, cryptically, that it is "decisive . . . not to get out of the circle but to come into it in the right way" (BT, 153). A precise phenomenological view, in other words, a proper methodological approach, is needed to get to the things themselves. One's fore-sight cannot be wavering, but has to be carried out with determination and precision. This new tone, emphasizing decisive action, seems at odds with the previous discussion of the fore-structure of interpretation, where Heidegger allows for the possibility that entities might not resist conceptualization (BT, 150). It also seems to collide with his previous analysis of projection as understanding "which is the kind of Being of Dasein in which it *is* its possibilities as possibilities" in other words, where they are let be as such (BT, 145). Getting into a circle in the right way is an unambiguous, agentic message to be heeded by the phenomenologist who wants to avoid a mis-grasping (*Vergriff*) leading her astray into "fancies and popular conceptions" (BT, 153).

Being thrust into the *Spielraum* of the hermeneutic circle, Dasein, in its concern with mineness, finds that it must weigh the different options, decide on proper entry points in order to pinpoint decisively the ultimate outcome of its game. Here we might begin to understand how Heidegger intends to use the dictum "Become what you are!" keeping in mind that one's factical existence is ontologically circumscribed as one's projected possibilities. This tautological moment (after all, becoming *is* potentiality) gives Dasein little metaphysical comfort in playing its cards in the here and now. Dasein's game is declared as most supreme (in other words, primordial) when it is permanently deferred into the mode of 'not yet'. Clearly, the commanding rule of the game is, higher than actuality is possibility (BT, passim). When do we dare say Dasein has truly arrived? Clearly, when it no longer worries about not yet being there—death itself must be the highest ontological possibility. Short of such finality, Dasein's primordial grasp on understanding itself is being in the radically individualized state (of anxiety) of 'being towards death' (compare BT(s), 234, n. ‡, where death is defined as 'being of nonbeing'). Dasein can truly assert 'I am' (in my mineness) when it no longer exists.[9] Even though Dasein is heavily invested in its community with others and depends on a common, shared cultural background in order to project its possibilities, it is called upon to separate off and totally involve itself in its solitary master game, because this is its superior task. Dasein is implored to project, play, or rather throw down its last dice—*faire bancot*, in other words, to risk everything, to set all one's assets on one card, only to be sure that the result is deadly.

Despite being socially embedded, Dasein, properly understood, is foremost concerned with itself, not with others. Decisions about projecting meaningful possibilities do not need the consultation of friends or family or their intervention in one's actions. In fact, others only hamper one's pursuit of authentic projections—precisely because their solicitude is, for the most part, a projection of their own self-interests onto my own. Ontologically speaking, one has to take great care to seek refuge in solitude or silence in order to make Being an issue for oneself. Heidegger's protestations notwithstanding, it is difficult to maintain that such an ontological quest is not suspect on normative grounds. I wish to claim that the only overlapping interest we might hold with others in a Heideggerian environment is that they also need to seek out Being while projecting their utmost possibilities—toward death. Such fatalistic bonding is rarely a viable practice of Being-with; it would deny a playful tarrying in the moment. The phenomenological playground is solipsistic and grim in its outlook on the fancies of the present, the fleeting moment, the joy of interacting with others in meaningful or trifle ways, for example, in gossip and jest (see below).[10] Thus, playing with one's choices qua projection becomes a solitary exercise of playing poker against imaginary foes or, really, playing Russian roulette with oneself—although in the latter case the *Spielraum* seems decidedly limited. For Heidegger, it must be the true calling of the hero (soldier) living out his utmost potentiality. The existential game seems at first open to different rules and interpretations, yet it is crucial to get into the circle in the right way that limits choices of rules radically. What is open to one's projecting imagination is the grim march toward death; the rules of the game are decidedly marked by thanatological ideology. Thanatological models are problematic, for they dismiss the actual facticity of being-in-the-world; they minimize the importance of intersubjective sociality, of playing and working with others; sharing living spaces, disputes and learning to resolve discord with each other peacefully and playfully.

Ethics and Poetics

Dichten and Denken

It has been noted that there is a certain violence of interpretation in Heidegger's texts. Deconstruction is always conflictual, seeking to "read texts for their moment of rupture, for the moment at which they conceal their conditions of possibility."[11] Joanna Hodge notes that Plato's violent gesture to banish the poets is similar to Heidegger's intention of getting rid of logocentric philosophy. Neither move is productive, according to Hodge.[12] I am sympathetic to this view that it is too facile to engage in an abstract negation of Western philosophy, though I think Hodge goes too far when she boldly claims that Heidegger has indeed left *Denken* behind and already favors *Dichten* in *Being and Time*.[13] Far from abandoning 'thinking' and turning to 'doing poetry', Heidegger attempts a 'destruction' of Western metaphysics and constructs a decisionist, normative existential phenomenology which does not value and celebrate the poetic play of difference and ambiguity.[14] He sets up a masculinist, agonistic game where a solitary (heroic) player makes his decisive move in silence in order to exist authentically.[15]

Even though Heidegger has had an important role as a 'fore-thinker,' pioneering what has been called deconstructive thinking and writing, it seems problematic to suggest that the early Heidegger uses poetic, nonstringent, antiagonistic argumentation and even goes as far as celebrating a ludic ambiguity in his search for hidden and heretofore abandoned meanings of Being. To the contrary, he seeks to articulate the ontological difference, which the later Heidegger recognizes as an elusive goal. However, in early Heidegger, such logic of difference collapses into a logic of sameness, of authoritarian identity where ambiguity is emphatically weeded out. This is accomplished by setting up a valorization of authentic modes of existence. Resolutely, Dasein projects itself toward death as its most authentic way of being.

Hodge perhaps is right to suggest that on one level existential ontology is descriptive and poetic, in the way in which it details a distinctive mode of everyday "busy play" and a different, reflective kind of way that understands that something is uncanny about Dasein's very being and understanding itself. Yet, despite his protestations to the contrary, Heidegger does not remain at this descriptive level (and he says very little about poetic comportment in his early writings). In no uncertain terms his fundamental ontology delineates the desirable *Spielraum* (of the solitary player) and maligns the poorly reflected (derivative) understanding that would involve other players (*Mitspieler*).

The Ethics of Authenticity and Solitary Decisionism

I wish to take issue with two camps of interpretation on the question of ethics in Heidegger's thought. One side, including Heidegger, strongly disavows that existential ontology has anything to do with ethics and the validation of a certain worldview.[16] The other side suggests that we can read an ethics of care into his work.[17] First, claims about an antiethics tend to take Heidegger's disavowals at face value: repeatedly, Heidegger assures us that his talk about disgenuine, inauthentic modes of being is not a devaluation of these modes; it amounts to a mere descriptive phenomenological work that pays attention to detail and fine-tunes use of language. Yet, it seems difficult to accept such assurances in light of what is mapped out as *the* strategic plan of action for Dasein. Certain rules need to be heeded if one wants to force one's way into the phenomenological playground (*Spielraum*) and stay on track.

Let me put forth two objections to the first perspective of antiethics. (1) The notion of forgetfulness exemplifies Heidegger's hermeneutic zeal of bringing into play the notions of authenticity and decisionism. There is nothing therapeutic about forgetting and abandoning the question of Being. Forgetfulness, rather, is a sign of repression, forced by infatuation with busy activities (idle talk, and so on). "Dasein comports itself towards it in the mode of average everydayness, even if this is only the mode of fleeing in the face of it and forgetting of itself" (BT, 44). Note that forgetting is devalued by its juxtaposion with flight, escape—the coward's response to facing a difficult and important situation. There is no indication in *Being and Time* that indecisiveness or delaying decisions are signs of the self's authentic existence. Conflicts have to be sought out and dealt with unwaveringly. Far from shunning normative judgment, Heidegger proposes an ethics that is intensely decisionist.

(2) Furthermore, since phenomenology is interpretative or hermeneutic, it must uncover the meaning of Being in the existential analytic of Dasein; it is, after all, important to come into the circle in the right way (BT, 153). I take this to be the motto, if not the imperative, of *Being and Time*. To penetrate the circle—an agonistic act that allows one to gain access to the things themselves—involves a clairvoyance about understanding as ability-to-be. Understanding is characterized by its ability to project, and Dasein is admonished to stay clear of everyday modes involving others in curiosity, idle talk, and ambiguity (see below). To the uninitiated (players), this hermeneutic circle is hermetically sealed. Quite clearly, it seems to me, Heidegger gives prescriptive commands if only to advise how the self needs to take issue with its own being, if only to focus on the self and in what ways it has to take issue with is own being.

Recently, an interesting revision has occurred that holds that Heidegger's early philosophy actually has an ethics. Far from being solipsistic, it refrains from insisting on absolute singularity and isolation. According to Hodge, "*Being and Time* can thus be read not as a failed move from the everyday to some other temporal structure, nor as a failed move from the relatively familiar structures of determinate being to an account of the indeterminacies of being, but as revealing the complexity of the temporal dimensions contained within the everyday and, analogously, as revealing the fullness of being in the existence of determinate being."[18] What exactly does "the fullness of being" amount to? The key to understanding Heidegger's ethics is the notion of resoluteness (*Entschlossenheit*). Dasein is ethically engaged insofar as it takes responsibility for itself, refuses to take responsibility for others, and recognizes that the self is positioned in opposition to others.[19] This defense of Heidegger's ethics is quite attractive, because it is able to elide a critical engagement with the question of authoritarianism. By refocusing the debate on an authentic ethic of self-care this position also elides the problem of a missing dialectical, playful encounter of the self and others. Thus, (bad) authoritarianism is reformulated as (good) quietist ethical engagement, since Dasein needs to take care of itself and cannot pretend to attend to others and do the thinking for them.

Given the emphasis and admonishment about primordiality and authenticity it seems doubtful that Dasein's "fullness of being" truly eschews solipsism and radical individualism. To make use of the play metaphor, the solitary player's goal is simply self-preservation qua self-realization without the 'noise' of the man. In this decisionist, bourgeois, and monological game, Dasein is solely concerned about its own destiny. For the later Heidegger, one's authentic destiny tends to be expressed in quasi-poetic terms and exemplified in solitary, masculine figures, such as a farmer, carpenter, or leading poet and thinker.[20]

Dasein's playground imposes limits to Dasein's choices in the here-and-now, because Dasein exists factically. Yet Dasein is cut off its inauthentic capacity to play along with others and to use common or communal rules in a social game. Being in the world with others poses more perils than Dasein can truly afford. Dasein's own authentic choice, in other words, projection, is all that matters in its decisionist game. The clash of a social ethics with a solipsistic ethics comes to the fore in the discussion on Dasein's deficient modes. As Heidegger's discussion of speech (*Rede*) and gossip (*Gerede*) makes abundantly clear, *Mitdasein* gets short-shrifted. Dialogical playfulness with potential *Mitspieler* is regarded with suspicion, and ethical concern for others is cast aside. In its anxious pursuit of the question of Being, Dasein loses a penchant for carefree or even serious play. Playing in the world is fraught with problems of distractions and curiosity. Ever distrustful of others' intentions, Dasein finds itself unable to play with others authentically. Heidegger's ethics exude a fascination with thanatological projection; and it is masculinist and solitary, for it disregards other yearnings, such as maternal sociality, affective (in other words, irrational!) predilections for life, life giving, and gaining parenting skills. Heidegger has not overcome the Cartesian model of metaphysics with its postulation of an ontological priority (and self-generating creation!) of the self. His preoccupation with authenticity precludes a playful encounter with other modes: care for others is denigrated to a mere curiosity, speaking with others is disfavored for genuine silence, and communication becomes trivialized as idle chatter or gossip.

Play in Ambiguity and Other Inauthentic Modes

When Heidegger claims that the silent assertion 'I am' is superior to the communicative assertion 'I speak', he implies that the latter condemns Dasein to lose its grip on the question of Being and to end up giving itself over to the 'they'.²¹ The self's genuine understanding and projection does not involve others (for example, in intersubjective communication). "Keeping silent authentically is possible only in genuine discoursing" (BT, 165). Yet, this kind of discourse is far from mere talk, because, after all, it would be incapable to "hear" its conscience (BT, 296). In fact it is reticence that "beats down" idle chatter.²² Thus reticence is the primordial mode of discourse and puts other modes out of commission with a tour de force. As such it brings to the fore Heidegger's dis-ease with superficial talk or gossip, in other words, that which is only concerned *that* something is being said, rather than nothing at all (cf. BT, 168). It is noteworthy that in Heidegger's version, talk is always only superficial.

Thus, radical individualism looms large in the existential analytic. Heidegger states that Dasein's "being-with others" (in other words, *Mitsein*) always spoils authentic self-projection. "Being-with-one-another in the 'they' is by no means an indifferent side-by-side-ness in which one another, a secret and reciprocal listening-in. Under the mask of 'for-one-another', an 'against-one-another' is in play" (BT, 175). Instead of truly engaging in a dialogue with one another, everyone acts competitively; it is an agonistic game where one needs to protect one's advantage by keeping an eye on the opponent's next move. Playfulness, especially in its intersubjective realization, is characterized by an agonistic and cunning mode. Mindfully playing with others always means to be on guard, to be suspicious of foul play, which is especially true when one has to engage in team play, in other words, trust one's teammate to play responsibly.

In the process of unmasking other players' intentions, one's own seem to fail in delivering the right messages, as well. One's dice throw (*Entwurf*) is more akin to a missed throw or a 'cast-away' (*Verwurf*). A certain interplay between three inauthentic modes (in other words, ambiguity, idle talk, and curiosity) of Dasein brings about such failure: "This ambiguity is always tossing [*zuspielen*] to curiosity that which it seeks; and it gives idle talk the semblance of having everything decided in it" (BT, 174). Authentic play that deals with "taking action and carrying something through" is hampered by the ambiguous playing expressed in the term *zuspielen*.²³ Decisive action is hindered by decoy moves. Those who seem to be set up as partners in the game turn out to be opponents. If mimicry is false or foul play, couldn't we imagine an authentic kind of playing-in-the-world? Such performative moves could amount to a fair and proceduralist ethical game where care would be taken to treat other players with benevolence to bring about a win-win situation. Heidegger begs to differ. He suggests that the Being of the three modes of Dasein is characterized by fallenness (*Verfallen*) of Dasein and a thrown Being-with-one-another (BT, 175). Therefore, a playing-in-the-world with others clearly is doomed to inauthentic existence, because they hinder one's free projection in taking care of one's issues. If one needs to speak, to communicate (to others), then one has already said too much. Authentic play, if there is such a thing, is the performative concern for the self, playing at draughts with one's very own board where the self is not reflected as an Other, but where one is indeed—in pure monological self-reflection—a mirror of one's own rationality (I = I).

Feminist philosopher Iris Young refers to Heidegger's concept of thrownness as a useful category to describe group affinity and membership. It gives, structurally and necessarily, cohesiveness to one's own experience of selfhood where the self is marked as a member of a certain ethnic, religious, or other kind of community and as such the self is truly marked by others.[24] Thrownness does not, however, establish such imagined identity as a 'factum', as Heidegger writes. Rather, one can abandon one's position and take up chosen communities, even those in opposition to the existing ones (see BT, 179). I am sympathetic to this interpretation and use of thrownness, as I stated earlier. Yet let me raise another issue here in the context of ethics. Interestingly, Young does not mention Heidegger's concomitant existentiale of fallenness, which is more extensively elaborated than is thrownness. Dasein errs, hustles, and drifts into alienation. Fallenness, or falling prey, is a defective self-understanding, a failed projection of one's possibilities (BT, 177–78). More important, Dasein simply is thrown into the world and exists factically. Heidegger remains silent on the pertinent issue of whether anybody "contributed" to that factum, say, birthing. Dasein is thrown, not born. "Being towards birth" is not part of the vocabulary of the existential analytic of Dasein.[25] While it makes sense to draw on some of the hermeneutic aspects of thrownness for a feminist ethical and political perspective, it seems pertinent to critique its masculinist, thanatological, and agonistic concomitant components as well.

In summary, in Heidegger's play-world, the subject and its self-understanding is always already solitary. Dasein never is in a meaningful relation with others (as a parent, or friend). Heidegger does not conceive of *Mitspieler*, other players, except perhaps, as mischievous spoilsports. Dasein's play ought not to masquerade, since ambiguity has to be kept in check. A player who seems to go through the motions and seems to grasp the rules of the game of authenticity but applies them only in a derivative sense or feigns the proper moves in order to get into the game in the right way is an undesirable spoilsport who ridicules the stoic mandate of resolutely steering into the authentic mode of being (toward death). In the final section of this essay, I want to briefly entertain a post-Heideggerian feminist perspective on play.

Toward a Feminist Ethics of Play

I wish to present two interconnected claims: feminist ethics could benefit from a concept of play, and playfulness needs to be conceived as ethical. Although I will hint at a vision of a feminist play ethics, I do not want to present the following as necessary and sufficient conditions but perhaps as cautionary tales learned from an encounter with play discourse in Heidegger's thought. Heidegger's play with authenticity is a kind of play, which is unsettling for feminists who have critiqued Western philosophy for its agentic and subjectivist drive.[26] Feminist playfulness does not have to be bound to authentic modes of existence and may even tinker with masquerade, ambiguity, and gossip to go against the grain of Western philosophy. Nevertheless, if such a perspective is still feminist in some meaningful sense (and not just relativist), certain limitations apply: while an endorsement of ambiguity indicates a departure from Western code ethics (deontological or utilitarian), a feminist play ethics steers clear of oppressive hierarchies, and it is aware that systems of class, race, gender, and nation are intertwined. Its political mandate is a play-from-below, a play that resists and ridicules hegemonic discursive practices. However, feminist play, insofar as it is discursive (*begrifflich*)—in the Heideggerian sense—is also agonistic. It cannot escape the agonistic horizon, except were it to perform prediscursively. As Heidegger's analysis of fore-conception demonstrates, simply to engage in an abstract negation of conceptual agonism is too facile. This point seems pertinent for those strands of feminist ethics, which wish to deny the existence of any forms of violence in their conceptual models.[27]

Departing from Heidegger, I would like to suggest that self-critical reflective praxis is a dialectical interplay with others, and such performance needs to pay attention to whether its play is resistant parody or whether it is simply a reactive parody of hegemonic community values.

After all, power is intimately linked to play, in other words, it is not the case that by saying no to power, we say yes to play. Mocking play behavior may be hurtful to those who are targeted, but it is important to be able to actualize different modes of play. Children's schoolyard behavior is particularly instructive. Child psychologists note that in the era of school violence, including shootings, it is important to increase, not diminish, unsupervised leisure time. Children probably learn negotiating and coping skills and temper violent behavior by engaging in and appreciating, for instance, gossip, and even expressions of mocking imitation in pretend play. At the same time, there ought to be an emphasis on violence prevention through formal mediation processes, which include a good deal of role-playing (of victim and accused, and of impartial judge).

The non-Western trope of the Coyote, a tragic-comic figure of the Dineh and the Omaha,[28] could serve to remind us that human play is shot through with both agonistic and quasi-nonagonistic perspectives.[29] Lugones, perhaps, puts it best when she writes of playfulness being "in part, an openness to being a fool, which is a combination of not worrying about competence, not being self-important, not taking norms as sacred and finding ambiguity and double edges a source of wisdom and delight."[30] Judith Butler advocates that "laughter in the face of serious categories is indispensable for feminism. Without a doubt, feminism continues to require its own forms of serious play."[31] Parodic play with oppressive categories (for example, redeploying the hurtful notion of 'queer' or 'fag') is an important instantiation of serious play. Such play is not a frivolous, in other words, politically irresponsible, play of *différance*.

Thus, let me revise Heidegger's existential analytic in order to offer a parodic perspective on a playful dwelling-in-the-world. I want to say yes, to ambiguity as a 'primordial' way of playing, yes to gossip and to superficiality or distraction (*Zerstreuung*); furthermore yes to 'never dwelling anywhere' (*Aufenthaltslosigkeit*) and importantly, yes to a cunning teasing and mockery of other's discourse as a way of checking up on them (cf. BT, 172–75). To be fallen to the world and obsessed with this trickster game is to mingle with others indifferently and to have nothing to say to one another, except in friendly or mocking talk. That would the kind of game worth playing—in any world but Heidegger's Todtnauberg.

Due to its featured characteristics of tarrying with gossip, distraction, and dispersion, curiosity is hounded down and weeded out of the existential analytic of Dasein. Why is curiosity always portrayed as restless? What is wrong with nontarrying? In fact, we are quite needy of solicitude inflected with light-hearted chat and curiosity, since they might strengthen social, communicative practices and help to build ties among strangers and friends. I would argue even further that gossiping very much strengthens our emotional bonds—and one need not be in graduate school to validate such "inauthentic" play therapy.

Why would I like to endorse 'risky practices' and encourage gossip and nomadic dwelling (the latter is also known as chosen communities among feminists)? In part, such a parodic play perspective serves as an antidote to Heidegger's shameful reticence about Auschwitz—a silence as monstrous as his infamous comparison of modern agrotechnology with gas chambers. Nothing is ambiguous about his postwar silence about the Shoah; his equation of agribusiness and genocidal destruction of a people reveals his romantic and reactionary longing for a deeply depoliticized Heimat.[32]

Insofar as Heidegger's antifoundational hermeneutics is shot through with agonistic, masculinist ideals, his approach appears to lack usefulness for a feminist ethics of play. While he notes the violence of fore-conceptualization, he continues to employ it in a decisionist way. Authentic playful comportment in the existential analytic of Dasein is reduced to a solitary and thanatological tarrying with the self. Curiosity leads Dasein astray—away from thinking and presencing my own finality or being-toward-death (BT, 348). In defiant resistance to such play, I suggest that feminists reevaluate and retool all so-called inauthentic or deficient modes of Dasein (for example, curiosity, ambiguity, gossip). I attempted to show that these modes actually motivate us to engage with others in a friendly way—as a playing with seriousness. Parodic masks are an important point of departure for such feminist play/ethics.[33]

Notes

1. Hans-Georg Gadamer, *Truth and Method* (New York: Seabury Press, 1975), 37.

2. "The appeal of the game, the fascination it exerts, consists in the fact that it becomes master of the player. Even when games are concerned in which one tries to fulfill tasks one has set oneself, it is the risk, the question of whether it "works," "succeeds," or "succeeds again" that exercises the game's attraction. The actual subject of the game (precisely those experiences make this clear in which there is only a single player) is not the player but the game itself" (Gadamer, *Truth and Method*, 95). For a critical discussion, see Georgia Warnke, *Gadamer: Hermeneutics, Tradition and Reason* (Stanford: Stanford University Press, 1987), 48–56.

3. For a critique of Gadamer's agonistic play and conservative politics, see María Lugones's

"Playfulness, 'World'-travelling, and Loving Perception," *Hypatia: A Journal of Feminist Philosophy* 2, no. 2 (1987): 3–19; and Warnke's *Gadamer*. Lugones chides Gadamer for employing play in a way that simply continues and reinforces the agonistic, in other words, combative strand in Western philosophical thought about play (*Spiel*). Gadamer's illustrations circle around winning and losing a game, taking risks in order to overpower, dominate, an opponent, and to take on role-playing as a way to attain a certain fixed conception of oneself (Lugones, "Playfulness," 15).

4. See Friedrich Nietzsche, *Birth of Tragedy*, in *Basic Writings of Nietzsche*, trans. and ed. Walter Kaufmann (New York: Random House, 1966), and a recent discussion of the debate by Mihai Spariosu, *Dionysus Reborn* (Ithaca: Cornell University Press, 1989); and Mechthild Nagel, *Masking the Abject: Genealogy at Play* (Lanham: Lexington Books, forthcoming).

5. I am thinking of a return of a volley, for example, in tennis, or in a war, where one returns the enemy's cannon fire with equal fire power.

6. It is often noticed that one does not begin to understand or reflect upon the grammar of one's native language before one has learned laboriously a second language. Thus, one takes one's native language for granted.

7. See Marge Piercy, *He, She, and It* (New York: Knopf, 1991).

8. Gadamer clarifies in *Truth and Method*, hermeneutics is not a novel exercise in interpretation (lest it would be confounded with a revolutionary language or poetics), but interpretation is already vested in a particular tradition, in a familiar cultural surrounding.

9. See Rainer Marten, *Der menschliche Tod: Eine philosophische Revision* (Paderborn, Germany: Schöningh, 1987) for a sustained discussion of Heidegger's thanatology.

10. To be sure, William McNeill's Heideggerian stance in *The Glance of the Eye: Heidegger, Aristotle, and the Ends of Theory* (Albany: State University of New York Press, 1999) argues that such an interpretation which I advocate is "shortsighted" (101).

11. Joanna Hodge, *Heidegger and Ethics* (New York: Routledge, 1995), 200.

12. Hodge, *Heidegger and Ethics*, 133.

13. Hodge, *Heidegger and Ethics*, 180.

14. This is not to leave out the possibility that the later Heidegger does turn to poetry. Following John D. Caputo ("Demythologizing Heidegger," *Review of Metaphysics* 41 [March 1988]: 519–46), Patricia Huntington argues that the later Heidegger in fact attempts to overcome violent conceptual discourse and advocates a noninstrumental, noncompetitive poetic ethics (*Ecstatic Subjects, Utopia, and Recognition: Kristeva, Heidegger, Irigaray* [Albany: State University of New York Press, 1998], 219).

15. See Huntington, *Ecstatic Subjects*, for a sustained analysis of Heidegger's masculinist ethics. Unlike Iris Young (*Justice and the Politics of Difference* [Princeton: Princeton University Press, 1990]), who argues for a feminist reevaluation of thrownness, Huntington claims that Dasein is not materially or socially engaged with its environment, so that Heidegger's ideal projection of Dasein is another instantiation of a traditional, masculinist-rational, stoic ethos (*Ecstatic Subjects*, 28–29).

16. E.g., Phillipe Lacoue-Labarthe, *La fiction du politique: Heidegger, l'art et la politique* (Paris: Christian Bourgois, 1987), and Jacques Derrida, *Of Spirit: Heidegger and the Question*, trans. Geoffrey Bennington and Rachel Bowlby (Chicago: University of Chicago Press, 1989).

17. E.g., Hodge, *Heidegger and Ethics*.

18. Hodge, *Heidegger and Ethics*, 183.

19. Hodge, *Heidegger and Ethics*, 202. I will not dwell on a sustained critique of Hodge's analysis here that would take issue with her characterization of Heidegger's ethics as being influenced by Christian values.

20. See Rainer Marten, "Leben und Vernunft: Thesen zur Ideologie menschlichen Selbsterhaltung und zur Neubestimmung menschlicher Selbstbejahung," *Zeitschrift für philosophische Forschung*, Bd. 38 (1) (1984): 19–38, 27.

21. Marten notes that in this case, Dasein has already made grave mistakes in its game and loses out. See Marten, *Der menschliche Tod*, 65.

22. Note that the translators of *Sein und Zeit* do not capture the vehemence and violence of the verb *niederschlagen* with their phrase that reticence "does away with 'idle talk.' "

23. The translators' term "toss" doesn't do justice to the meaning of *zuspielen*—for example, a (trump) card handed over to the opponent that seems to benefit that player but in reality it doesn't.

24. Young, *Justice and the Politics of Difference*, 46.

25. See Marten, *Der menschliche Tod*, 48.

26. *Fürsorge*, too, for Heidegger, has more to do with an interplay of domination and subordination than a genuine caring-for without a claim to domination as articulated by ethic of care theorists. Care in the end is always about a concern of the self (*Seiendes, dem es um sein Sein geht*, my emphasis) in a radically individualist way. We can say contra Heidegger that his *Fürsorge* masks genuine concern for others.

27. Sarah Hoagland, Marilyn Frye, Nel Noddings, and specifically, María Lugones and Linda Bell have developed play perspectives in feminist ethics.

28. See Dell Hymes, "Coyote, the Thinking (Wo)man's Trickster," in *Monsters, Tricksters, and Sacred Cows*, ed., A. James Arnold (University of Virginia Press, 1996), 108–37. It is a demigod, sometimes human, sometimes godlike, a being that defies structuralist analyses; its character is elusive, because it appears exceedingly intelligent in some tales while in others exceedingly stupid (like German trickster Till Eulenspiegel). The trickster of the Dineh and Plains Indians also takes on various shapes, such as rabbit, Ictinike (Omaha for monkey), spider, and demigod. Often stories describe an encounter where both rabbit and Ictinike trick each other. See Roger Welsch, *Omaha Tribal Myths and Trickster Tales* (Chicago: Sage Books, 1981).

29. Note that Donna Haraway also borrows the coyote simile for her famous socialist-feminist "Cyborg Manifesto" (*Simians, Cyborgs and Women* [New York: Routledge, 1991]).

30. Lugones, "Playfulness," 17.

31. Judith Butler, *Gender Trouble: Feminism and the Subversion of Identity* (New York: Routledge, 1990), x.

32. For a cogent clarification of Heidegger's "silence" and "forgetfulness," see Jean-Françoise Lyotard's book *Heidegger und "die Juden"* (Vienna: Passagen Verlag, 1988) in which he also takes issue with Lacoue-Labarthe's defense of Heidegger (cf. n. 16).

33. I thank Nancy Holland and Patricia Huntington for comments on earlier drafts. I have benefited from discussion with participants of the conference sponsored by the Society for Philosophy of the Contemporary World, Estes Park, August 1998.

Part Four

Thinking, Spirit, Moving Forward

11

From *The Forgetting of Air* to *To Be Two*

Luce Irigaray

Translated by Heidi Bostic and Stephen Pluháček

It is not so far from *The Forgetting of Air* to *I Love to You* and *To Be Two*. The same breath circulates. Sometimes it applies itself to saying its paralysis in our intellectual tradition: philosophy. At other times it frees itself and protects itself in order to love at the limits of life, or to provide room for an interval that safeguards the difference between the Being of woman and the Being of man.

In each one of these works, air appears as the element that goes hand in hand with Being. The "oblivion of Being," of which Heidegger speaks,

---

This essay was originally published as the introduction to the Italian edition of *L'Oubli de l'air*. It was written to commemorate the twentieth anniversary of Martin Heidegger's death in the Spring of 1976.

would redouble the oblivion of the fluid matter that made its constitution possible. Being itself would already be forgetting.

The memory of breath would permit us to reach another epoch of Being, where Being presents itself as two—man and woman—and not as split between appearance and essence, or the being and the becoming of every phenomenon, including the human. The air element, its imperceptible presence in every life, in every act of speaking, in every thought, would be then the path that permits a return beyond the foundation and the closure of metaphysics in order to discover again the breath and the spirit that they have captured—captivated in their logic. The frequenting of nature as empty clearing, the cultivation of breathing would provide a passage from the Western tradition to the Eastern culture that Heidegger, as well as others among recent philosophers, tried to make emerge from oblivion, tried to question as source both on this side of and beyond our Being, we hyperboreans.

But Heidegger does not easily leave the ground, whether it be that of the earth or that of *logos*. He questions, certainly, but he moves most often through certitudes, at the risk of being in touch with the "groundless." He does not call at random through the air. The air, for him, is already encircled, it is already used for something other than what it is: a source of life, including spiritual life.

When Heidegger is listening to the Japanese master, he is still seeking a discourse, a syntax, an art of saying otherwise—even if it means allowing nature to be the subject of it—more than an art of living, of breathing, silently. From Being, Heidegger is already attached to manifestation. He knows the sense of ειναι as "to breathe" but he forgets it, including as a path toward the lighting up of Being. It is to the making of a double of the living that he allies himself, to the preparation of a technique of safeguarding at the disposal of man, neither simple generation nor simple creation, but memory. This memory nevertheless is founded upon the oblivion of the poietic. Doubling life by a mastery of the tracing of its unfolding, by a savoir-faire with respect to its gathering and collecting into a whole, Heidegger forgets that life then redoubles itself in death. To "double" life is both to conserve it and to annihilate it. And it is not true that a cultivation of life needs death as its master, nor even as its horizon.

What it requires, rather, is to be respected for what it is, and not for another end than itself. The master of life, in this way, is he who teaches and safeguards the practice of breathing.

Of course, this bodily technique entails a mourning. Breathing signifies taking care of one's own life. This care supposes a distance from the one who gives us life: from she who has nourished the first breath with her blood, from she who continually nourishes it with her immediate surroundings.

Breathing inscribes in its rhythm the renunciation of the dream of fusional proximity to she who gives life or restores it: the mother, or nature. To breathe is to separate from her, to be reborn, and to give back to her a share of breath: through air, through praise, through work of life and of living spirit. To breathe is to leave prenatal passivity, to leave the infantile state, dependent or mimetic, to leave simple contiguity with the natural universe, in order to maintain and cultivate a status as an autonomous living being.

The gathering of our existence can be fulfilled through breathing. It is a vehicle both of proximity and of distancing, of fidelity and of destiny, of life and of cultivation. It is not necessary to depart for a foreign land to tear oneself away from proximity; breathing will suffice. And nothing can substitute for this intermingling in the self of a nearness that moves away from all immediate closeness: no voyage, no word, not even any form of death. Life is cultivated by life itself, in breathing. This practice produces a distance, an estrangement, a proper becoming that is a renunciation of adherence to the environment. The near becomes one's own, through air. But this proper is never property of the self. It corresponds to the shaping of a life that is never simply mine even if the task of its fulfillment is my responsibility.

Life is never simply mine, because it is always already received from the other and presence to the other, but also because it comes to be thanks to the shared air and atmosphere.

Heidegger speaks of the gathering of nature, of *phusis*, in the saying for its safeguard. In order to guard life, growth, appearing, he doubles them, collects them, names them, links them thanks to the *logos*. But he forgets the mastery of the proximity with air, the gathering of air; that is to say, he forgets the cultivation of life itself and of its relation with the surrounding world, with others, mastery then without violence, without a technique that takes living matter in a fabricated exteriority where it is exiled from its own becoming. Air is cultivated while remaining itself and in relation with itself. This cultivation is necessary for the becoming of each one, man or woman, but also to the becoming of the relation between the one and the other, of the relation between all.

If breathing estranges me from the other, this gesture also signifies a sharing with the world that surrounds me and with the community that inhabits it. Food and even speech can be assimilated, partially become mine. It is not the same for air. I can breathe in my own way, but the air will never be simply mine.

To breathe combines in an indissociable way being-there and being-with. Going out of the mother, I come into the air, I enter into the world, and into the community of living beings.

Speech, perhaps, can bring together access to what is one's own and access to the community. But which speech? Does it already exist? Is it still to be created? How will it realize the link between life and meaning? Through pronunciation? Through a different way of saying: arch-ancient and still to come?

For such an alliance, poetry does not suffice, even if it can set us on the right path. The same goes for song. To unite breaths through a common activity is not yet to exchange breath between us, nor moreover between us and nature.

The poet, perhaps, creates breath, exchanging with nature what he received from it. Lovers sometimes exchange breath participating in one another's life, and even creating from their life an additional breath.

Language, on other occasions, often risks using breath without creating it again, moving between fire and ice, expenditure and paralysis or capitalization of air. The one would come from love, the other from hate. Instead of the invisible dwelling in air that surrounds us imperceptibly, hate would imprison us in a circle. We would live within the limit traced by the freezing of air into ice. At least, such is the word of Empedocles on that which separates us, and Heidegger does not refute him, even if he says nothing about this original imprisonment of or in Being. He thinks that this closure results from a decision on our part: to be and to think are the same. The equivalence or the equality between "to be" and "to think" would constitute the foundation, the ground without ground, of man's dwelling in language. Sheltered by this operation that he masters through his activity, man would separate himself from the flow of life, from the link with she who engendered and nourished him, in particular from air.

He would also separate himself from breath, forgetting the bond of speech and wisdom with breathing. To live in the mother, to receive life from her, would be transformed illusorily into dwelling in language, receiving life from it.

Imperceptibly, the subject thus passes from the living to the dead, the word, especially the written word, rarely presenting itself as a reserve of air. Being-towards-death, such would man be if a word fabricated without concern for breath commands his essence. But such a destiny would elude him just when he claims to bring it under control. The *logos* itself would be a poison to him even before helping him to preserve the world from disintegration. He would prefer nevertheless to dwell in death rather than to emerge into the free air, in this outside where he dwells alone and where absence takes place. Where he is called to discover himself, solitary and confronted with the manifestation of difference(s).

I Love to You and *To Be Two* propose another relation to the air. Air now remains air: not fire, nor ice, nor emptiness. Air remains what gives autonomy to every living being.

Safeguarding the air between them, breathing it in moderation, he and she can meet one another, remaining two. She is no longer this infinite gift that loses itself in him without return. He is no longer this master of a bridge at the end of which there is no one, this shepherd of Being whose autological circle prevents approaching her.

She and he make their way on paths that can cross without ever merging. The other shore, the foreign shore is, for each one, the other.

To be sure, to perceive her in this way signifies, for him, renouncing the one who gave herself infinitely to him in the beginning, first of all in the form of fluids. In order to meet her, he must acknowledge the difference between her and him.

He must not build everything starting from her; he must not sense, look at, gather together, say everything starting from himself. Each one must build, feel, speak. And what she is will never be his own. He will never assimilate her, will never appropriate her without renouncing her and, moreover, himself. Without reducing her to a shadow of herself, to a distortion of him, without limits between them.

In order to prevent this, Being must always be accompanied by a limit and by a question, or two. I am not you, you are not me. Who am I? Who are you?

Strangers we are to one another, irreducible to the same Being. Being, then, is split in two, or, rather, is held in two and in the relation between.

Fidelity to Being thus supposes giving up the appropriation of the other without renouncing the proper, constructing the proximate starting from a proper that will not be appropriation. From then on, I approach the other thanks to the renunciation of him as me, or as mine. I support the other in an environment of air, letting him be in the autonomy of his breath rather than assimilating his Being through words.

Letting the other be obliges me to cultivate my own existence as autonomous, and thus sets me on the path toward the search for my own destiny. Moreover, safeguarding the unfolding of *phusis* in the other and in me, I give up a traditional privilege of mastery that brings under control being in general, whether it be human, animal, or cosmic. To cultivate no longer means simply to reduplicate, to name, to educate, to construct, or to create the already existent universe, but to leave it to its becoming while accepting that it affects my own, without robbing it of its singularity.

Only sexual difference can support such a movement, the difference that attributes to each one a *phusis* to take into consideration, a history and a relational world proper to each one. The subject here is no longer alone nor unique: it is always at least two, and its apprehension of the world is no longer univocal.

Speech thus enters a new epoch of its saying. Neither simple *logos* rationally gathering being for its safekeeping, nor simple poetry that sings of nature, love and gods; speech becomes a poetic tool assisting the birth and growth of human being. Another process of generation takes place, neither simply natural nor simply constructed. A sort of birthing and cultivating of the spiritual is realized between two subjects that accompany one another on the path of the discovery and care of their own Being. Such a task would permit escaping from a perpetual infancy linked to the fear of abandonment and solitude, as well as to the generalized reign of genealogical models. In all domains of culture, we have most often remained in, or returned to, parental roles, whether they be assumed by humans or gods. The cultivation of a horizontal relation between autonomous adult beings does not yet exist, because we have not thought sexual difference as a difference to safeguard without reducing it to the natural.

This new stage of a historial destiny would probably permit us to enter into a new epoch of the unfolding of Being, faithful to Western and Eastern traditions. This new epoch would lead us toward a more complete fulfillment of the human, while permitting us to resolve certain problems of our time: the peril that results from a too exclusive domination of technology, the submission of a part of humanity to the other in the name of universal values forgetful of *phusis* and Being, the disappearance of certain gods, the destruction of nature inside of and outside of us, and so on.

To be sure, we will find ourselves then without parental guardianship, without the demiurgic activity of world builders. We will be exposed before the question of Being, of our Being and that of the cosmos. More abandoned than ever to a destiny that we still must discover and deploy. We will also be more human. Not more men, as it is said, because we will be men and women.[1]

Carrying out such a journey, indicating such a path, I wanted to contribute to the becoming of my epoch and also to celebrate the work of Martin Heidegger. To succeed in this gesture implied not appropriating his thought, but respecting it in its difference. To pay homage to Martin Heidegger in his relationship to the earth, to the sky, to the divinities and to mortals presupposed for me the unveiling and the affirmation of another possible relation to this fourfold.

I began writing *The Forgetting of Air* a few days after Martin Heidegger's death, in May 1976. The task of continuing the philosopher's work imposed itself upon me without any other consideration.

His thought enlightened me at a certain level more than any other and it has done so in a way that awakened my vigilance, political as well as philosophical, rather than constraining me to submit to any program. To conceal such a light would be, in my opinion, a serious error and an ethical mistake for our culture. To gather in this light, to allow it to settle, to pass it on seems more valid to me. And this is what I have tried to do, with respect and gratitude.

To a great thinker, Martin Heidegger wrote, it sometimes happens that he is greatly mistaken. This admission of a limit in the discovery of truth on the part of a philosopher certainly merits an anniversary tribute.

Spring 1996

Notes

1. The French reads: "*Non pas plus hommes, comme il se dit, car nous serons hommes et femmes.*" The word *homme*, "man," is still widely used in French to mean "human." The sentence plays on this double meaning of *homme*.

12

"Through Flame or Ashes"

Traces of Difference in *Geist*'s Return

Ellen T. Armour

> The link uniting or reuniting masculine and feminine must be horizontal and vertical, terrestrial and heavenly. As Heidegger, among others, has written, it must forge an alliance between the divine and the mortal, such that the sexual encounter would be a festive celebration and not a disguised or polemical form of the master-slave relationship. Not a meeting in the shadow or orbit of a Father-God who alone lays down the law, who is the immutable spokesman for a single sex.
>
> —Luce Irigaray, "Sexual Difference"

Heidegger's importance to twentieth-century continental philosophy is a given among philosophers; his centrality to twentieth-century theology (via Paul Tillich, Rudolf Bultmann, and their heirs) is similarly well established among religionists. However, feminist philosophers and religionists attend to Heidegger primarily as a background figure—as precursor to existentialist philosophy and theology and, more recently, to deconstruction. In what follows, I will reverse the order of approach to Heidegger I just described. I will turn to the work of Luce Irigaray and Jacques Derrida as guides for my own reading of Heidegger. Through my reading I will seek resources in Heidegger's work that can support feminist philosophizing in areas where concerns with religion and difference—sexual and racial—intersect. To uncover resources is not to claim

Heidegger as a precursor to feminism's second wave. It is, rather, to mine this philosopher's work for what it can yield, under certain pressures, for projects that he may or may not have envisioned. In the reading of Heidegger I will offer, I aim to be deconstructive; that is, I will search for what traces itself through Heidegger's thought that undoes its surface logic and opens it toward differences of various kinds. Irigaray's approach to the philosophical tradition will provide particularly important cues for my approach. Beginning with *Speculum of the Other Woman*, in her readings of the tradition she seeks out feminine figures within it that serve as philosophy's unacknowledged resource.[1] By "feminine figures" I mean motifs marked as feminine by what Irigaray calls the West's cultural grammar. This grammar is constructed, in part, of hierarchical dualisms that rank mind over body, spirit over nature, ideality over materiality, transcendence over immanence, as well as men over women. These dualisms overlap with one another to create an association of masculinity with mind, spirit, ideality, and transcendence and femininity with body, nature, materiality, and immanence. Through a strategy she calls *mimetisme* (mimicry), Irigaray excavates a particular text's or thinker's use of female figures—woman, her associates (body, nature, matter), or both—in order to show the text's dependence upon them as resources. Irigaray positions herself (as reader/writer) as mirror for the text or thinker in question. Rather like a psychoanalyst (which she is), she poses reflective questions to the text or thinker that expose dynamics heretofore hidden. The reflection created by *mimetisme* disrupts the cultural grammar by exhibiting female figures' transcendence of the boundaries that seek to fix them in place. Disrupting this grammar and the economy it funds begins to make space for women to come into their own; that is, to figure as genuinely different rather than simply the other of the same.

Irigaray on Religion and Sexual Difference

It is a commonplace in feminist theology that if God is male, the male is God. Critique of masculinist language for deity has been central to the feminist theological project. As the epigraph cited above suggests, Irigaray makes a similar argument in essays in *Sexes and Genealogies* and in *An Ethics of Sexual Difference*.[2] The concept of a male god, she argues, serves as support and guarantee for male subjectivity while simultaneously denying subjectivity to women. Male subjectivity draws on female resources for sustenance. Entrance into subjectivity comes at the cost of the sacrifice of the maternal body. Man's confidence in his status as subject is sustained through the woman's gaze, which reflects man as he would like to be. The secure accomplishment of subjectivity is, however, perpetually foreclosed by unacknowledged costs. Man's need for woman-as-mirror places an other inside the subject, thereby disrupting the subject's claim to self-mastery, singularity, and wholeness. The maternal body constitutes yet another split in the subject. The unmourned loss of that body resides within the subject as lack. Irigaray argues that the longing for the mother is displaced onto the longing for the (male) God or gods (Irigaray, "Love of Self," in *Ethics*, 60–61).

As several scholars have noted, Heidegger figures prominently in Irigaray's exposure of the debt to the maternal that funds not only subjectivity, but other features of the West's cultural grammar.[3] Joanna Hodge argues that Irigaray describes the maternal sacrifice in Heideggerian terms, as an originary event.[4] An originary event does not occur once and for all at the beginning of a chain of events that it sets in motion. It is better described as "an omnipresent and recurrently affirmed set of parameters that open up certain lines of possibility while closing off others" (Hodge, "Irigaray Reading," 192). Irigaray uncovers traces of the primordial sacrifice through its memorialization and reenactment in such sites as philosophical texts, Greek tragedy, and Western Christianity. Heidegger's work constitutes an important site for excavating the forgotten sacrifice of the maternal body and its use as resource for thinking. The traditional four elements familiar to us from the pre-Socratics (earth, air, water, and fire) occupy a central role in this aspect of Irigaray's work. In *L'oubli de l'air chez Martin Heidegger*, Irigaray uses *mimetisme* to show that beneath Heidegger's explicit invocation of the motif of homelessness lies the unmourned maternal body.[5] That body, in the form of air, serves as resource for Heidegger's thinking, as I will explain below.

It seems clear that sexual *indifference* and traditional western notions of deity go hand in hand, but what about sexual *difference*, Irigaray's central concern? What connection could promoting a new sexual economy that accommodates women as subjects in their own right possibly have with religion? Several essays in Irigaray's oeuvre contain tantalizing invocations of religious motifs as critical to the project of realizing sexual difference (and enabling genuine relations between differends). In "Divine Women" Irigaray identifies God as the Other necessary for subjectivity's grounding and urges women to image the divine in female terms.[6] In "Sexual Difference" she argues that the difficult task of making genuine relationships between men and women possible requires a third (divine) term. "For this 'God' is necessary, or a love so attentive that it is divine" (Irigaray, *Ethics*, 19).

To find a philosopher—particularly a postmodern philosopher—invoking deity as necessary to *anything* may seem outlandish, particularly in light of feminists' longstanding critiques of religion's central role in women's subordination. With a few notable exceptions, Irigarayan scholars outside religious studies tend to pass quickly over this aspect of Irigaray's work.[7] Some have raised concerns about the dangers inherent in it.[8] A number of scholars have noted that Irigaray's later work, where most of her discussion of religion takes place, loses sight of an element considered critical in her earlier work; namely, thinking differences between women (such as race or sexuality) as essential to what *woman* means.[9] I have argued elsewhere that Irigaray's work with religious motifs is particularly vulnerable to this problem, especially those places where she urges women to image God in their terms.[10] As Irigaray herself argues, God is the linchpin in the economy of sameness that structures our cultural grammar. Because God's word *is* being, he serves as the guarantor that words can correspond to the things they describe. Moreover, it is God's resemblance to man that grounds man's subjectivity. As Feuerbach argued, God is man writ large, purified of his limits and faults. When Irigaray suggests to women that they form God in their own image, she recapitulates the logic of mutual reflection and thus courts the establishment of another economy of sameness. Is it just coincidental that the issue of differences *between* women recedes from sight on this terrain?

Moreover, Irigaray's evocation of religious motifs seems untimely, if not unseemly. God's displacement from his place at the center of existence and, ultimately, pronouncements of his death constitute signposts of modernity's reign. How can Irigaray's invocations of a deity be read as something other than nostalgic, misguided, or ironic? In "The Envelope: A Reading of Spinoza, *Ethics*, 'Of God,'" Irigaray takes note of the fact that the question of sexual difference arises in the epoch after the death of God (Irigaray, *Ethics*, 86). This, she thinks, is not coincidental. The god who has died is the one who could contain himself (give himself his own envelope, to use the metaphor in play in this essay). In "Love of the Other," Irigaray asserts that the philosophers who announced the death of God were not announcing the death of all gods for all time, but anticipated the coming of a new god, a "return of the divine in the festival, grace, love, thought" (Irigaray, *Éthique*, 133, my translation; see *Ethics*, 140). Perhaps, she asks, this is the time when a meeting between the sexes becomes possible.

But what sort of deity, if she is serious, does Irigaray have in mind? In "An Ethics of Sexual Difference," Irigaray gives Heidegger's famous statement "only a god can save us now" an ironic twist. She responds, "A moins d'un dieu, peut-être?" (Irigaray, *Éthique*, 124). The multivalence carried by the original French is easy to lose in translation. "At least a god, perhaps?" "Less than a god, perhaps?" "More than *one* god, perhaps?" The figure of divinity employed by Irigaray plays between all of these meanings. On the one hand, she invests this figure (ironically, perhaps?) with traditional divine powers. "At least a god, perhaps? [To] displace the limits of the possible, melt the ancient glaciers, a god who can make a future for us" (Irigaray, *Éthique*, 124, my translation; see *Ethics*, 128). Humanity's role in relation to this god appears limited. "We still have to await the god, remain in a disposition and an opening that prepares its return. And with it, for ourselves, in place of an implacable decline, a new birth, an other epoch of history" (Irigaray, *Éthique*, 124, my translation; see *Ethics*, 129). On the other hand, she portrays this vision of deity as subject to human effort. "This creation would be our opportunity . . . by means of the opening of a *sensible transcendental* that ad-vents through us, of which *we would be* the mediators and bridges. Not only in mourning for the dead God of Nietzsche, not waiting passively for the god to come, but by conjuring it up among and across us, within and between us, as resurrection or transfiguration of blood, of flesh, through a language and an ethics that is ours" (Irigaray, *Éthique*, 124, my translation; see *Ethics*, 129).

Following the figure of a sensible transcendental through Irigaray's work moves this vision of the sacred farther away from classically (mono)-theistic notions of deity and of transcendence. Traditional notions of deity, as diverse as they are, describe it (or often, him) as transcendent in two senses. Although not subject to the conditions of mundane material reality (change, time, decay death, division), God is the source of mundane reality. As such, then, God is envisioned as ideal spirit rather than material body, transcendent to the world, not immanent within it. Irigaray's choice of terminology here—*sensible* transcendental—indicates her attempt to think sacrality against the grain of this tradition. Exploring an example of a sensible transcendental at work will articulate the difference Irigaray is trying to produce.

I noted earlier that Irigaray's reading of Heidegger in *L'oubli de l'air* uncovered air as the unacknowledged milieu of Heidegger's thinking. As such, it functions as a sensible transcendental in Heidegger's work. Air is transcendent in that it constitutes the space of the clearing, which is the horizon for thinking. Air is sensible in that, although invisible to the naked eye, it is nonetheless material.

Air as a sensible transcendental is both less than a god and more than a god. As transcendent horizon for what is, air serves as source (and resource) for existence. And yet, in its materiality, it evokes not a distant transcendence—much less an immaterial one—but an immanent transcendence. Air resides *entre nous*, between us but also within us individually. Without it, we are nothing, yet we hardly notice its presence. Although it occupies these transcendent roles, it is not, properly speaking, *a* god. Air is too dispersed to be any *one* thing at all. In all these ways, air as a sensible transcendental figures the sacred in terms quite different from the logic of classical (mono)theism.

The figure of the sensible transcendental seems particularly promising as a productive route out of the link between sexual (in)difference and divinity. I say "sexual (in)difference" to suggest that an economy of sexual difference appears only through the cracks of the current sexual economy of indifference. In *L'oubli*, air funds a new relationship between masculine and feminine figures (*l'un* and *l'une*) that Irigaray portrays in the book's closing pages. I have described it elsewhere as a dance between masculine and feminine where the dancers repeatedly exchange places, effectively robbing the labels *masculine* and *feminine* of their traditional meanings.

In addition to serving as a possible (un)grounding ground for sexual difference and the relationship between differends, sensible transcendentals also offer significant potential for addressing two other issues associated with critiques of religion. Insofar as they disrupt the logic of (mono)theism that lies at the heart of the economy of sameness, they hold out the promise of (un)grounding a thinking of sacrality that could support differences in all their variety. They also promise to disrupt the dualisms that make up the West's cultural grammar (its body/soul dualism, its validation of transcendence over immanence, immaterial over material, and so on)—all of which many religionists argue are linked to

Western Christianity's legacy of sexism, colonialism, and environmental exploitation.

Sensible transcendentals hold out a great deal of promise, but can they fulfill it? Disrupting the logic of monotheism and the dualisms that surround it may be critical to making a place for *sexual* difference, but what about other differences? The fact that *L'oubli*'s last dance (un)-grounds sexual difference but leaves racial indifference unchallenged suggests caution. Is a sensible transcendental really capable of preventing sexual difference from foreclosing on racial difference?

My choice of Irigaray's work on Heidegger to describe sensible transcendentals is hardly random. Those familiar with Heidegger's work know that religious motifs shape its milieu. Indeed, Heidegger's importance to Irigaray's understanding of the connection between sexual difference and religion makes his work a logical site to explore with these questions in mind. His own troubled legacy of involvement with National Socialism makes his work a particularly challenging place to bring these questions. To carry out this experiment, I will read Heidegger's essay from 1953, "Language in the Poem: A Discussion on Georg Trakl's Poetic Work" (OWL, 159–98). I have been led to this essay by Jacques Derrida's reading of Heidegger in *Of Spirit: Heidegger and the Question* and associated texts.[11] While sexual difference is not Derrida's focus in *Of Spirit*, he points toward its traces in Heidegger's involvement with *Geist* (spirit) and *Geschlecht* (a complex term that means genre, gender, race, lineage, tribe, and so forth). Both terms figure prominently in questions about Heidegger's relationship to theology and racial or ethnic (in)difference, issues that focus Derrida's reading and with which I am also concerned.[12]

The complexity of these terms' history in Heidegger's oeuvre adds another layer of significance to their exploration. I noted earlier that Irigaray's work with religion in pursuit of sexual difference rendered her work vulnerable to recapture by an economy of sameness that she sets out to avoid. Sites where more traditional religious motifs figure prominently foreclose on Irigaray's early project, thinking differences between women. This keeps Irigaray's thinking of woman blind to the difference race makes to women, for example. Derrida's reading of Heidegger finds the figures of *Geist* and *Geschlecht* implicated in Heidegger's complicity with National Socialism. This legacy calls for caution in approaching Heidegger's work, especially for feminism struggling to get beyond racism's effects.

Let me begin the next section of this essay, then, by tracing what I find of interest in Derrida's inquiry into Geist's and Geschlecht's careers in Heidegger's thought, with a particular focus on the Trakl essay's place in that inquiry. I will outline Geist's place in relationship to Geschlecht in Heidegger's thought as a whole, as Derrida sees it. Then I will turn specifically to these terms' places within the Trakl essay.

Derrida on Heidgger, Religion, and Difference

Derrida's reading of Heidegger in these essays suggests that Geist and Geschlecht follow similar careers in Heidegger's work. Both terms constitute sites where Heidegger contests philosophy's bondage to metaphysical humanism and ontotheology, with limited success. Their association with these legacies motivates Heidegger to subject both terms to avoidance, to begin with. However, Derrida finds reason to ask about the precise meaning of *avoidance* in these cases. It cannot be the terms *as such* that Heidegger desires to avoid—especially in the case of Geist, which Heidegger employs in Being and Time right on the heels of announcing his intention to avoid it. In "Geschlecht" and "Geschlecht II," Derrida argues that Heidegger resists Geschlecht as defined in terms of current economies of racial and sexual difference, which are based in metaphysical humanism. Derrida argues, however, that Heidegger leaves open the possibility that Dasein could be productively associated with other configurations held out by Geschlecht's inherent multiplicity.

Derrida's reading exposes serious limitations to Heidegger's avoidance. Both Geist and Geschlecht turn out to harbor residues of metaphysical humanism and ontotheology. Derrida's analysis finds these residues implicated in Heidegger's involvement with National Socialism. Geschlecht and Geist both appear in the infamous rectorship address—Geist, now, unaccompanied by gestures of avoidance—where their metaphysical associations take on a National Socialist hue, in Derrida's analysis.[13] This public address, which Heidegger delivered upon assuming the rectorship of the University of Freiburg (upon invitation of the Nazi regime), is often cited as a damning piece of evidence that Heidegger subscribed to Nazi ideology. In this speech, Heidegger connects the university's mission to the character of the German people through their shared embodiment of Geist. Derrida notes that Heidegger's insistence on the character of the German people as spiritual (rather than biological or racial) may indicate a resistance to racism or anti-Semitism founded upon biological principles. Perhaps Heidegger spiritualizes National Socialism in hopes of saving it from itself, Derrida suggests. Invoking *Geist* for this purpose, however, risks capitulating to metaphysical humanism with its own history of intolerance.[14] As Derrida writes, "In the *Rectorship Address*, this risk is not just a risk run. If its program seems diabolical, it is because, *without there being anything fortuitous in this,* it capitalizes on the worst, that is on both evils at once: the sanctioning of Nazism, and the gesture that is still metaphysical" (Derrida, OS, 40).

My account of Derrida's reading of *Geist's* and *Geschlecht's* careers in Heidegger's work up to this point might make one suspicious of any claim that they could point beyond metaphysics in any way that could be helpful for feminism. In particular, what can Heidegger's work offer to feminism, which is already struggling to break free of racism's legacy? To toss Heidegger aside at this point would be premature, however. The other side of Heidegger's legacy that Derrida also discusses remains to be explored. Heidegger's essay on Trakl, where *Geschlecht* and *Geist* intersect again, occupies center stage in the refiguring of these terms that Derrida also finds in Heidegger's work. Derrida's reading of this essay points toward resources within it that link up with Irigaray's work with religion and sexual difference and exceed it in bringing racial difference into the picture as well.

According to Derrida, Heidegger finds resources in Trakl's poetry that carry thought beyond the boundaries of metaphysics and ontotheology. Heidegger excavates these resources through taking two phrases as guides to Trakl's poetry. The two phrases are "Spirit in-flames" and "the soul is on earth a stranger" (or "a strange thing is the soul on earth").[15] "Spirit in-flames" marks the limit of ontotheology. The notion of spirit that Trakl deploys here is neither Greek nor Christian, according to Heidegger. It is, rather, their originary origin. Greek and Christian concepts of spirit emerge from *Geist* in flames, but they also forget their origin insofar as they lose sight of a material transcendence and a connection with the meaning of being.

Geist's break with ontotheology is also borne through its alliance with *Geschlecht*. In Trakl's poetry, *Geist* gathers itself into *ein Geschlecht*. Drawing on his analysis of *Geschlecht* elsewhere, Derrida notes the impossibility of thinking *Geschlecht* as a unitary One. The very possibility of unity in *Geschlecht* is bound up with diversity. *Geschlecht*, in its polyvalence, contains an originary dispersibility that enables both division and unity.

Thus, linking *Geist* with *Geschlecht*—even *ein Geschlecht*—potentially carries it beyond metaphysics and ontotheology, whose economies rest on oneness.

When read with Irigaray in the background, the possible significance of this thinking of *Geist* in conjunction with *Geschlecht* grows. In reworking *Geist*'s transcendence in terms of materiality (fire) rather than in opposition to it, "Spirit in-flames" approaches a sensible transcendental. Moreover, *Geist*'s associations with *Geschlecht*—with an originary dispersibility that funds both current and future sexual and racial economies—suggest that this (possible) sensible transcendental might fund new economies of difference. It will be interesting to see whether their impact registers in this way in Trakl's essay.

"The soul is on earth a stranger" also points beyond ontotheology and metaphysics, according to Heidegger. Derrida notes that the phrase seems to lend itself to a traditional Platonic reading of body/soul dualism. The soul finds earth inhospitable because its true home lies elsewhere; the immaterial realm of the purely ideal (versus the merely material). However, Heidegger takes the phrase in a contrary direction. The earth constitutes the home the soul seeks rather than the trap it desires to escape. Remembering Irigaray's analysis of Heidegger's homelessness as evidence of the longing for the maternal body gives this phrase added significance. Once again, an element (earth, this time, versus air in *L'oubli*) traditionally associated with femininity stands as the true home. Moreover, the German word for soul, *Seele*, is feminine and, as Derrida notes, Heidegger maintains that traditional association. Thus, below what appears at first glance to be a traditional Platonic (and masculine) figure (immaterial soul breaking out of its material prison) one finds female figures leading the break with traditional philosophical thinking.

Even what seems at first to be the most traditional of the elements at work in this essay, the relationship between soul and spirit that it evokes, shows signs of pointing elsewhere. *Seele* (a feminine noun, remember) and *Geist* (a masculine noun) come together at first in a scene that bears the marks of a traditional sexual economy. *Seele* acts as *Geist*'s guardian in giving it shelter, reproducing the woman's traditional role as giver and man's as taker. However, these roles are reversed as well when *Geist* gives *Seele* to herself as gift (Derrida, OS, 104).

Derrida's reading of Heidegger's essay on Trakl points toward these intriguing elements in the essay, but lets them lie fallow in his own analysis. Particularly when read with Irigarayan eyes, these elements invite a fresh reading of Heidegger's essay in search of more evidence of their effects and their possible limits. It is to that reading that I now turn, with the following questions as my guide: "Spirit in-flames" offers a number of provocative hints that it may serve as a sensible transcendental. Will a reading of the Trakl essay confirm such a function? If so, will it also uncover any signs that "Spirit in-flames" also funds a new economy of sexual and racial difference? "The soul is on earth a stranger" similarly evokes images of a sensible transcendental yoked to sexual difference, if not racial difference. Do its effects run deeper in Heidegger's text? The association of both *Geist* and *Seele* with ontotheology and metaphysics— not to mention racism, in *Geist*'s case—raises a cautionary flag, however. My reading will have to keep watch for recapitulations of these legacies, particularly their associations with racism. Do possibilities of sexual and racial difference and intimations of a sacrality beyond traditional Western notions follow the same path? If so, what can following this path accomplish for feminism, and for feminist philosophy of religion? Are there limits to this path's efficacy?

Reading Heidegger Reading Trakl

Symptoms of sexual (in)difference, in particular, register strongly in this essay, as well as invocations of a sacrality that exceeds traditional Western notions. At the beginning of the essay, Heidegger identifies his interest in reading Trakl as investigating and heeding the site of Trakl's poetry. By this, he means not its physical location in ordinary time and space, but its *Ursprung*, if you will; that which gives rise to what Trakl's poetry offers to thinking. Heidegger resorts to another familiar term, *gathering* (*Versammlung*), to describe the aim of this encounter between the philosopher and the poet. What is it that gathers Trakl's poetry, that Trakl's poetry gathers and thus makes available for thinking? Access to this site or this *Versammlung* comes only indirectly, through following guides that reside within it. Heidegger selects "The soul is on earth a stranger" as the key to locating this site. Solitary masculine and feminine figures journey across a densely colored landscape filled with typical Heideggerian landmarks. The soul (*Seele*) serves as Heidegger's guide, as Heidegger's reader's guide, and as guide for masculine figures who appear along the way. *Seele* leads her followers to *Geschlecht* and to *Geist* as she takes them through a landscape at once strange and familiar (*Unheimlich*, one might say, though Heidegger does not use this term here).

As Derrida noted, Heidegger immediately rejects a Platonic reading of "the soul is on earth a stranger." Heidegger insists that nothing in the poem where the phrase appears would support reading it as a description of the (immaterial) soul's fall into earthly (material) existence. His interpretation of this phrase recapitulates other late Heideggerian themes. "The soul is on earth a stranger" describes the essence of the soul, Heidegger writes, but its essence resembles an event more than a static substance. *Seele* is always "under way" toward what she seeks, the earth. She seeks the earth "so that she might poetically build and dwell upon it, and thus may be able to save the earth *as* earth." (OWL, 163). The interplay of female markings with another of the traditional four elements that Irigaray associates with sensible transcendentals is striking, but only hints at what is to come.

Heidegger turns to other poems to further describe that toward which *Seele* is under way. References to the earth give way to references to the sky, evoking associations with yet another element (air)—indeed, the element that *L'oubli* uncovers as Heidegger's particular sensible transcendental. *Seele* is under way toward the blue of twilight; itself a gathering (*Versammlung*) of the end of the day, the beginning of evening, and the launch of the next day. This *Versammlung* takes on sacred connotations as well. Blueness as deployed by Trakl "gathers the depth of the holy in the depths of its bond. The holy shines out of the blueness, even while veiling itself in the dark of that blueness. The holy withholds in withdrawing" (OWL, 165).

A masculine figure appears under the blue sky of twilight at this point in Heidegger's essay. Heidegger turns to another of Trakl's poems that describes a vision of the holy that causes an animal's face to freeze. Heidegger reads this animal as "modern man," the rational animal, who has lost his home. Feminine figures appear as this man's traditional moorings in this scene, but rather than securing him, they call him to wander. *Seele*'s journey toward her home is now doubled in the figure of man whose search for *his* home is launched by an encounter with the holy, "the 'mirror of truth,'" that renders him speechless. In taking *Seele*, the stranger, as his guide, man himself becomes strange. The first sign of his strangeness appears in his relationship to *Geschlecht*. Heidgger notes that following *Seele* places man outside the traditional bonds that form *Geschlecht* (including kinship, race, tribe, family, "all of these in turn cast in the duality of the sexes," Heidegger says in OWL, 170). Yet to move outside *Geschlecht*—as currently constituted, at least—is also to begin to reestablish it in its more originary sense. *Geschlecht*, like man, has lost its way. The symptom of its decomposition and decay is "discord among sexes, tribes, and races" (OWL, 170) that has led to "an irreconcilable split" and so "casts [each kind] into unbridled isolation" (OWL, 171). This discord is not the inevitable result of *Geschlecht*'s duality, Heidegger says; in fact, the "proper cast" of *Geschlecht* lies "with that kind whose duality leaves discord behind and leads the way, as 'something strange,' into the gentleness of simple twofoldness following in the stranger's footsteps" (OWL, 171). Following the stranger, now figured as the lunar voice of the sister, leads man toward his true home *and* true *Geschlecht* (tribe, family, race, kind).

These evocations of sensible transcendentals figure a sacrality that exceeds traditional Platonic-Christian notions of divinity and transcendence. The holy appears once again in materiality—in the blue of twilight. It transcends not through abandoning the material realm but through withdrawing into materiality that both reveals and veils it. This figure of transcendence bears marks of sexual (in)difference as well. On one hand, the holy figures as a mirror of truth, a traditionally feminine position. However, rather than securing man in his speaking subjectivity, it silences him and drives him outside of himself. Heidegger's vision of an irreconcilable split within *Geschlecht* resonates with Irigaray's diagnosis of the (im)possible possibility of relationships between women and women and men and women, though without the dense analysis of the source of that split that Irigaray offers. At the same time, Heidegger's vision of healing is encouraging. Rather than suggesting that the cure lies in overlooking difference, *Geschlecht*'s centrality means Heidegger's vision unfolds toward an embrace of difference in many senses—sexual difference, yes, but also racial difference, ethnic difference, and so on. Yet feminists appropriate this vision with caution, I think. Rather than exploiting *Geschlecht*'s multiplicity, Heidegger envisions healing as the embrace of a "simple twofoldness" figured in terms of sexual difference alone. Moreover, the human masculine and feminine figures that appear from this point on in the essay are brother and sister, not lovers or even friends. Heidegger's vision, though figured by sexual differends, is hardly sexual at all. Thus, it falls short of the dance between *l'un* and *l'une* that Irigaray choreographs at the end of *L'oubli*. This dance, though limited in its effects by the absence of racial difference, permits and even encourages multivalent readings of its figures (*l'un* and *l'une*) in greater variety (as friends, as lovers, as figures of divine/human relations, as mother/son, father/daughter, and so on).

Yet another promising aspect of Heidegger's excavation of Trakl's site, the intersection where *Geist* and *Geschlecht* meet, appears on the horizon at this point in the essay. Heidegger ventures to name Trakl's site "apartness," which recalls the division enacted between man and *Geschlecht* (as currently constituted) by man's encounter with the holy. "Apartness," Heidegger writes, "is spiritual, determined by the spirit, and ghostly, but it is not 'of the spirit' in the sense of the language of metaphysics" (OWL, 179). Heidegger describes Trakl's site as a land that is "older, which is to say, earlier and therefore more promising than the Platonic-Christian land, or indeed than a land conceived in terms of the European west" (OWL, 194). Just as *Seele*'s distance from earth traced a path opposed to an immaterial notion of transcendence, so *Geist* resists associations with immaterial transcendence. It is spirit *as* material that Trakl's phrase, "Spirit in-flames" gives for thinking. Heidegger makes much of Trakl's choice of flame rather than breath or air (*pneuma*), the traditional Platonic-Christian metaphor, as his figure for *Geist*. Flame undoes the traditional metaphysical opposition between spirit and matter. The ethereal qualities of *pneuma*, on the other hand, reinforce this opposition, Heidegger argues.

Derrida greets Heidegger's emphatic attempts to separate Trakl's *Geist* from Platonic-Christian connotations (and Trakl from Christianity) with skepticism. Derrida's suspicion is linked to the ethical concerns that motivate *Of Spirit* and the *Geschlecht* essays. He brings to light traces of the same ethnocentrism that attends *Geist*'s appearance in the Rectorship Address. *Geist*'s originary meaning can only be thought in German, Heidegger insists—not even in Greek, Derrida notes, the other language and culture that Heidegger privileges. Heidegger trains his sights on *Geist* as figured by the intersection of Platonism and Christianity, but he ignores the third road that constitutes this intersection, Judaism. What of the Hebrew word for breath and spirit, *ruah*? What funds this omission, Derrida asks? What accounts for it, and what does it suggest about the dangers associated with *Geist* and ethnocentrism, especially given Heidegger's insistence upon *Geist*'s essential Germanness?

This is not to say that Derrida finds Heidegger's claim that Trakl's *Geist* points beyond ontotheology totally without merit. Derrida leaves open the possibility of a potential challenge to ontotheology in Trakl's *Geist*.

"Spirit in-flames. How to hear or understand this?" (Derrida, OS, 96). Significantly, that potential is linked to the issue of sexual (and other) differences through *Geist*'s link to *Geschlecht*. In the same poem that leads Heidegger to describe Trakl's site as a land, he finds it possible to think *Versammlung* in terms of *Geschlecht*. As Derrida pointed out, Trakl's site gathers into "ein *Geschlecht*," which is not, Heidegger asserts, a reference to "a biological fact at all, to a 'single' or 'identical' gender" (OWL, 195). Heidegger stresses sexual difference where Derrida in his reading stresses the dispersibility inherent in *Geschlecht* that takes sexual difference beyond its current binary and, in "Geschlecht II," beyond sexual difference alone. Together, they provide another promising element for feminist thinking. Not only is "ein *Geschlecht*" something of an oxymoron (what sense can it make to think a term layered with multivalences as a "one"?), but its dispersibility brings sexual difference into the company of many other differences that ground human diversity. Is it too much to hope that *Geschlecht* might ground sexual differences thought in and through racial differences, national differences, and so on, rather than in opposition to them?

Conclusions

I set out to determine whether a reading of Heidegger's essay on Trakl informed by Irigaray and Derrida could offer indications that following links between sensible transcendentals, sexual and racial difference, could be productive for feminism. The reading I have just given answers both yes and no. This reading suggests that following such a trajectory promises to benefit feminist philosophy of religion and feminism in general. Heidegger's essay, however, contains limits that prevent the full realization of that promise within its boundaries. I have noted the limits that affect sexual and racial difference, but what of this essay's attempts to break with Platonic-Christianity through "Spirit in-flames"? Are there limits to that aspect of Heidegger's thought, as well? The closing pages of *Of Spirit* raise that question. In connecting spirit with fire, Trakl exceeds ontotheology in refiguring its connection of transcendence with ideality. Yet Derrida's reading suggests that ontotheology remains strong enough in Heidegger's text to recapture "spirit in-flames" within its boundaries. In the last pages of *Of Spirit*, Derrida stages a dialogue between Heidegger and a group of theologians. The theologians first accuse Derrida's Heidegger of being antitheological, anti-Christian even. Heidegger rejects these appellations arguing that he is trying to think what made possible Christianity, its theology, and the Greek/Christian paradigm that funds it. He claims to be headed in the direction of an altogether heterogeneous origin. The theologians nod approvingly. Yes, they say, we have been after the same thing all along. Heidegger resists the accuracy of this claim, but the theologians reject his resistance, referring to a spirit that will keep watch over them, and that binds them together in a common project. Derrida leaves the dispute unresolved as the staged dialogue comes to an inconclusive end. Are the theologians and Heidegger, in fact, headed in the same direction? If so, are they headed outside ontotheology or not? And what about spirit? Derrida gives spirit the closing lines of the text: "The spirit which keeps watch in returning [*en revenant*, as a ghost] will always do the rest. Through flame or ash, but as the entirely other, inevitably" (Derrida, OS, 113).

Exploring this ending in its full complexity is beyond the scope of a brief conclusion, but important implications for my project can be drawn from it that bear on the promise and danger it carries. First of all, this ending, *Of Spirit* as a whole, and the readings in which I have engaged here warn us that to play with religious motifs—even after the death of God—is to play with fire in many senses.[16] *Geist*'s involvement in Heidegger's complicity with Nazism, the disappearance of women's diversity when Irigaray enters religious terrain, all suggest that religious motifs bring with them baggage that can derail one's original intentions.[17] Religious motifs share the same situation, then, that everything faces within a context still shaped by ontotheology and metaphysics. As Derrida and Irigaray both remind their readers repeatedly, getting beyond ontotheology and metaphysics is (im)possible. At best (at least, for now) we can find ways to disrupt this context's mastery and inhabit it differently. At the same time, routes toward disruption that could fund a different habitation have begun to appear. Is it only coincidental that Heidegger ends up calling upon sexual difference in his drive to break the bonds of ontotheology and metaphysics? As I noted earlier, Irigaray finds it logical that sexual difference becomes a question for thinking after the death of God. She goes on to suggest that the exploration of the ontico-ontological difference also necessarily preceded the question of sexual difference. To find the later Heidegger drawn toward sexual difference as he explores ground opened up by his previous account of the ontico-ontological difference suggests that the obverse of another of Irigaray's claims is also true. Not only do we perhaps need a god, or a love so attentive that it is divine, to achieve sexual difference, but we need sexual difference to evoke a sense of sacrality on the other side of ontotheology.

These explorations also suggest that *sexual* difference alone may not be sufficient for this task because of *its* tendency—especially in religion's terrain—to close itself off into an economy of sameness with a different standard. The openness that Irigaray advises us to cultivate as we await the coming of a new god, then, also needs to apply to the *entre nous*. Until and unless the differences-between-us receive more attention, we would do well to suspect that any new god appearing on the horizon and demanding our loyalty will be a ghost of the same.

Notes

1. Luce Irigaray, *Speculum of the Other Woman*, trans. Gillian C. Gill (Ithaca: Cornell University Press, 1985).

2. Luce Irigaray, *Sexes and Genealogies*, trans. Gillian Gill (New York: Columbia University Press, 1993). See especially "Divine Women," 57–72, in this volume. Relevant essays in *Éthique de la différence sexuelle* (Paris: Minuit, 1984); *An Ethics of Sexual Difference*, trans. Carolyn Burke and Gillian C. Gill (Ithaca: Cornell University Press, 1993) will be mentioned in due course. Where necessary, I have given my own translations of *Éthique*. In those cases, I include a reference to the Burke and Gill translation as well as the French original for the reader's convenience.

3. Tina Chanter and Ellen Mortensen both argue that Heidegger provides a mode of approach to sexual difference through its kinship to the question of Being. See Tina Chanter, *Ethics of Eros: Irigaray's Rewriting of the Philosophers* (New York: Routledge, 1995), chap. 4; and Ellen Mortensen, "Woman's Untruth and *le féminin*: Reading Luce Irigaray with Nietzsche and Heidegger" in *Engaging with Irigaray*, ed. Carolyn Burke, Naomi Schor, Margaret Whitford (New York: Columbia University Press, 1994), 211–28.

4. Joanna Hodge, "Irigaray Reading Heidegger," in Burke, Schor, and Whitford, *Engaging with Irigaray*, 191–209.

5. Luce Irigaray, *L'oubli de l'air chez Martin Heidegger* (Paris: Minuit, 1983).

6. "Divine Women," in *Sexes*, 64.

7. Exceptions from scholars outside religious studies include Kathryn Bond Stockton, *God Between Their Lips: Desire Between Women in Irigaray, Brontë, and Eliot* (Stanford: Stanford University Press, 1994); and Elizabeth Grosz, "Irigaray and the Divine," in *Transfigurations: Feminist Theology and the French Feminists*, ed. C. W. Maggie Kim, Susan M. St. Ville, and Susan M. Simonaitis (Philadelphia: Fortress Press, 1993), 199–214 (originally published in *Transitions in Continental Philosophy*, ed. Stephen Watson, Arleen Dallery, and Marya Bower [Albany: State University of New York Press, 1994]).

8. See Grosz, "Irigaray and the Divine" for a discussion of these critiques.

9. Most recently, see Elizabeth Grosz and Pheng Cheah, "Of Being Two: An Introduction," and "The Future of Sexual Difference: An Interview with Judith Butler and Drucilla Cornell," *Diacritics* 28 (Spring 1998): 3–18 and 19–42 respectively.

10. See Ellen T. Armour, "Crossing the Boundaries Between Deconstruction, Feminism, and Religion" in *Feminist Interpretations of Jacques Derrida*, ed. Nancy J. Holland (University Park: Penn State Press, 1997), 193–214; and *Deconstruction, Feminist Theology, and the Problem of Difference: Subverting the Race/Gender Divide* (Chicago: University of Chicago Press, 1999), chap. 4.

11. Jacques Derrida, *Of Spirit: Heidegger and the Question*, trans. Geoffrey Bennington and Rachel Bowlby (Chicago: University of Chicago Press, 1989). Hereafter cited as OS.

12. In following Derrida's lead here, I am not claiming that he has thought through the connections between these vectors in all their complexity. David Farrell Krell has argued convincingly that Derrida fails to follow sexual (in)difference all the way through *Geist*'s terrain. See Krell, "Spiriting Heidegger" in *Of Derrida, Heidegger, and Spirit*, ed. David Wood (Evanston: Northwestern University Press, 1993), 11–40. To a certain extent, then, I aim to cultivate what Derrida's work opens up but leaves lying fallow. Where my approach to Heidegger via Irigaray was relatively direct, my approach through Derrida is somewhat less so. *Geist* and *Geschlecht* (and sexual difference, racial difference, and theology) cross paths in the same text only in *Of Spirit*. However, Derrida explicitly connects *Of Spirit* to two essays on *Geschlecht* in Heidegger's work that were written in its proximity. "Geschlecht: Sexual Difference, Ontological Difference" (originally published in *Research in Phenomenology* 13 [1983]: 65–83; reprinted in this volume) concerns Heidegger's involvement with *Geschlecht* as sexual difference. "*Geschlecht* II: Heidegger's Hand," in *Deconstruction and Philosophy: The Texts of Jacques Derrida*, ed. John Sallis (Chicago: University of Chicago Press, 1987), 161–96, takes on Heidegger's use of *Geschlecht* in relation to race. Reading these essays with *Of Spirit* deepens the significance of the intersection between *Geist* and *Geschlecht*, and between theology and sexual and racial (in)difference, that *Of Spirit* makes it possible to think. For a fuller treatment of these issues, see chapters 3 and 5 of my *Deconstruction, Feminist Theology, and the Problem of Difference*. David Wood also argues that *Of Spirit* needs to be read as the next stage in Derrida's careful interrogation of the Heideggerian scene begun in *Margins of Philosophy*, trans. Alan Bass (Chicago: University of Chicago Press, 1982) and continued in the *Geschlecht* essays. See David Wood, "Responses and Responsibilities: An Introduction," in Wood, *Of Derrida*, 1–8.

13. See Martin Heidegger, "The Self-Assertion of the German University" (SA); reprinted in *Martin Heidegger and National Socialism: Questions and Answers*, ed. Günther Neske and Emil Kettering, trans. Lisa Harries (New York: Paragon House, 1990), 5–13.

14. For Derrida's reading of the rectorship address, see Derrida, OS, 31–40. For a fuller explanation of Derrida's analysis of the connections between metaphysical humanism and racism here and elsewhere, see chapter 5 of my *Deconstruction, Feminist Theology, and the Problem of Difference*.

15. "Spirit in-flames" is Derrida's translation of the combination of two lines from Trakl: *"Der Geist is das Flammende* and "Der Geist ist Flamme" as quoted by Derrida, OS, 84. "The soul is on earth a stranger" translates "Es ist die Seele ein Fremdes auf Erden," from Trakl's poem "Frühling der Seele" (Springtime of the soul) as quoted by Derrida, OS, 87.

16. See also, for example, the discussions of *Geist*'s association with evil and pain in Heidegger's work—aspects of the Trakl essay and *Of Spirit* that I have not been able to discuss here.

17. I am reminded here of Derrida's comment "I do not at all believe in what today is so easily called the death of philosophy (nor, moreover, in the simple death of whatever—the book, man, or god, especially since as we all know, what is dead wields a very specific power)." See "Implications: Interview with Henri Ronse," in *Positions*, trans. Alan Bass (Chicago: University of Chicago Press, 1981), 6.

13

Revolutionary Thinking

Gail Stenstad

> The originary and genuine relation to the beginning is revolutionary (*Revolutionäre*), bringing the hidden rule of the beginning again into the open through the turning over of what is conventional.
>
> —Martin Heidegger, *Grundfragen der Philosophie: Ausgewählte "Probleme" der "Logik"*

Most readers of Heidegger, while somewhat surprised at the radical-sounding language, would nonetheless be able to place this comment in a familiar context: the overcoming of metaphysics in the thinking of the question of being, along with the shifting away from the domination of enframing spoken of in "The Question Concerning Technology," and the transformative experience with language spoken of in several places in *On the Way to Language*. We expect to encounter comments about change or transformation here and there in Heidegger's thinking. Often, however, it seems that there are hints and pointers all around the notion of transformation, while an account of how this might actually occur, or what difference it might make to *us*, is not explicitly spelled out.

It seems so, but there is much more, if we can struggle with the rather difficult texts that give a more extended account of the possibility of radical transformation that opens up in a deeply questing-questioning thinking. Prior to the publication of volumes 45 and 65 of Heidegger's *Collected Edition* (*Gesamtausgabe*), it was principally *On the Way to Language* that addressed the deeper question of the way transformation takes place. That text makes fairly clear the way transformations of thinking and being move *through* and enact a transformation *of* language. But it is in *Beiträge zur Philosophie (vom Ereignis)* (GA 65) where we find the opening up and preparatory enacting of a way of thinking that yields the wherewithal to explicitly think the question of deep and decisive transformation.[1]

Why is it so important to understand transformation as opened up in Heidegger's thinking? This is not just an abstract discussion of an abstruse history of metaphysics. Heidegger's thinking points to the ways in which that history yet holds power and connects it to issues of deep concern to many: the drive for maximum organization and control, environmental devastation, and humans' use and abuse of one another. Although he does not mention this, the latter would surely also pertain to male dominance or patriarchy, and thus be relevant to feminist thinking. A central question is *how* can and does deep and genuine change come about? The problems (whether taken as individual problems or more insightfully seen as interwoven indications of a deeper "problem") are difficult and entangled and resistant. There have been many political theories and solutions proposed—in feminism, we have, at the very least, theories that have been characterized as liberal, socialist, and radical, along with various approaches through ethical theory, such as an ethics of care. While each of these has strengths and weaknesses that are not the subject of this essay, none of them has given or can give an account of transformation that does not circle back into the very metaphysical presuppositions about being and truth that also ground male dominance. While such feminist theorizing has undoubtedly had a part to play in some of the positive changes for women in the past three decades, problems have come to light. How can we account for the current backlash against feminism, if we cannot account for feminist transformation in the first place? Also, among feminist academics, theory building itself has been seriously questioned as a way of transforming thought and action.[2] Heidegger's thinking holds an intricate and powerful attempt to *say* how genuine change could take place; this is a radically different way of going because it is not an ethical or political theory (Heidegger has in fact been attacked from various quarters for "lacking" such a theory), or a theory of any kind. There are no prescriptions or plans of action to be found here. Neither are there any guarantees of success or pictures of some rosy future. However, *such saying and thinking of transformation requires and is itself radical transformation*. This goes much deeper than ethical or political theories and their attempts at problem solving. It goes deeper than the various metaphysical and epistemological theories and presuppositions within which ethics and politics are situated. It attempts to go deeper into "what" yields all those ways of thinking and being. Heidegger thinks the way in which, more than two millennia into the history of Western philosophy, genuine change, radical change, emerges only from that opening that is an a-byss (*Ab-grund*), yielding no ground on which to rest and build.

I would also suggest that to read Heidegger from the perspective of a feminist deeply engaged with those particular transformations enlivens what he says. It helps us see the potential range of impact of the otherwise abstract-sounding "end of metaphysics." Thinking and questioning with Heidegger in this domain—the domain of being, of god, of man—may open up a radically different way to proceed as feminists. The way that Heidegger's thinking of transformation and an atheoretical form of feminist thinking may deepen and strengthen each other in their revolutionary impact is the main focus of this essay.

Thinking Radical Transformation

In Heidegger, this transformative thinking has to do with our relation to and situation within the history of metaphysics. "What is past means nothing, but the beginning means everything. Therefore this ever more urgent questioning back into the beginning" (GA 45, 23).

To say that we are historical, in other words, that what is past shapes the present and in fact shapes us, is so noncontroversial as to be almost trite. To understand the range and depth of that shaping, and to contemplate whether and how we can change is another matter. In GA 45 and GA 65 Heidegger engages with this matter in terms of the thinking of the "first beginning" of Western philosophy with its metaphysical orientation, which already opens up the possibility of an other beginning for thinking.

To understand the thinking of the first and other beginnings requires understanding the distinction Heidegger makes between historiography (*Historie*) and history (*Geschichte*). The ways of thinking associated with each are distinguished as historiographical observation (*historische Betrachtung*) and historical reflection (*geschichtliche Besinnung*), to emphasize the distancing objectification in the former in contrast to the sense of engaged yet-in-play in the latter. In historiographical observation, the past is examined as something more or less statically present (in various narratives, for instance) within the (unreflected-upon) horizon and measure of the present. This procedure takes up an objectifying distance from what is past, which then can be taken as something to be studied as if it had no bearing on us now other than as something to enrich our experience in the present, letting us "learn from the past." (As if we are in charge, as if its power over us is somehow optional and a matter of choice.) But what if the past determines the present in such a way that to use the measure of the present to examine the past prevents us from seeing what "the past" really says to us (much less what is not said but nevertheless holds sway)? This is indeed the case, and is why the thinking of the first beginning is not a historiographical examination, but rather a historical reflection. In historical reflection there is a recognition not only that what has taken place already shapes and limits our thinking, but also that it does so specifically in regard to our relation to "the past." An important concomitant is that such thinking opens the possibility of being no longer (obliviously) limited in the same ways by the past, by the "history of Western thinking, which history we ourselves are" (GA 45, 188; see also 115). Historical thinking is concerned with a more originary experience of a beginning that still unfolds, such that we are no longer limited in the same way by "the past" or "the present," but rather can be open to an "other beginning." Thus, this thinking is, says Heidegger, revolutionary: it carries within it an enabling of radical transformation (GA 45, 33–43, 115, 188; GA 65, 8, 32, 84–86, 183–87, 456). How so? Consider how Heidegger sketches this out for us.

The first beginning is genuinely appropriated for the first time when its determining question ("what is a being?") is thought as the guiding question that shapes Western philosophy as metaphysics, evoking "answers" that emerge as various ways of determining being as grounding presence. As this (our thinking the first beginning *as such*) takes place, thinking is enabled to place the ground-question concerning the *Wesen* of being (the emerging-as-such of being).[3] A crucial point: the thinking of an other beginning is not the consequence or outcome of the thinking of the first beginning. The possibility of an other beginning opens up *within* the thinking of the first beginning; the thinking of the first beginning emerges only under way within and toward an other beginning. In GA 65 the words Heidegger finds to say this preparatory-transitory movement of the initiating thinking of the first and other beginnings are Anklang (echo, resounding, resonance, assonance), various forms of *Schwingung* (swinging, oscillating, vibrating), *Auseinandersetzung* (here, a sort of oscillating interplay that also carries the sense of clarifying-in-strife), and various forms of *spielen* (play). *Auseinandersetzung* is used specifically to name the way thinking sets the two beginnings into play with one another. *Anklang* echoes the nonrepresentable movement of thinking into the abyss (*Ab-grund*), thinking without grounding in any metaphysical sense, and *play* emphasizes the noncausality and goallessness involved here. The thinking of the first and other beginnings is in play as transformative resonance or vibrating: incalculable, uncertain, in-definite, nonrepresentable; it is utterly unplannable and there are no guarantees of success (GA 65, 57–58, 173, 286–87, 342, 381). To see how this works, think with Heidegger into the first beginning. "Therefore all metaphysics is at bottom, and from the ground up, what grounds, what gives account of the ground, what is called to account by the ground, and finally what calls the ground to account" (ID 125/58). As Heidegger's many careful considerations of the history of metaphysics have shown, such grounding presence, whether being as what is most general, or god as the highest and ultimate, is thought from out of *beings*. The first beginning of Western philosophy arose from within an emerging orientation (a "grounding attuning") of astonished wonder at the being of beings; beings, the must usual things, became unusual in that they are. *Their* being, in other words, what is common to them *as beings*, is posited as grounding presence (and thus beings come to be taken as what is present). Being is first differentiated from beings, as their ground, but that difference is then forgotten. Being is thought as and thus becomes a being. But in the ensuing history of the various metaphysical and theological names for and interpretations of being, the original differentiating move—whereby the being of beings first becomes a being that can then serve as ground—is forgotten and thus left unquestioned. Further, its grounding function is assumed and not questioned. Thus the question concerning the meaning of being is not raised, much less its emerging as such. Why ask for a ground *of* ground? and even less in theology: why ask for a ground *of* the highest and ultimate ground? (GA 65, 255, 436, 508).

The emerging and unfolding of the history of being did not influence only philosophers. Already with the Greeks, humans name themselves rational animals, the realm of truth becomes correct statements *about* beings, astonishment and questioning give way to a drive for calculable knowing and certainty, beings become objects of representation, and *techne* (relating to beings in order to understand and preserve their being) becomes machination, technique. All of that sounds so familiar: we stand in the culmination of the first beginning. However, thinking and experiencing this beginning for what it is, in its grounding, already grants the possibility of a transition to an other beginning. How so? The question about the being of beings that so captivated the Greeks does not arise. The presence of beings is simply taken for granted. Face to face with "objects" to which we are related in a way that is essentially a nonrelation (and in a situation in which we seem ever more in danger of becoming also no more than additional items in a standing reserve of units-for-use), *grounding* no longer seems so clear and obvious, nor does grounding presence—being, god—seem so securely to undergird beings. The experience that arises is that which Heidegger calls abandonment by being (*Seinsverlassenheit*). The security and certainty of ground and grounding—the traditional *function* of being—is refused, denied not by us, but apparently (so it seems at first) by "being itself." Being "should be there"—but is not. It is not *there*, serving its grounding function. And it *is* not, as thinking pursues it further, uncovering its historical emerging in thought and language. The ground falls away, shifting us into an abyss (*Ab-grund*) without ground (GA 65, 406–10). Thinking moves into ungrounding.[4]

One of the things that makes Heidegger's transformative thinking so difficult is the attempt to say something nonmetaphysical in our until now habitually metaphysical language. The image of *abyss* tends to call forth the kinds of thoughts it would if it were merely a spatial metaphor. But *abyss* here does not refer in the way in which metaphors do. Just as is the thought of be-ing, the thought of abyss is an attempt to bring the thinking to language in such a way that the thinker is displaced from conventional, being-bound tracks. Confronting something that makes one want to say "what *is* this? What?" Only to find that it continues retreating. It is sayable—almost, nearly, tantalizingly so—but not definable, not graspable conceptually in the way we usually expect. Be-ing, thought in the abyss of the refusal of grounding, is itself nothing. Nothing. Yet it says (shows) something in the movement of thinking.

There we are, in the midst of what have, for more than two thousand years, been being-grounded beings. Just where we have always been. Yet now, our thought is shifted to follow be-ing, into an abyss, finding itself following radically different paths of thought. *Within* a newly clarified thinking of the first beginning, we are already moving *toward* the possibility of an other beginning. This movement loosens the usual senses of *toward* and *within*. Within, we are "there"; moving-toward, we are "not yet there." Both at once.

In that "both at once," further movement emerges. In the thoughtful experience of abandonment by being and the growing uncertainty and questionableness arising in the refusal of grounding, thinking faces a compelling necessity to move for the first time *within* the forgetfulness of the differing of being and beings, and in so doing, it is enabled to move *outside* that presupposed difference and its oblivion, moving outside the closed circling of representations of present-at-hand beings. This move outside does not take place as an exit-from, or an evasive move; in the playing forth of the first and other beginnings, *within* and *outside* do not name clearly distinct spaces. They indicate the way in which thinking resonates transformatively in the interplay of the first and other beginnings. In thinking the first beginning as such, the other beginning *already* begins its emerging.

Abyssal thinking is far from vacuous; rather, it is an ungrounding that enacts an opening (*Er-öffnung*). Thus the refusal of grounding is not a simple drawing back or going away or nihilistic absence. Within the abyss, thinking moves toward an other beginning, which is itself already emerging, opening up. Heidegger wants to emphasize that this abyss is not a goal or even a way station. Abyssal thinking is in motion within an interplay of the first beginning and a nascent other beginning. And surely *beginning* suggests further movement. This initiatory thinking prepares for transformation while undergoing it. This requires letting go of any tendency to cling to old notions and ways, or to the experience of ungrounding as something merely negative, whether despairingly or in a heroically accepting way. It becomes more clear at this point why Heidegger says that the thinker would be shifted into a new attuning, every bit as much as the Greeks were at the first beginning, an attuning that "is not so much to be written as to be at work in the whole of initiatory thinking" (GA 65, 395; see also 86, 410–12).

This yields not only a radically different way of thinking but also opens the possibility of radically different ways of dwelling. Thinking and dwelling come together here in Heidegger's discussion of de-cisions, not thought psychologically but *as enacted* in thought and practice (actually, it is another way to say transformation). He does not write *Entscheidung* (decision) here but *Ent-scheidung*, to stress parting or de-parture, or even a tearing or rending. We are said to be torn to our freedom in this space of de-cision (GA 65, 412). This is de-cision as a radical parting of ways: dif-fering ways of thinking, dif-fering ways of dwelling (dif-fering: carrying apart, moving de-cisively down a different fork in the road). This de-cision simply does not get enacted according to any of the usual notions of power. It is not, in the usual sense, a decision made by an individual agent; rather it enacts itself in the unfold-ing of be-ing, in the playing forth of the thinking of the first and other beginnings (GA 65, 8, 86–88, 251–52, 380–82, 385, 407, 410–11, 484–88).

At the same time, without our thinking and choosing and doing, this would remain on the level of either vacuous abstraction or, worse, passivity in the face of some kind of determinism. De-cision as a movement within be-ing holds within itself particular "decisions," the consideration of which Heidegger includes to help show what is at stake in this region of de-cision. Will humans remain in the guise of subjects or rational animals, or will they be open to other ways? Will truth as correctness of representation, the art of arranging and reckoning life-experience, sustain its rule even in its degeneration? Or will an ungrounded disclosive clearing of self-showing and concealing emerge more freely and set itself into work? Will nature be degraded to nothing but a region for the exploitation of unrestrained calculation and management, or will the self-concealing, sheltering earth sustain and bear up an *other* world? Will the christianizing (and westernizing, one might add) of culture celebrate its triumph, enforcing the (groundless) presumption of a highest being as ground of all? Or will the need of facing and *thinking* all the way into what is named in GA 65 as the "passing by of the last god" (the radical undecidability regarding gods, which is yet another way of saying the experience of abandonment by being) open to de-cision? All these decisions are gathered in de-cision: "whether be-ing itself ultimately withdraws *or* whether its withdrawal as the refusal comes first to [its] truth and to an other beginning" (GA 65, 90–91). We encounter be-ing as we dwell in the midst of beings, confronting the absence of being, of ground. This encounter is transformative as it is thought and lived and enacted in the midst of the vibrating tensions between what we inherit and what we create; what befalls us and what we choose; what we are able to think and what we refuse to think; what we cling to and what we can let go of. We are shifted into an opening for transformation in the *Auseinandersetzung* of the first and other beginnings.

Feminist Thinking in the *Auseinanadersetzung*

So: what is it that makes this account of transformation *revolutionary*? And how is this powerfully relevant to feminist thinking? The key to the first question is that this thinking (a) moves always (b) within and toward (c) abyssal be-ing. Focusing on each part:

(a) As Heidegger also stressed in many other texts, this thinking is on the way, always in motion, not determined by a method, not settling for a quick fix or for mere problem solving.

(b) Within and toward. There is no structuring based on *arche* and *telos*. No fixed presuppositions, necessary starting point, rule(s), or aims. (As we will see, this does not mean there is nothing to hold in front of thinking, nor that this thinking is vacuously purposeless.)

(c) Abyssal be-ing. There is no ground in any metaphysical sense. To think the first beginning as such, resonates within and evokes or enables an other beginning which is not bound to or grounded on being, freeing thinking and other actions from the limits established by metaphysical presuppositions.

It should be very clear that this is nothing like the production of theory. Theory-building was always an enterprise linked to metaphysical thinking, with the thinking of being, with the thinking of *arche* and *telos*, with striving for truth. The history of metaphysical thinking always drives toward the positing of being as the representable (theoretically intelligible), ever-present ground of beings. In the transformative thinking under discussion, what is prepared for and "produced" is not some idea to which one could be related in thought, but is the transformation that takes place. "This preparing does not consist in acquiring provisional knowledge as the basis for later gaining actual knowledge. Rather preparing is here: opening the way, yielding to the way—essentially, *attuning*" (GA 65, 86). This attuning cannot—based on everything said above—be one, determinately changed way of thinking and living. It is multiple (GA 65, 22).

This multiplicity of ways and possibilities is an important thing to remember when seeing how this is helpful to feminist thinking. Although Heidegger, in his listing of questions that laid out particular de-cisions, did not mention women, surely such changes and emerging possibilities as have begun to open up for women in the past few decades are decisive in the sense discussed above. That is, de-cision as *Er-öffnung*, as an opening into the tensions of the *Auseinandersetzung* within the thinking that confronts the absence of grounding being. This is also, at the same time, an opening to the possibility of new ways of living. We can add a question to Heidegger's list. Will women continue to be defined and limited by a being-bound patriarchal hierarchy, or will women and men have the courage of the abyss, to open ourselves to other ways of thinking and living with each other? To enter the region of such de-cisions may well call for the kind of revolutionary thinking Heidegger has opened up for us. Insistent standing on the ground of being (and its most popular form, god), and clinging to the "truths" grounded on it, results in a circling within the same old limits. (It is not difficult to situate much of the backlash against feminism within that tired circling.) Also, to bring the thinking opened up for us by Heidegger into play with issues of such pressing concern to many of us may help us to better understand what Heidegger is trying to say.

An important feature of this transformative thinking is its radically different relationship to theory. The thinking opened up here is not the production of a better theory (as was already stated), nor is it opposition to theory (or to metaphysics). "If seen within the bounds of an expressly given difference between beings and being, and compared historiographically with metaphysics, reckoned in its going forth from *beings*, it might seem as if the questioning within the other beginning . . . is a simple and crude *reversing*. But . . . mere reversing . . . empowers what is reversed, and secures its previously lacking stability and completeness" (GA 65, 436). This thinking moves outside the bounds determined by metaphysics. It is not antitheoretical, but rather atheoretical.

Within feminist thinking, this is not a totally new way to go. It has been very much a minority approach, since for the most part feminist discussions (especially, but by no means only, among academics) have been involved with the production or development or criticism or enactment of theoretical perspectives. For about fifteen years, such intensive engagement with theory-building has also come in for quite a bit of criticism. A major criticism has been that the prominent feminist theories (liberal, radical, socialist) speak primarily from and to the experience of white, middle-class, well-educated women. In the quite understandable desire for a viable political strategy, coupled with the assumption that such a strategy requires a theoretical base, we may well have deleted or at least trivialized the voices and experiences of the majority of women. Adherence to theorizing and theories has also been criticized for the formation of in-groups and out-groups. Then the divisions and lack of agreement become issues in themselves and we think, "if only we could devise the ultimate feminist theory, the one on which we could all agree." This amounts to saying, "if only we were all the same."

Concerned with giving adequate thought to these criticisms, I once wrote:

> The practice of theory-building presupposes some philosophical notions that serve to validate the contents of theories: truth, reality and objectivity. A theory seeks to give an objectively true account of the domain of reality with which it is concerned. The best theory is that which most closely approximates the true and the real. The root assumption is that there really *is* one truth, one reality, and that it is the business of philosophy to give an account of it. The rider is that it is our responsibility to conform our lives to it.[5]

Metaphysically grounded philosophy, both secular and religious, has for more than two thousand years exacted conformity to predetermined standards for thought and action, a conformity that has been especially onerous for women. Surely we do not need to repeat this yet again; this is what the criticisms of feminist theory-building tell us. In response (and with Heidegger in the background), I proposed an *anarchic* way for feminist thinking to proceed.

A-byssal Thinking as Anarchic Feminist Thinking

Anarchic feminist thinking emerged as an explicitly atheoretical way of thinking that would be subversive of patriarchal theory and practice, creatively going beyond conventional bounds, deviating from expected goals and methods, un-ruled. As atheoretical thinking, it would not work from, posit, or yield objective distance, transhistorical truths, hierarchical orderings, or a unitary reality. It would be characterized by persistence in questioning, openness to ambiguity and a multiplicity of interpretations, and attentiveness to the strange within the familiar. All of those aspects involve letting tensions (between question and answer, between one answer and a differing answer, between meanings, and between what is familiar and what is strange, especially when the familiar becomes also strange, as it has in so many women's experiences) remain in play, keeping thinking in motion. Preserving the tensions that keep thinking moving is not "motion for the sake of motion." To maintain such tension and fluidity in thinking is to resist the long-standing tendency to settle for one explanation, one voice, one truth.

Readers of Heidegger encounter the tension between the strange or uncanny and the familiar over and over again, particularly in the thinking discussed above, where we move into the ungrounding of being, at the same time that the old familiar presuppositions about being and the nature of beings begin to explicitly emerge into thought. Feminists are acquainted with this making-strange in the works of, among others, Mary Daly, Luce Irigaray, and Susan Griffin. The effect of this making-strange is to decenter the familiar, the taken-for-granted, the true, the real, and so on. The boundaries set for our thinking by familiarity are transgressed. Lingering patriarchal presuppositions and internalizations shift and move and perhaps are even evicted. The previously unthinkable becomes thinkable. Anarchic thinking is boundary thinking, pushing at the very boundaries of the thinkable, stretching them, rearranging them, breaking them. The practice of thinking at (also toward and within) the boundary transforms thinking and transforms us, those who think.

Susan Griffin's *Woman and Nature* remains a powerful example of transformative, an-archic thinking. It is not a theory-building work. It is, in its own way, a deeply thoughtful historical reflection (*geschichtliche Besinnung*), in precisely the sense discussed by Heidegger in GA 45 and GA 65. Griffin begins and proceeds by quoting and paraphrasing the voices of the philosophers, the theologians, the scientists, the engineers, the technicians. These echoing and reechoing patriarchal voices are all very familiar. Plato, Aristotle, Aquinas, Bacon, Descartes, Kant, and Schopenhauer. Copernicus, Kepler, Newton, Boyle, and Bohr. The *Malleus Mallificarum*, Pavlov, and Freud. The foresters and the doctors. All speaking from an ever-increasing objective distance, analyzing, ordering, establishing hierarchies, proclaiming the truth, defining reality, dividing the real into useful strata and manageable units. Reading and thinking along with Griffin, one experiences the almost numbing impact of the devaluing and silencing of women that the unfolding history of Western philosophy and religion enforced. The familiar becomes strange. To *think* our history in this way opens fissures where questions can enter, where alternative interpretive possibilities can be considered, and where an other beginning can begin to emerge and other voices begin to speak. In the last pages of *Woman and Nature*, women's voices find their own ways to speak, tentatively at first, but not bound to old limits, or to the being, however named, which validated those old restrictions.[6]

This is not strictly parallel to Heidegger's thinking of the first and other beginnings. The beginning of patriarchal social structures is older, by at least two or three thousand years, and is also more geographically diverse than the beginning of Western philosophy that is Heidegger's focus. (This is not to say that he is oblivious to those older roots of the Western metaphysical tree, especially the one originating in the move from tribal gods to the biblical god.) Nevertheless, it serves to show how the kind of thinking he opens up is not restricted to that one area. Also, many of those speaking with the most oppressive voices negating women are precisely the ones who are also key figures in the history of Western metaphysical philosophy and religion. Metaphysical presuppositions, especially the ones that link man and being (women and nonbeing), man and reason (women and unreason), man and god (women and Eve, women and the devil), structured and reinforced male dominance as it unfolded in Western history. Just as does Heidegger's thinking of the question of being that impelled the first beginning, Griffin's evocative writing places us in the interplay of the old, familiar limits with newly emerging possibilities.

Anarchic thinking is a powerful way of opening up as yet unthought possibilities and strategies for further thought and action. Anarchic thinking adds to but does not attempt to abolish other modes of thinking. For example, if I were to say that no one should "do theory," I would be, in effect, setting up an-archy as an *arche*. That would not only be prima facie absurd, but would also operate within a rigid either/or framework that is counter to what I have said about the way in which anarchic thinking affirms multiplicity. It would fall into the trap of mere reversing noted by Heidegger. The insights attained by theorists have been very valuable. However, as an anarchic thinker, I do not hold to the results of such thinking as capital-T Theory (as establishing or naming Truth or Reality, or as speaking universally). I view the work of theorists as clarifying particular areas, as positional analyses applicable within clearly demarcated limits. This leaves thinking open to other, perhaps very different, analyses, based on other women's situations and experiences.

Another dichotomy to be wary of is the apparent clash of anarchy and purposefulness. "No *arche*" does indeed mean "no *telos*"; there is no one, overarching end. However, that by no means implies utter purposelessness. One need have no unitary starting point or theoretical basis to feel outrage about oppression and engage with its transformation. One may have intentions and aims and plans, and act on them creatively and constructively without a theory that unifies and justifies this thinking and acting. Annette Baier and Lorraine Code have reiterated this in regard to moral thinking.

> Perhaps the most radical effect of feminist moral critiques is their demonstration that moral theories close off more possibilities of discernment and action than they create. A more productive route is to claim broader scope for engaged yet thoughtful *practices*.... Although a critical, deliberative morality is a more modest option than theory construction, it has a greater potential to accommodate the subtleties of the experiences of real, gendered, historically located subjects.[7]

This matter of purpose is of course closely linked to one of the major bogeys of philosophy: the fear of relativism. I could focus this a bit more sharply with a couple of questions. What is the relation of anarchic thinking to normativity, and to feminist political concerns? Is anarchic thinking a case of "anything goes," utter relativism? No. Otherwise I could hardly call myself a feminist (I would have to admit that the oppression of women is acceptable). But as I suggested above, it should be fairly clear that one does not need a theoretical basis to take the normative position that such oppression is wrong. In a later chapter in the same book in which she discusses atheoretical moral practice, Lorraine Code goes deeper into the matter to develop an approach to epistemology that is also atheoretical, not grounded on the old metaphysical presuppositions. She questions the kind of epistemological thinking and practices that unrealistically attempt to unify the experiences of women (and men) through a universalizing, theoretical approach.

> No single, monolithic scheme has been able to claim adequate explanatory power; and projects to devise such a scheme have been impressive for their failure to acknowledge their gaps, exclusions, and suppressions. Yet the fact that the scheme that has claimed absolute authority has proved wanting does not count as a reason to conclude that no scheme is better than any other.... relativism is stopped in its feared slide into nihilism, solipsism, or subjectivism by the "brute facts" of the world and by the discursive limits of speaking positions. Sexism, racism, and environmental harm are as demonstrably part of the world as tables and chairs, though they are open to more varying interpretations.[8]

I have called for an-archic boundary thinking as one way of moving within and forward from the ungrounding that disrupts metaphysical, hierarchical limits. Code suggests another way to think anarchically: holding to a "middle ground." In discussing this, she emphasizes our refusal to fall into the trap of engaging in the adversarial mode of doing philosophy. (Recall here, too, all the times Heidegger says that thinking has nothing to do with polemics or argumentation or proving.) The adversarial mode assumes the opposition of fairly entrenched positions, one of which will eventually be victorious (more convincing, more correct, more true). The middle ground is more like a region than a point-position, flexibly accommodating a wide range of possibilities. "The middle ground is located within experiences, histories, social structures, material circumstance. Its occupants are committed to examining the resources and contradictions their experiences yield. Its openness is a source of power in which the productiveness of an ambiguity that refuses closure can be realized."[9] Closure is precisely what philosophy-as-usual aims at, precisely because of its historical attachment to truth grounded on being. Here we can see where atheoretical feminist thinking and the historical, transformative thinking of Heidegger begin to converge. A deeper look in both directions (or, following Code, making room for both in a middle ground) should both strengthen feminist thinking and show more clearly the deep relevance of Heidegger's thinking.

A question that could well arise at this point is that I am emphasizing creativity and commitment, but at times it might seem as if the kind of thinking Heidegger discusses is almost passive (being-open-to, being-shifted, attuning, de-cision that is not forced or willed) This would, I believe, be a serious misreading of Heidegger, falling into another specious either/or dichotomy, this time between active, forceful thinking and passive thinking. Transformative, an-archic thinking is neither active and forceful in that sense ("masculine," in the traditional patriarchal stereotyping), nor passive (in terms defined through a lack of forceful action). "The thoughtful questioning must above all have reached an originariness in affirming power, which lays aside all programmatic heroism and he-man antics in order to be strong enough to experience what is nothing in be-ing itself" (GA 65, 266). Anarchic thinking is revolutionary in that it empowers through enabling us to avoid being trapped in these dichotomies. Heidegger was well aware of this, pointing out that the old, metaphysically structured dichotomies keep us engaged in evading fundamental de-cision. "*Either* get stuck in the end and its course and that means the renewed variations of 'metaphysics' that become more and more coarse, groundless and aimless (the new 'biologism,' etc.) *or* begin the other beginning, i.e., be resolved for its long beginning" (GA 65, 229; see also GA 65, 12).

Perhaps some of the current backlash against feminism comes from entrapment in these dichotomies. Masculine or feminine, true or false, powerful or powerless, "pro-life" or pro-choice, and so on. Code's anarchic middle ground may open a space for thoughtful discussion rather than mere adversarial battles. An-archic thinking could begin to see what is decidedly strange in these familiar structures and allow space for other, nondichotomous options for thinking and action. Heidegger's historical reflection enables us to go deeply into the origins of the presuppositions undergirding the entrenched ideas and values that so often get in the way of even beginning to think or discuss alternatives.

The transformative thinking that has been the theme of this essay could indeed be *revolutionary*, as Heidegger said. It would be, however, a revolution without a violent, adversarial character, without a mere reversing of old structures, without a theoretical basis or predetermined plan of action. It would be more like an organic transformation: cohesive but multiply enacted. The forms of life that could be empowered by this revolutionary thinking are as yet barely thought and imagined. However, thinking is under way in the ungrounding abyss, imagining and creating the possibilities yet to come.

Notes

1. All translations from GA 65 in this essay are mine. GA 65 has, however, been published in English translation as *Contributions to Philosophy (From Ereignis)*, trans. Parvis Emad and Kenneth

Maly (Bloomington: Indiana University Press, 1999). For readers who only have access to the English translation, the page numbers to which I refer (in the German text) can be found in the margins of the English translation.

2. For a clear statement of this type of criticism, see María Lugones and Elizabeth Spelman's "Have We Got a Theory for You! Feminist Theory, Cultural Imperialism, and the Demand for 'the Woman's Voice.'" *Women's Studies International Forum* 6, no. 6 (1983): 573–81.

3. The question of how to bring *Wesen* into English continues to be one of the most difficult and contentious issues for Heidegger translation. The matter is further complicated in GA 65 by his use of *Wesung*, often in the phrase *Wesung des Seyns*. Regarding *Seyn*, Heidegger makes a distinction between metaphysical and nonmetaphysical senses of "being." *Sein* (being) usually indicates the metaphysical sense: the representation of constant presence posited to serve as ground of beings. *Seyn* (be-ing) indicates a nonmetaphysical sense: nonrepresentational, saying movement and abyss rather than presence and ground (I put the hyphen in be-ing to mark the distinction in a way that emphasizes movement.) Regarding *Wesen*, it ordinarily means being, entity, nature, or essence. When Heidegger is merely referring to a historical usage, "essence" can carry the meaning. But in most of the instances where the word is used in GA 65 (and elsewhere), essence in the traditional sense is precisely what Heidegger does not want to say with *Wesen* (much less with *Wesung*), any more than he wants to say "grounding presence" with *Seyn*. Consider some of the other ways *Wesen* has been brought into English. "Presencing" conveys the motion involved, but *Wesen* says more than that; further this translation risks confusion with *Anwesen*. "Root-unfolding" again says motion, but risks being heard as a reifying spatial metaphor. Likewise with "in-depth-sway," though perhaps the risk is somewhat less. "Emerging as such" can hardly be reified, but *Wesen* says more than just emerging. Likewise with "coming-to-pass" (though here, the "to pass" suggests the notion of "staying" that is needed). All these ways of bringing *Wesen* into English say something of the thinking, but not without difficulties. Simply leaving the word in German has its own difficulty, namely, that it works well only for those who are very familiar with the German texts. Instead of arguing for one "best" translation of *Wesen*, I prefer to see the multiple possibilities as openings for thinking, openings that would not be there if we were trapped in a mistaken attempt at correct representation of what, after all, cannot be represented.

4. This is not to say, of course, that *Seinsverlassenheit* only first occurs now, in the thinking of the end of metaphysics. In the first beginning, with the positing of the being of beings as a being (the positing and then forgetting of the ontological difference), being, Heidegger says, has already withdrawn from beings. The being that had been in question (the being of beings) becomes merely another being, albeit in the form of a constantly present ground. "*Abandonment of and by being* means [also] that be-ing abandons beings" (GA 65, 111). Metaphysical thinking rests on a grounding being, and goes no deeper. Said another way, from the very beginning of metaphysical thinking, *Seinsverlassenheit* accompanies *Seinsvergessenheit*. This was, however, not explicitly thought as such. In the thinking of the first and other beginnings, forgetting of and abandonment by being are thought explicitly as such. For an extended discussion, see GA 65, 110–20.

5. Gail Stenstad, "Anarchic Thinking: Breaking the Hold of Monotheistic Ideology on Feminist Philosophy," *Woman and Values: Readings in Recent Feminist Philosophy*, Marilyn Pearsall, ed. (Belmont, Calif.: Wadsworth, 1993), 248.

6. Susan Griffin, *Woman and Nature: The Roaring Inside Her* (New York: Harper and Row, 1978).

7. Lorraine Code, *What Can She Know: Feminist Theory and the Construction of Knowledge* (Ithaca: Cornell University Press, 1991), 107–9. See also Annette Baier, *Postures of the Mind: Essays on Mind and Morals* (Minneapolis: University of Minnesota Press, 1985), 232.

8. Code, *What Can She Know*, 321.

9. Code, *What Can She Know*, 321.

14

Stealing the Fire of Creativity

Heidegger's Challenge to Intellectuals

Patricia Huntington

Heidegger grants the twentieth century an immense legacy. And yet the task of identifying precisely what gives an *enduring quality* to his thought remains an issue for thought. He will go down in history as the greatest philosopher of Being, having surpassed even the Greeks, and he will be credited with a long list of vibrant contributions to philosophy.[1] Still, Heidegger will not be recognized as seriously relevant to political theory. Or if he is granted a certain relevance, then it will only be in a tangential manner as one who gave birth to specific questions about language and technology that have been taken up and advanced in a more politically nuanced manner by other scholars.[2] When considered solely as a sustained effort to think Being, Heidegger's life endeavor appears to feminists, myself included, as offering no pivotal basis upon which to recast the perennial problems of philosophy in light of a decisive and critical interest in gender.[3] The question of a feminist reading of Heidegger thus stands in a similar relation to Heidegger as it does to many canonical figures. Such a reading can only take his most important insights—such as his critiques of subjectivity, linear history, and representation—diagnose how his manner of posing these critiques remains masculinist, and transmute his ideas into a form more amenable to feminist theory. Such projects are of great importance to feminism because they fulfill the two goals of evaluating tradition critically and reconstructing new paradigms and values in light of critique.

In *Ecstatic Subjects,* I undertook a preliminary look at some of the limits and promises of Heidegger's thought for feminist social theory. As important as it is to continue such work, I believe that it does not deliver a decisive answer to the question, What gives Heideggerian thought its enduring quality? That is why such work, no matter how valuable, cannot quiet the nagging intuition that Heidegger's legacy simply cannot be surpassed and overcome, for something in his thought endures beyond revisionist approaches. Feminism acknowledges that it stands in an uneasy relation to tradition in that it both wants to overcome yet remains parasitical upon tradition. Rather than accepting this tension because life is historical and no reflection transpires in a vacuum, I suggest that more is at work. Heidegger's thinking, like that of all great figures, endures because the ultimate subject of his thought can, when rightly understood and actualized, deliver us to a lived reality: well-being.

Heidegger's search for an *originary thinking* has been labeled quietist at best and retrograde at worst. Ironically it is only before the matter of originary thinking that we begin to touch upon what endures in Heidegger's thought. In this essay, my primary intent is not to rescue originary thinking from the charge of quietism nor to defend the claim that Heidegger's corpus offers the best resources for political theory. Although I will comment on political matters at the end, I proceed on the assumption that Heidegger's thought points to a *lived possibility of well-being* that defies the distinction between the political and the apolitical, and is decisively nonpolitical but not antipolitical. Instead of employing my earlier revisionist approach, I venture to take Heidegger's thinking on its own terms, as it is, without modification. This task is not distinctly feminist, but also not necessarily antifeminist. My basic thought is that we can, as intellectuals, both feminist and nonfeminist, come to hear what endures in Heidegger's legacy only when we face his most offensive challenge: *that we do not understand ourselves as intellectuals*.[4]

As feminists and social theorists, we all know and write about the fact that we live in a truly frightening age. And Heidegger's ultimate diagnosis of our disease—that what we lack most is thought—appears in the face of the urgency of our social problems (problems such as nuclear war, racism, the battery of women) a bit silly, uninformed, naive, and antiquated. Worse, Heidegger fails altogether to supply us with new values and to engender a transvaluation of values. Yes. But philosophy cannot get over Heidegger, because it intuits there is something true about what he says, that we intellectuals are still not *thinking*. If there is a chance for us as intellectuals to face earnestly what Heidegger teaches us—that to *think* is to open out on *radical freedom as thinkers*—then we must make his teaching concrete by asking what challenge it poses to each of us *as an intellectual*.

What Heidegger tells us as intellectuals is that we rarely comprehend the source of all our reflections; that is, we rarely ask, What compels us to think? If self-understanding is a condition of undergoing existence well and of theorizing well about how to foster well-being in society, then perhaps Heidegger's challenge to intellectuals has value for each of us as a concrete living subject, independent of the task of fostering a transvaluation of values. Heidegger's seemingly naive challenge is this: as intellectuals we only begin to think and understand ourselves as thinkers on condition that *we relinquish the belief that we are the source of our own creativity and life of ideation*. No matter how limited his vocabulary or how faulty one may find the language he employs, Heidegger's thought endures because it turns us toward the possibility availed to us now to take a leap and, through coming to understand what compels us to think, become free as thinkers.

On Truth and Falsification

Heidegger asks the singular question that, he thinks, terrifies all of us as intellectuals, whether we are conservative, radical, progressive, or traditional; whether beset upon solving the problems of human suffering in a playfully avant-garde or a pedantically serious manner. That question is,

What is the source of thinking? Or better, Why are we not yet thinking (WD, 3/WT, 6)?[5] To ask this question is not an epistemological problem. When he tells us that we are still not thinking, Heidegger is not suggesting that no philosopher prior to him has endeavored to figure out how the mind works, how we can know. He is not implying that reflection does not occur and all the time. This question points to a more basic truth: that the source of all reflection can only be *understood* though a *living engagement* with it. Paradoxically, it cannot be *known* through *reflection on, ideation about,* or *conceptualization of* who and what we are.

The immediate implication is so astounding that we must dismiss it or tame it. For Heidegger says that *all* the many and varied forms of reflection we invent as philosophers—no matter how great their differences, suppositions, moral and political commitments—place the human agent in the position of arrogating to itself the source of all creativity, all ideation. How could this be? Numerous schools of thought, beginning with existentialism and moving through phenomenology to multiple brands of postmodernism, have already decentered agency and the belief in mastery, in fact have carried the process of decentering well beyond the idea that all thought is situated to the much more radical claim that humans are not the source of authorship and do not control the life of an idea. Have we not in the twentieth century, whether by rationalism's greater acknowledgment of the fallibilism of reason or by deconstructive methods, carried Heidegger's insight into the limits of agency further than he ever did? Is this not especially true in postmodern political philosophy, in feminism and postcolonial theory, where the limitations of all systems of reflection are being fleshed out in terms of their manifold pernicious effects in *real life?* So it seems.

Yet by appropriating and moving beyond Heidegger, we falsify the very reality that his entire life endeavor sought to reveal. The postmodernist feminist task of delimiting reason remains, as it well knows, within the bounds of representation and conceptualization. To mark off systematically wherein those limitations lie and to develop methodologies that displace the focus of theory away from subjectivity to language or what constitutes subjectivity, however noteworthy such projects may be, does not bring reflection up against its most supreme limitation: that the source of human thinking is nothing human, stems not from the human power to appropriate, invent, or generate. The source of thinking is not reason, it is not the mind, it is not emotion, it is not mood, it is not desire, and it is not language. One can only know the source of thinking concretely and not abstractly, not theoretically, not through conceptualization, not through textual analysis. One must, Heidegger tells us, "leap" into the engagement with what calls for thinking (WD, 4/WT, 8).[6] And in that active engagement one understands in a preeminent sense that she or he is not the author of thought even though thinking happens. Heidegger's challenge cannot be so readily tamed. He does not claim that human reflection is tainted by language, horizons of meaning, desire, the unconscious, and other forces that humans control only partly. His is a much more radical claim: human beings are not the source of (their) thinking.

Thus, as a philosopher, I can only begin legitimately with my true confession. To speak of thought as a neo-Kantian practice of delimiting reason from within the bounds of reason, as I did in *Ecstatic Subjects*, is *to falsify* the significance of what Heidegger does; it is to stand outside the medium within which his thought moves. It is not that one cannot, as I did, successfully supplement Heideggerian ontology and then spin out a vibrant social theory. If we employ the term *falsify* to mean that it is incorrect to cull Heidegger's corpus for insights that can inform social theory, then so employing Heidegger is no falsification. Yet inventiveness does not think with Heidegger. Thus, if by falsify, we mean to lead astray, to cover over the pathway back to what Heidegger spent his lifetime attempting to bring into view, then all such inventive projects falsify Heidegger's thought. This falsification consists in giving the impression that we have understood (or could understand) what is most radical or originary in Heidegger when we cut ourselves off from *what engaged* Heidegger's thinking.

Here we reach a peculiar conundrum, for to engage what Heidegger's thought points toward is not to care whether or not we get Heidegger correct in terms of scholarship. It is to intimate the possibility of being a freethinker. Yes, this is exactly true. So why not invent a transmutation of Heidegger? Where revisionist interpretations go astray is not in getting Heidegger incorrect. All projects of fixing Heidegger in order to make him useful for social theory begin from the correct intuition—that this issue is not Heidegger, but rather our own freedom—and yet treat Heidegger's *thought* reductionistically. Instead of being engaged *independently* by what his thought points toward and discovering firsthand what it means to think on our own, such projects reflectively *place* Heidegger's work in its historical context, *circumscribe* how his textual corpus delineates a system of ideas, then critically *mark off the limits* of that system, and happily *skip over* the deeper possibility of a lived engagement with the reality addressed by, but not reducible to, his work. Such projects never enable us to answer the question, What is the source of all thinking? If we want Heidegger to assist us in facing this question, then we must, as I failed to do, differentiate *rigorously* and *categorically* between the *project of delimiting reason* and the Heideggerian notion of *thinking* (*Denken*).[7]

Neither Absolute System nor Perspectivalism Deliver Radical Freedom

In *Ecstatic Subjects*, I pressed Heidegger's ontological insight, that all beings are autodisclosive, into the service of a perspectival theory of knowledge, an interactive ethics, and a model of utopian society based on difference.[8] Perspectivalism strives to delimit theory as absolute system without lapsing into moral relativism. From Heidegger's ontology I generated two precepts in support of a perspectival theory of knowledge. The first precept is that because no system of representation can contain Being as a whole, all ideas reflect the standpoint of subjects whose historically embodied condition influences how they represent reality. In *Identity and Difference*, Heidegger disputes the Hegelian logic of identity when he argues that reason and reality do not mirror each other in perfect transparency. For want of making this asymmetrical relation available to conceptualization, I treated the Heideggerian notion of Being as an excess, a reservoir of possible meanings that exceeds any given horizon of meaning, any system of ideation, any symbolic matrix, or any historical ethos tacitly understood by a society or generation. The *es gibt*, the granting, I suggested, denotes the fact that human beings are historical. In a given historical epoch certain ways of viewing reality reign, with the necessary correlate that other ways of comprehending life journey recede into the background and remain foreign to our sensibilities.[9]

The second precept is that because all beings are autodisclosive, no entity ever presents all its faces at once; all entities defy containment in a concept. The implication is that human beings have an infinity within them, a singularity, such that however much any two people come to know each other, they remain inexhaustible wellsprings for each other in illuminating the nature of life. From here I pressed well beyond Heidegger. My idea was that Heidegger's genius consists in his revealing how history weds us to limited forms of perception and reflection; his weakness, in his failing to comprehend that social conditions further inform and constrain how a given person views the world. I posited the concept of mediation to denote the lived ethical practice requisite to becoming a critical and decentered subject. To become decentered requires that I mediate—that is, raise to awareness—the preconscious ways I evaluate the social totality and imbue it with meaning from out of a particular conceptual horizon. Since we never get out of some perspective, the best we can do is mediate it. If I take this task to heart, I argued against Heidegger, then I must recognize my intersubjective dependence on others.[10]

Finally, I linked the ethical moment in this model to a vision of the ideal society. Unlike traditional utopian thinking, this ideal has to be based on two moments. The first moment generates a model for the next historical stage of social change. But the second moment is formal and not substantial. It suggests that a utopian ideal must not center entirely on a positive image of a "humane society for all times." Instead, it must harbor within itself the ability to formally delimit itself. It must foster an awareness of the impurity of all original myths because all traditions are tainted; and it must mark off the impossibility of any society arriving at complete transparency to itself, since no social symbolism can contain the singularity of all genuine human need nor curtail the unforeseeable consequences of human action.[11]

Yet this interpretation of Heidegger errs in two egregious ways—egregious for our own self-understanding. First, to *treat* Being as language, as the reservoir of possible meanings left out of a given conceptual horizon, is to *conceptualize* Being, instead of *engaging* the autodisclosive world of things as they reveal themselves from out of themselves. To conceptualize Being as the limit of representation enables us to decenter subjectivism through awareness of perspectivalism. But it is not to decenter myself; it does not get beyond subject-ism.[12] When I label Being the excess of meaning in any ideational system, I continue to regard Being as that upon which "I" draw in order to generate my own reflection, critical or not. Drawing on "Being" as reservoir for my productivity tacitly subordinates the self-generating disclosiveness of others to my production, my thought, my creativity. I critique representation and metaphysics but without negating the habit that underpins conceptual-based thinking (metaphysics).[13]

Hence everything hinges on the second issue of becoming decentered and not on the debate over which paradigm—perspectivalism or system—delivers the best foundation or antifoundation for ethics and politics. The issue upon which the art of concretion stands and falls is this: does not the same habit sustain both poles of the debate? Isn't it the habit of making myself, if not the source of ideation, then the source of the activities and methodologies that show ideation to be limited? Heidegger's thinking presents a harder challenge than becoming aware, through critical mediation, of this habit and on the basis of that awareness tempering its operation. Just as Kierkegaard says there is a huge abyss between understanding and understanding, so too does Heidegger's legacy issue the challenge that there is an immeasurable difference between decentering and decentering. For to decenter metaphysics and representation through the categories I develop in theory (excess and mediation) is not to become *concretely* decentered in actuality. Even actualizing the intersubjective practice of becoming aware of my embodied interests as a situated knower can decenter me only *up to a point*. To become *radically decentered* requires that I negate the very habit of conceptualization.

When we compare the two conceptual paradigms, it seems perfectly transparent and indisputable that perspectivalism is the antithesis of system. It seems blatantly obvious what the stakes are, which paradigm is aligned with which consequences. For to advance ideation as system is to eliminate the marginalized, but to win perspectivalism is to learn from history and life and thus to foster a new multicultural ethics, a new poetics, a new form of life. Compared so, as I argued in *Ecstatic Subjects*, the latter is richer than the former, promises a better future, and reflects historical growth, ironically by disputing the model of progress. But when we examine perspectivalism and system qua activity—the activity of giving reasons and the activity of showing the limits of reason—then neither proves antithetical to the other, but instead are shown to be variations of the same. What Heidegger teaches is that the "other" of system, actively or verbally understood, is not perspectivalism. The "other" of rational abstraction is not the more experiential practice of intersubjective knowing. Beyond all perspectives, beyond the conceptual distinction between rational system and embodied perspective, lies freedom.

In *Gelassenheit*, Heidegger makes it amply clear that Being can be reduced neither to a given conceptual horizon nor to the conscious meditation of horizon as horizon (G, 48–50/DT, 72–74). Thinking begins where horizon leaves off. Thinking begins in freedom. Defined negatively, freedom is freedom from the compulsion both to give reasons and to delimit the giving of reasons. Positively understood, Heidegger calls freedom releasement from all conceptual horizons.[14] But releasement obtains on condition that I negate the habit of regarding my "self" as the one who is or is not critically aware of the limits of perspective, as the one who creates and produces systems of ideation or their replacements, ideational antisystems. Defined positively, freedom points to a most radical and concrete possibility: that thinking can arrive at a coincidence with the source of thinking. "I" can become decentered on condition that I relinquish "willing"; that is, the idea that *I engender thinking* (G, 5/DT, 79). The egregious error is not that I misunderstand Heidegger. It is rather far more serious: I misunderstand myself as thinker.[15]

Intellectualism as Un-ease

What does it mean to think *nonconceptually?* This question defies a conceptual response. It can only be answered actively by leaping into an engagement with what grants thinking. Strictly speaking, the leap is not a category and cannot be explained as a formula. It can only be taken. I can only leap. What can be diagnosed, however, is how I avoid the leap, how I fall into conceptualization. What Heidegger teaches philosophers is that talent and genius and analytic clarity are not enough to guarantee that we are thinking. He requires intellectuals, encourages intellectuals, to see that intellectualism is a compulsive habit, one that indeed makes us discontent and this discontent, against what philosophers claim, is no virtue to prize. All intellectual creativity, no matter how much genius it exhibits, how much talent or skill it portrays, remains a habitual art of conversion, a chemistry whereby we sever *technē*—the techniques of writing, conceiving, reflecting—from *poiēsis*, from the Event that discloses what shows itself forth for thinking (VA, 16/QCT, 13).[16]

To be an intellectual is to be a contradiction: intellectuals are called upon to think, to reach deeper into the source of reality than do other people; yet no human, intellectual or no, is the source that sustains thinking. We are to think, and yet radical thinking is not an activity that lies within our power to undertake through will. Heidegger tells us that as intellectuals we suffer from a disease, a fundamental un-ease with the fact that we span the tension between the Event of Appropriation and the world of beings (see TB). This anxiety—that we are driven to grasp the world of beings and yet we know not what motivates us to reflect—already suggests the possibility of misunderstanding ourselves as thinkers. For the most part, we tend not to think about this tension, as it seems so insignificant. There is an answer immediately available to us and it seems not to matter that it is a circular answer: that our natural predilection as intellectuals drives us to reflect.

But as philosophers we are never content to accept a vicious circle; we add greater justification. We say that human beings are the rational animal and thus it follows, without delineating the logic here, that intellectuals are the guardians of the culture's and nation's integrity and wellbeing. Intellectuals produce Socratically, we say; intellectuals produce citizens who can bear well the responsibilities of the polis (democracy) and who can sift through the traditions of old and make sound decisions about what to retain and what to give up. After all, we know that there are no bloodless origins, no original myths that are not tainted by the blood spilled in historical battles to preserve the alleged purity of the nation.

Yet do I, do we as intellectuals, thereby overcome our un-ease, do we resolve the contradiction, have we escaped the vicious circle? Have we dispelled our un-ease with the fact that we are compelled to reflect for reasons we know not why? No, not at all. When we fail to think originarily, then we instead learn to speculate about our contradiction, we learn to live with it by postulating it as natural and originary. We theorize anxiety as primordial, as what cannot be wholly overcome, as that which, when mediated though not overcome, makes us the best possible citizens in the polis even though we remain imperfect. At least awareness of anxiety, we claim, makes us more flexible and less dogmatic about our values (though it's difficult to account for why we still polemicize so much that we become enclosed in the ivory tower when the whole polis is at stake). Finally, we admit, if we are honest and sincere, that we live without why, that the rationalists got it all wrong. Yet by prematurely accepting the idea of living without why, we lose our most vital possibility: that there can be a nonanxious relation to the groundlessness of human existence.

When we settle for the contradiction as contradiction, when we accept the un-ease of our ontological condition as a necessity by rationalizing how to live with it, we miss the target of self-understanding. Worse, this acceptance is no passivity, but rather active defiance, a deliberate leap away from and not to the source that compels us to think (GA 5, 236/

QCT, 100). In this act, we fail to become what we are: thinkers. We convert un-ease into outright disease, with all the psychological machinations required to sustain the habit of flight. Hard as we try, we cannot conceptualize our way into a coincidence between what we say (that humans are not the masters of language, thought, Being) and what we do (the activity of appropriating reflection to ourselves). Freedom's possibility—*the possibility of the self's arriving in an operational coincidence with its becoming*—defies our conceptual grasp and, far more basically and significantly, fails to abate the deep yearning to arrive, kinetically, at repose in what we do, in our productivity.

The reason this coincidence defies our grasp is not, contrary to current belief, because wishing for it is a mark of disease. The disease is not the tension embedded in the reality that we are called to think and yet cannot master the source of thinking. Anxious flight from the task called for by this contradiction unleashes the disease. That disease consists in refusing to believe in the possibility of a truly nonanxious mode of life. Freedom from anxious concern becomes impossible only when we defy its possibility. The contradiction, that we think but do not engender thought, can become understood on condition that it is transformed, via the leap, into a paradox. To be a paradox means that I understand myself and become fulfilled as thinker when I let something else fund creative thinking and dictate what calls for thought. The primary and key issue that Heidegger teaches is this: *we, intellectuals and by extension all humans, enter into a coincidence with the activity of thinking on condition that we take seriously the possibility of a nonanxious relation to groundlessness*. And that act requires a yet more basic condition: *that we negate the idea that we are the source of thought, of creativity*.

Stealing the Fire of Creativity

I want to draw out the significance of Heidegger's claim that we are not yet thinking as a diagnosis of the disease of intellectualism, but in terms he rarely discussed. In particular, I want to undermine the view that any theory that centers on the corporeal and prethematic basis of thinking effectively captures what Heidegger attempted to think. I begin by differentiating semiotics, understood as it is by Kristeva as bound up with the unconscious and with prethematic bodily drives, from conscious intentionality. The latter takes it scope from a system of meaning, while the former focuses on processes that break down meaning or expose every horizon of meaning to be finite and limited. For Heidegger, thinking, as a matter of heart, defies this distinction.[17] Yet to the extent that human beings can distinguish *operatively* within themselves between conscious and bodily intentionality, it is not unfitting to say that the refusal to think and the consequent fall into representation issue effects on two planes simultaneously, the plane of ideation (objectivity) and the plane of sensible experience (subjectivity). It follows that any theory that attempts to posit corporeal processes as more primordial than rationalization fails to deliver us to an engagement with that which originates thinking.

Heidegger tells us that the drive to reflect operates in intellectuals as a compulsive habit, an addiction, the source of which we never fully comprehend because we neglect to diagnose its operation on the spot (SG, 13–22/PR, 3–9). When delivering a public lecture, for example, I count on the fact that thinking *will happen for me*. Certainly I have knowledge, but I bank on something more: that insight descend and an influx of energy fund my performance. Intuitively I gamble on the arrival of both the *disclosure* and the *funding*. For I know that my performance will not be good enough if I cannot "think" spontaneously and if I don't deliver my reflections with just the right level of "energy" and tone of voice to draw people into my process of ideation and be persuasive. Then, perhaps in a quiet moment, after my success was had, I walk away empty, somewhat depressed, and claim that this is the price exacted by performance, that being funded by that energy moves me up the roller coaster of elation, while its inevitable contrary, depression, follows as natural consequence of "my" output. Heidegger's work suggests that we suffer the roller coaster of elation-depression, and find no repose in the creative performance, for having misunderstood the source of both the insight and the spontaneity.

The Event of Appropriation gathers me into the possibility to think freely, to freely engage that which is granted. It gathers me through a call (WD, 83–86/WT, 117–21).[18] I *intuit* that something calls, glimpse something inchoate pressing to show itself. And I undergo the gathering as the movement whereby I am *attuned* to what struggles to appear. This Event, of being appropriated and oriented by the call, is essentially poietic and thus dynamic. It demands a specific poietic response, that of attendance. I am to attend to the granting in a manner that fits both senses

Stealing the Fire of Creativity   363

of the term. I am to attend in the sense of cultivating what emerges at first as only an inchoate intuition and thereby let it come forth slowly into its aspects. But the activity of cultivation also requires that I be attentive, vigilant. To what? To the possibility that I can make an appropriative gesture. For want of vigilant attending to what calls, I will mistake the granting as my own *insight*. For want of patient holding to the *attunement* that gathers me onto a path for thinking, I will seize the gentle movement of the gathering and convert it into *raw energy* to fuel my performance. So it is that thoughtlessness, in the blink of an eye, issues in a thoroughly misguided interpretation of both the Event (the source of thinking) and myself (as thinker).

Heidegger wants us to ask with pathos and sincerity, What happens between the granting and the intellectual performance? How is it that intellectuals "experience" the Event of Appropriation as a mere echo of attunement, as if being gathered were merely a spontaneous drive of "mine"? How is it that the unpredictable arrival of a thought is so taken for granted that instead of pondering it, intellectuals merely assume that this is the way things "happen" when they perform and produce? Heidegger's corpus suggests that between the granting and the possible irruption of the compulsive drive to reflection extends a vast abyss. When all I experience and know are the arrival of insight and the spontaneous emergence of drive, I have failed to leap across the abyss and receive the granting. Far worse, I have leapt in the opposite direction, fled from the call, and by this act of flight catapulted myself headlong into the abyss. That tumultuous fall instantaneously transmogrifies the twin moments of the Event of Appropriation, the disclosing and the attuning, into debased and reduced forms.

To refuse a poietic response to the Event is at root a supreme appropriative gesture. It constitutes an act of defiant severing myself from the source that funds and sustains thinking; in that act, I center myself as the source of creativity and the measure of what is real and unreal, true and untrue. Like Prometheus, I steal the fire of creativity, I lay claim to the fire both as disclosure (illumination, vision, insight) and as funding (energy, drive, mood, psychosomatic state). This act of theft or possession, by severing the disclosure from its genuine source, constitutes an alchemy, a physical art of converting a higher possibility (creative freedom) into a lower one (human inventiveness). Ironically, my chemical art transmutes me as well and not for the better. By this supreme act of appropriation, I consign all my activities to the realm of *technē*, my reflections all lost to the poietic origin of thought.[19] As a thinker, I become unmoored, lost to the source of my creativity, because I manipulate the granting, bend it to my purpose, and govern willfully over the substance and manner of my production, the ideas and values, the artistry and style of performance. In all such conversions I mistakenly regard creativity as my own power of spontaneous genius.

This refusal to engage the Event splits my psychic life in two, into my life of conscious ideation and my preconscious psychosomatic life, which I believe funds all my productivity. The Event is a reciprocal movement issuing in the granting and my being gathered toward the granting. Thus, in the defiant act, a double conversion occurs. I translate the simple *intuition* that something calls, I know not what, into *my insight* (as if I already understand the call). And I simultaneously convert the dynamic aspect of *being gathered and attuned*, I know not how or by what power, into *raw energy* from which I proceed to drink greedily every new possibility for my ongoing productivity, my continual *giving birth* to my ostensible self through production. I can then conceptualize the granting in eventlike terms, such as absencing, becoming, chora, excess; and I can thematize the process of ideation as midwifery. But what passes unnoticed is that my act constitutes a willful possession of what is granted and unleashes a habit and momentum, an addictive siphoning off of the power funded by the granting. What I label "involvement with that which situates me" and what I claim not to create but only to "deliver" amount to flat and one-dimensional imitations of the genuine Event and the true midwifery of originary thinking. The whole world is lost through the appropriative gesture, both the world as free play wherein each thing attains to repose in its dynamic self-revealing and the promise of harmony with my own self-showing. A tremendous amount of activity on my part transpires in that defiant act but I pay it no heed, witness it not, and yet claim to have undertaken self-examination, to hold more critical distance on myself than others, to be decentered.

The key issue I want to bring forward is that the act whereby I appropriate the source of creative thinking to myself undermines all subsequent efforts to decenter myself through critical reflection and reveals my existence to be contradictory. The leap away from the Event of Appropriation has both a *possessive moment* and a *generative moment*. The first moment is the act of appropriation, while the second moment is a reflexive retrieval in which I generate a theory indicating that I am not the source of thinking. This second action, because abstracted from a genuine engagement with the granting, engenders falsification by covering over the possessive theft; it serves psychologically to reinforce the habitual momentum whereby I refuse thinking and keep my hands in control of the stolen goods, the reins of creativity. All conceptualization entails, as previously noted, an act of converting intuition into "my" insight, disclosure into concept, thinking into classifying or delimiting systems of classification. That Promethean act is a supreme act of possession. Still, the Event haunts me, and for this reason, if I am sensitive and ingenious, I say, "I did not invent the notion. The idea just came to me." Even this reveals confusion. For "ideas" don't come to me. Thoughts do. To call that intuition an idea is not only to neglect, to let lie fallow that which stirs unformed yet presses to appear. It is a disavowal of my defiance. At once I possess the idea as my own and disavow the act of possession without in actuality refusing the theft. I intuit that I am not the source of thinking or creativity and yet for all my ingenuity I am not in earnest; I never take the intuition seriously enough to follow it onto the path of thinking.

This ingenious attempt to decenter myself reveals my contradiction. For what happens when I attempt, via reflection and not the leap, to get rid of the idea that I possess ideas and measure reality according to them? After the initial possession of an insight, I make a second move in an attempt to resolve the felt contradiction that I do and do not own insight. I undertake an act of reflexiveness, the movement whereby I use reflection to delimit reflection, the so-called ethical praxis of self-mediation. In an effort to cast away rationalism and the concept of genius, I pay homage to the source of ideation by thematizing it. This second move appears to be the "step-back" to the origin of thought (TB, 30), it appears to deliver me into the Event. But in actuality it is a second act of severance from origin. Instead of taking a leap, I "reflect" on what originates reflection and objectify the source as a concept: as my conscience, as my unconscious, as language, as the unthought meanings in a symbolic matrix, as power. But no matter what concept I choose as label for the origin of thought, the contradiction of my life, much to my dismay, has not been dispelled. I talk about how reality has a slippery floor in my preferred vocabulary, whether that of phenomenology, deconstruction, or psychoanalysis. But in all this, and no matter how valid my insights, *I remain the one who determines* how to image the groundlessness of thinking; *I measure* which label is most appropriate; *I posit* the source as source. In no case have I engaged directly what lies before conceptualization, what grants. I never refuse to appropriate the intuition of disclosure or renounce the tendency to generate my own flow of ideas about the limits of ideation.

This brings me to touch briefly on how I appropriate the dynamic aspect of the Event. Again, there is a possessive and a generative moment. I am gathered into an attunement that turns me toward what calls and orients me to engage it. But I immediately interpret, and thereby possess rather than engage, the gathering. For the gathering lifts me out of myself, stands me before the abyss, and, no longer standing in myself, I feel without mooring. I panic. I struggle to identify my locus as quickly as possible and by doing so I secure an anchor in myself once again, make myself the locus of perception and knowledge. I refuse to be turned around and shown what subsists according to itself. Like the prisoners in Plato's cave, I prefer to be my own anchor, to place my eyes at the center of reality, and so I mis-interpret the gathering as "my" subjective experience, "my" spontaneous seeing. I grasp (possess) the "being gathered," stop the decentering, contain it as my experience, then "use" it as energy to "fund" (generate) my intellectual production. Here, too, I suffer the nagging intuition that the gathering cannot be reduced to an experience because I do not generate the turning by my will. So, in a second act of reflection, I hasten to articulate how that which funds my production transpires before any volitional act on my part. I assign manifold labels to this funding: the mysterious kinesis of life, psychosomatic energy, or the power generated by fissures in meaning. Still I cannot evade the contradiction of my existence.

After seizing control over the reins of the intellective process, I disingenuously set myself up as midwife. My theories all claim that I am spontaneously drawn into what funds thinking, that I am only a midwife for what defies rational explication. But my actions renege when I don't trust the granting to reveal itself and instead through effort of will presume that the granting is a mere power of mine whose express goal is to fund my vision, makings, and doings. I adopt the role of a disingenuous midwife when *I draw upon* the granting only to the degree that it enables me to spin out ideas by my own sights. Far from being in actuality a genuine midwife, I never pause long enough and with enough patience to let myself be drawn deeper into the Event that I might become a medium through which something truly spontaneous shows itself forth. In this I reveal my self-centeredness. For I believe that I am the one who "gives birth to ideas" and that only the fuel comes from beyond. But the uniqueness of the Event can be reduced to no mere "generic power" for my task; rather, it is an invitation that I refuse.

Whether I diagnose what occurs in ideation or in the process of giving birth, I find that the act of possession and my subsequent production deliver only stillborn babies. I take disclosure, render it static *as concept*, and thereby leave unthought and unappreciated what compels me to think and to create. And when I take the gathering and treat it *as experience*, I reduce the call to spontaneity to a stillborn flight, a call that beckons though I never risk the leap. Above all, when I regard myself as midwife, I disavow the reality that what calls for thinking requires me to let it give birth to itself through careful attendance and not by manipulation. Heidegger challenges us, intellectuals all, to understand that we are neither the seed of creativity nor the hand that quickens the gestation and guarantees a healthy delivery, but only the medium through which things show forth. What talent and genius can never grasp is that, even when by talent's hand I rightly conceptualize the nature of the groundlessness of existence, something vital evades my grasp. What I can never give birth to by my own hand is the radical and spontaneous freedom through which all things show themselves forth.

Neither genius nor skill delivers me to my own radical freedom as thinker. For in all the machinations of reflection and all manner of human inventiveness, I am unable to get beyond taking myself as measure of what is. My many and varied attempts at self-decentering are to no avail; I remain always in my way, always at the center. The only way around this contradiction is to leap and in that leap discover the paradox that, though I am called to think, something else must sustain me in the activity of thinking. Happily so, for only if another source grants thinking, can I be displaced genuinely from posing as the founder of thinking. Only when thinking is freed from the compulsive habit of taking myself to be the measure for how to engender what is, do I become harmonized to the genuine role of midwife. Then do I find the repose that alone obtains when, on pain of refusing to appropriate creativity as a power of mine, I arrive at a dynamic coincidence between what I say (that I am not the source of thinking) and what I do (refuse to govern over the nature of the production that lets be the self-showing of all things).

Why Not Steal the Fire?

I offer a fine apologia for Heidegger, one indicating why we should not kill Heidegger in the course of time, as his work, like that of all great thinkers, stands before the tribunal of history. But why does this matter? What's wrong with stealing the granting and elaborating it as my insight into the world and what I think must be accomplished in life? If we adhere strictly to the ultimate concern of Heidegger's thought, then supplying an answer to this question risks perpetuating the illusion that we can know the value of nonconceptual thinking by reflecting on it abstractly. To even ask about value is already to relegate originary thinking to a sphere foreign to it. As Plato does in the *Republic*, I nonetheless offer a double answer. Heidegger's answer, as was Plato's, is that thinking is *immanent activity*. Short of knowing that activity from within its operation, no argument about the greatness of its value ever falls on willing enough ears. Thus, Plato gives a second answer. Through telling the myth of Er, he effectively says, if the argument for immanent activity does not suffice, I concede to evaluate thinking in terms foreign to its activity. Plato proceeds to warn that those who does not follow the good in this life will come back in a worse state in the next life.[20] Although the answer differs in Heidegger's case, I follow Plato in suggesting what Heidegger won't say: that without radical freedom as a thinker, I will never abide in harmony with myself, I will never be free of anxious concern, and, as a consequence, I won't let each individual be in her or his radical singularity.

Radical freedom is that activity alone that sustains nonconflictual relations to everything: to self, to others, to animals, to things, to world, to symbols, to drives, to desire. What makes nonconceptual thinking diametrically opposed to all other forms of reflection is that it knows nothing of ordinary polemics because it takes its point of reference from neither past nor future.[21] What grants thinking is a wellspring that has no bottom but always gives forth. The unique source of thinking is the intrinsically wondrous. When gathered into the Event of Appropriation, I thus am relieved of anxiety and arrive at the only truly immanent activity, the wondrous engagement with the self-showing of all things. Although Being needs human beings to come forth, so too in its embrace am I, as intellectual, set free from mistaking myself as the measure of all things. I land in the world of singular universals, where each thing stands beyond measure. Most remarkable is that thinking, as a self-generating activity, unfolds as a purely *constructive* activity. A sure sign that I have not leaped beyond conceptualization is that anxious concern still drives me to want recognition and to want to distinguish myself from others through polemics. What grants thinking gives of itself freely and has no enemies; neither hatred nor preference contains it, neither desire nor fear taints it. In the ceaseless holding to that which grants thought, so too am I relieved of anger and want, am I opened out on the wondrous singularity of each person and every living thing.

If, upon release from the compulsive anxiety that drives intellection, I am still called to effectuate social change, then I must regard *radical freedom* and *social liberation* as two distinct and irreducible dimensions of existence. And the paradox is this: social liberation, no matter how greatly it attenuates anxiety and alleviates oppression, cannot deliver us to the equanimity that enables us to live well. Yet what's the alternative? For radical freedom, though it harmonizes me to existence, does not build society! Heidegger insistently tells us that originary thinking does not directly fund action, does not erect a value system, is not useful (WD, 161/WT, 159). If equanimity does not deliver us from circumstance and suffering, then aren't we stuck with quietism and the most non-Heideggerian of all questions, What value brings equanimity? No, we are not stuck with quietism. The task of implementing new values and social systems, however, unfolds in a sphere and as an activity of reflection that, while extremely valuable in its own right, harbors the constant temptation to neglect to cultivate radical freedom, that freedom alone that returns us to a dynamic repose with our individual life journey. Conversely, even though thinking yields no project, it does not follow that thinking is inimical to accepting that humans need a form of life.

So we can say that radical freedom poses this challenge: be free. Only then can you pick your form of life well. Heidegger was not concerned with this latter project, because he was leery of all projects. The paradox is this: thinking alone sets us free from the grip of the anxious desire for recognition, from dissatisfaction with other human beings, from the subtle ways in which we define our worth against others. If we want to quiet competition, Heidegger's work suggests, no form of life will ever suffice, though some may be more encouraging in this regard than others. No amount of critical reflection ever suffices for me to live well among others, if I do not venture to discover that "I" am not the source of reflection. Beyond the moral virtues that can be had by psychological maturation lies a qualitatively distinct humility, one that, in eliminating all residual struggle for recognition, enables me to let be.

In light of the possibility of radical freedom, the sociohistorical challenge becomes both more simple and more difficult. For it will not suffice to undertake a transvaluation of myths and values simply in terms of political liberation. We must ask instead, How can we retell (as opposed to rewrite) myths in such a fashion that they point us to what no society can deliver and every society needs: radical freedom? Over the years I have come to identify several primary reasons why the Left has not been able to win against conservative forces. Besides lack of money, the most basic reasons are two: habitual momentum and intuition of freedom's possibility. Conservatism always has greater momentum on its side in that traditional values become solidified into ideational and behavioral habits over long periods of time. What is more basic still and difficult to admit, however, is that people's reluctance to give up traditions stems not simply from familiarity and comfort, though certainly that. A more obtuse and serious reason why the Left cannot dispel traditional values and replace them with thick substitutes is that people *intimate* that traditional myths contain a doorway to radical freedom, to the repose that alone can cure them of nostalgia for rest. I am not claiming that fundamentalists and traditionalists are more willing to face the groundlessness of human existence, to leap beyond habit and to freedom, than are progressive revolutionaries who face their death on a daily basis. But the task of rejuvenating old myths is an exceedingly difficult one.

Given the difference between radical freedom and liberation, that task requires two things. It requires that, as a society, we emancipate ourselves from the misinterpretations of traditional myths that have led people to neglect to provide the optimal social and material conditions requisite to encourage people to seek freedom; and yet it must also recover what is potent in those original myths. The critical-historical approach to the first task mistakenly asks, How can we undertake a transvaluation of old values and yet, in writing new myths, bring people to understand the limitations of all myths? But the second task shows the impossibility of such an approach when it suggests that, short of encouraging radical freedom, no form of life can sustain itself with sufficient critical awareness to deliver radical freedom; only a leap can do that. It does no good to replace old religions with new ones if all valorize a cultural system of beliefs but have no inkling of freedom. Enlightenment critique may be better than the resources of tradition from a political standpoint. But radical freedom is better than both tradition and critique, because it alone harmonizes all individuals to the equality of the radical uniqueness of individuated personal journey.

Originary thinking need not proceed by a return to historical beginnings because the leap to freedom exists in the now. Yet to the extent that the primary role of myth is not to delineate values but rather to point us toward the originary possibility of radical freedom, then every historical beginning contains within it the seed of that originary possibility. Original myths, if genuine, point to the freedom that lies before all developmental processes, individual and historical. Myths point to this freedom because they carry the power of poetic word. The poetic word, in its most radical operation, is neither a concept nor an image. Rather than performing the critical task of abstracting from reality in order to reflect on it conceptually or metaphorically, the poetic word points to the possibility of a direct and concrete engagement with that which discloses itself. *Mythos* delivers us to thinking. That deliverance attunes each of us individually, and harmonizes all people equally, to the specificity of each person's journey. Each is given back to the radically individuated character of existence, the singular and self-contained quality of her or his life. This singularity yields an equanimity more stable than all certainty or conviction. It enables each person to accept what every other is and in that acceptance none is defined for or against any other person or thing.

Thus to seek social change with an eye to freedom is not to dismiss politics, but rather to point political projects back to freedom's possibility. This implies something hard to face. If at the end of Western history, the goal of a transvaluation of values seems necessary, then this is not because a new value system can make us radically free. To the contrary, and this was Nietzsche's point, the call for a transvaluation of values arises not fundamentally because the old myths have lost their intrinsic power to recall us to freedom. Rather, generational sensibilities lead us mistakenly to believe that original myths point back to the value system of the classical world and not to the original freedom availed within them now. The conservative tradition mistakenly conflates myth with a cultural value system. As progressives, women like myself are tempted to make the same mistake. Instead of hearing the call of myth to freedom, every new generation tends to grasp the words of the last generation solely as a system of concepts and values. Interpreted conceptually, traditional myths are offensive to those of us who have borne the brunt of their historical and fallen transmutation into mere values. These values harm us and engender liberation struggles.

Yet it remains important to face the offense and to hear these myths nonconceptually. For if original myths were merely cultural, then they would house only the timeworn vocabulary and age-bound values of their era. This would hold for new myths as well. And all myths would be reducible to the historical and relativistic perspective of a given society or group. But if *mythos* is contained within myth, then treating myth only as a system of ideation that reflects the peculiar sensibilities and limitations of an age or group would cloud over the vital function of myth to point us to equanimity. If, then, our inceptive myths have worn out, is this not due simply to our inability to think? Certainly history has changed our sensibilities in ways that enable us rightly to resist the negative effects of the values of older times, even if those values spin off from reductionist interpretations of original myths. But the challenge persists. New values necessarily employ vocabularies that are no less susceptible to debasement, to being reduced to a closed system of ideas and values. While some of us prefer the possible side effects of making dogma out of the new to those of old values, we are left with two age-old problems: What about myth is efficacious enough to encourage people to accept the upheaval of a transvaluation of values? and, What about myth can secure the future against crimes in the name of a new dogmatics? My answer is that originary myths point us to radical freedom. For this very reason, there is no ultimate need to write new myths or generate a new dogmatics, though there may be a need to retell original myths.

If we were to write new myths, and I would advise against it, the ultimate purpose in doing that would have to be to reawaken the most fundamental operation of *mythos*. If feminism rests content with the historical goal to replace old values with new ones, it may evolve forms of life consistent with women's liberation. But it is not obvious how subjects will be free enough to sustain those forms of life well. The project of critical mythologizing strives to resolve this dilemma by propounding a multicultural value system while simultaneously teaching children to critique all values, to understand that all values are limited. The question posed by Heidegger is whether critical mythologizing—understood as the replacement of old myths with entirely new ones—must fail. Unless it rejuvenates and deepens the premonition that the original myths of tradition already contain within them the richness of *mythos*, then the retelling of myths will effectuate a horrific deracinating from that which points beyond itself toward radical freedom. If instead of retelling myths we rewrite them, then critical mythologizing will fail, because language and myth are not the ground of existence but only the pointers to that which sustains us in freedom. The best that a critical retelling of myth could attain—and this would be a genuine accomplishment—would be to recover the originary power of myth to point beyond itself toward the source of creativity. Myth cannot directly deliver us to freedom. In retelling new stories, the difficult task will be to revive a lost sensibility that the words do not constitute the message but only point the way. It is thus utterly vital to emphasize that the fundamental reason we cannot hear myth's deepest call is because we don't think and not because history has made us aware of the pitfalls of tradition.

What wrestling with Heidegger teaches us is that critique alone remains too hollow, too skeptical, to give people the very integration of sincerity and humility that critical mythologizing requires. How can people simultaneously adopt a heart-bound and sincere willingness to embrace multicultural values with the utmost seriousness and yet regard them playfully and with complete humility as unable to deliver ultimate freedom by themselves? How can people both believe and critique without self-contradiction? Can we square the circle of combining thick cultural values with Enlightenment critique? Not so long as we fail to think. The only mooring substantial enough to prevent values from supplying the ultimate anchor of existence, and thereby deteriorating into dogma, is radical freedom. The only compass accurate enough and properly oriented to grant distance on all values without corroding the decisive action requisite to all social struggles, is freedom. Critique without radical freedom threatens to lapse into emptiness, skepticism for skepticism's sake, a paralyzing inability to take any values seriously. Tradition without radical freedom inevitably takes itself far too seriously to let others be freely. In order to strike the balance between risking the venture of meeting the future anew and remaining intensely aware that no venture of establishing values can deliver radical equanimity, I must venture to become free.

The historical project of a transvaluation of values presupposes that we should reinvent mythologies and values rather than live without them. Old myths no longer speak to progressives. And the Enlightenment does not speak to most people's need to conserve something of tradition. Perhaps as intellectuals we should follow Nietzsche's lead and pose as the "last men" or the bridge to freedom's possibility. In that case we should by all means retell myths in a contemporary language. But rather than resting content with the project of melding culture with critique, why not bring *mythos* back into its proper operation: to point out that freedom is won through a leap. As Kierkegaard reminds us, every generation has to start again in order to find its way to being contemporaneous with the beginning, that is, to enter into the now-time of freedom, humanity's original possibility.²² And Heidegger warns that only freedom, and not the humanly powered effort to fit the square peg of critique into the circle of thick values, can harmonize the human heart to the demands of the time, while allowing human beings to face the supreme task: to recall, listen to, and heed the fact that each individual's freedom defies containment in every system of ideas and values.

Notes

1. At a minimum, this list would include Heidegger's unique hermeneutical phenomenology, his critique of transcendental phenomenology, his challenges to some of the most basic presuppositions of modern philosophy (the transparency of the self, the Cartesian starting point for philosophy, foundationalism), the sources, ancient and modern, of the technological era, and the singular contribution of his work to poetics.

2. Jacques Derrida and Jean Luc Marion have adapted Heideggerian insights to social theory; Herbert Marcuse offered a more political analysis of technological rationality, and this work has been carried forward most notably by Andrew Feenberg. Trish Glazebrook, Carol Bigwood, and Michael Zimmerman, among others, have advanced Heideggerian notions in developing ecological theories. See the Selected Bibliography.

3. See, as examples, Sandra Lee Bartky's critique "Originative Thinking in the Later Philosophy of Heidegger," *Philosophy and Phenomenological Research* 30 (1970): 368–81, and her constructive use of the Heideggerian notion of attunement in *Femininity and Domination: Studies in the Phenomenology and Oppression* (New York: Routledge, 1990), chap. 6; Iris Marion Young, "House and Home: Feminist Variations on a Theme," in *Intersecting Voices: Dilemmas of Gender, Political Philosophy, and Policy* (Princeton, NJ: Princeton University Press, 1997), 134–64; Carol Bigwood, *Earth Muse: Feminism, Nature, and Art* (Philadelphia: Temple University Press, 1993); and my *Ecstatic Subjects, Utopia, and Recognition: Kristeva, Heidegger, Irigaray* (Albany: State University of New York Press, 1998), esp. chaps. 1, 2, 4–6.

4. In this essay, I employ two voices. I work in the "we" voice, yet this is not the imperialist we but rather a personal we. Heidegger's thought challenges intellectuals, especially philosophers, in a very particular manner. It is possible to discuss earnestly this challenge only in concretely personal terms. For this reason, I employ the "we" in this essay to refer to intellectuals. Occasionally the "we" takes on a reference more narrowly to feminist theorists or at times more broadly to humanity. Such references are indicated in context. In the section "Stealing the Fire of Creativity," the "I" voice addresses ways that my work in *Ecstatic Subjects* fell prey to the disease of intellectualism that Heidegger spent his life diagnosing, even though I wrote all about Heidegger.

5. WD/WT in its entirety explores this question; see also Heidegger SG/PR.

6. That one enters thinking through a leap becomes highlighted as a sustained theme throughout WD/WT and no single passage captures its significance. It is also taken up throughout PR, see esp. 53, 60–61, 68, 78, 88–89, and passim.

7. Throughout the mature works such as WD/WT, SG/PR, and G/DT, Heidegger employs the general word *Denken* to distinguish thinking from all other types of reflection. In G/DT, Heidegger sometimes refers to thinking as "das besinnliche Denken" or meditative thinking in contrast to "das rechnende Denken" or calculative thinking (WD, 13). Yet calculative thinking encompasses far

more than crass instrumentalism. Reginald Lilly's introductory comments to PR prove most helpful. Lilly notes that thinking challenges not only representational thinking (*Vorstellen*) but "conceiving" (*begreifen*) and all intellection or "cognition" (xiv–xvii).

8. Huntington, *Ecstatic Subjects*, chap. 5, provides the key.

9. Huntington, *Ecstatic Subjects*, 168–69.

10. Huntington, *Ecstatic Subjects*; on Being as Excess, see 176 and 198; on critical mediation and ethical subjects, see 173, 188–94, 198–200.

11. Huntington, *Ecstatic Subjects*, 194–202.

12. See William J. Richardson, *Heidegger: Through Phenomenology to Thought* (The Hague: Martinus Nijoff, 1963), for his discussions of "subject-ism" on 176, 321–28, 363–64, 381–82, 420, and 629; cf. Heidegger's preface, in which he addresses Richardson's thesis that there is a Heidegger I and II and that the issue of subject-ism divides the two phases of thought (R, VIII–XXIII).

13. The difference between naming and labeling merits its own essay. I think we have profoundly misunderstood Heidegger when we take language to be the origin of human existence. In Heideggerian thought, there is no personified name for that which grants thinking. What grants thinking is real; one can only know this by engaging the granting. In order to write about the granting, Heidegger must continually "name" it. The activity of naming, as an activity, always presents a challenge to listeners and readers. Both that to which naming points and the activity of naming defy comprehension through speculation. What naming points toward can always be misunderstood and reduced to a noun, a nominative case, a proper name. Thus there is an important sense in which every naming of that which grants thinking—Being, language, Saying, granting, *es gibt*, Event of Appropriation—is subject to abuse. Any of these terms, when taken as labels, reduces the Event to an objectified thing. To some extent Heidegger's poetic naming (source, wellspring) is less susceptible to this reduction than are the philosophical words (Being). Yet even these can be misunderstood. Every naming, insofar as it can be converted into a noun, transmutes the name into a label and evinces a failure to engage and understand through that engagement that which grants thinking.

14. For the full discussion of horizon, see also G, 36–39, 57–58/DT, 63–66, 79–80. The question of radical freedom, discussed in "On the Essence of Truth" (BW, 117–41) and "Letter On Humanism" (BW, 193–242), finds its mature expression in those works, such as G/DT, WD/WT, TB, SG/PR, that move beyond transcendental-horizonal thinking and thus beyond will.

15. Important to note is that from this perspective it makes no difference how Heidegger acted politically, but only whether his work can point me toward self-understanding.

16. Heidegger develops the theme that reason as *technē* begins as a form of *poiēsis* (a bringing-forth of that which shows itself for thinking) but becomes increasingly lost to *poiēsis* as philosophy unfolds from its inception with Plato to its culmination in Nietzsche. Crucial texts include PD, all the Nietzsche lectures, and QCT. For a summary of this story, see Huntington, *Ecstatic Subjects*, 180–87.

17. See Heidegger, WD/WT, part II, lectures IV through VI.

18. Heidegger develops the notion of the "Event of Appropriation" in TB. Gathering appears throughout the late works, see esp. WD/WT, part II, lecture III; and all essays in EGT.

19. See Heidegger's comments on how we "unhinge our essence" (NII, 366/N4, 223) and thereby turn ourselves into "standing-reserve" or disposable objects (VA, 31/QCT, 27).

20. Plato, *Republic*, trans. G. M. A. Grube (Indianapolis: Hackett, 1974). Book 2 brings forward the notion of immanent activity, books 4 and 6 defend the view that the rational life is an immanent activity, and book 10 relates the myth of Er.

21. By virtue of resting in itself, freethinking has no polemic. But we could also say that polemic attains its proper sphere in the struggle to let that which calls for thinking come into thought. The primary enemy of this struggle is speculation. Thus, thinking may be called upon, in a given thinker's work, to don the mask of ordinary polemics, the way Kierkegaard did with his pseudonymous authorship or Nietzsche by posing as the last man. But here polemic is shifted to a higher plane, the heroics

involved in setting all people and things free. Here polemic is employed to shock us into opening our eyes to the possibility of the leap to radical freedom. In essence, thinking has no polemic and only strategically must take one on.

22. Ursula LeGuin grapples with this concern in *The Dispossessed* (New York: HarperCollins, 1974).

Contributors

ELLEN T. ARMOUR is associate professor and chair of religious studies at Rhodes College in Memphis, Tennessee. She is the author of *Deconstruction, Feminist Theology, and the Problem of Difference: Subverting the Race/Gender Divide*, Religion and Postmodernism Series (University of Chicago Press, 1999).

CAROL BIGWOOD teaches philosophy at York University (Atkinson College). She has published articles on gender theory, art, and William Blake's illustrations. Her book *Earth Muse: Feminism, Nature, and Art* (Temple University Press, 1993) draws on the work of Heidegger, Merleau-Ponty, Irigaray, and Brancusi. She is currently writing a post-apocalyptic work of fiction that takes place in Northern Ontario, as well as painting and drumming as often as she can.

HEIDI BOSTIC is assistant professor of French at Michigan Technological University. She is co-author, with Stephen Pluháček, of "Thinking Life as Relation: An Interview with Luce Irigaray," *Man and World* 29 (1996): 343–60.

JOHN D. CAPUTO is the David R. Cook Professor of Philosophy at Villanova University, where he has taught since 1968. His most recent books include *More Radical Hermeneutics: On Not Knowing Who We Are* (Indiana University Press, 2000), *The Prayers and Tears of Jacques Derrida: Religion Without Religion* (Indiana University Press, 1997), and *Deconstruction in a Nutshell: A Conversation with Jacques Derrida* (Fordham University Press, 1997). He has also been co-directing a series of conferences titled "Religion and Postmodernism" at Villanova, featuring Derrida in dialogue with contemporary theologians and philosophers of religion, the first of which has been published as *God, the Gift, and Postmodernism*, which he has co-edited (Indiana, 1999). Professor Caputo is also editor of the Fordham University Press's book series Perspectives in Continental Philosophy.

TINA CHANTER received her Ph.D. from the State University of New York at Stony Brook. She is author of *Ethics of Eros: Irigaray's Rereading of the Philosophers* (Routledge, 1995), and *Time, Death, and the Feminine: Levinas with Heidegger* (Stanford University Press, forthcoming). She has edited *Feminist Interpretations of Emmanuel Levinas*, (Penn State Press, 2001), and is the author of articles on figures such as Beauvoir, Derrida, Kofman, Kristeva, Hegel, Heidegger, Irigaray, Lacan, Levinas, and Merleau-Ponty and topics such as theory and tragedy, sex and gender, time and temporality, and film theory. She has contributed to journals such as *Differences, Signs, Philosophy and Social Criticism, Philosophy Today, Research in Phenomenology*, and the *Graduate Faculty Philosophy Journal*.

JACQUES DERRIDA is director of studies at the École Practique des Hautes Études en Sciences Sociales and also teaches at the University of California, Irvine, and the New School. Recent English translations of his works include *Politics of Friendship, Monolingualism of the Other* OR *The Prothesis of Origin, Of Hospitality, Adieu to Emmanel Levinas*, and *Religion* (which he edited, with Gianni Vattimo).

TRISH GLAZEBROOK received her Ph.D. from the University of Toronto in 1994. She is assistant professor of philosophy at Moravian College, and has taught at the University of Toronto, Colgate University, and Syracuse University. A board director of the International Association of Environmental Philosophers, she is the author of *Heidegger's Philosophy of Science* and the editor of a forthcoming collection of essays on Heidegger's critique of science, and has published further on Heidegger, ancient and modern science, environmentalism, and feminism.

JENNIFER ANNA GOSETTI is assistant professor of philosophy at the University of Maine. She taught previously, as Quentin Lauer Fellow, at Fordham University. She is a translator of the forthcoming Heidegger volume *Phenomenology of Religious Life*; has authored several articles on phenomenology, language, and aesthetics; and is currently at work on a book about Heidegger and Hölderlin.

NANCY J. HOLLAND is a professor of philosophy at Hamline University. In addition to having produced numerous articles, she is the author of *Is Women's Philosophy Possible?* (Rowman and Littlefield, 1990) and *The Madwoman's Reason: The Concept of the Appropriate in Ethical Thought* (Penn State Press, 1998), and the editor of *Feminist Interpretations of Jacques Derrida* (Penn State Press, 1997).

PATRICIA HUNTINGTON teaches contemporary continental philosophy at Loyola University of Chicago. She is the author of *Ecstatic Subjects, Utopia, and Recognition: Kristeva, Heidegger, Irigaray* (State University of New York Press, 1998). She co-edits New Critical Theory, a book series published by Rowman and Littlefield. In an effort to raise funds to meet the health care needs of indigenous communities in Chiapas, Mexico, she originated and directs the Chiapas Solidarity Project.

LUCE IRIGARAY is a leading female philosopher and thinker of the twentieth century. In addition to holding a Ph.D. in philosophy, she is a poet and a trained psychoanalyst and linguist. She has been a director of research at the Centre National de Recherche Scientifique in Paris. Her authored books include *Speculum of the Other Woman; This Sex Which Is Not One; Elemental Passions; Marine Lover of Friedrich Nietzsche; The Forgetting of Air in Martin Heidegger; An Ethics of Sexual Difference; Sexes and Genealogies; Je, Tu, Nous: Toward a Culture of Difference; I Love to You: Sketch of a Possible Felicity in History;* and *Thinking the Difference: For a Peaceful Revolution* as well as *Le souffle des femmes*, an edited collection of feminist spirituality, and most recently *Between East and West*, a work currently being translated by Stephen Pluháček.

DOROTHY LELAND is professor of philosophy and associate provost at Florida Atlantic University. She has published a number of essays of interest to feminist and continental philosophers, including essays dealing with the thought of Richard Rorty, Julia Kristeva, Luce Irigaray, Gloria Anzaldúa, Sartre, and Husserl.

MECHTHILD NAGEL is assistant professor of philosophy at SUNY Cortland. She co-edited, with Andrew Light, *Race, Class, and Community Identity*, vol. 1 of Radical Philosophy Today Series (Humanity Books, 2000).

STEPHEN PLUHÁČEK teaches philosophy at Michigan Technological University. He is the translator of Luce Irigaray's book *Between East and West*. He co-authored, with Heidi Bostic, "Thinking Life as Relation: An Interview with Luce Irigaray," published in 1996.

GAIL STENSTAD is chair of the Department of Philosophy and Humanities at East Tennessee State University. She is associate editor of the journal *Heidegger Studies* and a member of the board of directors of the International Association for Environmental Philosophy. She has written on Heidegger, Merleau-Ponty, feminist thinking, and environmental thinking and is especially concerned with questions concerning the transformations that are needed if we are not to destroy the earth and one another. Her philosophical work finds its context in living with, caring for, and learning from six dogs and all the other animals and the plants at home on a twenty-two acre Appalachian hill that is both wild (old woodland) and cultivated (food and flower gardens, water gardens).

IRIS MARION YOUNG is professor of political science at the University of Chicago. Her two most recent books are *Inclusion and Democracy* (Oxford University Press, 2000) and *Intersecting Voices: Dilemmas of Gender, Political Philosophy, and Policy* (Princeton University Press, 1997).

Selected Bibliography

A list of works by Heidegger cited in this anthology can be found in the Abbreviations at the beginning of this volume.

Arendt, Hannah. *The Human Condition*. Chicago: University of Chicago Press, 1958.
Armour, Ellen T. "Crossing the Boundaries Between Deconstruction, Feminism, and Religion." In *Feminist Interpretations of Jacques Derrida*, ed. Nancy J. Holland, 193–214. University Park: Penn State Press, 1997.
———. *Deconstruction, Feminist Theology, and the Problem of Difference: Subverting the Race/Gender Divide*. Chicago: University of Chicago Press, 1999.
———. "Questions of Proximity: 'Women's Place' in Derrida and Irigaray." *Hypatia: A Journal of Feminist Philosophy* 12, no. 1 (1997): 63–78.
Bartky, Sandra Lee. "Originative Thinking in the Later Philosophy of Heidegger." *Philosophy and Phenomenological Research* 30 (1970): 368–81.
———. "Shame and Gender." In *Femininity and Domination: Studies in the Phenomenology of Oppression*, 83–98. New York: Routledge, 1990.
Beauvoir, Simone de. *The Second Sex*, trans. H. M. Parshley. New York: Vintage, 1952.
Benhabib, Seyla. *The Reluctant Modernism of Hannah Arendt*. London: Sage, 1996.
Berry, Philippa. "The Burning Glass: Paradoxes of Feminist Revelation in *Speculum*." In *Engaging with Irigaray*, ed. Carolyn Burke, Naomi Schor, and Margaret Whitford, 229–46.
Bigwood, Carol. *Earth Muse: Feminism, Nature, and Art*. Philadelphia: Temple University Press, 1993.
Birmingham, Peg. "Ever Respectfully Mine: Heidegger on Agency and Responsbility." In *Ethics and Danger*, ed. Arlene B. Dallery and Charles E. Scott, with P. Holley Roberts, 109–23.
———. "Logos and the Place of the Other." *Research in Phenomenology* 20 (1990): 34–54.
———. "The Subject of 'Praxis': Review of 'The Thracian Maid and the Professional Thinker: Arendt and Heidegger' by Jacques Taminaux." *Research in Phenomenology* 29 (1999): 215–25.
———. "The Time of the Political." *Graduate Faculty Philosophy Journal* 14, no. 1–15, no. 2 (1991): 25–45.
Bowles, Brian. "Heidegger and the Absence of the Body: The *Zollikoner Seminare*." *International Studies in Philosophy* (forthcoming 2001).
———. "Heidegger's Retrieval of Aristotelian πάθος: On the Place of 'the Bodily' in Heidegger's Thought." Ph.D. diss., Loyola University of Chicago, 2001.

———. "Sensibility and Transcendence in *Kant and the Problem of Metaphysics*." *Philosophy Today* 44, no. 4 (2000): 347–65.
Brown, Alison Leigh. *Fear, Truth, Writing: From Paper Village to Electronic Community*. Albany: State University of New York Press, 1995.
Burke, Carolyn, Naomi Schor, and Margaret Whitford, eds. *Engaging with Irigaray: Feminist Philosophy and Modern European Thought*. New York: Columbia University Press, 1994.
Cladwell, Anne. "Fairy Tale for Politics: The Other, Once More." *Philosophy Today* 41 (Spring 1997): 40–50.
Caputo, John D. *Demythologizing Heidegger*. Bloomington: Indiana University Press, 1993.
———. "Dreaming of the Innumerable: Derrida, Drucilla Cornell, and the Dance of Gender." In *Derrida and Feminism: Recasting the Question of Woman*, ed. Ellen K. Feder, Mary C. Rawlinson, and Emily Zakin, 141–60. New York: Routledge, 1997.
———. *The Prayers and Tears of Jacques Derrida: Religion Without Religion*. Bloomington: Indiana University Press, 1997.
———. " 'Supposing Truth to Be a Woman...': Heidegger, Nietzsche, Derrida." *Tulane Studies in Philosophy* 32 (1984): 15–21.
Carlson, Thomas A. *Indiscretion: Finitude and the Naming of God*. Chicago: University of Chicago Press, 1999.
Chanter, Tina. *Ethics of Eros: Irigaray's Rewriting of the Philosophers*. New York: Routledge, 1995.
Cheah, Pheng, and Elizabeth Grosz, eds. "The Future of Sexual Difference: An Interview with Judith Butler and Drucilla Cornell." *Diacritics* 28 (Spring 1988): 19–42.
Cimitile, Maria Christine. "The Truth in Mimesis: Phenomenological Transformation in Gadamer, Heidegger, Irigaray." Ph.D. diss., University of Memphis, 1999.
Cixous, Hélène. *Reading with Clarice Lispector*. Edited and translated by Verena Andermatt Conley. Minneapolis: University of Minnesota Press, 1990.
Collard, Andrée, with Joyce Contrucci. *Rape of the Wild: Man's Violence Against Animals and the Earth*. Bloomington: Indiana University Press, 1989.
Cornell, Drucilla. *Beyond Accommodation: Ethical Feminism, Deconstruction, and the Law*. New York: Routledge, 1991.
Dallery, Arleen B., and Charles E. Scott, with P. Holley Roberts, eds. *Ethics and Danger: Essays on Heidegger and Continental Thought*. Albany: State University of New York Press, 1992.
Derrida, Jacques. *Circumfession: Fifty-Nine Periods and Periphrases*. In *Jacques Derrida*, by Geoffrey Bennington and Jacques Derrida, 3–315. Chicago: University of Chicago, Press, 1993.
———. "Geschlecht: sexual difference, ontological difference." *Research in Phenomenology* 13 (1983): 65–83. Originally published in *Martin Heidegger*, ed. Michel Haar (Paris: *Cahier de l'Herne*, 1983).
———. "Geschlecht II: Heidegger's Hand." Translated by John P. Leavey, Jr. In *Deconstruction and Philosophy: The Texts of Jacques Derrida*, ed. John Sallis, 161–96. Chicago: University of Chicago Press, 1987.
———. "Heidegger's Ear: Philopolemology (*Geschlecht* IV)." Translated by John P. Leavey, Jr. In *Reading Heidegger*, ed. John Sallis, 163–218.
———. *Of Spirit: Heidegger and the Question*. Translated by Geoffrey Bennington and Rachel Bowlby. Chicago: University of Chicago Press, 1987.

———. *Points...: Interviews, 1974–1994*, ed. Elizabeth Weber, trans. Peggy Kamuf et al. Stanford, Calif.: Stanford University Press, 1995.

———. *Politics of Friendship*. Translated by George Collins. New York: Verso, 1997.

———. *The Truth in Painting*. Translated by Geoff Bennington and Ian McLeod. Chicago: University of Chicago Press, 1987.

Derrida, Jacques, and Christie V. McDonald, "Choreographies: Interview." In *Feminist Interpretations of Jacques Derrida*, ed. Nancy J. Holland, 23–41. Originally published in *Diacritics* 12 (Summer 1982): 66–76.

Diefelt, Wanda. "Toward A Latin American Feminist Hermeneutics: A Dialogue with the Biblical Methodologies of Elisabeth Schuessler Fiorenza, Phyllis Trible, Carlos Mesters, and Pablo Richard." Ph.D. diss., Northwestern University, 1990.

Diprose, Rosalyn. *The Bodies of Women: Ethics, Embodiment and Sexual Difference*. New York: Routledge, 1994.

———. "Ethics and the Body of Woman: Hegel, Nietzsche, Heidegger." Ph.D. diss., University of South Wales, 1991.

Dreyfus, Hubert L. *Being-in-the-World: A Commentary on Heidegger's Being and Time, Division I*. Cambridge: MIT Press, 1991.

duBois, Page. *Sowing the Body: Psychoanalysis and Ancient Representations of Women*. Chicago: University of Chicago Press, 1988.

Elam, Diane. "Is Feminism the Saving Grace of Hermeneutics?" *Social-Epistemology: Journal of Knowledge, Culture, and Policy* 5 (October–December 1991): 349–60.

Elliot, Terri. "Making Strange What Had Been Familiar." *The Monist* 77 (October 1994): 424–33.

Fóti, Véronique M. *Heidegger and the Poets: Poiesis/Sophia/Techne*. Atlantic Highlands, N.J.: Humanities Press, 1991 [1995].

Frascati-Lochhead, Marta. *Kenosis and Feminist Theology: The Challenge of Gianni Vattimo*. Albany: State University of New York Press, 1998.

Glazebrook, Patricia. "From *Physis* to Nature, *Techne* to Technology: Heidegger on Aristotle, Galileo, and Newton." *Southern Journal of Philosophy* 38 (Spring 2000): 95–118.

———. "Heidegger and Experiment." *Philosophy Today* 42 (Fall 1998): 250–61.

———. *Heidegger's Philosophy of Science*. Perspectives in Continental Philosophy, no. 12. New York: Fordham University Press, 2000.

Gosetti, Jennifer Anna. "Language and Subject in Heidegger and Kristeva." *Philosophy Today* 43, supplement (1999): 76–87.

Graybeal, Jean. *Language and "The Feminine" in Nietzsche and Heidegger*. Bloomington: Indiana University Press, 1990.

Griffin, Susan. *Woman and Nature: The Roaring Inside Her*. New York: Harper, 1978.

Grosz, Elizabeth. "Irigaray and the Divine." In *Transfigurations: Theology and the French Feminists*, ed. C. W. Maggie Kim, Susan M. St. Ville, and Susan M. Simonaitis, 199–214. Minneapolis: Fortress Press, 1993. Originally published in *Transitions in Continental Philosophy*, ed. Arleen B. Dallery, Stephen H. Watson, and E. Marya Bower, 117–28. Albany: State University of New York Press, 1994.

Guignon, Charles, ed. *The Cambridge Companion to Heidegger*. Cambridge: Cambridge University Press, 1993.

Hatab, Lawrence. *Ethics and Finitude: Heideggerian Contributions to a Moral Philosophy*. Lanham, Md.: Rowman and Littlefield, 2000.

Hirschboeck, Paula. "Soul Making Women: A Philosophical Exploration of Imaginal Feminisms." Ph.D. diss., Union Institute, 1992.

Hodge, Joanna. "Forgetting: Europe, Tradition, Philosophy." *Journal of the British Society for Phenomenology* 26 (October 1995): 255–67.

———. "Heidegger, Early and Late: The Vanishing of the Subject Between Ambiguity and Duplicity." *Journal of the British Society for Phenomenology* 25 (October 1994): 288–301.

———. *Heidegger and Ethics*. London: Routledge, 1995.

———. "Heideggerian Temporalities: Genesis and Structure of a Thinking of Temporality." *Research in Phenomenology* 29 (1999): 119–40.

———. "Irigaray Reading Heidegger." In *Engaging with Irigaray*, ed. Carolyn Burke, Naomi Schor, and Margaret Whitford, 191–209.

———. "Nietzsche, Heidegger, and the Critique of Humanism." *Journal of the British Society for Phenomenology* 22 (January 1991): 75–79.

Hokka, Tuula Margareta. "Writing of the Soil, Smoke of the Sun: Perspectives on the Poetry of Eeva-Liisa Manner and Its Modernity" (in Finnish). Ph.D. diss., Helsingin Yliopisto, Finland, 1991.

Holland, Nancy J. "Derrida and Feminism." *APA Newsletter on Feminism and Philosophy* 91, no. 2 (1992): 40–43.

———. "Heidegger and Derrida Redux: A Close Reading." *Hermeneutics and Deconstruction*. Selected Studies in Phenomenology and Existential Philosophy 10, ed. Hugh J. Silverman and Don Ihde, 219–26. Albany: State University of New York Press, 1985.

———. *The Madwoman's Reason: The Concept of the Appropriate in Ethical Thought*. University Park: Penn State Press, 1998.

———. "Rethinking Ecology in the Western Philosophical Tradition: Heidegger and/on Aristotle." *Continental Philosophy Review* 32 (1999): 409–20.

———, ed. *Feminist Interpretations of Jacques Derrida*. University Park: Penn State Press, 1997.

Huntington, Patricia. "Between the Scylla of Discursivity and the Charybdis of Pantextualism." *Human Studies* 21 (April 1998): 197–206.

———. *Ecstatic Subjects, Utopia, and Recognition: Kristeva, Heidegger, Irigaray*. Albany: State University of New York Press, 1998.

———. "Fragmentation, Race, and Gender: Building Solidarity in the Postmodern Era." In *Existence in Black: An Anthology of Black Existential Philosophy*, ed. Lewis R. Gordon, 185–202. New York; Routledge, 1997.

———. "Heidegger Meets Bloch and Reich: A Heretical Material Phenomenology." *Philosophy and Social Criticism* 25 (July 1999): 103–9.

Irigaray, Luce. *Elemental Passions*. Translated by Joanne Collie and Judith Still. New York: Routledge, 1992.

———. *An Ethics of Sexual Difference*. Translated by Carolyn Burke and Gillian C. Gill. Ithaca: Cornell University Press, 1993.

———. *The Forgetting of Air in Martin Heidegger*. Translated by Mary Beth Mader. Austin: University of Texas Press, 1999.

———. *I Love To You: Sketches for a Felicity Within History*. Translated by Alison Martin. New York: Routledge, 1996.

———. *Marine Lover of Friedrich Nietzsche*. Translated by Gillian C. Gill. New York: Columbia University Press, 1991.

———. *Sexes and Genealogies*. Translated by Gillian C. Gill. New York: Columbia University Press, 1993.
———. *Speculum of the Other Woman*. Translated by Gillian C. Gill. Ithaca: Cornell University Press, 1985.
Jones, Steven E. "Disconnected Connection: The Road to Being a Black Man." Ph.D. diss., University of Maryland, College Park, 1996.
Kisiel, Theodore. *The Genesis of Heidegger's Being and Time*. Berkeley and Los Angeles: University of California Press, 1993.
Klawiter, Maren. "Using Arendt and Heidegger to Consider Feminist Thinking on Women and Reproductive/Infertility Technologies." *Hypatia: A Journal of Feminist Philosophy* 5, no. 3 (1990): 65–89.
Kolb, David. *The Critique of Pure Modernity: Hegel, Heidegger, and After*. Chicago: Chicago University Press, 1986.
Kompridis, Nikolas. "Heidegger's Challenge and the Future of Critical Theory." In *Habermas: A Critical Reader*, ed. Peter Dews, 118–50. Oxford: Blackwell, 1999.
Krell, David Farrell. *Lunar Voices: Of Tragedy, Poetry, Fiction, and Thought*. Chicago: University of Chicago Press, 1995.
———. "Spiriting Heidegger." In *Of Derrida, Heidegger, and Spirit*, ed. David Wood, 11–40. Evanston: Northwestern University Press, 1993.
Kristeva, Julia. *Desire in Language*. Edited by Leon S. Roudiez. Translated by Thomas Gora, Alice Jardine, and Leon S. Roudiez. New York: Columbia University Press, 1980.
———. *The Kristeva Reader*. Edited by Toril Moi. New York: Columbia University Press, 1986.
———. *Revolution in Poetic Language*. Translated by Margaret Waller. New York: Columbia University Press, 1984.
Lauterbach, Sarah Steen. "In Another World: A Phenomenological Perspective and Discovery of Meaning in Mothers' Experience of Death of a Wished-for Baby." Ph.D. diss., Columbia University's Teachers College, 1992.
Llewellyn, John. *The Middle Voice of Ecological Conscience*. New York: St. Martin's Press, 1991.
Lugones, María. "Playfulness, 'World'-traveling, and Loving Perception." *Hypatia: A Journal of Feminist Philosophy* 2, no. 2 (1987): 3–19.
Lugones, María C., and Elizabeth V. Spelman. "Have We Got a Theory for You! Feminist Theory, Cultural Imperialism, and the Demand for 'the Woman's Voice.' " *Women's Studies International Forum* 6, no. 6 (1983): 573–81. Reprinted in *Women and Values*, ed. Marilyn Pearsall. Belmont, Calif.: Wadsworth, 1993, 18–29.
McAfee, Noëlle. "Abject Strangers: Toward an Ethics of Respect." In *Ethics, Politics, and Difference in Julia Kristeva's Writing*, ed. Kelly Oliver, 116–34. New York: Routledge, 1993.
McCumber, John. *Metaphysics and Oppression: Heidegger's Challenge to Western Philosophy*. Bloomington: Indiana University Press, 1999.
McHugh, Patrick. "Culture and Masculinity: Critical Impasses in Twentieth-Century Social Narrative and Discourse." Ph.D. diss., State University of New York at Binghamton, 1988.
McWhorter, Ladelle, ed. *Heidegger and the Earth: Essays in Environmental Philosophy*. Kirksville: Thomas Jefferson University Press, 1992.

Martinez, Roy. "Existential *Angst* and Ethnic Cleansing." *Soundings: An Interdisciplinary Journal* 77 (Spring/Summer 1994): 201–10.

Marx, Werner. *Is There a Measure on Earth? Foundations for a Nonmetaphysical Ethics.* Translated by Thomas J. Nenon and Reginald Lilly. Chicago: University of Chicago Press, 1987.

Mortensen, Ellen. *The Feminine and Nihilism: Luce Irigaray with Nietzsche and Heidegger.* Oslo: Scandinavian University Press, 1994.

———. "Woman's (Un)Truth and *le féminin*: Reading Luce Irigaray with Friedrich Nietzsche and Martin Heidegger." In *Engaging with Irigaray*, ed. Carolyn Burke, Naomi Schor, and Margaret Whitford, 211–28.

Mullen, Amy. "Purity and Pollution: Resisting the Rehabilitation of a Virtue." *Journal of the History of Ideas* 57 (July 1996): 509–24.

Nagel, Mechthild. "Play in Culture and the Jargon of Primordiality: A Critique of *Homo Ludens*." In *Diversions and Divergences in Fields of Play*, ed. Margaret Carlisle Duncan, Garry Chick, and Alan Aycock, 19–29. Play and Culture Studies, ed. Stuart Reifel, vol. 1. Greenwich, Conn.: Ablex, 1998.

Odell-Scott, David W. *A Post-Patriarchal Christology.* Atlanta, Ga.: Scholars Press, 1991.

Okhamafe, E. Imafedia. "Heidegger's *Nietzsche* and Nietzsche's Play: The Question of Wo(man), Christianity, and Humanism." *Soundings: An Interdisciplinary Journal* 71, no. 4 (Winter 1988): 533–53.

Oliver, Kelly. "Nietzsche's Woman: The Poststructuralist Attempt to Do Away with Women." *Radical Philosophy* 48 (Spring 1988): 25–29.

———. *Womanizing Nietzsche: Philosophy's Relation to the "Feminine."* New York: Routledge, 1995.

Olkowski, Dorothea. "If the Shoe Fits: Derrida and the Orientation of Thought." In *Hermeneutics and Deconstruction.* Selected Studies in Phenomenology and Existential Philosophy 10, ed. Hugh J. Silverman and Don Ihde, 262–69. Albany: State University of New York Press, 1985.

Pearsall, Marilyn, ed. *Women and Values: Readings in Recent Feminist Philosophy.* Belmont, Calif.: Wadsworth, 1993.

Pepper, Susan Elizabeth. "Women and Narrative: Reinterpreting the Tradition." M.A. diss., University of Calgary, 1993.

Petro, Patrice. *Joyless Streets: Women and Melodramatic Representation in Weimar Germany.* Princeton: Princeton University Press, 1989.

Ramsey, Eric Ramsey. *The Long Path to Nearness: A Contribution to a Corporeal Philosophy of Communication and the Groundwork for an Ethics of Relief.* Atlantic Highlands, N.J.: Humanities Press, 1998.

———. "Suffering Wonder: Wooing and Courting in the Public Sphere." *Communication Theory* 8 (November 1998): 455–75.

Richardson, William J. *Heidegger: Through Phenomenology to Thought.* The Hague: Martinus Nijoff, 1963.

Rodemeyer, Lanei. "Dasein Gets Pregnant." *Philosophy Today* 42, supplement (1998): 76–84.

Sallis, John, ed. *Reading Heidegger: Commemorations.* Bloomington: Indiana University Press, 1993.

Schrag, Calvin O. *Communicative Praxis and the Space of Subjectivity.* Bloomington: Indiana University Press, 1989.

———. *The Self After Postmodernity.* New Haven, Conn.: Yale University Press, 1997.

Schürmann, Reiner. "Heidegger and Meister Eckhart on Releasement." *Research in Phenomenology* 3 (1973): 95–119.
Serequeberhan, Tsenay. *The Hermenuetics of African Philosophy: Horizon and Discourse.* New York: Routledge, 1994.
Sheehan, Thomas. "Heidegger." In *A Companion to the Philosophers.* Blackwell Companions to Philosophy 12, ed. Robert L. Arrington, 288–97. Malden, Mass.: Blackwell, 1998.
———. "Martin Heidegger." In *The Routledge Encyclopedia of Philosophy*, ed. Edward Craig, 307–23. New York: Routledge, 1998.
Shepardson, Charles. " 'Adequatio Sexualis': Is There a Measure of Sexual Difference?" In *From Phenomenology to Thought, Errancy, and Desire*, ed. Babette E. Babich, 445–71. Dordrecht: Kluwer, 1995.
Sikka, Sonia. *Forms of Transcendence: Heidegger and Medieval Mystical Theology.* Albany: NY: State University of New York Press, 1997.
———. "The Philosophical Bases of Heidegger's Politics: A Response to Wolin." *Journal of the British Society for Phenomenology* 25 (October 1994): 241–62.
———. "Questioning the Sacred: Heidegger and Levinas on the Locus of Divinity." *Modern Theology* 14 (July 1998): 299–323.
Staskowski, Andrea C. "Conversations with Experience: Feminist Hermeneutics and the Films of West German Women." Ph.D. diss., University of Iowa, 1990.
Stenstad, Gail. "Anarchic Thinking: Breaking the Hold of Monotheistic Ideology on Feminist Philosophy." In *Women and Values*, ed. Marilyn Pearsall, 248–53.
———. "Attuning and Transformation." *Heidegger Studies* 7 (1991): 75–88.
———. "The Last God: A Reading." *Research in Phenomenology* 23 (1993): 172–84.
———. "Thinking What Is Strange." *Heidegger Studies* 10 (1994): 185–94.
———. "The Turning in *Ereignis* and Transformation of Thinking." *Heidegger Studies* 12 (1996): 83–94.
Thiele, Leslie Paul. *Timely Meditations: Heidegger and Postmodern Politics.* Princeton: Princeton University Press, 1995.
Tucker, Otto Bruce. "A Phenomenological Conversation: A Philosophical Insight into Consciousness, Competition, and Culture." Ph.D. diss., University of North Carolina at Greensboro, 1997.
White, Stephen K. "Heidegger and the Difficulties of a Postmodern Ethics and Politics." *Political Theory* 18 (February 1990): 80–103.
———. *Political Theory and Postmodernism.* Cambridge: Cambridge University Press, 1991.
Wood, David, ed. *Of Derrida, Heidegger, and Spirit.* Evanston: Northwestern University Press, 1993.
Wright, Kathleen. "Heidegger's Hölderlin and the Mo(u)rning of History." *Philosophy Today* 37 (Winter 1993): 423–35.
Young, Iris Marion. "House and Home: Feminist Variations on a Theme." In *Intersecting Voices: Dilemmas of Gender, Political Philosophy, and Policy*, 134–64. Princeton: Princeton University Press, 1997.
Ziarek, Krzyzstof. "Love and the Debasement of Being: Irigaray's Revisions of Heidegger and Lacan." *Postmodern Culture* 10, no. 1 (1999) (online).
———. "Proximities: Irigaray and Heidegger on Difference." *Continental Philosophy Review* 33 (2000): 133–58.
———. "Sexuate Experience: Irigaray and the Poetics of Sexual Difference." In *The*

Historicity of Experience: Modernity, the Avante-Garde, and the Event. Evanston: Northwestern University Press, 2001.

Zimmerman, Michael E. "Feminism, Deep Ecology, and Environmental Ethics." *Environmental Ethics* 9, no. 1 (1987): 21–49.

———. *Heidegger's Confrontation with Modernity: Technology, Politics, and Art.* Bloomington: Indiana University Press, 1990.

———. "Implications of Heidegger's Thought for Deep Ecology." *Modern Schoolman* 64 (1986): 19–43.

———. "Rethinking the Heidegger–Deep Ecology Relationship." *Environmental Ethics* 15 (Fall 1993): 195–224.

Index

"abject" literature, 218 n. 19
abyssal thinking: as anarchic feminist thinking, 344–49; Heidegger's concept of, 340–42
Adams, Carol, 223
adikia, Heidegger's discussion of, 189–90
Aesop, 192 n. 13
aidos, Heidegger's discussion of, 181–82, 193 n. 40
air metaphor, in Sappho's work, 173–75, 192 n. 18
aletheia, Heidegger's concept of, 24, 60, 155–58, 182–86
alterity: Derrida's concept of, 40 n. 37; Heidegger's discussion of, 209–13
Althusser, Louis, 83
"Anarchic Thinking: Breaking the Hold of Monotheistic Ideology on Feminist Philosophy," 40 n. 37
anarchic thinking, Stenstad's concept of, 40 n. 37, 344–49
Anaximander, 189–90, 193 n. 32, 195 n. 61
Andenken, Heidegger's concept of, 196
androcentrism, ecofeminism and, 229–30
Angst, Heidegger's concept of, 244–46
anthropocentrism: Heidegger's analysis of science and, 227–30; objectivity and, 234–40
antiethics, in Heidegger's work, 297–99
Antigone, Heidegger's interpretation of, 46, 150, 198, 209–16, 216 n. 2
Anzaldúa, Gloria, 119–22
Aphrodite (Greek goddess), 168–71, 176–90, 191 nn. 6–7, 194 n. 43
Apollonian aesthetic, play in context of, 290–91
apple metaphor, Heidegger's use of, 183–86, 194 n. 42

Arendt, Hannah: Heidegger and, 47; on human meaning of building, 286 n. 3; labor *vs*. work, concept of, 273; in Western canon, viii
Arisaka, Yoko, 41 n. 39
Aristotle: Heidegger and, 34, 47–48, 76–77, 150; *ousia* concept of, 101–2; philosophy of science and, 224–27, 241–46; on Sappho, 173; in Western canon, viii
Armour, Ellen, 16, 39 n. 35, 48, 316–32
asexuality, in Dasein, 57, 59–61
attunement: *Auseinandersetzung* and, 343–44; Event of Appropriation, Heidegger's concept of, 362–67; Heidegger's concept of, 10–12, 20–21; play theory and, 291–92
"Attuning and Transformation," 12
Augenblick, Marxist ideology and, 86–87
Augustine (Saint): Derrida's discussion of, 151–52, 158, 163 n. 10; Heidegger's discussion of, 46, 149–63
Auseinandersetzung: feminist theory and, 342–44; Heidegger's concept of, 49, 338–42
Austen, Jane, 136, 279
aute, concept of, in Sappho's work, 190
authenticity: ambiguity of play, 299–302; Beauvoir's discussion of, 138–39; in *Being and Time*, 11, 33–36, 44–45; conflictual culture and, 116–22; Dasein and, 91–95; ethics of, 297–99; Heidegger's concept of, 40 n. 37, 126 n. 5; oppression and, 122–26; psychotherapy and, 109–16, 126 n. 4; they-self concept and, 133–34
"Authenticity, Moral Values, and Psychotherapy," 109–10

Baier, Annette, 49, 347
Bartky, Sandra Lee: early assessment of Heideg-

ger by, 3–5, 7–9, 11; mood/attunement discussed by, 10–12, 14
Basic Problems of Phenomenology, The, 80–81, 244
Beauvoir, Simone de, 75; on biology and psychology, 130; ecofeminism and, 222–24, 247–48; Freud and, 139–41; on gender division of labor, 108 n. 9; Heidegger and, 45, 47; house and home discussed by, 253–54; on housework, 267–69; on preservation and futurity, 272–77; on scripts for women, 131; they-self concept and, 136–39; in Western canon, viii; on women's temporality, 99
Befindlichkeit, Heidegger's concept of, 291–93
Begriff: agonistic play and, 293; Heidegger's concept of, 80–81, 184
Being: as *Kampf*, 159–60; radical transformation of, 338–42; representation of, 356–59; Sappho's work and concept of, 184–86
Being and Nothingness, 110
Being and Time: authenticity/inauthenticity in, 11, 33–36, 44–45; bodily dimension in, 40 n. 38; *Dichten* in, 296–97; ecofeminist theory and, 246; fate and destiny in, 236–40; gender discussed in, 43–44, 233–34; key concepts in, 3, 9–11; mortality in, 95–98; play discussed in, 290–304; self-realization in, 23–28, 30, 80–83, 216 n. 2; structure of care in, 102–7, 149; they-self concept in, 131–36, 141–44; uncanniness discussed in, 244–46; Wittgenstein's work and, 110. See also *Sein und Zeit*
Beiträge, 238–39, 335–36
Benhabib, Seyla, 288 n. 36
Bentley, Richard, 226
Berkeley School, 45, 110–12, 126 n. 2
Berne, Eric, 128–31, 139, 143, 144 n. 1
Berry, Philippa, 40 n. 35
Bérubé, Michael, on Western canon, viii
Besinnung, Heidegger's concept of, 243–46
Biehl, Janet, 229, 234, 247
Bigwood, Carol, 5–6, 10, 12–15, 18, 20, 22, 39 n. 28, 374 n. 2; on eastern thought in Heidegger, 48; on Sappho and Heidegger, 46, 165–90
Binswanger, Ludwig, 109, 114
Black Nationalism, 124–25, 126 n. 15
"Black Women in Academia: A Statement from the Periphery," 125
Blatner, William, 126 n. 2

blindness, Derrida's discussion of, 154–58
Boddington, Paula Ruth, 232
bodies: gender neutrality of Dasein and, 141–44; in Heidegger's work, 74–83, 192 n. 15, 217 n. 17
Bodies of Women: Ethics, Embodiment, and Sexual Difference, The, 40 n. 37
Böhlendorff letter, 213, 218 n. 23
Borderlands/La Frontera, 119–21
Bordieu, Pierre, 123
Boss, Medard, 109, 114
Bostic, Heidi, 48, 309–15
Bowles, Brian, 40 n. 38
Brandon, Robert, 126 n. 2
breath imagery: Irigaray's use of, 310–15; of Sappho, 174–75, 193 n. 25
Buege, Douglas, 223
building (construction), Heidegger on duality of, 255–57, 286 n. 2
Bultmann, Rudolf, 316
"Burning Glass: Paradoxes of Feminist Revelation in *Speculum*," 40 n. 35
Butler, Judith, 303

Caldwell, Anne, 40 n. 37
Callicot, Baird, 238
capitalism, Dasein and, 83–88
Caputo, John, 15, 37 n. 6, 38 n. 12, 39 n. 28, 46, 149–63, 305 n. 14
care ethics: authenticity in Heidegger and, 297–99; ecofeminism and, 235–40; feminist interpretation of Heidegger and, 88–90; Heidegger's structure of care, 102–7, 149–63; play theory and, 302–4
Carty, Linda, 125
Casey, Edward, 270–71, 286 n. 2
Catholicism, assimilation of Native Americans through, 118–19
Chanter, Tina, 16, 44–45, 73–107, 332 n. 3
Cheney, Jim, 223, 229–30, 235–36
"Choreographies," 157
Christianity: Heidegger on woman and, 37 n. 7; Heidegger's Christian soldier motif, 152–53, 159
Cimitile, Maria Christine, 40 n. 38
Circumfession, 46, 151–52, 156–58, 163 n. 10
Cixous, Hélène: on feminist writing, 235; on Heidegger, 37 n. 8
class structure: conflictual culture and, 121–22;

Index   391

home in context of, 278–82; in Western canon, vii–ix
Code, Lorraine, 49, 223, 347–49
Coleridge, Samuel Taylor, 235
Collins, Patricia Hill, 124–25, 126 n. 15
communicative ethics: Heidegger and, 20; scripts of they-self and, 131–44
Confessions of Augustine, 150–63
conflictual culture: assimilation of Native Americans and, 117–19; authenticity and, 116–26; borderland as metaphor of, 119–21; Dasein (human being) in context of, 44–45, 109–26; Marxism and, 121–22; oppressive social structures and, 116–22
constancy, Dasein and, 108 n. 11
"Conversations with Experience: Feminist Hermeneutics and the Films of West German Women," 37 n. 7
Corbin, Henri, 62
Cornell, Drucilla, 17, 159
Coyote (folk figure), play theory and, 303–4, 306 n. 28
creativity, Heidegger's legacy for feminists and, 361–67
Cuomo, Chris, 223
Curtin, Deane, 223

Dallmayer, Fred, 160
Daly, Mary, 345
"Dasein Gets Pregnant," 40 n. 37
Dasein (human being): attunement and, 11, 13–14; authenticity/inauthenticity in, 91–95, 297–99; Black Nationalism and, 124–26; care ethics and, 89–90; "conflictual culture" and, 44–45; *das Man* and, 110–22; death and, 95–98, 156–58; in Derrida's *Geschlect* essay, 54–72; ecofeminism and, 14–15, 231–34; fore-structure of, 294–97; gender neutrality of, 3, 6–7, 27–28, 37 n. 7, 38 n. 12, 44, 57–72, 141–44, 231–40; Heidegger's concept of, 1; history and temporality in, 98–107; inauthentic form, conflictual culture and, 118–19; Marxist labor theory and, 83–88; meditative thinking and, 28–36; militarism of, 159–61; ontological "being" and, 76–83; oppression and authenticity and, 123–26; play in context of, 290–91; projection as understanding and, 291–92; psychotherapy and, 109–10; self-understanding and, 23–28, 42 n. 43; structure of care and, 102–7, 150–69; they-self concept, 131–44; throwness concept and, 300–302; transactional analysis and, 130–31; uncanniness of, 210–13; "who" of, 91–95; world in context of, 90–91
das Man: authenticity and oppression in, 123–26; conflictual culture and, 118–22; Heidegger's concept of, 110–12, 115–16; they-self concept and, 131–44
death: Dasein and, 95–98, 156–58; language and, Derrida's discussion of, 143–44
d'Eaubonne, Francois, 222
Deconstruction, Feminist Theology, and the Problem of Difference: Subverting the Race/Gender Divide, 39 n. 35
deconstructionism, feminist theory and, 8–9, 38 n. 12
deep ecology, ecofeminism and, 228–30, 235–40
Deifelt, Wanda, 37 n. 7
de Lauretis, Teresa, 254, 278, 280–82
demoralization disorders, inauthenticity and concept of, 116
Demythologizing Heidegger, 37 n. 6, 38 n. 28
Denken (thought), Heidegger's concept of, 31, 243–46, 296–97, 374 n. 7
Derrida, Georgette Safar, 156–58
Derrida, Jacques: alterity discussed by, 40 n. 37; Anglophone reception of, 6; blindness discussed by, 154–58; "Circum-fession" of, 46, 151–52, 156–58; *Geschlecht* essays, 53–72; Heidegger and, 6–7, 14, 36 n. 2, 37 n. 7, 38 n. 12, 43–44, 50 n. 1, 75, 165, 191 n. 2, 197, 213–14, 217 n. 9; Irigaray and, 16, 40 n. 35; religion and difference in Heidegger and, 14, 323–30, 333 n. 12; on Sappho, 173, 193 n. 24; on sexual difference, 45, 47, 141–44, 322–23; on social insights in Heidegger, 374 n. 2; "weeping women" discussion of, 154–58, 163 n. 10; in Western canon, viii
"Der Zeitbegriff in der Geschichtswissenschaft," 226
Descartes, René: Heidegger and, 44, 47–48, 76–80, 90, 92, 226, 237; play theory and, 290–91; in Western canon, viii
desire, Sappho's discussion of, 183–86
Despres, Carole, 287 n. 12
"determinism/responsibility" problem, 140–41
deute, concept of, in Sappho's work, 189–90
Devall, Bill, 228
de Volterra, Daniele, 154, 157–58

"Dialogue on Language, A," 180–82, 216 n. 2
Diamond, Irene, 223
Dichten, Heidegger's concept of, 296–97
Die Frage nach dem Ding, 225–26, 237–38
difference feminism, Heidegger and, 37 n. 7
Dionysus: philosophers' discussion of, 177; play in context of, 290–91
Diprose, Rosalyn, 40 n. 37
disclosure, Heidegger's notion of, 24
"Disconnected Connection: The Road to Being a Black Man," 41 n. 38
Discourse on Thinking, 30, 245
dispersion, neutrality of Dasein and, 65–72
"Divine Women," 318–19
Doricha (slave woman), 170, 192 n. 13
Dreyfus, Hubert, 45, 110–11, 126 nn. 2, 10
duBois, Page, 35, 193 nn. 33
Du Bois, W. E. B., 230–34, 235, 236
dwelling. *See also* home (*Heimat*): feminist concept of, 269–72; Heidegger's concept of, 254–57, 286 n. 2

Earth Muse: Feminism, Nature, and Art, 5, 13–15, 18
Ecce Homo, 155
ecofeminist theory: androcentrism and, 228–30; anthropocentrism and objectivity in, 234–40; gender neutrality and, 230–34; Heidegger and, 14, 20, 41 n. 39, 47–49, 160–61, 221–48, 351–52, 374 n. 2
economic policy, feminist rejection of home and, 288 n. 21
Ecstatic Subjects, Utopia, and Recognition: Kristeva, Heidegger, and Irigaray, 5, 15–16, 352, 355–56, 358–59
ego, 129, 139; Heidegger's poetics and, 208–9
Elam, Diane, 7–8
Elliot, Terri, 40 n. 37
Engaging with Irigaray, 17, 39 n. 31, 40 n. 35
Enlightenment philosophy, care ethics and, 88–90
"Envelope: A Reading of Spinoza, *Ethics*, 'Of God,' " 319–23
equanimity, Heidegger's concept of, 12
ereignis, Heidegger's concept of, 207, 210–13
Eros, Sappho's work in, 177–78, 193 n. 29
Eros the Bittersweet, 193 n. 24
Erstreckung, Dasein and, 66–72
ethics: of authenticity, 297–99; Heidegger and, 33–36, 40 n. 37, 47–49; poetics and, 296–302

Ethics of Eros: Irigaray's Rewriting of the Philosophers, 16
Ethics of Sexual Difference, An, 8, 317–23
ethos, ethics and, 40 n. 37
Event of Appropriation, Heidegger's concept of, 361–67
"Existential Angst and Ethnic Cleansing," 41 n. 38
existentialia, Dasein and, 81–82, 102
existentialism: home and housework in context of, 267–69; they-self concept and, 133–34, 138–41

"Fairy Tales for Politics: The Other, Once More," 40 n. 37
falsification, truth and, 353–56
Feenberg, Andrew, 374 n. 2
femininity: Heidegger's concept of, 19–20, 45; Western canon definition of, vii–ix
Femininity and Domination, 5, 9
Feminism and Nihilism: Luce Irigary with Nietzsche and Heidegger, 5, 15–16
feminist theology, Heidegger and, 18–19, 22, 39 n. 35
feminist theory: anarchic feminist thinking, 344–49; Augustine as interpreted by Heidegger and, 159–63; *Auseinandersetzung*, 342–44; dwelling motif in, 254–57; ecofeminism and, 221–48; embodiment metaphor and, 74–83; Heidegger as source for, debate concerning, 4–5, 21–22, 33–36, 43–49; Heidegger's work and, history of commentary, 2–36; house and home in context of, 252–86; late twentieth-century shifts in, 6–36; legacy of Heidegger and, 351–74; Marxism and, 86–88; play ethics and, 302–4; poetic language and, 197–98, 217 n. 5; positive assessments of Heidegger in, 5–7; radical transformation, 335–49; rejection of home in, 277–82; spirituality and, 10–11; they-self concept, 131–44; Western canon critiqued by, vii–ix
feminist transformation theory, 140–41
Ferguson, Ann, 140–41
finitude, Heidegger's work in, 23–28
Fink, Eugen, 192 n. 15, 290
Finn, Geraldine, 232
Flax, Janet, 232
fore-conception (*Vorgriff*), Heidegger's concept of, 292–97

forest clearing metaphor, Heidegger's use of, 240–46
forgetfulness, Heidegger's concept of, 297–99
Forgetting of Air, The, 309–15, 318–23, 327–30
Forms of Transcendence: Heidegger and Medieval Theology, 18
Foucault, Michel: misogyny in work of, 193 n. 35; in Western canon, 75, viii
Frascati-Lochhead, Marta, 5, 18–19, 21–22
freethinking, legacy of Heidegger and, 371–74, 375 n. 21
Freiburg lectures (Heidegger), Saint Augustine discussed in, 46, 149–63
French intellectuals, Heidegger and, 9, 38 n. 16, 75
Freud, Sigmund, 8, 128–31, 135–36, 139–41; eros concept of, 177–78; language theory and, 205
Friedrich, Paul, 191 n. 6
Fürsorge, 56, 91, 306 n. 26
futurity, Beauvoir on preservation and, 272–73

Gadamer, Hans-Georg: concept of authenticity, 114; hermeneutics of, 305 n. 8; play concept of, 47–48, 289–90, 304 n. 2, 305 n. 3
Galileo, 226, 238
games: authenticity and, 289–304; in transactional analysis, 129–30
Games People Play, 144 n. 1
Geist, Heidegger's concept of, 48, 316–32, 333 n. 12
Gelassenheit, Heidegger's concept of, 160–61, 198–209, 214–16, 217 n. 14, 245, 358–59
gender: bias of, in Western canon, viii–ix; ecofeminism and neutrality in, 230–40; Heidegger's contribution to study of, 3, 5–6, 19–21, 37 n. 7, 45–49; home in context of, 257–60; neutrality, in Dasein, 3, 6–7, 27–28, 37 n. 7, 38 n. 12, 44, 57–72; race and, 39 n. 35; technology and, 41 n. 39
Genet, Jean, 235
Germania, Heidegger's discussion of, 198–202
Gesamtaugabe, 49, 149, 335
Geschlecht essays, 6–7, 36 n. 2, 37 n. 7, 43–44, 50 n. 1, 322–30, 333 n. 12
Gestell, Heidegger's concept of, 31–32, 34–36, 187–90, 225–27, 239–40
Geworfenheit, Heidegger's concept of, 203–9, 214–16, 292
Glazebrook, Trish, 20, 47, 221–48, 374 n. 2

Gosetti, Jennifer Anna, 40 n. 37, 46, 196–216
Goux, Jean-Joseph, 17
Graybeal, Jean, 5–6, 10, 12, 37 n. 7; assessment of Heidegger by, 12–14
Greek philosophers: Asian influence on, 178, 193 nn. 32–33; blindness as metaphor for, 154–55; ecofeminism and Heidegger's view of, 241; Heidegger's discussion of, 31–36, 42 n. 44, 45, 152–53, 166–70, 178–86 193 n. 32; scientific discourse and, 224–27
Green, Judith, 236
Griffin, Susan, 49, 223, 345–46
Guignon, Charles, 44, 109–16; authenticity and oppression and, 123–26; conflictual culture and, 116–22

Haar, Michel, 217 n. 12
Habermas, Jürgen, 20; on Heidegger's pseudoconcreteness, 37 n. 6
Hale, Janet Campbell, 117–19
Hall, Harrison, 126 n. 2
Hallert, Judith P., 195 n. 58
Harlow, Elizabeth, 236
Hartmann, Heidi, 86
Hartsock, Nancy, 40 n. 37
Haugeland, John, 126 n. 2
Hayden, Delores, 287 n. 12
Hebel, Johann Peter, 203
Hegel, G. W. F.: on sexual difference, 54; in Western canon, viii
Heidegger, Martin. *See also* specific concepts and works: anthology feminist interpretation of, 1–36, 41 n. 41; Augustine and, 150–69; *das Man* concept of, 110–22; Derrida's *Geschlecht* essays, 53–72; dwelling concept of, 252–86; early-late divison in work of, 29, 42 n. 45; ecofeminism and, 221–48; embodiment metaphor, 74–83; feminist theory and legacy of, 351–74; *Geist* concept of, 316–32; Marx and, 83–88; philosophical contributions of, 351–52, 374 n. 1; play and authenticity in work of, 289–304; poetics and, 196–216; psychoanalytic theory and, 128–44; Sappho and, 165–90; as source for feminist theory, 5–36, 37 n. 7, 43–49; structure of care and, 102–7
Heidegger: Through Phenomenology to Thought, 42 n. 45
"Heidegger and Derrida Redux," 7
"Heidegger and the Difficulties of a Postmodern Ethics and Politics,' 20

Heidegger and the Problem of Knowledge, 110
"Heidegger's Hölderlin and the Mo(u)rning of History," 39 n. 28, 40 n. 37
"Heidegger's *Nietzsche* and Nietezsche's Play: The Question of Wo(man), Christianity, and Humanism," 37 n. 7
Heidegger's Philosophy of Science, 20
"Heidegger's Retrieval of Aristotelian [παθος]: On the Place of 'the Bodily' in Heidegger's Thought," 40 n. 38
Heraclitus, 193 n. 32
hermeneutics: feminist theory and, 7; Gadamer's concept of, 305 n. 8; play theory and, 290; *Spielraum* and, 294–96
Hermeneutics of African Philosophy: Horizon and Discourse, The, 41 n. 38
heroism, Dasein and authenticity of, 122
Historicity of Experience: Modernity, the Avant-Garde and the Event, 16
history (historicity; historicality): authenticity and, 113–16; conflictual culture and, 122, 126 n. 12; as destiny, Heidegger's discussion of, 199–202; *Geschehen* concept, 101–2, 108 n. 14; Heidegger's categorization of, 333–42; home metaphor and feminist theory of, 267–77; language theory and, 206–9; law of encounter and, 213; Marxism and materialist concept of, 86–88; preservation ethics and, 274–77; radical transformation and, 336–42; temporality and, 98–107
Hodge, Joanna, 16, 39 n. 31, 296–99, 305 n. 19
Hokka, Tuula Margareta, 37 n. 7
Hölderlin, Friedrich, Heidegger's discussion of, 198–216, 216 n. 2, 218 n. 23
"Hölderlin's Hymn, 'The Ister,'" 46, 203–9, 216 n. 2
Hölderlin's Hymnen "Germanien" und "Der Rhein," 198–202
Holland, Glen A., 144 n. 1
Holland, Nancy, 3, 40 n. 37, 43–49, 128–44; ecofeminism in work of, 20; on Heidegger, 7–8, 38 n. 12
Holocaust: Heidegger's comments on, 162, 304; preservation ethics and, 275–77
home *(Heimat)*: commodification of, 260–63; as critical value, 282–86; feminist theory and concepts of, 252–86; Heidegger's concept of, 47, 161–62, 244–46; rejection of, by feminists, 277–82; woman as nostalgic home, 257–60

homemaking: feminist concept of, 269–72; preservation and, 272–77
Homer, Heidegger and, 177–78
Honig, Bonnie, 254, 278–82
hooks, bell, 278, 281–82
horizons, Heidegger's discussion of, 359, 375 n. 14
Horkheimer, Max, 223
"House and Home: Feminist Variations on a Theme," 40 n. 37
Housekeeping (film), 267
housework, Beauvoir's discussion of, 267–69
human mortality, Heidegger's work on, 1
Hume, David, in Western canon, viii
Huntington, Patricia, 1–36, 43, 49, 305 nn. 14–15, 351–74
Husserl, Edmund: language theory and, 205–9; phenomenology of, 202; on sexual difference, 54, 69

identity politics: authenticity and oppression in, 124–26; commodification of home and, 260–63; homemaking in context of, 270–72
immanence: home and housework in context of, 267–69; transcendence and, 272–73, 321–23
immediacy, Heidegger's concept of, 171–73
individuation, philosophy of home and, 284
intellectuals: Heidegger's legacy for, 352–74; unease of, 359–61
interpretation, Heidegger's concept of, 292–93
Introduction to Metaphysics, 198–202, 241
Irigaray, Luce: anarchic feminist thinking and, 345; Anglophone reception of, 6, 15; ecofeminism and, 235; on Heidegger, 8–9, 15–17, 22, 36 n. 2, 40 n. 35, 46–47, 309–15; house and home discussed by, 253–54, 256–60, 278, 281; *mythos* concept discussed by, 17–18; originary thinking of, 9, 38 n. 15; religion in Heidegger and, 48, 317–23, 325–26, 330–32; Sappho and, 173–75; on sexual difference, 9, 17–18, 20–22, 45, 170, 317–23; on violence and sexism, 159
"Irigaray Reading Heidegger," 16, 39 n. 31
"Is Feminism the Saving Grace of Hermeneutics?," 7

Jaggar, Alison, 20
Jones, Steven E., 41 n. 38
Joyless Streets: Women and Melodramatic Representation in Weimar Germany, 37 n. 7

Jünger, Ernst, 159

Kampf, Heidegger's concept of, 159–60
Kant, Immanuel: Heidegger and, 80; "play" tradition and, 290; on sexual difference, 54; in Western canon, viii
Keller, Helen, 122
Kenosis and Feminist Theology: The Challenge of Gianni Vattimo, 5, 18–19
Kermode, Frank, 114
Kierkegaard, Soren, Heidegger and, 40 n. 37, 110–11, 152, 358, 373–74, 375 n. 21
King, Martin Luther, 122
Kisiel, Theodore, 149
Kittay, Eva Feder, 232
Klawiter, Maren, 37 n. 7
Kompridis, Nicholas, 20
Krell, David Farrell, 170, 333 n. 12
Kristeva, Julia: Heidegger and, 13, 19, 45–46; on language, 202–9, 210–16, 218 n. 19; Platonic chora of, 98–99; on poetics, 197–98, 201–2, 217 n. 5; semiotics of, 202–9, 361–62

labor: Beauvoir on housework as, 267–69; Dasein and, 84–88; gender divisions of, 108 n. 9, 288 n. 22
Lacan, Jacques, 75; Irigaray and, 8; language theory and, 205
Lahar, Stephanie, 223
Lakatos, Imré, 223
language: feminist interpretation of Heidegger and, 357–59, 375 n. 12; Heidegger on poetics and, 197–202, 217 n. 9; phenomenological ontology of, 202–9; uncanniness of, 210–13; *Wesen* of being, meanings of, 337–38, 350 n. 2
Language and "The Feminine" in Nietzsche and Heidegger," 5, 12–13
"Language in the Poem: A Discussion on Georg Trakl's Poetic Work," 322
lanthanein, in Greek philosophy, 182–86
"Last God—A Reading, The," 12
laughter, Heidegger on philosophy and, 166–68, 191 n. 3
Lawrence, D. H., 129
legein, Heidegger's concept of, 184, 194 n. 49
Leland, Dorothy, 44–45, 109–26
Lesbos, in Sappho's work, 178, 187–88, 193 n. 34
lethe, Heidegger's concept of, 24, 155–58
"Letter on Humanism," 161, 244

Levinas, Emmanuel, 48, 97, 107 n. 4, 108 n. 17
liberalism, authenticity and, 114
liberation, Heidegger as source for, debate concerning, 4–5, 369–74
Lincoln, Abraham, 122
Llewellyn, John, 20, 221
Locke, John, in Western canon, viii
logos, Heidegger's concept of, 18, 174–78, 184–86, 310–15
Long Path to Nearness: A Contribution to a Corporeal Philosophy of Communication and the Ground work for an Ethics of Relief, The, 20
Lugones, María, 48–49, 234, 304 n. 3
Luther, Martin, 152–53
lyric imagery, of Sappho, 173–75, 192 n. 20

Madwoman's Reason: The Concept of the Appropriate in Ethical Thought, The, 40 n. 37
"Making Strange What Had Appeared Familiar," 40 n. 3
Malcolm X, 122, 126 n. 12
Malinowski, Bronislaw, 130–31
Mansfield Park, 279
Marburg lectures (Heidegger), gender neutrality of Dasein in, 44, 56–57, 68–72
Marcuse, Herbert, 374 n. 2
marginal practices, conflictual culture and assimilation of, 118–19, 126 n. 10
Marion, Jean Luc, 374 n. 2
Martin, Biddy, 254, 278, 280–82
Martinez, Roy, 41 n. 38
Marx, Karl: Heidegger and, 83–88; in Western canon, viii
Marxism, conflictual culture and, 121–22
masculinity, of poets, assumption of, 197, 216 n. 4
McAfee, Noëlle, 40 n. 37
McNeill, Will, 240, 244–45
McWhorter, Ladelle, 41 n. 39
Meaning of Aphrodite, The, 191 n. 6
meditative (originative) thinking: Heidegger's concept of, 4, 11–12, 17, 28–36, 352–56, 368–74, 374 n. 2; Irigaray's concept of, 9
Memoirs of the Blind, 151–52, 154–55
memory, in Heidegger and Sappho's work, 186–90
Merchant, Carolyn, 224
Merleau-Ponty, Maurice, 75, 102 n. 4
Metaphysical Foundations of Logic, 27–28, 231–34

metaphysics, Heidegger's work as departure from, 28–36
militarism, in Heidegger's work, 152–53, 159–60
Mill, John Stuart, viii, 108 n. 9
mineness *(Jemeinigkeit)*, Dasein and, 92–95, 108 n. 10
Mitsein: care ethics and, 89–90; neutrality of Dasein and, 68–72
Mohanty, Chandra, 254, 278, 280–82
Monica, Heidegger's omission of, from analysis of Augustine, 150–69
mood: Bartky's discussion of, 10–11; Heidegger's concept of *(Gestimmtheit)*, 10–11
morality: authenticity and, 116, 126 n. 6; Beauvoir on sexism in, 137–39
Mortensen, Ellen, 5, 15–16, 332 n. 3
motherhood, Dasein and, 100–101
Mother Teresa, 122
mother tongue, Heidegger's concept of, 203–9
Mullen, Amy, 40 n. 37
Muses, Heidegger's discussion of, 186–90, 194 n. 55
mythos: Heidegger's concept of, 17–18, 371–74; logos and, Sappho's link between, 175–78, 184–86

Naess, Arne, 228–30, 238
Nagel, Mechthild, 47–48, 289–304
naming, Heidegger's concept of, 357–59, 375 n. 13
nationalism, philosophy of home and, 283–86
National Socialism, Heidegger's involvement with, 15, 126 n. 8, 160, 218 n. 21, 221, 323–26
Native Americans: conflictual culture and oppression of, 117–22; ecofeminism and, 223
nature, Heidegger's discussion of, 224–25, 241–46, 311–15
nearness, in Heidegger and Sappho's work, 184–86
necessity, Heidegger's discussion of, 166–67
Neoplatonism, Heidegger's discussion of, 152–53
New Testament, Heidegger's discussion of, 152–53
Newton, Isaac, 225–27
Nietzsche, Friedrich: blindness metaphor and, 155; ecofeminism and Heidegger's discussion of, 242–46; Heidegger's interpretation of, 32, 34, 37 n. 7, 48–49, 192 n. 15, 375 n. 21; on love and time, 190, 195 n. 62; "play" tradition and, 290; on sexual difference, 54; sexuality in work of, 177; transvaluation of values, 371; in Western canon, viii; will to power, Heidegger's analysis of, 159–60; Zarathustra myth and, 191 n. 8
"Nietzsche's Woman: The Poststructuralist Attempt to Do Away With Women, 38 n. 12
Nietzsche volumes, ecofeminism and, 241–46
nihilism, Heidegger and, 15
Norton, Bryan, 236
nostalgia: gender context of home and, 257–60; preservation and, 274–77
Notebooks of Malte Laurids Brigge, 244

objectivity, anthropocentrism and, 234–40
Odell-Scott, David W., 5–6, 10, 18–19, 22
Odyssey of a Native Daughter, 117–19
Oedipus myth: blindness and, 154; temporality and history and, 98–99; transactional analysis and, 129–30
Of Spirit: Heidegger and the Question, 48, 322–23, 330–3323, 333 n. 12
Okhamafe, E. Imafedia, 37 n. 7
Okrent, Mark, 126 n. 2
Oliver, Kelly, 38 n. 12, 157
O'Neill, R. V., 230
"On the Essence of Truth," 245
On the Way to Language, 46, 143, 207–9, 334–35
ontological being: Dasein and, 76–83; *Gelassenheit* and, 217 n. 14
oppression, authenticity and, 122–26
oral tradition, Sappho's work and, 174–75, 193 n. 24
originary thinking: Heidegger's concept of, 4, 11–12, 17, 28–36, 352–56, 368–74, 374 n. 7; Irigaray's concept of, 9
"Originative Thinking in the Later Philosophy of Heidegger," 4
"Origin of the Work of Art," 198–203, 245
Ortega y Gasset, José, 38 n. 17
Ortner, Sherry, 246
Other: death and Dasein and, 97–98; they-self concept and, 133–36
ousia, Heidegger's discussion of, 101

Paris, Ginette, 193 n. 28
Parmenides, 179, 183, 193 n. 32
patriarchy: anarchic feminist thinking and,

345–49; commodification of home and, 260–63
perception, Heidegger and theories of, 37 n. 7
Petro, Patrice, 37 n. 7
Phaedrus, 193 n. 24, 211–12
phallocentrism: Derrida's discussion of, 155–58; hermeneutics and, 7
phenomenology: in Heidegger's work, 30–36, 217 n. 14; of language, 202–9
Phenomenology of the Religious Life, 149–63
Philososphical Investigations, 110
Physics, 47, 224–27, 241–42
Pindar, 178
Plato: on Eros, 177–78; Heidegger's discussion of, 32, 34, 42 n. 44, 48, 152–53, 211–12; maternal chora, 98; mimesis critique of, 290; originary thinking and, 368; on philosophy, 166; on Sappho, 173; on sexual difference, 54; in Western canon, viii
Platons Lehre von der Wahrheit, 60
"Plato's *Pharmakon*," 193 n. 24
play: agonistic play, 291–96; ambiguity and inauthenticity and, 299–302; authenticity and, 289–304; feminist ethics of, 302–4; Heidegger's concept of, 47–48
Pluháček, Stephen, 48, 309–15
Plumwood, Val, 223
poeisis, Heidegger's discussion of, 187–90
poetics: ethics and, 296–302; feminine in, Heidegger's discussion of, 196–216; feminist theory and, 197–98, 217 n. 5; Heidegger's commentaries on, 32–36, 37 n. 7, 46, 162–63, 178, 186–90, 305 n. 14, 359–61; Irigaray's discussion of, 312–15; Kristeva's discussion of, 197; language and, 198–209; of Sappho's, 173–75
Pöggeler, Otto, 218 n. 21
Political Theory and Postmodernism, 20, 37 n. 7
politics: authenticity and oppression and, 124–26, 126 n. 14; feminist view of home and, 278–82; Heidegger's work in relation to, 1–2, 15–16, 20, 36 n. 1, 39 n. 31, 47–49, 218 n. 21, 351–52, 374 n. 2
postmodernism: Heidegger in context of, 9; truth and falsification and, 354–56
Post-Patriarchal Christology, A, 5, 10, 18
postphenomenology, feminist interpretations of Heidegger and, 7
poststructualism: Heidegger and, 14; Irigaray and, 9

power: language of poetics and, 199–202, 217 n. 12; sexuality and, in Dasein, 61–62
Powers of Horror, 218 n. 19
Pratt, Minnie Bruce, 278
Present Age, The, 111
preservation: Heidegger's concept of, 47; homemaking as, 272–77
privacy, philosophy of home and, 284–85, 288 n. 36
projection, agonistic play and, 291–96
"Proximities: Irigaray and Heidegger on Difference," 16
pseudoconcreteness debate, Heidegger's philosophy in context of, 4, 9–10, 14, 37 n. 6
psychoanalysis: authenticity and, 109–26; Berne's transactional analysis, 128–31; feminist theory and, 8–9; gender formation theories, 140–41; Heidegger's philosophy and, 44–45, 109–12
"Purity and Pollution: Resisting the Rehabilitation of a Virtue," 40 n. 37

"Question Concerning Technology, The," 225, 237, 334–35
"Questioning the Sacred: Heidegger and Levinas on the Locus of Divinity," 18
"Questions of Proximity: 'Woman's Place' in Derrida and Irigaray," 16

race: authenticity and oppression and, 124–26, 126 n. 14; conflictual culture concept and, 44–45; ecofeminism and, 230–34; gender and, 39 n. 35, 41 n. 38; home in context of, 278–82
radical freedom, legacy of Heidegger and, 368–74
Ramsey, Ramsey Eric, 20
rationality: ecofeminism and, 247–48; as male province, vii
ready-to-hand objectivity, Dasein and, 78–79, 102 n. 3
Rektoratsrede, 36 n. 1
relativism, anarchic feminist thinking and, 347–49
releasement, Heidegger's concept of, 30–31, 42 n. 46
religion: Derrida on Heidegger's concept of difference and, 323–26; feminist theory and, 37 n. 7; Heidegger's discussion of, 11–13, 48–49, 149–63; Irigaray on sexual difference and,

317–23; Native American conversion to Catholicism and, 118–19
repose, Heidegger's concept of, 12
Republic, 290, 368
res cogita, Dasein and, 77
res extensa, Dasein and, 76–77
Revolution in Poetic Language, 13, 197–98, 218 n. 19
Richardson, William J., 42 n. 45, 375 n. 12
Ricoeur, Paul, 113–14
Rodemeyer, Lanei, 40 n. 37
Room of One's Own, A, 230–34
Rousseau, Jean-Jacques, in Western canon, viii
Rubin, Gayle, 86
Ruddick, Sara, 287 n. 18
Ruether, Rosemary Radford, 222–23, 244–45

safety, philosophy of home and, 283–84
Said, Edward, 279
Salleh, Ariel Kay, 223, 229
Sappho: fragments of work of, 193 n. 26; Heidegger's poetics and, 46, 165–90
Sartre, Jean-Paul, 75, 102 n. 4, 110, 132
Schrag, Calvin, 20
scientific discourse: androcentrism and, 227–30; ecofeminism and, 224–27; language theory and, 206–9
scripts theory: Beauvoir's discussion of, 137–39; they-self concept and, 132–33, 140–41; in transactional analysis, 128–31
Second Sex, The, 131, 136–39
Seele, Heidegger's concept of, 324–30
Seinsfrage, Heidegger's concept of, 29
Seinsgeschichte, Heidegger's concept of, 31, 35
Seinsverlassenheit, Heidegger's concept of, 339–42, 350 n. 4
Sein und Zeit, 55–57, 59, 66, 68–72. See also *Being and Time*
self: ambiguity of play and, 300–302; authenticity and, 112–16; feminine abode of, 213–16; Greek concept of, 42 n. 44; Heidegger's concept of, 23–28, 77–83, 90–91, 196–98; uncanniness and, 209–13
semiotics, Kristeva's discussion of, 202–9, 361–62
Serequeberhan, Tsenay, 41 n. 38
Sessions, George, 228
Sexes and Genealogies, 8, 317–23
sexual difference: Derrida's concept of, 44, 53–72; Heidegger's concept of, 40 n. 37, 44–49, 53–72, 141–44; Irigaray's concept of, 9, 17–18, 20–21, 314–15, 317–23; religion and, in Heidegger's work, 323–26
sexuality, in Sappho's work, 176–78
shame, Bartky's discussion of, 10
"Shame and Gender," 5, 11–12, 14, 37 n. 7
Sheehan, Thomas, 42 n. 45
Shiva, Vandana, 223–24
Sikka, Sonya, 18
slavery: conflictual culture and, 121–22; origins of philosophy and, 166–71; preservation ethics and memory of, 275–77
Slicer, Deborah, 229
social structures: authenticity and oppression in, 116–22; Dasein and, 111–26
social theory, Heidegger and, 15–16, 20, 33–36, 351–52, 374 n. 2
Socrates, 150
somatophobia, 75, 102 n. 1
Sophocles, 178
spatiality, Dasein and, 66–72, 81–82
Speculum of the Other Woman, 9, 20–21, 235, 317
speech act theory, Dasein and, 63
Spielraum, Heidegger's concept of, 290–92, 294–96
Spelman, Elizabeth, 49
spirituality, in Heidegger's work, 10–12, 20–21, 38 n. 17, 48–49
standpoint epistemology, 40 n. 37
Staskowski, Andrea C., 37 n. 7
Steiner, Claude M., 143–44, 144 n. 1
Stenstad, Gail, 12, 40 n. 37, 41 n. 39, 43, 48–49, 334–49
Stone, 161
structuralism, language theory and, 205
subject-ism, Heidegger's Being and, 357–59, 375 n. 11
subjectivity: in Heidegger, feminist assessment of, 12–15, 196, 216 n. 2; religion and sexual difference and, 318–23
suprapolitical thought, Heidegger's work as, 2
surplus value, theory of, Dasein and, 84–85, 102 n. 6

techne, Heidegger's discussion of, 31–32, 225–27, 239–40, 359–61
temporality: death and Dasein and, 96–98; history and, in Dasein, 98–107; of preservation,

273–77; spatiality and, 81–82; structure of care and, 103–7
Thales, 8, 166–68, 191 nn. 4–5
Theaetetus, 166
Themis, 187, 194 n. 57
theologica crusis, 154–55
theory-building: *Auseinandersetzung* and, 343–44; radical transformation and, 333–42
"they," Dasein and dictatorship of, 91–92
they-self: Beauvoir's discussion of, 137–39; Heidegger and feminist theory of, 131–44; sexual difference and, 141–44
thinking: anarchic feminist thinking, 344–49; ecofeminism and Heidegger's discussion of, 237–40; radical transformation of, 333–42; Sappho and Heidegger's discussion of, 183–86, 194 n. 48
Thinking the Difference, 8
This Sex Which Is Not One, 9
throwness, authenticity and play and, 289–304, 306 n. 23
Thus Spoke Zarathustra, 168–69, 191 n. 8, 194 n. 56
Tillich, Paul, 316
To Be Two, 309, 313. See also *Forgetting of Air*
"To One Who Died Young," 201
"Toward a Latin American Feminine Hermeneutics: A Dialogue with the Biblical Methodologies of Elisabeth Schuessler Fiorenza, Phyllis Trible, Carlos Mesters, and Pablo Richard," 37 n. 7
Trakl, Georg, 162, 201, 216 n. 2, 324–30
transactional analysis, 129–31, 144 n. 1
Transactional Analysis in Psychotherapy, 144 n. 1
transcendence: Heidegger's *Geist* and, 328–30; immanence and, 272–73, 321–23
transformation, Heidegger's concept of, 335–49
Tronto, Joan, 287 n. 18
truth: anthropocentrism and objectivity in, 237–40; falsification and, 353–56; Heidegger's concept of, 24–28
"Truth in Mimesis: Phenomenological Transformation in Gadamer, Heidegger, and Irigaray," 40 n. 38
"Turn," Heidegger's concept of, 42 n. 45
"Turning in *Ereignis* and Transformation of Thinking, The," 12

Unamuno, Miguel de, 38 n. 17
uncanniness, Heidegger's concept of, 209–16, 244–46

understanding, play as projection of, 291–92
"Using Arendt and Heidegger to Consider Feminist Thinking on Women and Reproductive/Infertility Technologies," 37 n. 7
utopia: in Heidegger's work, 357–59; Irigaray's discussion of, 17–18

Van Gogh, Vincent, 191 n. 2
Van Lennep, D. J., 269–70
Vattimo, Gianni, 18–19
Verdeckungen, Dasein and, 70
Verstellungen, Dasein and, 70
Verwindung, Heidegger's concept of, 19
violence: Heidegger's discussion of, 199–202, 217 n. 12; play and, 296–97, 303–4
Vom Wesen des Grundes, 62
von Clausewitz, Karl, 159
Vorhandensein, Dasein and, 69–70, 77–79

"Wandering Stranger, The," 201
Warren, Karen, 223, 230, 242–43, 246
Weiss, Helene, 231
Wesen of being, Heidegger's concept of, 337–42, 350 n. 2
Western canon: feminist transformation of, viii–ix; Heidegger's challenge to, 1–2; male dominance of, vii–ix
Westra, Laura, 223
What Is Called Thinking?, 49; Aphrodite in, 179–82; ecofeminism and, 239–40, 242–46; women discussed in, 166–69
Whitbeck, Caroline, 227
White, Stephen K., 20, 37 n. 7
Whitford, Margaret, 17
Wittgenstein, Ludwig: Heidegger and, 110; in Western canon, viii
Wollstonecraft, Mary, in Western canon, viii
Woman and Nature, 345–46
Woman at the Foot of the Cross, 154–55, 157–58
"Women's Time," 99
Woolf, Virginia, 230–36
Wright, Kathleen, 39 n. 28, 40 n. 37

Young, Iris Marion, 40 n. 37, 47, 252–86, 301–2, 305 n. 15

Ziarek, Krzysztof, 16, 18
Zimmerman, Michael, 20, 221, 229, 374 n. 28